D1665560

Triumph of the Fatherland

Social History, Popular Culture, and Politics in Germany
Geoff Eley, Series Editor

Triumph of the Fatherland

*German Unification and
the Marginalization of Women*

BRIGITTE YOUNG

Ann Arbor

THE UNIVERSITY OF MICHIGAN PRESS

2002 2001 2000 1999   4 3 2 1

A CIP catalog record for this book is available from the British Library.

Library of Congress Cataloging-in-Publication Data

Young, Brigitte, 1946–
    Triumph of the fatherland : German unification and the
marginalization of women / Brigitte Young.
        p.   cm. — (Social history, popular culture, and politics in
Germany)
    Includes bibliographical references and index.
    ISBN 0-472-10948-0 (cloth : acid-free paper)
    ISBN 0-472-08536-0 (pbk. : acid-free paper)
    1. Women in politics—Germany.   2. Women's rights—Germany.
3. Feminism—Germany.   4. Marginality, Social—Germany.
5. Democracy—Germany.   I. Title.   II. Series.
HQ1236.5.G3   Y68   1998
305.42'0943—ddc21   98-40080
                                                              CIP

To my late grandfather, Alois Lessmann,
who taught me the values of justice and equality

and

Birgit

Contents

Preface

Being a witness in Berlin at the historic moment when the Wall opened on that memorable evening on November 9, 1989, and watching the process of unification unfold was like viewing the toppling of a mountain.[1] Nobody could have foreseen on that joyous night that the international political order was in the process of being completely transformed. The collapse of the East German state system and the emergence of a "civil society" in which women demanded a political role in the newly emerging social order made me realize that such systemic transformations touch on important social science questions of the relations between the state and civil society.

Here we have a "natural experiment" (Offe 1992), the dimensions of which could not be reproduced even under laboratory conditions, in which an entire political elite was being delegitimized and members of the civil society were suddenly rising up and claiming they could "run" the state themselves. And into this political vacuum East German feminists stepped and proclaimed that "Without Women There Is No State."[2] Of course, we know from hindsight that this is not what happened. In that "moment of madness" (Zolberg 1972) when "all seemed possible," however, one thing was clear: the relations between the East German state and its citizenry had taken a turn that could not be reversed.

I became interested in this transformation of an entire state and civil society, but how could I link several different empirical strands theoretically? At the center was German unification, an event triggered by the revolution of 1989. Then there was the collapse of the East German state and the importation of "new" state structures from the West. And, finally, East

---

1. I was in Berlin from September 1989 until 1991, first on a Social Science Research Fellowship and then as a faculty member at the Free University of Berlin.

2. This was the title of the "Manifesto for the Independent Women's Movement" written by Ina Merkel for the first public women's gathering in the GDR on December 3, 1989.

German women activists demanded to be involved in this restructuring of state and civil society.

The complexity started because the East German state ceased to exist and became united with the West. That meant that suddenly two states became one and the East German feminists entered a political space that was already occupied by Western feminists. So, a contraction in the number of states accompanied an increase in the diversity of social actors with different strategies and goals in trying to gain access to the policy-making process during unification.

Given this contraction in the number of states and increase in feminist political actors, I decided to center my research around the notion of the state. The emphasis on the state permits us to focus on the East German and West German states before unification; the period of the "stateless state" in East Germany after the collapse of the Wall; the West German state during unification; and the opportunity structure these political regimes provided for feminist mobilization.

Simultaneously, we can bring East German women into the picture by focusing on their political activities during these different state periods. They were involved in bringing down the German Democratic Republic state, and they tried to gain access to the decision-making arena of German unification, a project that they were "forced" to share with their West German sisters. Why they failed and how the West German institutions of the state blocked the actions of both East and West German feminists is the central question of this research. Finally, what was the outcome of this negotiated unification process and its effect on women in both parts of Germany in the post-unification period?

This case study of German unification and the role of West and East German feminists trying to contest the existing power structure is unique for several reasons. Not only have we become eyewitnesses to the impact of the West German social market economy on GDR women socialized under conditions radically different from those in the West, but we are able to analyze the impact of a negotiation process that, despite their eagerness to participate in it, virtually ignored the presence and input of East and West German feminists and female political activists. Unification thus provides scholars with a natural opportunity to reflect on German state and civil society relations.

The scholarly research I present relies on: interviews with feminist political activists involved in the East German uprising[3] and with East and West German feminists who have been involved in political action during the negotiating process of German unification; records of the East Ger-

---

3. See the section on the specifics of gathering information in the appendix.

man Independent Women's League; documents collected on the Central Round Table at the Federal Archive in Potsdam; newspaper articles; and many secondary sources on German unification that have since been published.

I also gained invaluable insight into the dynamics of East and West German feminist politics from my personal involvement in West German university politics and from my participation in peace activities. I was the principal organizer of the working group Politics and Gender within the German Political Science Association (DVPW) and chaired the first feminist panel ever to be held at a German Political Science Congress, in Hannover in October 1991. This institutional experience within the West German university structure did much to sensitize me to what Eva Kreisky (1994) has called the German legacy "of the state as the highest male-bond."[4] At the same time, these institutional activities also brought me into contact both as a speaker at professional conferences and as a listener, with many West German, and later also East German, feminist academics. These meetings, in addition to the formal interviews, documents, and records, provided me with much informal material on the role of German feminists during the negotiation stage of German unification.

I was also involved in the East-West collaboration of women pastors and women peace activists who organized a "Night Prayer" at the French Dome (Französiche Dom) in East Berlin during the Persian Gulf Crisis, on March 9, 1991. It was the first time that East German women pastors were permitted to hold a service in the French Dome. My involvement with East German church women and their peace activities within the confines of the Protestant Church gave me another view of an important segment of East German opposition groups. The group meetings were held at the homes of women pastors,[5] permitting me an insight into the private lives of these activists. More important, I gained an understanding of the importance of the "living rooms" in private homes in which so much of the political work was done by the opposition groups during the 1980s.

A high point for me occurred when I was asked to speak at the French Dome in Berlin on March 9, 1991, on the politics of the Gulf War in front of Jewish, Muslim, Protestant, and Catholic women and men. Two weeks later I spoke at the weekend Conference on Peace at the Erfurt "Predigerkirche" before a standing-room crowd of over a thousand people from

---

4. Universities are part of the German state. For example, Germans have to take a loyalty oath when entering university service.

5. These meetings were held in the home of the well-known East German pastor Ruth Misselwitz, who founded the equally well-known "Peace Circle" in Pankow in 1981. The members as well as the pastor were subject to constant harassment by the East German State Security (Stasi).

East and West Germany. This experience among East German church activists again gave me some understanding of how the Protestant Church in East Germany was able to organize these large weekend gatherings throughout the 1980s, thereby providing a meeting ground for feminists, gays and lesbians, environmentalists, human rights activists, antimilitarist and anti-Socialist Unity Party of Germany (SED) individuals. I came to realize the true meaning of the Protestant Church providing an "umbrella" for the gatherings of all the various opposition groups for whom a public space did not exist during the state socialist period.

The Erfurt "peace gathering" was memorable for another reason. For the first time I was able to get a glimpse into the lodgings of high-ranking communist functionaries and foreign guests visiting the GDR. Being a guest of the city of Erfurt, I was put up at the former SED Guest House (Gästehaus—Rat der Stadt Erfurt), where Leonid Brezhnev supposedly spent the night and also where, as German irony would have it, the West German finance minister, Theo Waigel, stayed in 1990. Not only did I share these famous lodgings with a prominent church elder from West Berlin, but the butler of the Guest House was a relic of the old communist time who not only offered us the most exquisite French wines from the house cellar but also entertained us until the morning hours with stories of the dignitaries who had stayed in the suite I was to occupy for the weekend. Two things impressed me in particular. First, virtually everything was made in the West. The bathroom robes and towels still had the labels from a West German company.[6] Second, and to my greatest surprise, I marveled at the worst Hollywood kitsch I had ever seen (two green bathtubs big enough to hold several grownups), and I was generally puzzled by the boudoir atmosphere of the suite. That the Guest House did have a "certain reputation" was confirmed the next day when women from Erfurt curiously asked, "What does it look like inside?" Seeing such lodgings with my own eyes brought home the feeling of cynicism the GDR political elite must have had toward its own system. While ordinary citizens could not find in the stores of the GDR simple replacement parts for repairs, the SED hard-liners relied on goods exclusively imported for them from the West.

A study of such a "moment of historic madness" could not have been completed without the help of many women and men in both parts of Germany. I thank them, some not wanting to be acknowledged openly, for their patience and goodwill in answering the interview questions at times when they themselves felt that "history was bulldozing them to the

---

6. I asked the butler if these items had been purchased after 1989, and he assured me that they had been there prior to 1989.

ground." In particular, I wish to thank Ina Merkel, Tatjana Böhm, Eva Schäfer, and Eva Maleck-Lewy for their very detailed information on the Unabhängiger Frauenverband (UFV, Independent Women's League). I would also like to acknowledge the assistance provided by Nannette Maennel, editor of the UFV's journal, *Weibblick,* and the staff at the UFV office in Berlin, for their help in reconstructing the "history" of the UFV.[7]

I would also like to thank Anne Hampele for sharing her unpublished dissertation chapters on the UFV and for her willingness to grant me several interviews. Only with these detailed insights did I begin to understand the formation and organizational structure of the Independent Women's League. I also thank Christine Kulke for digging up her unpublished dissertation (1967), which was the first West German study to deal with the SED's policies toward women during the 1950s and 1960s. My gratitude also goes to Sabine Berghahn, who provided me with her invaluable knowledge and her many informative articles on the abortion case and the German legal system.

I could not have written this work without intellectual and emotional support from Margit Mayer, Birgit Sauer, and Sabine Lang. I thank both Birgit and Sabine for the transatlantic ferrying of the many books and newspaper articles I was always in a rush to receive. Their critical reading and discussions of the theoretical outline of the manuscript and continuous encouragement to persevere proved invaluable. Our many meetings and joint projects have greatly inspired me intellectually.

I also wish to thank my colleagues who gave so generously of their time in both the early stages of conceptualizing my ideas in the research proposal and later in reading the entire manuscript. Particular thanks go to Sue Fischer, Sociology Department, Wesleyan University, whose conceptual guidance was much appreciated in the early stages of writing the research proposal. In addition, I thank Rita Mae Kelly, director and chair, School of Justice Studies, Arizona State University, who gave generously of her time and of her written work to help me think through the concept of gender.

The manuscript was read in its entirety by Gerard Braunthal, Myra Marx Ferree, Lily Gardner-Feldman, Peter Rutland, David Titus, and Birgit Sauer. The critiques of these scholars touched upon their areas of expertise and were invaluable for rewriting the manuscript. I thank them for their time and their much appreciated suggestions. In particular, I wish to thank David Titus not only for reading the final manuscript but also for providing feedback after I had written the introductory chapter. He was instrumental in pointing the way to the larger theoretical issues of the rela-

---

7. See appendix for interview information and data gathering.

tionship between state and civil society. I thank Gerard Braunthal for his meticulous reading of the manuscript and for suggesting tough organizational choices, which helped to streamline the argument. I am also indebted to Lily Gardner-Feldman for her suggestion to use the notion of the "different" German states as an organizing principle to link the various themes of state and civil society.

I would also like to thank the Information Officer, Hannelore Koehler, at the German Information Center, New York, for her prompt assistance in providing much needed information. After considerable brainstorming, Julia Perkins came up with the title of the book, which says it all! I also thank Julia for battling with my German prose. None other than Mark Twain had already referred to the German language as "a sort of luminous intellectual fog which stands for clearness among these people."[8]

The manuscript could not have been completed without the help of the generous funding I received. Indirectly, the Social Science Resource Council (SSRC) postdoctoral fellowship made it possible for me to be in Berlin at the time of the collapse of the Wall. Wesleyan University provided me with several summer research grants to go to Germany and interview people. Finally, the financial support of the Center for German and European Studies, School of Foreign Service, Georgetown University, Washington, D.C., enabled me to write the manuscript during the 1994–95 academic year. I thank Sam Barnes, Greg Flynn, Jeff Peck, and Roger Chickering for providing such a collegial atmosphere in which to complete the project.

It was an extraordinary coincidence that my presence at the Center for German and European Studies coincided with that of the visiting Adenauer professor, Uwe Thaysen, from the University of Lüneburg, and chief editor of the German journal *Zeitschrift für Parlamentsfragen*. His presence at all sixteen meetings of the Central Round Table in Berlin as the sole Western observer proved invaluable for my research. His willingness to provide access to the still unpublished stenographic reports from these meetings led to many reevaluations of my earlier positions. I am deeply indebted to him for sharing this information and for the many long and stimulating discussions we had on German politics.

Last but not least, I thank Bruce Spear for saving the manuscript (and my sanity) from the invasion of computer viruses that appeared once the manuscript had been completed.

Finally, I dedicate this book to the past and to the future: to my late grandfather, Alois Lessmann, and to my daughter, Birgit. It is my grand-

---

8. Mark Twain, "A Tramp Abroad," app. D, vol. 2: "The Awful German Language" (1880).

father, born in the region of the former "Sudentendeutschland," a dedicated socialist, who gave meaning to the notion of political struggle for justice and equality. It is he, with his strong, unwavering political beliefs, who shaped my understanding of the world at a time when the post–World War II German and Austrian generation had to cope with the "sins of their fathers and mothers." And to my daughter, who, as a feminist, made me realize that her generation is facing many of the same problems we had hoped to have resolved. As a single parent, I gained from my relationship with my daughter the strength and conviction to struggle for women's empowerment.

Abbreviations of West and East German Organizations

AfNS   Amt für Nationale Sicherheit (Office for National Security), East Germany

ASF   Arbeitsgemeinschaft Sozialdemokratischer Frauen (Working Group of Social Democratic Women), West Germany

AL   Alternative Liste (Berlin), (Alternative List), West Germany

BDF   Bund Deutscher Frauenvereine (Federation of German Women's Associations), East Germany

CDU   Christliche Demokratische Union (Christian Democratic Union), West Germany

CSU   Christliche Soziale Union (Christian Social Union), West Germany

DA   Demokratischer Aufbruch (Democratic Awakening), East Germany

DJ   Demokratie Jetzt (Democracy Now), East Germany

DBD   Demokratische Bauernpartei Deutschlands, East Germany

DDR   Deutsche Demokratische Republic (German Democratic Republic)

DFD   Demokratischer Frauenbund Deutschlands (Democratic Women's League of Germany), East Germany

DGB   Deutscher Gewerkschaftsbund (German Labor Union League), West Germany

DSU   Demokratische Soziale Union (Democratic Social Union), East Germany

EEC   European Economic Community

EU   Europäische Union (European Union)

FDP   Freie Demokratische Partei (Free Democratic Party), West Germany

FDGB   Freier Deutscher Gewerkschaftsbund (Free Democratic Labor Union League), East Germany
FDJ   Freie Deutsche Jugend (Free German Youth), East Germany
FRG   Federal Republic of Germany
FRT   Frauenpolitischer Runder Tisch (Women's Political Round Table), East Germany
GDR   German Democratic Republic
IDFF   Internationaler Demokratischer Frauen Federation (International Democratic Women's Federation), East Germany
KPD   Kommunistische Partei Deutschlands (Communist Party of Germany)
LDPD   Liberale Demokratische Partei Deutschlands (Liberal Democratic Party of Germany), East Germany
Lilo   Lila Offensive, East Germany
LISA   Women's Working Group within the PDS, East Germany
MdB   Mitglied des Bundestags (Member of the Bundestag), Germany
MfS   Ministerium für Sicherheit (Stasi), (Ministry for Security), East Germany
NDPD   National-Demokratische Partei Deutschlands (National Democratic Party of Germany), East Germany
NF   Neues Forum (New Forum), East Germany
ÖTV   Gewerkschaft Öffentliche Dienste, Transport und Verkehr (Union for Public Service, Transport and Traffic), West Germany
PDS   Partei des Demokratischen Sozialismus (Party of Democratic Socialism), East Germany
SDS   Sozialistischer Deutscher Studentenbund (German Socialist Student League), West Germany
SDP   Sozialdemokratische Partei, East Germany
SED   Sozialistische Einheitspartei Deutschlands (Socialist Unity Party of Germany), East Germany
SOFI   Sozialistische Frauen Initiative (Socialist Women's Initiative), East Germany
SPD   Sozialdemokratische Partei Deutschlands (Social Democratic Party of Germany), West Germany
UFV   Unabhängiger Frauenverband (Independent Women's League), East Germany
VL   Vereinigte Linke (United Left), East Germany
ZiF   Zentrum für Interdisiplinäre Frauenforschung (Center for Interdisciplinary Women's Research), Humboldt University, East Berlin

Introduction: Feminisms and the German Political Regimes

The Role of Women in the East German Uprising

The East German uprising was not a male "revolution."[1] Politically active women joined the revolution and demanded a political role in the reconstruction of the new East German state and society. In spirit they followed in the footsteps of the most well-known German bourgeois women's rights activist, Louise Otto-Peters, who had declared in Leipzig 150 years earlier that the participation of women in the affairs of the state is not only a right but a duty (Zetkin 1960; Frevert 1986; Gerhard 1991). Even if the East German uprising in the fall of 1989 was not "the hour of women,"[2] the political visibility of East German women activists prior to, during, and after the collapse of socialism was in stark contrast to the largely male-dominated revolutionary activities in other East European countries (Tatur 1992; Einhorn 1993; Funk and Mueller 1993; Rueschemeyer 1994).

East German women such as Bärbel Bohley, Ina Merkel, Tatjana Böhm, Ulrike Poppe, Vera Wollenberger, and Ingrid Köppe became household names even in the West and shared the headlines with such prominent men as Jens Reich, Gerd Poppe, Wolfgang Ullmann, Konrad Weiß, Wolfgang Thierse, and Gregor Gysi. In the 1980s Women for Peace, founded in protest against the conscription of women for unarmed military service, was the first group in the GDR to organize nationally and to appear publicly (Bärbel Bohley, interview). Wolfgang Ullmann, one of the founders of the citizen group Democracy Now and a member of the Cen-

---

1. In fact, there is much disagreement about whether the collapse of the East German state was a revolution at all. See Thaysen 1992.

2. Graf von Krockow (1994) details the story of the strength of women (his sister and women generally) who persevered in Pomerania from 1944 to 1947 while the men were absent or too demoralized to fend for their families.

tral Round Table in Berlin, paid homage to the contribution women made during the critical months of the East German "awakening" in a speech before the German Reichstag in Berlin:

> Without Bärbel Bohley the New Forum and the shape it took is unthinkable. Without Ulrike Poppe Democracy Now would exist as a prominent intellectual elite but not as a citizen movement. Without Vera Wollenberger the connection between the 1988 Rosa Luxemburg demonstration and the fall of 1989 would have been forgotten. Without the perseverance of Tatjana Böhm the *Social Charta* would not have been produced, and without the toughness of Ingrid Köppe the Round Table would not have issued the spectacular ultimatum on January 8, 1990, to dissolve the Office of National Security. What do these women stand for? They not only stand for great political successes; they also stand for a change in meaning, associated with "peace" and "democracy." In the revolution, in which these women played such an important role, "peace" and "democracy" simultaneously meant being "human." . . . Alone the presence of these women made it possible that children could be present at the large Berlin demonstration on November 4, 1989, and could experience an unforgettable event: adults, men and women, claimed the highest authority of the country for themselves.[3]

No claim is made that all East German women took part in the political uprising, that the politically active women spoke for the majority of GDR women, nor that all women political activists identified with a feminist cause.[4] It is even difficult to speak of East German women as "feminists" at the time the Wall collapsed. Feminism was a much contested concept in East Germany and, as I will explain in more detail later, was initially rejected as an import from the West.[5] Whether women identified as feminists or not, a sizable number of women took part in the emerging citizens' movement in the fall of 1989, and over three thousand politically

---

3. In the last sentence Ullmann refers to the largest demonstration ever to take place in East Germany in which people rose up and demanded en masse freedom of speech and freedom of association and other radical reforms. Wolfgang Ullmann spoke these words in the Berlin "Reichstag" on June 16, 1990; cited in Thaysen 1990: 211–12.

4. For example, Bärbel Bohley, one of the initiators of "Women for Peace" and its successor, the "Initiative for Peace and Human Rights," rejects the notion of feminism, because she suggests that women, men, and children were equally oppressed in the GDR (interview, 1993).

5. Yet even in West Germany the concept of feminism remains contested, and an uneasy relationship continues to exist between women's politics and feminist politics.

active women, with many more sympathizers, organized in the national Independent Women's League (UFV) and asserted that "Without Women There Is No State" (Hampele 1996).[6]

The most important aspect about these women is not their social engagement in creating women's cafés, women's shelters, and feminist bookstores, which they did.[7] More important for this analysis is their political engagement and their demand for empowerment in the political arena. Their battle cries—"We want more than a fatherland," "Without Women There Is No State," and "Others make politics for women; we make politics ourselves"—were aimed at mobilizing women, influencing the political arena, and providing the bases for political manifestos (*Argument Extra* 1990; Schwarz and Zenner 1990). On November 1, 1989, the GDR women's journal *Für Dich* had organized a Round Table discussion with prominent women academics from Humboldt University and the Academy of Sciences in Berlin to discuss the situation of women in the GDR. The participants subsequently issued an open letter to the Central Committee of the Socialist Unity Party of Germany (SED) to demand that women's issues be included on the agenda for the planned Twelfth Party Convention of the SED (Kahlau 1990).

Starting in October and taking off after November 9, 1989, feminist political groups appeared not only in Berlin; women organized in virtually every city in the former GDR. The Lila Offensive (Lilo), the Socialist Women's Initiative (SOFI),[8] the Women's Joint Working Group within the Party of Democratic Socialism (PDS) (LISA), the First Women's Awakening (EWA), the Self-Help Initiative for Single People (SHIA), Women Foreigners in the GDR, among many others, expressed their concern that women's issues played virtually no role in the political discourse toward the construction of a more democratic and pluralistic polity (Kahlau 1990; Winkler 1990). Despite different ideological and regional backgrounds and diverse individual concerns, politically active women shared the common goal that "We best represent our own interests."[9] In their demand to act as political subjects East German feminists shared

---

6. This slogan became the title for the manifesto of the Independent Women's League (Unabhängiger Frauenverband), authored by Ina Merkel.

7. Within a year and a half *The Handbuch. Wegweiser für Frauen in den fünf neuen Bundesländern* (1990) published the addresses of an extraordinary regional variety of women's projects and associations in virtually every small city in the former GDR. In many cities women occupied and finally claimed offices of the former State Security (Stasi) to house their new projects.

8. Subsequently renamed Women's Solidarity Initiative.

9. This was one of the many slogans of the East German Independent Women's League.

with George Bernard Shaw's Hypatia Tarleton the desire "to be an active verb."[10]

To realize this desire, women from all walks of life and political ideologies came together on December 3, 1989, at the theater Volksbühne in Berlin to create the first East German women's movement, the Independent Women's League. Over twelve hundred women responded to the rallying cry "If you don't struggle, you will end up in the kitchen,"[11] and in one of the most memorable moments for the participants they threw off the yoke of the state-sanctioned women's organization, the Democratic Women's Union (DFD), declaring their independence from the SED and its approach to solving the "women's question."

Having launched this feminist organization, members of the UFV fought to gain representation at the Central Round Table in East Berlin and also at the regional Round Tables,[12] sometimes with comical effects. In Leipzig the demand that feminists participate in the local Round Table met with sarcastic remarks that, if women were permitted to be seated, then people wearing glasses also had the right to representation (Ferree 1991–92; Hampele 1991). Nevertheless, members of the UFV did gain political access. A crucial point for women came when the UFV was seated at the Central Round Table in East Berlin at the first meeting on December 7, 1989; Tatjana Böhm, of the UFV, was asked to join the cabinet of Hans Modrow's transitional government in January 1990 as "minister without portfolio,"[13] and Lothar de Maizière appointed Marina Beyer to the Office for Equality of Women and Men after the landslide election of the conservative Allianz für Deutschland (Alliance for Germany) on March 18.

Anne Hampele has argued that these appointments showed that women were politically important in the process of the GDR transformation process and at the same time showed the willingness of the UFV to participate in institutional politics (Hampele 1991). The UFV's crowning piece was its *Social Charta,* one of the most important documents adopted by the Central Round Table in Berlin on March 5, 1990, and subsequently passed by the East German parliament (Volkskammer) on March 7, 1990 (Thaysen, Central Round Table Stenographic Report, 15th meeting).

---

10. George Berhard Shaw, theater production, *Misalliance.*

11. The German rhyme was "Wer sich nicht wehrt, kommt an den Herd."

12. The East German Round Tables (established at the national, regional, and local levels) functioned as "crisis instruments for the establishment of democratic legitimacy." These bodies are thus to be seen as "institutions of transformations of more or less closed political systems" (Thaysen 1992a: 7).

13. The Modrow government came to power on November 17, 1989, and invited eight ministers without portfolio from opposition groups to join the government on January 22, 1990.

Barely noticed in the West, the UFV's innovative draft paper on "The Essential Elements of a Political Strategy to Achieve Equality between Women and Men" was also adopted by the Central Round Table at the next to the last meeting.

At this "moment of madness" after the Wall collapsed, when the universe of "normal" political events was suspended and "all was possible," when people had become masters of Berlin and Leipzig, and when "dreams became possibilities" (Zolberg 1972), East German feminist activists, liberated from the constraints of the state, seized the moment and declared that no longer could they be pushed aside as had happened to women in previous German revolutions. Instead, they demanded a voice in the construction of a new East German state system. This period of feminist "ecstasy and delirium" came to an end when the East German voters in their first free election on March 18, 1990, signaled their overwhelming readiness for, and acceptance of, German unification.

In the second period, starting with the parliamentary election campaign in February and ending with German unification in October, East German feminists were forced to change their strategy and direct their attention to the West German system. The dream of an independent socialist democratic East German state was nullified by the election results, which altered not only the space in which East German feminists acted politically; the election also meant they had to share the political stage with West German feminists. In contrast to the first moment of madness, in which the East German political terrain was the "playing field" for movement activities, the subsequent period was largely circumscribed by the rules of West German party politics.

While the first meetings between feminists from the East and West were voluntary and based on curiosity to meet the sisters who had been separated by the Wall for over forty years, the second period forced East and West feminists into one soon-to-be shared political space. This cohabitation did not prove to be happy for either side. The initial expectations that East German feminists would energize the West German movement and that West German feminists would be sympathetic to East German fears and concerns remained unfulfilled and turned the initial euphoria that accompanied the first meetings into disappointment by the beginning of the 1990s (Böhm 1992; Hampele 1992; Schenk and Schindler 1993; Ferree 1994; Sauer 1994a).

By the time the first East-West Women's Congress took place at the Technical University in West Berlin in April, "war" had broken out between the sisters (Helwerth and Schwarz 1995). The reasons for this animosity are complex. Suffice it to say that feminists in the East and West, despite their common language and their shared interest in the future of a "women-friendly" united Germany, soon realized that their forty-year socialization as ideological enemies prevented the formation of a common identity as a "Volk of sisters" (Nickel 1992; Helwerth and Schwarz 1995).

Despite these feelings of "otherness" and "strangeness" that developed between feminists on both sides of the by-then defunct concrete Wall, Eastern feminists in the Independent Women's League, Western feminists in the autonomous informal grassroots networks, and women activists in East and West German political parties, parliaments, and labor unions struggled during the unification negotiations to have a part in the policy-making process. The result has been disappointing. East and West German feminists were unable to influence the unification process. The first State Treaty to create a Monetary, Economic, and Social Union between the Federal Republic of Germany and the German Democratic Republic went into effect on July 1, 1990. This treaty mentioned women only once, along with the handicapped, as two groups whose special needs had to be considered (Süssmuth and Schubert 1992: 45).

In the Unification Treaty, which was to establish the political unification of the two Germanies on October 3, 1990, pressure from both East and West German women activists and women politicians did lead to the insertion of policy goals in Article 31 regarding equal rights, balance between work and family life, child care, and finding an acceptable abortion regulation for the East and West. Only the decision to find a common abortion regulation by December 31, 1992, had a clear mandate compelling the first united German parliament to act. The other provisions were purely symbolic, to take effect at some unspecified future time. For example, the language was couched in unspecific policy goals to "develop further the legislation on equal rights for men and women" (Lemke 1993: 148).

The only irony of the largely male-centered unification process was that the abortion issue nearly derailed the entire Unification Treaty (Böhm 1991–92). While feminist issues did not figure in the negotiations for German unification, the East and West German negotiators faced the task of reconciling two fundamentally different approaches to the abortion issue. East German women had possessed the right to terminate a pregnancy within the first twelve weeks, whereas in the West women were exempted from criminal prosecution only if they qualified under one of four indicators (rape, fetal deformity, medical reasons, social hardship) (Berghahn 1993a). The majority of the West German CDU and CSU pushed for the West German law to take effect on the day of unification in the East (Riemer 1993). The East German chief negotiator, Günther Krause, realized, however, that he did not have his country's support for such a drastic measure. In a rare moment of cooperation between East and West German feminists and women activists in East and West German political parties, they succeeded in producing a parliamentary stalemate in Bonn that was resolved only by the intervention of Chancellor Kohl and his instructions to the two chief negotiators, Wolfgang Schäuble and Günther Krause, not to let the abortion issue derail the unification process (Schäuble 1991). The compromise solution was to retain the two-state provisions until the united German parliament could pass a single law by December 31, 1992 (Berghahn 1995; Maleck-Lewy 1995).

Initially, East German women celebrated this postponement in the hope that the more liberal East German regulations might be given a chance to become law in the united Germany (Böhm 1991–92), and West German women hoped, at least, that the West German abortion law would be decriminalized. In the end the compromise legislation that emerged from the all-German parliament landed once again, as had been the case with the liberal abortion bill in 1974, in the Constitutional Court. The 1993 court's ruling disappointed the expectations of both East and West German women. The court's restrictive interpretation of the right of women to terminate an unwanted pregnancy was "a slap in the face" particularly for women in the East (Hanewinckel 1993). The debate on the abortion issue, which will form an important aspect of the unification analysis in the following chapters, showed once again that there could be no talk of either a West or East German feminist contribution to German unity (Riemer 1993).

The Puzzle

We are confronted with an interesting puzzle. Why did East German women gain such political visibility during and after the collapse of socialism? How can we explain why their political mobilization and the efforts of West German feminists and women activists in labor unions and political parties had virtually no influence on the political agenda of the unification process? Different theoretical frameworks can be brought to bear on these issues.

At one level the rise of East German feminists was the result of a political vacuum created by the collapse of the East German state. The very real "withering away of the state" did provide feminists with the opportunity to fill this empty space and convinced them that they could climb to the pinnacle of political power and usher in a "women-friendly" state. According to such theories of revolution, the rise of feminist mobilization is correlated with the collapse of state power. Conversely, feminists are "swept aside" once the state is newly constituted. In their search

for political inclusion and empowerment during times of political transformation, the East German feminists' rise and subsequent decline differs
little from other revolutionary periods such as the French, Russian, and/or
Cuban Revolutions (Gerhard 1991–92). These cases share the sudden
eruption of a political vacuum and a certain social uncertainty that permits the "entrance of the marginals" onto the political stage until they are
again cast aside by the events of "normal" politics (Zolberg 1972).

This answer certainly has some merit for several reasons. It does highlight the emergence of marginal groups during times of political upheaval
and links the rise and failure of such popular mobilizations to the pre- and
postrevolutionary political structures. It is less satisfying in that the determinants of the success and failure of such movements are derived from
structural variables of state power, and the explanation for the demise of
such groups is both deterministic and defeatist.

It is deterministic because "cycles of protest," the beginning of protest
activity, the peak of the cycle, and the subsequent decline, are related to
the revolutionary cycle of the political system. It may be true that protest
groups are more likely to emerge in a political vacuum. This does not
mean, however, that their decline is a necessary condition of state consoli-
dation.

Linking the "fortunes" of the protest groups to revolutionary patterns is defeatist because this spurt of revolutionary action virtually always
ends up in disillusionment. The moment when "all is possible" vanishes
into the twilight of historical pessimism, as Aristide Zolberg has reminded
us: "What we remember most is that moments of political enthusiasm are
followed by bourgeois repression or by charismatic authoritarianism,
sometimes by horror but always by the restoration of boredom" (1971:
205). Unfortunately, the East German revolution seems to have left
behind exactly such feelings of disillusionment, particularly among
women in the East. "That women are the losers of German unification" is
not only one of the most cited clichés in the writings of East German
women; it reflects reality (Ferree 1995). Whether this feeling of disillusionment was a foregone conclusion is an altogether different matter.

A second theory for understanding the failure of the East and West
German feminists to influence the unification process draws upon the
social movement literature. In particular, the resource mobilization and
political opportunity approaches provide important insights into the
mobilization of collective actions. The resource mobilization approach
focuses on the internal resources and the organizational capacities of the
movements and argues that the variability of resources either constrains or
facilitates the mobilization of people (McCarthy and Zald 1977). The

strength of the resource mobilization approach is its emphasis on the organizational prerequisites of a movement to act strategically within its wider political environment (Rucht 1996).

Some East German feminists have concluded that the reason feminists were marginalized during the unification process may be found in the internal dynamics of the East and West German movements and, in particular, in the weakness of their organizational structures (Schenk and Schindler 1993). At a superficial level there is some evidence to support such a resource mobilization argument. During the fateful months of German unification three groups/movements with different ideologies, organizational structures, strategies, and goals were unable to find a common denominator to enable them to pool their resources. The groups were the newly emerging feminist movement in the East, organized in the Independent Women's League; the West German "autonomous feminist movement," organized in informal grassroots networks; and the "institutionalized feminists," who are not organized in formal organizational structures but are situated within the traditional political structures of West German political parties and labor unions (Young 1996).

These three groups, whether organized in movements or acting as individuals in the traditional arena of German party politics, did not stand idly by while the negotiations for unification were in process. Yet they failed to unite under a common organizational umbrella and mount a concerted effort to challenge the process of unification. Given this profile of deeply divided German feminists, it seems reasonable to conclude that the meager outcomes for women from the unification process were due to the organizational deficiencies of the movements themselves.

I am not convinced, however, that this is an accurate reading of the situation, for two reasons. Most important, the singular focus on the internal dynamics of a movement leaves out the crucial role the German state played in blocking the feminist initiatives. Mayer argues that the blind spot in the resource mobilization approach is the failure to study the relationship between movements and the state: "Hence, the state's functions, reactions, and the many possible relations between social movements and the state remain outside the perceptual horizon of the research" (1991a: 469). Yet, by neglecting the external political context, the resource mobilization approach is unable to theorize situations in which the very success of the organizational structures/resources of movements is dependent on particular political contexts. If the "political opportunity structure" changes, the movements often fail (Tarrow 1994).

This is exactly what happened in East Germany between the first period, which ended with the East German parliamentary elections in

March, and the Bonn orientation, which started within the parliamentary election campaign.[14] Large-scale demonstrations, one of the most success-ful "repertoires" of feminists during the period of the "stateless state" in East Germany, were no longer suited to a West German political context organized around national party politics (Tilly 1978; Tarrow 1994; Rucht 1996). This neglect of structural and cultural change in the resource mobi-lization approach, according to Mayer, is not accidental. It is based on the basic liberal concepts holding sway in American public philosophy. The national specificity of the assumptions and theoretical premises have not only shaped American social movement practice but have also been incor-porated into the premises of American movement research, which make this approach much less appropriate for the European political context (Kitschelt 1991; Mayer 1991a; Rucht 1991).

A more promising theoretical framework to explain the inability of East and West German feminist movements to influence the unification negotiations also has its roots in social movement research and focuses on the political opportunity structure (Tarrow 1994). Instead of looking at how movements develop, as is the case with the resource mobilization approach (Melucci 1988), Tarrow argues that "movements are created when political opportunities open up for social actors who usually lack them" (1994: 1). It is the "when" of social movement formation rather than the "how" that is the crucial element in Tarrow's framework. In contrast to the resource mobilization approach and its emphasis on internal resources, "theorists of the political opportunity structure emphasize the mobilization of resources external to the group" (85).

In this emphasis on the political environment Tarrow singles out four factors that are most conducive to movement mobilization. The first refers to the opening up of access to participation. This opening up of opportu-nity can refer to electoral access. It can also refer to transnational access, as was the case with the Helsinki Accords and the opportunities it pro-vided for East European dissidents to keep track of the human rights vio-lations in their countries in the 1980s.

Second, Tarrow identifies the importance of electoral realignments in opening political opportunities. The realignment was an important factor in the U.S. Civil Rights Movement of the 1950s, which capitalized on the switch of Southern racial "exclusionists" to the Republican Party, in the process strengthening the "inclusionist" wing of the Democratic Party. Even in authoritarian systems, political instability may encourage collec-

---

14. There is a certain overlap between the first and the second period. The East German state period definitely ended with the parliamentary elections of March 18. The Bonn orien-tation had started, however, with the introduction of the West German party system into the election campaign.

tive action as the many historical peasant uprisings in repressive systems have shown.

A third aspect for movement success is the presence of influential allies. Whether these allies are "friends in court" or "friends in the political parties" or the Protestant Church in Eastern Germany, they are important actors to protect activists.

Finally, conflicts within and among elites are the fourth factor that Tarrow singles out in providing an incentive to unrepresented groups to take collective action. The division among elites may not only encourage collective action; it also may help groups of the disaffected elites who are out of power join forces with the protesters (1994: 85–89).

In this taxonomy of the dimensions of movement mobilization Tarrow answers critics who have questioned whether the social movement literature developed in the West can be applied to former state socialist systems (Joppke 1995). Because state socialist systems lack the constitutional guarantees of a representative system, Joppke argues, the very notion of opposition within them is contradictory. The opposition faced two irreconcilable choices: "either to accept the normative principles of the regime and try to make the latter live up to its ideals (revisionist choice), or to invoke standards of free expression and independent action, but that cannot be accepted by the regime unless it abrogates its constitutive principles (choice of dissidence)" (13).

Tarrow acknowledges that the suppression of social movements is the hallmark of authoritarian states but nevertheless argues that the "centralization of power in repressive states offers dissidents a unified field and a centralized target to attack, once the system is weakened" (1994: 93). An example is Gorbachev's move to renounce the Brezhnev doctrine, which left not only the Eastern European hard-liners struggling for survival; Gorbachev's visit to celebrate the GDR's forty-year existence on October 7, 1989 energized the East German opposition against the ruling elite (Glaessner 1991).

If we move from this general level of the East German political opportunity structure providing space for movement development to applying Tarrow's four specific dimensions to the East German feminist movement, the approach fares less well. The four factors are the opening up of access to participation, shifts in ruling alignments, the availability of influential allies, and the cleavages within and among elites. Starting with the first criterion, feminists and women political activists certainly had access and were represented at the Central Round Table and the various Round Tables at the regional and local levels, they occupied a cabinet position in the East German transitional government of Hans Modrow, and they were included in the conservative government of Lothar de Maizière after the March elections. Yet this unusual political participation did not, as Rucht pointed out for the other East German opposition groups, lead to a stronger power position: "In retrospect, the brief intermediate situation between the breakdown of the old regime and the key decisions towards German unification was merely an experimental and mainly discursive playground without lasting consequences" (1996: 26).

Concerning shifts in ruling alignments and their salience for collective action for the East German feminist movement, again the answer is ambivalent. The tremendous instability caused by the collapse of the state socialist system and the delegitimation of the SED government did provide feminists with a new political space and opened the "universe of political discourse" to a feminist discourse (Jenson 1991). At the same time, this instability was too fluid to provide much orientation for the feminist movement. Such instabilities are thus not only conducive to movement success; they also constrain it.

Third, if we focus on the presence or absence of allies for East German feminists, we again fail to hit the mark. East German feminists had few friends in the East and the West. They could not count on the conservative forces organized in the East German electoral coalition Alliance for Germany that won in March, nor could they rely on help from the political system in Bonn. They had essentially three options, and none of them provided a political opportunity structure for women. They could ally with the PDS (the successor party to the SED), but by doing so they would alienate women who were members of the church and the local feminist grassroots organizations. At the same time, the PDS was largely a discredited party in the eyes of the majority of the East German population (Rucht 1996).[15] A second option was an alliance with the West German autonomous feminist movement. This proved impossible, however, for a variety of complex reasons that will be explained more fully in the coming chapters. Finally, the UFV could form an alliance with the Green Party–GDR. In fact, the Green Party and the UFV entered into an electoral alliance for the East German parliamentary elections in March 1990, yet this election coalition did not bring any gains to the UFV. Since the UFV was placed second on the party lists, it did not gain any seats in the East German parliament and the Green Party–GDR refused to transfer any of the mandates to the UFV (Hampele interview 1992; Schäfer interview 1995). East German feminists found themselves in the unfortunate situation of not having influential friends to facilitate movement success.

---

15. This is no longer the case; the PDS has gained new popularity and has become a strong defender of GDR identity since the early 1990s.

Finally, the fact that the elites were divided in East Germany had no bearing on the feminist movement "insofar as the elites had basically lost their formal power base" (Rucht 1996: 27).

These criticisms of Tarrow's four dimensions of the political opportunity structure do not imply that this approach holds no theoretical merit for studying the determinants of the rise of the East German feminist movements and the subsequent failure of the West and East German feminists to gain any influence in the decision-making process for German unity. It does mean, however, that the approach has to be modified so as to take into account the specificities of the German state systems in the East and the West and their impact on movement development.

Theoretical Issues and the "Political Opportunity Structure" of the German State(s)

Trying to answer the questions of why East German feminists mobilized in the fall of 1989 and demanded political empowerment and why they, and feminists in the West, failed to influence the unification process raises several interesting theoretical issues. At one level this story could be told from the perspective of the rise and decline of social movements in democratic and nondemocratic societies and what it tells us about the fate of such movements. Such a research agenda would fit theoretically with studies exploring the disempowerment of social organizations that mobilized around the time of the collapse of communism (Müller-Enbergs, Schulz, and Wielgohs 1991; Poppe, Eckert, and Kowalczuk 1995).

At a broader theoretical level the questions raise issues of the relationship between the state and civil society in a state socialist system in which "the society had withered away" (Meuschel 1992). Without a doubt the GDR was a system in which any mobilization was the exclusive privilege of the political elite (Joppke 1995); at the same time, a sizable number of opposition groups did challenge the regime in 1989 (Müller-Enbergs, Schulz, and Wielgohs 1991). Thus, the question arises how specific members in systems in which the "society had died" (Meuschel 1991) surge at a particular historic moment and demand political empowerment. More specifically, we can ask whether there was something inherent in socialist ideology and the GDR's emphasis on the trinity of women as mothers, workers, and political functionaries that predisposed women to political activism under specific historic conjunctures (Schubert 1980; Diemer 1989). Did socialism create a "new [East German] woman" who burst onto the stage of world history in the fall of 1989, as the Russian woman activist Alexandra Kolontay (1920) had envisioned socialism would do?

These are important research questions and will form part of the inquiry into why East German feminists mobilized in the fall of 1989 and challenged the state socialist system. My major interest, however, is to gain insight into the relationship between the state and civil society. Specifically, the question I wish to address is how particular states impact on movement mobilization. German unification was selected as a case study because it tells a story not only of one state system and its "opportunity structure" for feminist mobilization (Kitschelt 1985, 1986, 1990; Tarrow 1994; Rucht 1996); instead, we are confronted with three different state systems. The three state configurations that provided the "playing field" for the East German feminists were the state socialist system; the "stateless state" system of the GDR that started with the collapse of the Wall and ended in March 1990; and the West German state system that became increasingly important as a point of movement orientation starting with the election campaign in February. In addition, there were two different feminist movements (East and West German) that developed in isolation from each other and were forced to share a common political space after the decision was taken to unify the two countries.

East German feminists found themselves not only in the very difficult situation of having to adjust to three completely different state systems. They were also forced to enter a "stage" that was already occupied by West German feminists and in which the rules of the game had been carved out by these actors. For East Germans it meant that the structural elements of the state (different forms of representation, forms of repression, the nature of the party system, forms of interest intermediation, electoral opportunities) not only varied from one system to the next. In fact, the very form of the state system, its ideological foundation, and the cultural symbolism that provided East Germans with a system of reference were demolished and supplanted by the ideological state model of its former enemy. This experience is a singular event in modern history (Offe 1991). No other state has ever been swallowed up in its entirety and replaced with completely different legal, administrative, economic, political, and cultural structures and, in the process, inherited the former enemy's Weltanschauung in toto.

In our attempt to analyze the relationship between movement activities and particular state structures, three analytically distinct but empirically linked processes have to be considered: first, the extent to which state systems impact on the resource development of movements (organizational structures, political allies, strategies and goals, access to information); second, the extent to which social movements can gain access to the decision-making arenas; and, third, the extent to which institutions can block such collective action (Kitschelt 1985).

To advocate a strategy of linking social movement activities to state(s') opportunity structures does not mean that I intend to develop a general theory of social movements or state theory. Instead, I advocate developing middle-range conceptualizations, that provide causal relations between properties of movements and opportunity structures in a given political context. By focusing on the opportunity structures of the different German state configurations and their impacts on the feminist movements, we may come closer to understanding the marginalization of feminists during the unification process. Such a study may add new insights into the West German state structure and its continuing "almost methodological elite distrust" and distance from its citizenry (Offe 1990).

To link movement activities to macropolitical variables of state structures requires a microsociological approach focused on: the organizational structures of the East and West German feminist movements linking the center to the grassroots activists; the action repertoire they used in mobilizing collective action (Tarrow 1994); the cultural "frames" they employed to construct meaning (Snow and Benford 1992); the coalitions they made with other political actors (Klandermans 1990); and the access they had to the media and to government information. Constructing such a resource catalogue enables us to derive insight into the different resource capacities of the East and West German movements and gain some understanding of the variety of resources the two feminist movements used to contest for power and gain access to the West German policy-making process (Gelb 1990).

Such a focus could lead to a set of inquiries that asks whether the organizational structures and strategies of the East German feminist movement, developed within the context of an East German "stateless state," proved less successful when these resources were applied to gain political access in the West German political party system. At another level it lends itself to questions of whether these differences in the organizational strength, action repertoire, and cultural symbols of the East and West German feminists were at the very center of their mutual antagonism and prevented the creation of a "common feminist front."

At a more general level the focus on the role of the two feminist movements in Germany could add to the large comparative literature on the different models of women's participation and activism in other postindustrial Western democracies. Many scholars have pointed out that these countries have policies that are superficially similar with regard to women's rights, and yet these processes have proceeded in different ways and with different impacts in each country (Hernes 1987; Katzenstein and McClurg Mueller 1987; Gelb 1990; Nelson and Chowdhury 1994; Stetson and Mazur 1995).

Second, the microsociological approach must be linked to macropolitical variables of state structures. In contrast to the societal approach that characterizes Tarrow's concept of the opportunity structure, I find Kitschelt's statist analysis of political opportunity structures more useful for explaining the impact of German state structures on the dynamics of the feminist movements. Kitschelt focuses on the national institutional opportunity structure, which he labels "political regimes" existing in each country,[16] to discover the effects of institutional constraints on social movement mobilization. His argument is based on the assumption that access to the political sphere is dependent not only on the resources movements can extract from their environment and employ for their protest action. Equally important is the access of social movements to the public sphere and political decision making that is "governed by institutional rules, such as those reinforcing patterns of interaction between government and interest groups, and electoral laws. These rules allow for, register, respond to and even shape the demands of social movements that are not (yet) accepted political actors" (Kitschelt 1986: 62).[17]

"Political regimes" can be distinguished along a continuum of "open opportunity structures" and "closed opportunity structures" (Eisinger 1973). Systems with opportunity structures open to societal demands are characterized by four systemic characteristics. First, a number of political parties articulate social demands in the electoral arena. Second, the legislative rather than the executive branch dominates in the policy-making process. Third, a pluralist pattern of intermediation exists between interest groups and the executive branch rather than a corporatist system with a structured bargaining model. Finally, nonaccepted political actors have access to the process of forming policy compromises and consensus (Kitschelt 1985).

Utilizing the framework of the relative openness of the political regime's opportunity structure, researchers have concluded that systems with open political structures are more likely to co-opt the movements and

---

16. This framework of particular national policy styles is also found in Richardson 1982, in which he develops the notion of "dominant policy style." Other scholars have referred to the "political culture of policy making" and have argued that in many European countries the institutional organizations of power determine the context, and therefore the negotiated outcome, of most policy issues. Focusing on such macropolitical policy styles, scholars have found that in Germany "politics shape policies," in contrast to the American case, in which "policies shape politics" (Dyson 1982; Beyme 1985; Katzenstein 1987).

17. Kitschelt's approach has much in common with the neo-institutional perspective, which emphasizes the ways in which institutional arrangements structure the political space, tactics, strategy, and goals of political actors. In particular, scholars in the field of political economy have argued that historically evolved institutional arrangements shape the goals of economic actors and structure their strategic interactions (Katzenstein 1978; Berger 1981; Zysman 1983; Streeck and Schmitter 1985; Hall 1986; Campbell, Hollingsworth, and Lindberg 1991; Steinmo, Thelen, and Longstreth 1992).

convert them into interest groups such as with the American feminist movement, which Gelb characterizes as "interest group feminism" (1990). Closed opportunity structures such as the German model, on the other hand, have largely prevented greater participation of social movements, which consequently have had little policy impact. Movements have therefore adopted much more confrontational strategies organized outside traditional party and policy channels (Kitschelt 1985; 1986).

Distinguishing political systems by type of national "political regime" and asking how they affect organizational movements—their strategies to contest political power and gain access to the policy-making process—provides a comparative framework that focuses on the impact of the three different German state systems on the mobilization of East and West German feminist movements. Such an approach not only explains the variations in the movements' resources but also provides a political institutional explanation for the marginalization of both feminist movements during the decision-making process leading to German unification.

Applying this approach across the three German state systems, however, is not without theoretical problems. If we use Kitschelt's conclusion that the West German political system is a closed opportunity structure for both movement participation and policy gains, we must also recognize that such a comparison only makes sense within Western democratic systems. Variations of openness are measured along a continuum and are used to draw inferences about the nature of different liberal democracies and their degree of responsiveness to new societal actors and new social movement issues. Thus, the Western concept of a closed opportunity structure cannot be easily transferred to an authoritarian Marxist-Leninist state, which is established on the very premise of representing the interests of all its people as workers and farmers. The very idea that there are social cleavages outside of class is antithetical to Marxist-Leninist ideology (Glaessner 1991).

This statist opportunity structure approach still has merit, however, even in such repressive Marxist-Leninist states as the former GDR. Despite overall repressiveness in the GDR, some resistance did emerge there in the 1980s. Peace activists, lesbian and gay groups, human rights activists, and feminist scholars found a political sanctuary under the roof of the Protestant Church and in some departments in the universities in the 1980s (Dölling 1990b; Richter and Zylla 1991). The Protestant Church and some of the state-loyal universities functioned as "influential friends" (Tarrow 1994) and helped not only to protect the opposition groups but also to incubate resistance. At the same time, the opposition groups that burst into the public arena in the fall of 1989 bore all the markings of having formed in protected "niches" (Gaus 1983). The structure and strategies of the nascent feminist movement, a topic I will pursue in the following chapters, were thus historically conditioned by the "political regime" of the GDR and explain its variation from its West German feminist counterpart.

Yet the political opportunity approach is wanting in one crucial respect. It fails to take into account the specific practices of the women's movement (Kontos 1986; Riedmüller 1988; Kulawik 1991–92). Feminist scholars have consistently argued that the "new social movement" literature is wedded to traditional political science and sociological paradigms of organizational politics and therefore devalues the women's movements' concern with collective identity formation as "cultural," "privatistic," "particularistic," and "underpoliticized" (Kulawik 1991–92).[18] It should not come as a surprise, therefore, that many "male-stream" movement analyses see in the women's movements little more than cultural entities (Rucht 1988; Melucci 1989).

There are at least two theoretical pitfalls in such an interpretation. First, it easily leads to an artificial divide between the supposedly "apolitical" women's movement and the "political" new social movements. Rucht created a typology according to which women's movements are characterized along the axis of an "expressive logic of action," which corresponds to an identity-oriented strategy, as opposed to movements that express an "instrumental logic of action," which implies a power-oriented strategy. These different movement logics result in the former pursuing actions that focus on "reformist divergence, subcultural retreatment, and countercultural challenges." These "soft" feminine strategies are then contrasted to the "hard" male power-oriented strategies of groups that strive for "political participation, bargaining, pressure, and political confrontation" (Rucht 1990: 163).

These typologies are not only highly normative; they also miss the political aspect of feminist collective identity formation. Kulawik has pointed out that "the definition and formation of new personal and collective identities have to be regarded as a constitutive element of the politics of social movements" (Kulawik 1991–92: 69). An orientation toward cultural practices is thus not a sign of weakness. Instead, a change of "cultural" codes is always also an act of struggling to change power relations.

Rucht's typology reveals a second pitfall of identifying the women's movements as little more than engagement in cultural practices. By linking the "expressive logic" of the feminist movements to women's intrinsic

---

18. This discussion about the supposed "apolitical" nature of the women's movement has to be understood within a European context. Certainly, the American women's movement is not considered apolitical. The German autonomous feminist movement, however, is regarded as a cultural movement among a large section of the new social movement theorists, a characterization that I strongly reject.

"female values," Rucht essentially falls into the trap of creating an opposition between politics and culture. Women are thus reduced to their essentialist position of being different because of their biological characteristics. Two faulty assumptions follow from such a position. First, it invites biological determinism (Scott 1988). And, second, it creates two exclusionary categories: men and women (Flax 1990). Two hidden assumptions are carried in such a meaning system. If the biological categories are "natural," then any changes in the relationship between men and women are precluded a priori. On the other hand, if women and men are viewed as distinct types of beings, the relation of dominance and subordination between the sexes is hidden (Flax 1990). This essentialist view leads to a conception of gender relations that "veil" the institutional power relations inherent in all social relations. Yet gender relations are relations of domination (Scott 1988). This means that social relations are structured hierarchically, based on the perceived differences between women and men. Or, to express it differently, gender structures the very essence of power relations.

It is this lack of conceptualizing gender relations as power relations that is at the very root of many traditional social movement theories. Whether there are specific exclusionary mechanisms of the state that influence and even determine the practices of the women's movements is thus never even asked. Yet such a "gendered" insight into how the state influences the very practices of movements is, I will argue, the very basis for discovering why feminists failed to gain access to the policy-making process during German unification.

The next section presents an outline of this gendered aspect of the institutional political opportunity structures of the West German political regime. I will focus on the specific exclusionary mechanism of the West German system that created a "gender bias" against the participatory demands of feminists during the negotiations toward German unity. That I have excluded the East German state from such a gendered analysis has to do with strategic considerations rather than with the belief that the East German national regime did not have specific gendered effects on feminists. The West German state was simply the main player in unifying the two countries. The East German state not only did not play a subsidiary role; it played virtually no role in this process.

The Gendered Political Opportunity Structure of the West German Political Regime

Was the marginalization of feminists and their goals the result of a gender bias inherent in the West German state system that blocked the access of East and West German feminists to the policy-making process? Can we

isolate specific "institutional exclusionary mechanisms" in the German
state that were specifically antithetical to feminists' participation and concerns during the process of unification? By focusing on the specific
moment of German unification we can not only understand the unfolding
of this case study at a particular historic conjuncture; we can also derive
some generalizations about the German state and specific actors in civil
society. German unification and its exclusion of feminist actors offers a
snapshot of a "concentrated historical moment" in which the exclusionary
mechanisms of the state came into full force. Such a unique situation does
not occur during periods of "routine policy making" in which the powers
of the state do not come into play as overtly as they did during the process
of unification.

Posing the question only in terms of women being excluded from the
decision-making process invites the immediate objection that, in fact, the
entire opposition movement of the former GDR was unable to influence
the unification process and, therefore, feminists are not unique in their loss
of political influence. The political irrelevance of the opposition groups
after March 18, 1990, certainly makes it clear that women were not the
only losers in the unification process.[19] The political opposition groups
represented at the Central Round Table—such as Democratic Awakening,[20] Democracy Now, Green Party, Initiative for Peace and Human
Rights, New Forum, and United Left—all went down to electoral defeat
on March 18. Having formed into three major electoral groupings,
together they received no more than 5.05 percent of the popular vote.[21]

Despite this exclusion of all opposition groups from the treaty negotiations for German unity, the primary explanation for why feminists
failed to have policy access has to do with a "double gender marginalization" that feminists experienced, and continue to experience, in the German polity in the postunification phase. This double gender marginalization refers to specific institutional and cultural exclusionary mechanisms
intrinsic to the "parliamentary group state" (Steffani 1990; Schüttemeyer
1994) and the corporatist system of economic bargaining (Young 1996).

The parliamentary group state (*Fraktionsstaat*) refers to the increas-

---

19. For an explanation of why the East German opposition groups failed to actualize
their agenda after November 1989, see Joppke 1995; and Rucht 1994, 1996.

20. Members of "Democratic Awakening" joined the CDU and DSU in the election
coalition of "Alliance for Germany" for the Volkskammer election on March 18, 1990.

21. The political groupings consisted of Coalition '90 (New Forum, Democracy Now,
Initiative for Peace and Human Rights); Greens-UFV (Green Party, Independent Women's
Group), and the action coalition United Left (the Carnations, United Left). See Müller-
Enbergs, Schulz, and Wielgohs 1991: 367.

ing importance of the party parliamentary groups (*Fraktionen*)[22] in the Bundestag. These *Fraktionen* have assumed the former role of the parties and party bosses, and the newer literature not only often detects a more rigid, less open system with fewer access points in the German state system; it also points to an increasing centralization of the state system (Thaysen 1976; Steffani 1990; Schüttemeyer 1994).

Parliamentary groups have become the most crucial single actor in the process of recruiting and nominating political leaders, determining political direction and specific policy decisions, organizing parliamentary procedures, determining the basic right of parliamentary debates, and deciding which members are assigned to which committees. Taking into account that any party career advancement needs the endorsement of the *Fraktion,* that deputies can exercise influence only if they have the backing of the parliamentary group, and that any legislative bill has to survive the scrutiny of the *Fraktion,* it has become a truism that "a member without a parliamentary group is a member without any influence" (Steffani 1990: 288). These *Fraktionen* have become "gatekeepers of legislation" (Schüttemeyer 1994), and, by virtue of their hierarchical, closed, highly disciplined practices, they have made women deputies outsiders within the power structure. Feminists are thus confronted with a catch-22 position: if they want to advance their career, they cannot champion feminist issues; if they decide to operate independently of the party hierarchy, they are devoid of influence (Steffani 1990).

Second, the German system of corporatist interest intermediation also acts as an exclusionary mechanism for feminists and their issues. Corporatism, unlike pluralism, with its emphasis on individual access to the policy-making process, is a system of exchange between capital and labor through bargained agreements between strong, encompassing class associations at the national or industrial level with procedural and political facilitation by the state (Schmitter 1979).

In contrast to Anglo-Saxon countries, German politics is not only, or not even foremost, reducible to competition within political institutions. Instead, most bills introduced in parliament have already been preformulated within this complex process of societal concertation. Corporatism differs from the pluralist model of interest organization in that only a limited number of groups receive political status; membership in these groups is often compulsory. They are noncompetitive and hierarchically ordered,

---

22. The parliamentary groups are similar to the American congressional caucuses. I will, however, continue to use *parliamentary group* and not *caucus.* German scholars have not Americanized this term in their English translations to express the difference between the two institutions.

have a representational monopoly, and retain full control over leadership selection and interest articulation (Schmitter 1979). At the same time, these corporatist institutions (labor unions, employers associations, economic chambers, economic associations and societies, central bank, and economic policy institutes) are not among the formal state institutions (parliament, executive, administrative bureaucracy). These institutions, however, are linked to the state via the administrative bureaucracy and the political parties (Lehmbruch 1979; 1984).

Thus, the societal groups involved in corporate decision-making appear outside the state but in reality are linked through multiple channels to the state. The corporate state, which Gramsci (1971) has referred to as "the state in its inclusive sense," includes "an ensemble of socially embedded, socially regularized, and strategically selective institutions, organizations, social forces, and activities organized around the making of collectively binding decisions for the general polity" (Hirsch 1990; Jessop 1995). In corporatist systems the difference between state and society is blurred. Not only are "state institutions, norms, and practices diffused throughout civil society: social forces have also gained access to state institutions" (Katzenstein 1987: 10).

This inclusionary pattern of post–World War II West German political-economic class compromise, which crystallizes around elite bargaining among the leaders of mass apparatus parties and the centralized associations of economic producers, has also created its own patterns of exclusion (Jessop 1979; Panitch 1979; Esser and Fach 1981; Hirsch 1986; 1990). The very rise of what Kitschelt (1990) has called "Left-Libertarian" political parties[23] in political settings characterized by corporatist interest intermediation has to be seen as a "backlash" against these existing exclusionary institutional rules and styles of collective decision making. Corporatist systems are thus at one and the same time inclusive and create their own patterns of exclusion.

The German model of party and *Fraktionsstaat* and the specific style of corporatist interest intermediation have produced a largely "illiberal liberal" constitutional order of German "democracy" that is decidedly state-centered and has an inherent distrust of the forces and capacities of civil society (Kirchheimer 1966; Narr 1977; Kitschelt 1985; Hirsch 1986; Offe 1990; Young 1996a). In this German "fetishization of the state" and

---

23. Left-Libertarian parties are, for example, the West German Greens and other environmental and ecological parties. According to Kitschelt, they are "'Left' because they share with traditional socialism a mistrust of the marketplace, of private investment, and of the achievement ethic, and a commitment to egalitarian redistribution. They are 'libertarian' because they reject the authority of private or public bureaucracies to regulate individual and collective conduct" (Kitschelt 1990: 180).

state institutions an almost "methodological elite distrust [exists] in a citizenry that is held to be in need of a constant paternalistic supervision, control and education." The German model contains a strong element of institutional distance from the citizenry, who may not pass the test of democratic worthiness defined by the existing political elites (Offe 1990). This state-defined and state-enforced "constitutional culture" is reflected in the strong constitutional position of the German party system, by the lack of any significant direct democratic modes of citizen participation, and "by the strong position of the Federal Republic's constitutional court with its power to review and challenge the conformity of parliamentary legislation and political parties to what are believed to be substantive value commitments of the constitutional order" (249).

In addition to these general "illiberal" tendencies in the German state, at least two aspects of the parliamentary process and the corporatist elite bargaining model have an impact on women in particular and add to their marginalization and ineffectiveness: first, the right to frame a discourse; and, second, the very structure of "old boys' networks."

The "framing" concept draws on the notion of action frames that provide a shared understanding among participants of collective actions (Snow and Benford 1988). Concepts such as cognitive frames, ideological packages, or cultural discourses all "describe the shared meanings that inspire people to collective action" (Tarrow 1994: 22). In "framing" feminist issues, for example, West German women deputies faced a handicap not encountered by German male deputies. Not only do they struggle for distributional politics—"who gets what, when, and how"—they also fight for the right to "name oneself" (Jenson 1991) and gain representation *as feminists.* This involves legitimizing both one's self-definition as a feminist and one's deployment of feminist discourse. From this perspective "politics can be seen as a process in which actors create their constituencies by generating support for their preferred formulation of their own collective identity and for the enumeration of interests which follows from that collective identity" (50).

During the negotiation stage of German unification German feminists tried to challenge the male discourse in the parliamentary "universe of political discourse," the terrain in which actors struggle over definition, about who has a right to make claims, how to construct meaning, and where politics occurs. Yet this "universe of political discourse" remained impermeable to the discourse centered around feminist issues. The *Fraktionen* (as institutional exclusionary mechanism) acted not only as "gatekeepers of legislation" but also as "gatekeepers over discursive practices." It is this issue that is gender specific and has marginalized, and continues to marginalize, feminists and their agenda in the German parliament.

Second, concerning the basic gendered identity of the German state itself, Eva Kreisky (1984) recently advanced the argument that the German state was conceptualized on the basis of a "mystical male bond" that is inherently exclusionary toward women. This belief in the "state as the highest male bond" emerged around the turn of the century to legitimize the existing all-male state from the first challenges of women activists. This was not an isolated crackpot theory; it was an accepted social theory of the day. Germany was the first and only country to introduce the "scientific concept" of male bonds that found its echo throughout the literary cultural establishments during and after World War I (in the work of Hermann Hesse, Thomas Mann, Ernst Jünger) and in the writings of social theorists such as Max Weber, Carl Schmitt, and Hans Blüher. The National Socialists put into practice a concept of the state as the highest form of male bonding with an apparatus of terror, a concept that had already become the mainstream in German state theory and culture by the 1920s.

In this identity of the state as a "male bond," woman is always the "other," the foe (Carl Schmitt, cited in Kreisky 1994). It is, of course, true that the German state of today is no longer an expression of male bonding. Yet the ideal of male bond as a psychological pattern of behavior and a mental construct does not rely on the actual existence of such gendered cliques. The very idea of such a "masculinist" state identity can continue to flourish in changed environments in which such bonds no longer exist (Sombart 1988). Wendy Brown has argued that the state can be masculinist without intentionally or overtly pursuing the "interests" of men precisely because the multiple dimensions of socially constructed masculinity have historically shaped the multiple modes of power circulating through the domain called the state (1992: 14).

The continuing aspect of masculinist state power is particularly evident in the bureaucratic dimension of German state power. Not only is bureaucratic politics the central organizing principle of German corporatist welfare capitalism; the civil servant culture (*Beamten*), with its values of abstract rationality, formal proceduralism, rights orientation, and hierarchy, is the very basis of the bureaucratic apparatus (Kitschelt 1990; Offe 1990; Kreisky 1994). This overly bureaucratic aspect of German politics produces at least two moments of masculinity. First, the instrumental rationality of the bureaucratic order that constitutes both the foundation of bureaucratic order and the process of bureaucratic rationalization rests on the notion of domination (Weber 1978). This particular expression of domination "through regimes of predictability, calculability, and control" appears to be, as Wendy Brown suggests, constructed on the ultimate value of control and will to power. Such an emphasis on bureaucratic masculinist values of domination stand in relation to the more dominant female values of "need-based decision making, relationality, substantive rationality, and responsibility" (Brown 1992: 27; see also Ferguson 1984).

Second, the German bureaucratic value system is deeply infused with rituals that create "insiders" and "outsiders" in this exclusive male club. Belonging to the inner circles of the highly respected German civil service (the essence of German statehood) continues to be laden with symbolic, ritualistic, male bonding rites that take place in drinking places (*Kneipen* or *Gosthöuser*), which are less hospitable to women than to men. These rites are built around high alcohol consumption and sexist jokes (Kreisky 1994). Braunthal also documented the same aura of a preferred all-male atmosphere as part of the ritual of Social Democratic Party meetings. The male majority will continue to meet in bars and restaurants and thereby give the impression that women are unwelcome and that the male party members would prefer to make decisions among themselves (Braunthal 1983; Kolinsky 1993).

Not even the republicanization and democratization of the bureaucratic system, upon which the German state system rests, has been able to crack this highly ritualistic male "carrier culture." Behind the aura of secrecy and closed-door negotiations the "structural conservatism of the German bureaucracy" has turned feminist politics into nonevents (Häussermann 1977). The result is that there is not only a "policy implementation deficit" of feminist issues; there is the very absence of feminist discourse in the policy formulation process.

Metaphorically, the German state can be compared to an "apricot,"[24] soft and fleshy on the outside with a hard, inaccessible kernel around the very structure of German power. The increasing concentration of power is the inverse of the large pluralistic presence of German women in the new all-German parliament. As the political parties opened their doors to large numbers of female deputies during the 1980s and the state became more "feminized," the very center of state power contracted and, once again, became devoid of women's influence (Krieger 1991; Hoecker 1995).

Of course, women are not entirely excluded from the German state system. They have benefited as employees of the welfare state, as consumers (child care, health care, prenatal clinics), as clients (recipients of social services), and are visible as political representatives in government and the German labor unions. Yet the integration of women into the German political system is that of "policy takers" and not as "policy shapers"

---

24. Hannah Arendt compared the German National-Socialist state to an "onion." Peeling layer after layer of onion skin resembled the peeling of the various layers of Nazi power that remained ephemeral (Arendt 1968).

(Offe 1985). Women do not have access to the very center of political decision-making processes in either the political parties or the parliamentary
group state, the *Fraktionsstaat,* and they are not integrated into the corporate bodies dominated by economic organizations and administrative
bureaucracies.

The continuing resistance to the institutionalization of feminist
demands was at the very center of the German unification process. These
institutional exclusionary mechanisms antithetical to feminists' participation and concerns, however, are not unique to unification. As pointed out
earlier, unification only provided a "perfect snapshot" into this relationship between state and feminist politics. The more important result of this
study is to demonstrate that this double gender marginalization preceded
German unification and continues to operate in the postunification German political system. As a result, feminists not only face a closed opportunity structure; they face, above and beyond this, a gendered closed opportunity structure of the state.

Methodological Issues: What Is Feminism and Who Is a Feminist?

One of the most difficult methodological problems is the issue of feminism.
The problem stems from the fact that there were, and continue to be, three
different feminist/women's groups that were engaged in the pursuit of gender politics during unification but which did not agree on what constitutes
feminism, who is a feminist, and what the boundaries are between feminist
politics and women's politics (Ferree 1994; Helwerth and Schwarz 1995).
Since these differences form an important aspect of the larger research
project, I will address only the definitional issues at this point and leave the
substantive explanations for these variations for later chapters.

The concept of feminism in West Germany is largely associated with
the "autonomous" feminist movement that emerged in the early 1970s.
Feminism, according to this interpretation, means autonomy both from
men and from formal political institutions. The politics of autonomy
focused on the creation of a "counter-society" outside the existing social
and political institutions. Only in the 1980s did the autonomous feminist
grassroots groups become more receptive to institutional politics (Ferree
1990; Kontos 1990; Kulawik 1991–92).

Parallel to this autonomous feminist movement are the "institutional" feminists (*Politikfrauen*) situated within traditional German political institutions, who pursue "women's politics." Women's politics, in contrast to feminist politics, subscribes to the ideas of liberalism and focuses
on eradicating gender discrimination from within the traditional institu-

tional structures (Kontos 1990). In this respect German "institutional" feminists share some similarities with the American model of "women's rights" and "interest group feminism" (Gelb 1990).

To chart the relationship between West German institutional feminists and autonomous feminists is, to say the least, problematic. The autonomous feminist movement continues to harbor great skepticism toward the state and toward men generally. At the same time, much evidence exists of a considerable blurring of lines between feminist and women's politics and also among grassroots activists and feminists working within the traditional political institutions. This is particularly noticeable in the Green Party. Women deputies subscribe to the goals of the autonomous feminist movement; at the same time, they are working within the institutional channels of power (Krieger 1991). Yet, on another level, even institutional feminists who pursue women's politics have started to come closer to defining themselves as feminists. Rita Süssmuth, the former first minister of women and present president of the Bundestag, produced a shock wave within her party when she identified herself as a feminist (Holzhauer and Steinbauer 1994).

The demarcation line remains drawn between the two feminisms in terms of the contradictory goals they pursue. Autonomous feminism is still geared toward a fundamental restructuring of social institutions with the goal of supplanting present capitalist relations with a more environmentally conscious alternative economy and a decentralized, grassroots political system (Kontos 1986). In contrast, institutional feminists direct their struggle toward substantive equality within the given liberal social market system.

This picture of the differing West German types of feminism became even more complicated with the "entrance" of East German feminists organized within the Independent Women's League. The UFV understood itself as an independent, political, and feminist organization representing East German interests. The usage of *independent* referred to its independence from the SED and from the much-hated official GDR women's group, the DFD. It did not mean independent of state institutions and of men (Sauer 1994). In fact, the UFV constituted itself with the specific goal of participating in institutional politics. The founding mothers of the UFV envisioned real changes coming only from a parallel strategy of feminists working in the traditional public arena and others engaged at the grassroots level in various women's projects (i.e., women's centers, cafés, feminist bookstores, battered women's shelters) (Schenk 1990).

In contrast to the autonomous feminists in the West, the UFV saw the realization of social transformation only in conjunction with men. Having stood side by side with East German men against the socialist state, they did not target men as their adversaries (Lewis 1993). This solidarity with men was expressed in some of the pamphlets at political demonstrations in the fall of 1989. A Lilo pamphlet read: "We are fighting for a socialist society without patriarchal relations! Together with men!" In their emphasis on universal equality GDR feminism is best described as a type of "humanistic" feminism, with an emancipatory vision of a universal humanity, in which women and men can meet as equals and develop as human beings (Helwerth and Schwarz 1995).

There were also political women activists in East Germany who did not identify themselves as feminists. These activists, such as Bärbel Bohley, Ulrike Poppe, Vera Wollenberger, Ingrid Köppe, Katja Havemann, and Bettina Rathenau, had already been politically active in the 1980s and were some of the founding members of the first opposition groups organized at the national level, such as Women for Peace, the Initiative for Peace and Human Rights, and Real Peace (Frieden Konkret) (Poppe 1995). Being women, according to Bohley, was never the overriding criterion for creating these groups, and gender issues were not at the center of their concerns. Nevertheless, they did discuss the increasing militarization of the society and human rights violations and what could be done about them among women (Bohley interview).

While these women repudiated feminism as such, they did share with feminists some of the same goals that were based on "political pluralism, political freedoms, human rights, freedom of speech, grassroots democracy, separation of powers, rule of law" (Poppe 1995: 270).[25] The dividing line between the two groups, however, was their attitude toward the PDS, the successor party of the SED. In contrast to the UFV, which was rather close to the PDS and whose members even volunteered to be placed on the electoral party lists of the PDS, women activists who had opposed the GDR regime in the 1980s refused to have any contact with the party (Schäfer 1995; Hampele 1996).

This summary of the different East and West German feminist movements and of women political activists in both parts of Germany who did not necessarily subscribe to a feminist identity while sharing some of the values and goals with feminists should sensitize the reader to the complexities of German gender politics. In the following chapters I will clearly indicate which group is being discussed, whether they are East or West Germans, whether the focus is on women's politics or feminist politics, and whether the actors are West German institutional feminists or women political activists from the East.

---

25. These values were announced by the "Initiative for Peace and Human Rights" on "Human Rights Day," December 10, 1987.

Synopsis

The first chapter has a historical focus. Despite the divergent development of East and West German feminist thought after 1945, the two movements share a historical legacy that influenced the development of these movements in the post–World War II period. Understanding the development of feminist thought prior to 1945 is crucial to understanding the development of the particular feminisms in the East and West after 1945. That feminism did not develop in the East under state socialism prior to the late 1980s is as significant as the rise of the feminist movement in the West in the 1970s. Whether a feminist movement developed, and how it developed, will be explained within the context of the political opportunity structures of the respective regimes. How these structures shaped the organization, ideologies, action repertoires, and cultural frames of meaning of the feminist groups and the extent to which they gained, or failed to gain, access to the policy-making process is the subject of chapter 1.

The second chapter shifts to the collapse of the Wall in November 1989 and the beginning of the East German "stateless state" period, which ended with the start of the parliamentary election campaign in February. In this section I will describe the Central Round Table period of governing and how it shaped the mobilization of the first indigenous East German feminist movement. The "withering away" of the authoritarian state structures permitted at one level the "entrance of the marginals" onto the East German political scene. This stateless state period, however, had a Janus character. "All was possible" in the short run, but the lack of a political orientation, in the long run, constrained rather than facilitated the success of the East German feminist movement.

The third chapter is about the "forced" political reorientation of East German feminists toward Bonn and the start of the process of German unification. This period encompasses the time from the parliamentary election campaign to German unification in October. During the negotiation stage of German unification not only did East German feminists have to adjust their strategies to a completely different political environment, but they also entered a political space that was already occupied by West German feminists and institutional feminists. This chapter will analyze this reorientation toward the politics of Bonn from the perspective of the "clash" between two different feminist movements and will examine the extent to which the East and West German feminist movements, albeit not in concert, used their resources to contest for power and try to influence the negotiation process of German unification.

The fourth chapter turns to an analysis of the specific "exclusionary mechanisms" of the West German political opportunity structure and tries to explain why both the West and East German feminist movements failed to influence the unification process. I differentiate between primary and secondary phenomena. Chapter 4 focuses on the primary phenomena for the disempowerment of feminists during the decision-making process that lay in both the formal and informal exclusionary mechanisms of the German state (executive, parliament, judiciary, administrative bureaucracy) and the corporatist system, which effects a double gender marginalization in both the political and economic arenas. In particular, I focus on the controversial abortion issue in both the parliament and the Federal Constitutional Court.

The secondary phenomena include the internal problems within the Independent Women's League and the rivalry between the East and West German feminist movements and will be discussed in chapter 5. Although the secondary phenomena do not explain the exclusion of feminists from the negotiation stage of German unification, we should nevertheless heed Dostoevski's warning that "only in gambling does nothing depend on nothing" and therefore scrutinize the strategies and goals of the two movements during unification. It is, of course, a hypothetical question worth pondering whether the outcome would have been different for feminists on both sides of the former Wall had the Independent Women's League, the West German autonomous feminist movements, and the institutional feminists combined their energies to contest the largely male-centered unification process. Chapter 5 concludes with the theoretical arguments about the general gender bias of the German state that was brought to bear with all its force on feminists during the process of unification. I will argue against the "exceptionalism" of German unification and show that, while it was a "meta-policy-making" process involving singular and systemic changes,[26] the double gender marginalization was not a unique process confined to German unification. I will try to demonstrate that the continuing disadvantage experienced by East and West German feminists and by women in general in the postunification phase is part of this same gender bias in the German state.[27] The final chapter argues for a methodological framework to analyze and compare the gendered nature of the

---

26. Dror (1968) differentiates between specific policies and "metapolicy," the latter being how to make policy about making policies. I thank Bill Gormley, Department of Government and Public Policy, Georgetown University, for pointing out the difference between "routine policy" and meta-policy-making.

27. A recent survey carried out on behalf of the Federal Ministry for the Family, Senior Citizens, Women and Youth came to the conclusion that 62 percent of Germans in the West and a full three-quarters in the East feel that women remain considerably disadvantaged in comparison with men in German society (*Week in Germany*, May 10, 1996: 2).

transition of Eastern and Central European countries in order to go beyond the mere cataloguing of negative effects and come to understand the specific formal and informal institutional and cultural mechanisms of particular political and social systems that are antithetical to women's participation and concerns.

CHAPTER 1

Political Opportunity Structures and Feminist Protest in Thought and Practice: The German Historical Legacy and Women's Mobilization in East and West Germany, 1945–1989

The Common Historical Legacy

For nearly one hundred years (1848–1945) the shared historical legacy of all German women, except during the short permissive period of the Weimar Republic, is that of struggling to find a political voice and space in the mostly conservative political environment of the nineteenth and early twentieth centuries. Strongly ideological women's movements emerged in the nineteenth century that split not only along the lines of "bourgeois" and "proletarian" women's movements (Frevert 1986). Even the bourgeois women's movement witnessed divisive struggles between the radicals and the conservatives, which the latter increasingly won after 1908 (Evans 1976; Greven-Aschoff 1981).

The conservative political culture and exclusionary state policies of the German Empire on the one hand and polarized women's movements on the other are two sides of the same coin. In their polarized historical development the women's movements mirrored the equally polarized political developments of Germany in the nineteenth and twentieth centuries.

Nineteenth-Century Feminism and the Kaiserreich

In nineteenth-century Germany there were at least four groups of women occupying different social and economic status positions. First, there were the women and daughters of the bourgeois middle and upper classes who did not have the right to work (except for single women occupying positions as governesses, teachers, or society ladies). In the second group there were the women who worked in agriculture, trade, and commerce. Then there were the factory workers (single or married with children). The last group was confined to the single maids and domestic servants. The first leaders of the women's movement came largely from the middle and upper classes (Nave-Herz 1988).

The creation and the ensuing development of the bourgeois feminist movement has to be seen in the context of the revolutionary defeat of 1848. Although the origin of the German feminist movement dates back to the social and democratic movements of 1848, the Allgemeiner Deutscher Frauenverein (General German Women's Association) was only founded in 1865 in Leipzig. Louise Otto-Peters (1819–95), the first president of the association, influenced by the democratic ideas of "freedom, equality, and independence" was forced to retreat from the revolutionary radicalism and democratic idealism of 1848 (Evans 1976).

Enacted in the aftermath of the revolution, the 1851 Law of Association (fully rescinded only in 1908) forbade women in Prussia, Bavaria, and Saxony and in many other parts of the empire to engage in political actions (the right of assembly and association) (Evans 1976; Brand, Büsser, and Rucht 1986). Only in Hamburg, Bremen, Baden, and Württemberg did women have full rights to participate in politics. In addition, women had few legal rights. According to the Prussian Civil Code, they were not regarded as "legal persons." It was the husband who was the head of the family and the legal guardian of his wife. Until the replacement of the Prussian Civil Code with the Civil Code of 1900, she could not work, sign a contract, or engage in litigation (Evans 1976).

Banishment from political activities after 1851 forced the bourgeois women's movement to break links it had maintained prior to 1848 with the "democratic-liberal" political movement (Frevert 1986). The only avenue left for the women's movement of the 1870s and 1880s was to concentrate on issues that were regarded as "safe" from state repression: the improvement of women's education and the right to work. These demands did not challenge the existing political order nor aim at equality between women and men (Evans 1976). The political ban not only shaped the organizational structure of these early women's rights groups; it also shaped the very identity of bourgeois women and how they framed their demands.

Women's rights activists framed their "rights discourse" in the language of "motherhood as a profession" and elevated an essentialist position of "women's ethics" across class lines (Riedmüller 1988). The proposals were put forth in accordance with the accepted conservative social and moral system to "benefit society" and "the advancement of humanity" and emphasized women's traditional role of "devotion," "love," and "sacrifice" (Evans 1976; Nave-Herz 1988). This new ethics saw the role of women confined to such typical women's professions as teacher and social worker. It is therefore not surprising that the bourgeois women's movement directed most of its energies toward education. Starting in the 1870s, the movement championed the right of girls to attend "Gymnasium" and to gain access to the universities. Even in this struggle for the right to educate women, however, the bourgeois women's movement restricted itself to demands that were considered safe and within the purview of women's "natural" areas of moral concern (Brand, Büsser, and Rucht 1986).

Even those activists who regarded economic issues and the "right to work" as central to the emancipation of women were primarily concerned with the hellish conditions in the factories and their impact on social morality. Louise Otto-Peters not only championed a decent wage for working women; she and her colleagues made the increasing pauperism of working women the center of their agitation while at the same time defending the right of women to work in factories (Gerhard 1991).[1] These early bourgeois champions of women's rights believed the struggle to upgrade the working conditions of women would improve social morality (Frevert 1986).

Bourgeois feminists also criticized the limited educational opportunities middle-class women had to achieve an independent economic existence. With the increasing impoverishment of the middle class, bourgeois women had few opportunities but to work as poorly paid governesses, society ladies, or as assistant teachers.[2] They were not permitted to assume the headship of girls' schools, nor could they achieve equal status with male teachers. It is thus not surprising that women teachers provided the largest body of support for the feminist movement (Evans 1976).

In this climate of social and political conservatism and state repression, the role of the General German Woman's Association started to

---

1. Because of the increasing wage reductions and the oversupply of workers after 1848, the tailors and cigar workers in Leipzig introduced a ban to exclude women from working in factories. The hostility toward women is expressed in the verse: "First, get rid of the tailoress, who takes the bread from us tailors!" ("Schafft ab zum ersten die Schneidermamselln, die das Brot verkürzen uns Schneidergeselln!") (Kuczynski 1963: 81).

2. From 1825 until 1861 the number of women working as teaching assistants increased from 705 to 7,366 in Prussia (Nave-Herz 1988: 16).

decline in the 1880s. It became increasingly fragmented, suffered numerical losses, remained timid and conservative (Evans 1976). Only the 1890s ushered in organizational changes in the women's movement. On March 29, 1894, the many different women's societies and associations that had sprung up in the fields of welfare and charity formed an umbrella organization, the Federation of German Women's Associations (BDF), uniting thirty-four women's associations. Within a year the new association had sixty-five member associations with some fifty thousand members.[3] This organizational change also marked a new turning point for the bourgeois feminist movement. It became more radicalized around the goals of political equality and the right to vote and the struggle against the state's regulation of prostitution, abortion, and sexual freedom (Greven-Aschoff 1981; Nave-Herz 1988).

The new radicalization of the women's movement had to do with a combination of factors internal to the movement itself as well as to changes in the political environment. First, the slow but increasing access to educational opportunities permitted women to play an increasingly independent role in economic life in the 1890s. Second, the resignation of Otto v. Bismarck also made possible the upsurge of organizational activities of many associations after the lapsing of the Anti-Socialist Law in 1890. There were other changes in the social structure brought about by the "continuing process of Germany's headlong industrialization; the growth of the tertiary sector of the economy with its expansion of employment opportunities for middle-class women, associated with the general economic upturn after the end of the Great Depression of 1896; a rapid expansion . . . of the numbers and the professional consciousness of women schoolteachers" (Evans 1976: x).

The BDF, however, was from its inception riven between factions of the Right and the Left.[4] The Left was no longer willing to adhere to the political marginalization of women. In an unprecedented move they persuaded the BDF to challenge the provisions of the new Civil Code that had been ratified in the Reichstag in 1896 and continued to be disadvantageous to women. Although it was too late for any amendments to be made to the Civil Code, the Left was able to pass a resolution at their

3. In 1908 the BDF was able to rival numerically the left-wing liberals with a membership of 133,000. It had a membership of 150,000 in 1908, making it—numerically at least—one of the most influential organizations in Imperial Germany (Evans 1976: 145).

4. This ideological dispute was also reflected in the various publications issued by the federation. The official organ of the BDF was the *Central Paper of the Federation of the German Women Associations* (*Centralblatt des Bundes Deutscher Frauenvereine*). In addition, *The Woman* (*Die Frau*) was the official organ for the Right and the *Women's Movement* (*Frauenbewegung*) for the Left (Greven-Aschoff 1981).

meeting condemning the law as "an expression of one-sided man's law (*Männerrecht*)" (Evans 1976: 41). This ascendancy by the Left leaders (Minna Cauer, Marie Stritt, Anita Augspurg) was viewed with great misgivings by the Right (Auguste Schmidt, Helene Lange) who resented the radicalization and controversy that the new issues raised in the BDF. The heated conflicts that dominated the BDF for the next years were the issue of female suffrage and the issue of prostitution and sexuality. With the rise of Marie Stritt as president of the BDF in 1902, the radicals were able to impose their views on the BDF. The conservatives continued, however, to reject the "new ethics" espoused by Helene Stöcker in the newly formed Federation of Protection for Mothers and Sexual Reform. This federation raised publicly the issue of sexuality, advocated cohabitation without marriage, espoused the support for single mothers, and advocated the repeal of the anti-abortion law (para. 218). The conservative leaders within the BDF saw in these demands a rejection of marriage and family as a protective institution for the "general welfare" and voted against the admission of the Federation to the BDF (Evans 1976; Greven-Aschoff 1981; Nave-Herz 1988).

For the conservative Gertrud Bäumer, who subsequently became the president of the BDF in 1910 until 1919, the central woman's role remained that of motherhood. Even before Bäumer ascended to the presidency, the radicals' influence started to wane in 1908, and the BDF moved to the Right. A campaign organized by the moderates and a new group of conservatives "aimed at reversing the trend towards radical feminism within the BDF and eliminating the influence of all those within the BDF who supported it" (Evans 1976: 149). While the immediate cause for the decline of the radicals was the defeat to abolish Section 218 of the Civil Code, it was the ouster of the radical president of the Federation, Maria Stritt, that opened the BDF to the new move to the Right championed by Gertrud Bäumer. Female emancipation, to Bäumer, meant "that since as far as women were concerned motherhood and marriage were 'specifically female,' a strengthening of this aspect of women's life could now be regarded as an act of female emancipation. If she [woman] limits herself to house and family, she is under certain circumstances acting in this way more in accordance with the ideals of the women's movement than if she goes into any male profession" (155). This conservative view of women became the dominant strand within the BDF. More important, German feminism moved closely to the nationalism and authoritarianism that became the dominant ideology prior to World War I and, as will be shown later, was tantamount in linking motherhood to the service of the state.

The Proletarian Women's Movement

The bourgeois women's movement was not the only national representative of women's issues in the nineteenth and early twentieth centuries. It had to share the stage with the proletarian women's movement. Despite the different ideological worldviews of the two movements and their different priorities, they agreed on many of the emancipatory goals for women: the need for political equality, equal pay for equal work, improved working conditions, the protection of mothers, improved educational opportunities, and the right to work. They both faced the intensified competition from bourgeois and working-class males in the labor market. Single bourgeois women fought to gain entrance into the middle and higher professions, whereas proletarian women struggled against the exclusion of women from the labor process, a demand frequently voiced within their own proletarian organizations (Nave-Herz 1988).

Proletarian women's priority was the economic aspects but always as subordinate to male-defined class issues. Clara Zetkin in 1889 appeared publicly at the International Worker Congress and introduced the theoretical relations between the "emancipation of women" and "the emancipation of labor from capital" (Gerhard 1991). Yet she never questioned the basic Marxist premise and Lenin's conviction that the equality of women is bound up with the proletarian class struggle (Kulke 1967). Bebel (1990), echoing Engels, argued that women's emancipation becomes reality only when the social contradictions between capital and labor are abolished. In a similar vein Zetkin spoke out against the demand of bourgeois activists to achieve equal pay for equal work. Only when the means of production were taken from private hands, she argued, would the demand "equal pay for equal work" result in the emancipation of women. Therefore, she saw as futile the integration of women into the work force without a change in property relations (Zetkin 1979). Following the ideological path of Engels, Bebel, and Lenin, Zetkin never veered from the basic Marxist tenet that the destruction of private property was the prerequisite for the emancipation of women. Beer argues that some of Zetkin's writings are ambiguous enough to cause speculation that she may have had some doubts about subordinating women's questions to the class question. Yet she never carried this doubt to its logical conclusion of questioning class as the primary contradiction in capitalism. Given the official Marxist interpretation on this issue, and given that she needed the protection of the party for her political activities, she remained faithful to the official Marxist interpretation of theorizing class as the primary contradiction (Beer 1984).

Clara Zetkin started to lose power and influence over the proletarian women's movement increasingly after 1905 to Luise Tietz. In 1911 she still spoke at a rally on International Women's Day against war and remained loyal to the revolutionary theories. These views, however, lost her the support of the Social Democratic leadership of the party. As long as she was the editor of the newspaper *Die Gleichheit* (Equality), she was able to introduce her ideas to a general working-class public. In 1915 Zetkin was arrested, and this incident was used by the party to criticize her for the high intellectual standard of the paper denying—so her accusers claimed—proletarian women "easy" access to the socialist goals and the women's organization. She was subsequently forced to give up the editorship, and she decided to join the Left faction of the party (Spartacus) in 1917. With the founding of the Communist Party in 1918, the proletarian women's movement was split between the socialist and the newly formed Communist Party (Nave-Herz 1988) that separated the revolutionaries from the reformers and was not unlike the division between the radicals and the conservatives that had occurred in the bourgeois women's movement already at the turn of the century.

Although the bourgeois and proletarian women's movements were separated along ideological lines "on the nature of women's rights and on women's place in society" (Kolinsky 1993), they shared a common fate in being forced into the position of "petitioners" rather than independent activists. They shared this fate even though the proletarian women's movement was always linked to and anchored within the Social Democratic and later the Communist Party, while the conservative women's rights activists had no ties to the liberal or conservative parties prior to the lifting of the political ban in 1908. Regardless of their location within or outside traditional political structures, proletarian and bourgeois women's activist groups depended either on state-sanctioned "free spaces" or male-sanctioned spaces within the socialist parties. Even Clara Zetkin's launching of the socialist newspaper *Equality,* which became her main vehicle for agitating and educating for working women's rights from 1892 until 1917 (Gerhard 1991), has to be seen in the light of her dependency and subordination to the Social Democratic Party.

Window of Political Opportunity: World War I

The first window of political opportunity for the bourgeois women's movement ironically came with the start of World War I, which Frevert calls the "father of women's emancipation" (1986: 146). These first steps toward public visibility had little to do, however, with women's own demands for emancipation and everything to do with the state's interest in mobilizing all Germans for the war effort. This need of the state to embrace women in the "service of national culture and greatness" coincided with the desire of the bourgeois women's movement to escape from their political isolation. In their eagerness to be rescued from political nonexistence, they in turn endorsed wholeheartedly the state's imperative that all Germans support the war effort. Women were thus "liberated" from their nonpolitical state of affairs only to sacrifice themselves willingly for the greater goals of the state. Gertrud Bäumer, the chair of the Federation of German Women's Association (BDF), spoke of the exhilarating feeling of being able to throw off the yoke of representing women's particular interests and being permitted to "become one" with the larger experience of this "great and serious endeavor of all national forces to grow together for a common cause" (qtd. in Frevert 1986: 147).

It is the tragedy of German bourgeois women's history that it was World War I that provided women's rights activists the first political opportunity structure to change their identity from nonpolitical actors to "political citizens." This opportunity was granted only because the Kaiserreich shaped the very form women's representation as collective actors was permitted to take. An autonomous reconfiguration of gender roles along nonnationalistic lines was never politically feasible for the bourgeois activists. They were permitted a political role but only to express loyalty and unconditional readiness to make sacrifices for the fatherland, a role bourgeois women eagerly accepted. Although the Kaiserreich continued to bar women from political participation, Marie Bernays from the BDF enthusiastically proclaimed that in their support for the war, women were made to feel and identify as "political citizens representing general interests" (Frevert 1986: 147).

The state's nationalistic incorporation left a tragic birthmark on the bourgeois women's movement. Even before the National Socialists came to power, the movement was receptive to the ideals of "motherhood" being tied to the service of "father state." These women activists needed no Nazi strong-arm tactics to persuade them that the proper role of women was in their sacrifice to the state. The antecedents of this ideology already lay in the Kaiserreich and in the particular way bourgeois women experienced political inclusion. That Gertrud Bäumer was able to proclaim feminism as a "Germanic movement" in the 1920s shows a historic continuity rather than a break in bourgeois women's ideology (Brand, Büsser, and Rucht 1986).

The Constraints of the Weimar Republic on Movement Mobilization

The end of World War I and the beginning of the Weimar Republic provided all German women the first real opportunity structure to become political citizens. The right to vote, championed foremost although not exclusively by the proletarian women's movement since the 1890s, became a reality. In addition, the Weimar Constitution ensured that "women and men have basically the same rights and duties" (Bridenthal and Koonz 1984: 33). The long struggle for educational reforms for girls, championed by the bourgeois women's movement since 1870s, paid off as these reforms became institutionalized (Brand, Büsser, and Rucht 1986). Women were quick to avail themselves of these newly created political and social rights. With the first national elections nearly 10 percent of delegates were women, and between 5 and 10 percent entered the state legislatures (Bridenthal and Koonz 1984).

Yet the much celebrated political emancipation of women in the Weimar Republic was, as Bridenthal and Koonz point out, quite fraudulent. In particular, the continuity of socioeconomic structures and the cultural legacy of a patriarchal ideology continued to dominate all institutions of German economic and political life and diminished the impact of the political freedoms on women. In addition, political instability and increasing polarization between the political Left and Right led not only to an ever-widening split between the bourgeois and the proletarian movements but also to factional splits within the bourgeois movement itself and in the socialist camp.

First, the split between the SPD and KPD meant that the remaining dominant conservative wing of the SPD party separated itself from all its "radical outgrowths," "extreme feminists," and "women's rights activists." Motherhood became ideologized and declared as the highest destiny for women. The party even recommended that single working women should at least show a "mental state of motherhood" in their professional activities (Brand, Büsser, and Rucht 1986), although all socialist parties did at least pay lip service to the right of women to work, to equal pay for equal work, and to health care and other social programs. These demands were framed, however, at one level within a discourse of strengthening and humanizing the family at another in the need for special "protective legislation" restricted to women workers (Bridenthal and Koonz 1984).

It is not without irony that, while access to the ballot box created for socialist and conservative members of the women's movements a political opportunity never before available, the structure of Weimar party politics largely canceled out this newly gained political space. In fact, the involvement of conservative women in Weimar party politics not only restricted the little autonomy they had achieved in the women's rights associations but also prevented them from framing their messages independent of the larger party goals. With political inclusion in the party structures, bourgeois women activists were saddled with new responsibilities and duties.

In contrast to the Socialist Party, which had always opposed an autonomous women's organization, the conservative and liberal parties prior to women's gaining the vote had little interest in incorporating women in the party ranks. Yet, once the vote was given to women, they eagerly courted the new potential of women party members. Both conservative and liberal parties placed leading women's rights activists in top positions of the party structure. At the same time, bourgeois and liberal women's rights activists saw in their integration into traditional party organizations the advantage of struggling from a more favorable position for equal rights. This collaboration between parties and women's rights activists also meant, once again, that the emancipatory interests of women became wedded to the larger political goals of German parties. Both left-wing and right-wing parties told women, "We need you." And the conservative parties even added, "Without you Germany will collapse and fall into the chaos of Socialism" (Bridenthal and Koonz 1984: 41).

Of course, these conservative women's rights activists did not necessarily disagree with this nationalistic message. Nor did they disagree with the parties' framing their role in traditional terms of motherhood and housewives. They invariably saw themselves as playing a special role in the spiritual revolution of Germany. Nevertheless, the representation of women and their issues was in the hands of male party leaders, and women had little influence over these issues. Whether women were active in the Democratic Party, in the Catholic Center Party, or in the Nationalist Party, they strove for greater attention to women's issues.

This situation was no different and was perhaps even more pronounced in the Socialist Party. SPD women demanded a greater share in party offices, party budgets, and influence as their constituencies increased. The denial of such requests was invariably couched, however, in misogynist claims against the political behavior of women in general. As more women voted for the conservative parties, even SPD women were held hostage to the male claim that women's suffrage had cost the SPD the majority in the Reichstag. Given these anti-women sentiments within the socialist parties, it is not surprising that neither the Social Democratic Party nor the Communist Party ever translated women's issues into party politics (Bridenthal, Grossmann, and Kaplan 1984). Attaining suffrage was thus an ambivalent achievement for women. All parties were eager to attract women voters. At the same time, women and women's issues were either instrumentalized, as with the conservative parties and their emphasis on the special moral role of women to fight against socialism, or they were marginalized, as within the socialist parties.

The situation was no better if we look at the recruitment of women into the party structures of both the Left and the Right. Well-known women's rights activists were placed at highly visible top-rank positions. At the less-visible, lower-ranking levels, however, women were largely absent. And even those placed in high-ranking party offices were not intended as role models to encourage other women to enter politics. These women activists did not use their offices to further the goals of women; "they relaxed their efforts at further change and turned their attention to national issues" unrelated to the goal of furthering women's emancipation (Bridenthal, Grossmann, and Kaplan 1984: 54).

The End of the "First Women's Movement" and Its Legacy

Yet even this limited political opportunity structure available to all German women during the Weimar Republic was once again brutally closed off with the coming to power of the National Socialists in 1933. Given the absence of autonomy from both the conservative and socialist parties, the women's movements suffered the fate of the Weimar Republic: they disappeared. In this disappearance of the "first women's movements" the conservative and liberal women's rights activists played an important role. Many conservative and liberal women's rights activists joined the ranks of National Socialism and served with enthusiasm. Claudia Koonz best expresses the dialectical relations between Nazi men and Nazi women in the destruction of women's emancipation and democracy: "Women Nazis used the benefits of emancipation to destroy emancipation while men Nazis exploited democracy to demolish democracy" (1987: 53). A long hiatus followed the disappearance of the first women's movement in the 1930s until the "second women's movement" emerged and energized a new generation of West German women in the early 1970s. In the East such a movement did not appear until the late 1980s. Despite this long dormancy, the women's question was by no means dead in either the western or eastern part of Germany after 1945. Indeed, the historical legacy of the German proletarian and bourgeois women's movements, both as ideological constructs and as symbols, figured prominently in the reconstruction of the "new" women in the immediate post–World War II period. In both East and West Germany the state drew on selective aspects of the shared historical legacy and represented these aspects as the "true" representation of German womanhood. In the East it was the ideological inheritance of the proletarian women's movements that figured in the party elite's claim that socialism would lead to the emancipation of women. In contrast, the West German leaders emphasized the role of the mother of the nineteenth century and idealized this interpretation as the true nature of women.

How to integrate women into the post–World War II German social order and how to reconstruct their representation were ideological questions that even figured into Cold War rhetoric. Statements issued by the Office of the Military Government–U.S. Zone in Munich (Boehling 1995), the West German authorities (Moeller 1993), and Soviet sources (Merkel 1990) revealed different conceptions of women's role. In constant comparison with the other side, they propagandized on the radio, later on television, in print media, as well as through official pronouncements that the West Germans and Americans rejected the mobilization of women "following a Russian model" (Moeller 1993). The Soviet model of "leveling of differences" (*Gleichmacherei*) was seen by many CDU/CSU critics as leading "to the destruction of the family, as women were compelled to work in occupations for which they were unsuited, and would deny women the possibility of fulfilling their obligation as wives and mothers" (Moeller 1993:57).

In East Germany the official tone was one of pity for West German "housewives" whose horizons did not expand much beyond their newly acquired washing machines (Merkel 1990). In both cases the official West and East German pronouncements viewed the other's ideal women as victims. The Soviets and East Germans saw in the West German women little more than slaves to consumerism; the Westerners saw in their Eastern counterparts little more than unfree working "Muttis" (*Mommies*). In both cases a powerful picture laden with historical significance was transported across the borders. By constructing pictures of women in one country as housewives and consumers, and in the other as "being as good as men," the roles of woman, mother, and worker were used on both sides for ideological legitimation, that is, to justify the different developments of the two postwar German political and social orders (Merkel 1994). These "cultural signposts" that played such an important role in the reconstruction of the new Germanies after 1945 resurfaced during the debates on German unification and, once more, opened up the ideological question about the proper representation of women in the newly configured German political order. Thus, the historical legacy of feminist thought is far from dead; in fact, it is very much alive today in the united Germany.

The historical legacy has left its imprint on how the immediate post–World War II East and West German states constructed an ideal type of womanhood for future generations to follow. These state activities also left an impact on the very identity of the feminist movement that emerged in the West in the 1970s. Even the absence of such a development in the East is, as I will argue later, shaped by the way the socialist state dealt with the women's question throughout its forty years of existence. The different "political regimes" that emerged in the post–World War II period help shed light on why in one political system a feminist movement developed, why it was foreclosed in the other, and, more important, why the East German feminist movement that finally did emerge in 1989 differed so vastly from the West German example. Given that the pre-1989 developments are critical to our understanding of why there were two different movements that "collided" during the unification process, the following section will provide some background on the political opportunity structures of the two post–World War II German states and their impact on feminist developments in the West and women's politics in the East.

Feminist Mobilization in the West

The emergence of the West German feminist movement in the early 1970s was part of a process found in virtually all industrialized countries. Such movement mobilization has been analyzed from the perspective of systemic value changes that included a shift from materialist to postmaterialist values (Inglehart 1977); as a result of the emergence of new conflict lines due to the ever-increasing process of rationalization and the "colonization of the life-world" (Habermas 1981); as a phenomenon that has its origin in the crisis of modernity (Offe 1985, 1990; Brand, Büsser, and Rucht 1986); as a result of crises of the Fordist production model (Hirsch and Roth 1980; Roth 1991, 1994; Mayer 1991c); as the outgrowth of the contradictions in advanced industrial societies (Barnes et al. 1979; Dalton and Kuechler 1990; Rucht 1990, 1991); or as linked to the transformation of capitalism toward an organized, "postindustrial" social formation (Kitschelt 1985). These theoretical frameworks have in common a view of the emergence of social movements as a "qualitatively new" aspect of citizen politics (Dalton, Kuechler, and Bürklin 1990). The newness of these groups involves everything from an ideological rejection of "old politics" to an emphasis on the different political origins, structure, style, and goals of such movements (Brand, Büsser, and Rucht 1986; Dalton and Kuechler 1990). Moreover, the designation *new* in these movements is justified, as Offe pointed out, "to the extent that they persist outside the universe of 'old' political parties and their electoral politics" and thus redefine the "boundaries of institutional politics" (1990: 232, 1987).

The emergence of the feminist movements in the Western industrialized countries belongs to this general trend of movement mobilization ranging from the American civil rights movement to movements focused on issues of peace, human rights, gay and lesbian politics, and environmental and ecological concerns. Despite similarities in timing of the movements and their joint origins in a crisis of late capitalism, the feminist movements differ in one respect from others: they collectively struggle against patriarchal domination (Kontos 1986; Riedmüller 1988). The

German feminist movement in particular shares with other social movements the struggle against the increasing commodification of the private sphere and shares the bourgeois concerns for more substantive rights for women. It is equally concerned with the "proletarian" emphasis on the equality of women in the labor market and shares with environmentalists the fear of the increasing destruction of our natural resources. Equally important is the fight against militarization, the concern for human rights generally, and the protection of social welfare provisions. The feminist movement thematizes these concerns along the dimension of "patriarchal domination."

Other new social movements do not analyze these conflicts along gendered lines. As a result, feminist movements are not only new social movements (Kontos 1986). In fact, in their struggle for equality, for inclusion in the public sphere, in their continuing concern with distributive issues and with reproductive rights, feminist movements have much in common with the early labor movements and the women's rights movements of the nineteenth and early twentieth centuries. Thus, the particular mobilization of German feminists in the 1970s is, despite its general affinity to other feminist movements, the result of the unresolved contradiction in the FRG's conservative construction of "womanhood."

The Conservative Political Context of the FRG

The emergence of the West German feminist movement has to be seen within the very conservative context that existed in West Germany after 1949 (Moeller 1993). Rejecting both the models of National Socialism that politicized the family for political ends and the East German emphasis on equality defined in terms of "workers," West German politicians resurrected the conservative-Catholic idea of the "naturalness" of women's proclivity for the family and motherhood. Until the 1970s the West German ideal of "wife-mother," the arrangement by which women were to combine the roles of wife and mother (Ostner 1994; Ferree 1995), remained largely unquestioned.

Women did achieve one important victory in 1949. The FRG's Basic Law formally guaranteed the equality of women and men. Article 3, Paragraph 2, of the Basic Law guarantees the equality of men and women, while Article 6 guarantees the protection of marriage and the family. Yet this statement of equality is a proclamation without much content. Lawmakers saw in this clause no special obligation to realize the equality of women (Berghahn and Fritzsche 1991). Essentially, "the Basic Law proclaimed that 'men and women have the same rights,' but it did not question that a woman's principal identity was as a wife and mother." The reason for this limited interpretation of women's rights is to be found in the provisions regulating marital relations that go back to the Civil Code of 1900 and remained, with some changes in the 1950s, in effect until the 1970s. The Civil Code stipulates that husbands have extensive rights over their wives. Paternal rights encompassed not only the final say of what was in the children's best interest; it also gave husbands the right to determine what was in the best interest of their wives and their marriage. Since the family was seen as the "organic basis of state and society," woman's sub-ordination of her individual rights was justified for the good of the larger whole (Moeller 1993). While women did receive the right to vote in 1918, family relations continued to be based on the inviolable rights of husbands over marital relations.

The integrity and the inviolability of families was based on the idea that men were paid a male wage to support a dependent wife and children. This meant that the post–World War II social order was based on the notion of "familialism," in which there is an assumed natural compatibil-ity between the male breadwinner and the female nurturer subsidized with state transfers (Esping-Andersen 1995). In this reconstructed German social order women were guaranteed full equal rights with men; on the other hand, they continued to form an integral part of German families.

It should not be surprising that in this official reconstruction of the post–World War II West German woman the "negative" example of the East German conception played a major role. Officially, the East Germans decreed that the woman's role in the new socialist state was that of worker-mother (Ferree 1995). In separating themselves from the East German model of women, the West German political elites promulgated that there was only one type of family that was "normal" and that the Eastern vari-ant was outside the Christian notion of family as the organic cell of state and society (Moeller 1993; Ostner 1995).

Even the reforms of the Civil Code in 1957 did little to change this strongly held belief in the inviolability of the family and the particular place a woman had in it. In fact, the newly formulated Equalization Law was ingenuous in that it recognized that a woman could no longer be expected to act as "agent of the husband," as the 1900 Civil Code had stip-ulated. The reformed code instead stated that "the wife fulfills her obliga-tion to contribute to the support of the family by running the household" in accord with her own accountability. Women were given the "'power of the keys,' the right and obligation to manage the household" (Moeller 1993: 201). This law was a progressive act in that it did recognize the legal equality of mothers and wives with husbands and fathers. At the same time, this "equality of worth" was based on the acknowledgment of differ-ences. The basic notion that the home was the woman's most important workplace was never challenged. As a result, this separation between a public arena of men and a private arena continued to be seen as the natural order of things for the generations growing up in postwar West Germany.

The Autonomous Feminist Movement

The West German "autonomous" feminist movement that emerged in the early 1970s was born in negation. It rejected the German historical legacy of women's experiences as well as the conservative reconstruction of womanhood of the FRG. Specifically, it rejected the idealization of motherhood, which became the celebrated experience for West German women in the 1950s and 1960s; it rejected the proletarian legacy and its idealization of the woman "worker"; it rejected party politics and any closeness to the state; and, finally, it rejected males. In their emphasis on autonomy German feminists referred to both autonomy from the state and autonomy from males (Gerhard 1992). To many feminists the state was little more than an apparatus of male control and domination, and thus feminists rejected initially the participation in established political institutions.[5] Only activities outside of these institutions promised a chance for "self-determination" (*Selbstbestimmung*) (Kulawik 1991–92).

It was the position of German women in social relations that shaped the development of the autonomous feminist movement. Both the intensity and content of the specific "grievances" of German feminists explains the contrasting development of the movements in the United States and Germany. Although the American feminist movement of the 1960s was the precursor in ideas, arguments, and protest practices to German feminist collective actions (Kitschelt 1986; Ferree 1987), the German movement could not rely on the American political and cultural symbolism of a "rights discourse" to frame its grievances and demands. American feminists' success was based on their capacity to utilize politically familiar and "culturally appropriate frames of meaning." These cultural symbols are important for movement mobilization, because "movements frame their collective action around cultural symbols that are selectively chosen from a cultural toolchest and creatively converted into collective action frames by political entrepreneurs" (Tarrow 1994: 119). American feminists could thus frame their grievances in a rights discourse that included rights to education, rights to own property, emphasis on political and civil rights, and the right not to be discriminated against (Ferree 1987). Given Germany's weak link to liberalism and its inegalitarian political culture, this

---

5. This very strong initial rejection of the state was somewhat relativized in the 1980s when autonomous feminists aimed to influence the policy-making process in areas that affected women directly (Feree 1987; Kontos 1994).

rights discourse found little resonance and familiarity in the German context (Kitschelt 1985).

Cultural Frames

Given the roots of the autonomous feminist movement in the socialist student movement of the 1960s, the class-theoretical and political economy discourse provided the cultural frames around which the German movement mobilized consensus for collective action. These "socialist" frames of meaning remained important even after the feminists split from the socialist students' movement in the early 1970s.

The feminists' decision to form their own autonomous movement in the early 1970s arose from their refusal to subordinate the woman's question once again to the class issue and from the continuing indifference of the Left leadership to address gender issues, such as the restrictive abortion law known as para. 218, which became the focal point of feminist agitation (Schwarzer 1981; Meinhof 1988; Sander 1988).[6] The autonomous feminist movement has remained socialist, however, inasmuch as its theoretical categories continue to emphasize the organization and division of labor as a main structure of domination and conflict in capitalist societies (Kulawik 1991–92).

This theoretical embeddedness within a socialist frame of reference shaped the very understanding of feminists' strategies to achieve social change. They came to the conclusion that gender relations are based on "a structure of domination" that exists beyond individual males and is inherent in capitalist and patriarchal relations (Kulawik 1991–92). Only a "fundamental opposition" to the existing social and political order seemed to hold promise for social change and the creation of a new order based on solidarity relations rather than competitive market ethics (Kitschelt 1985). In its emphasis on a fundamental opposition to the existing social and political systems and the call for structural transformations, the German feminist movement differs substantially from the American model. In fact, Brand has argued that the German autonomous feminist movement should be regarded as a "cultural revolutionary women's emancipation movement" rather than an American type of "women's rights movement" (Brand 1986).

Not only does the German feminist movement differ from the American "interest group feminism" (Ferree 1987; Gelb 1990), it also differs from the first German women's movement, which disappeared with the

---

6. Para. 218 goes back to the 1871 Reich Criminal Code Book, which declared abortion a criminal act.

onset of National Socialism. This break between the first and second movement is, however, not absolute (Klinger 1986; Kontos 1986; Riedmüller 1988). Autonomous feminists continue in the footsteps of their "great-grandmothers" in their fight for the abolition of the restrictive abortion regulations (para. 218); they still struggle against a gendered division of labor in which they are assigned a large proportion of work that is unpaid; and they continue to struggle against the high degree of exclusion in political opportunity structures.

At the same time, they differ in the very concept of the meaning of *feminism,* a term that the conservative bourgeois women's movement did not use. In order to separate itself from this women's movement legacy, the autonomous movement used the concept of feminism from the very start. *Feminism* came to mean "a radicalization of the principle of femininity against the biologically based concept of the 'natural' role of women in society and an emphasis on a more woman 'suitable' society" (Riedmüller 1988). In this definition the autonomous movement left behind the ideological baggage of the proletarian emphasis on "work" as the emancipatory strategy for women. Instead, it endorsed the position of "radical feminism," which sees a fundamental opposition between men and women. The oppression of women is seen as a direct result of patriarchal relations. This theoretical construct owes much to Carol Gilligan (1982) and her thesis that women and men are socialized into two moral systems: one emphasizes care, relations, empathy, and the other is based on a system of rules and rights. Inherent in this notion of feminism is the concept of duality, and/or the "politics of difference" (Klinger 1986). Because women and men are socialized into different moral systems and because the values of males are always ranked as superior to those of women, women's concerns with "human relations" are by definition secondary. As a result, issues that concern women remain "private" and have no political relevance.

In subscribing to a "politics of subjectivity" aimed at politicizing the private sphere as a locus of power and domination, autonomous feminists politicized such concepts as the "body," "nature," "culture," "sex," "gender," and "violence." Instead of accepting their great-grandmothers' hegemonic definition of womanhood as being synonymous with motherhood, the new women's movement took the stance that "the personal is political" and made the politics of subjectivity the center of political agitation. The theoretical reliance on the politics of subjectivity, however, and its embeddedness within a politics of difference has left the autonomous movement in some difficulty in defining the boundaries to the "mothercult" that were inherent in the first women's movement. As pointed out previously, from the Kaiserreich to the Federal Republic, the representation of women was constructed around family and motherhood. Autonomous feminists found themselves in a theoretical contradiction that has remained unresolved to this day. They constituted themselves in the very rejection of this historical mothercult. At the same time, they rejected the ideas of a "male society" and focused on the politics of difference.

This theoretical contradiction burst into the open as more and more feminists became integrated into the labor market and others remained "only housewives." The position of women as either in the labor market, as "only housewives," or as those who worked outside the home and were at the same time mothers brought forth different factions in the movement (Riedmüller 1988). A split along the lines of women as "professionals" and women as "mothers" erupted that continues to this day. That feminists had difficulty conceptualizing the relations between women and mothers was readily apparent when the theme of the Third Summer University for Women in Berlin in 1978 was targeted to discuss the issues surrounding "Women and Mothers."

The conflict became particularly virulent among the various feminist factions within the Green Party and was further fueled by the Chernobyl nuclear power plant accident in 1986, which was seen as one more proof of the increasing destruction of the environment by a male-dominated value system. In endorsing a politics of difference, Gisela Erler introduced a "Mother Manifesto" in the Green Party in the mid-1980s to highlight the increasing concerns of mothers not only with the task of raising children but also with ecological survival in general (Kulawik 1991–92). Some feminists condemned this emphasis on the "new motherliness" (*neue Mütterlichkeit*) as a fetishization of the "mother issue" (Schwarzer 1981). The condemnation of this trend increased as some feminist theorists even suggested the withdrawal from the present social system into a utopian, subsistence society (Bennhold-Thomsen 1987; Mies 1987).

The irony of this conflict between professionals and mothers is that, while the autonomous feminists tried to escape the "motherly mystique" of the past, by pursuing a politics of difference they opened the door inadvertently to this mothercult from which they so desperately tried to escape (Klinger 1986).

Anti-Institutional Politics

Aside from these definitional issues that separate and at the same time unintentionally link the first with the new feminist movement, the most crucial difference is expressed in the autonomous feminist movement's refusal to work within existing institutions to achieve social change. Nevertheless, there has been a rapprochement between feminists and institutional politics that started in the 1980s, a move that will be addressed later in this section (Ferree 1987; Riedmüller 1988; Kontos 1990, 1994). It is true, however, that, despite this change of direction toward a more state-centered politics, the autonomous feminists remain skeptical toward the state and about party politics in general (Kitschelt (1990).

This inherent anti-stateness within the autonomous feminist movement is not surprising given women's historical experience with traditional politics. The most rudimentary acquaintance with German history was sufficient to convince the new generation of postwar feminists that women's issues had not fared well in any of the political regimes. Women's issues had either been instrumentalized in the name of the state or political parties or feminist issues were subordinated to class politics. Not wanting to repeat the mistakes of their forebears, the autonomous feminists took a step away from the old politics and focused on the creation of a "countersociety" that became known as the "project culture." In this emphasis on creating "counter-public space," women put their energies into "projects," creating women's centers, cafés, anti-authoritarian daycare centers, feminist bookstores, journals, magazines, and shelters for battered women (*Frauenhäuser*) (Ferree 1987; Riedmüller 1988; Kulawik 1991–92; Gerhard 1992).

This determination to stay outside the traditional political structures is not unique to feminism. Kitschelt (1985) has shown that the closed opportunity structure of the German party state system has made it difficult for movements in general to gain access to the policy-making process. Social movements confront a party system largely unresponsive to issues that cut across class lines; they confront a more secretive political system and a state that continues to be concerned with internal stability, order, and conflict avoidance and which reacts quickly to exclude any potentially "destabilizing" elements that do not fit class-based interest politics.

This specifically German exclusionary "policy style" and the subsequent formation of the Green Party outside the traditional party structures are two sides of the same political dynamic (Kitschelt 1985). As environmental activists failed to gain participatory policy opportunities in the traditional parties and failed to achieve any substantive policy gains, the ecological Green Party constituted itself in opposition to the existing party systems and its corporatist logic (Markovits and Gorski 1993).

This inability to gain access to the party and state structures not only "forced" social movements into working outside traditional party channels; the less egalitarian and highly bureaucratic political culture also gave rise to a more radical, noncompromising feminist movement. The militancy of the German autonomous movement can be seen both in its "anti-organizational ideology" and in its anticonventional "action repertoire"

(Tilly 1986; Kitschelt 1990; Rucht 1990). In its militancy the German variant of feminism differs not only from the American "interest group feminism," which has relied foremost on mass membership organizations, lobbying activities, and close ties to political parties to influence the policy-making process (Katzenstein and McClurg Mueller 1987; Gelb 1990). It also differs both in structure and technique from the first women's movement.

The older women's movement was organized in identifiable institutional structures with an elected leadership, and their preeminent political space was the parliament and political parties (Brand 1986; Rucht 1990). This dependency on the traditional political structures severely circumscribed not only the forms the organization could take but also the strategies the women's activists could utilize to voice their concerns.

In contrast, the novelty of the autonomous movement, which it shares with all other social movements, is the expansion of the meaning of the political. Rejecting the bureaucratic notions of politics that "conflicts can be resolved in meaningful and promising ways through *etatism,* political regulation, and the proliferating inclusion of ever more claims and issues on the agenda of bureaucratic authorities" (Offe 1985: 819), the feminist movement negated the traditional methods of party organization and interest representation (Kitschelt 1989, 1990).

In this rejection of old politics and in its endorsement of an anti-organizational ideology, the autonomous feminist movement has no institutional center, no organizational umbrella, no identifiable leaders, and no elected speakers (Brand 1986). The movement can best be described as what Neidhardt has termed "networks of networks" (Neidhardt 1985). Instead of formal organizations providing a mode of communication, personal networks of communication play an important role for their mobilization (Melucci 1984; Kaase 1990). These networks of networks and their low degree of institutionalization is not due to an "immaturity" on the part of the movement. Rather, they have become a permanent feature of all social movements (Kaase 1990).

These networks of different groups, initiatives, and local projects are relatively tightly knit through informal coordination and personal communications. The women's centers, autonomous *Frauenhäuser,* pregnancy and sexual counseling services, rape crisis centers, anti-authoritarian day-care centers, lesbian groups, feminist bookstores and publishing houses, large festive women's gatherings (*Frauenfeste*), women's congresses, demonstrations, women's groups located within the ecological and peace movements, and the many local and national feminist newspapers and journals function as an infrastructure to mobilize women into action and to spread news and new ideas (Brand 1986). The organizational structure of these projects and initiatives is based on nonhierarchical and collective decision making and is embodied in the slogan "women help women." This experience of women helping women is "considered a requisite in shaping an independent female identity" (Kulawik 1991–92: 76).

Parallel to the continuing existence of these informal networks of networks is an increasing professionalization and institutionalization of parts of the autonomous feminist movement (Brand 1986; Ferree 1987; Riedmüller 1988; Kontos 1990). Whereas the first phase of movement activities in the 1970s started with unpaid independent projects, the second phase witnessed the drive to more professionalization in the 1980s. No longer was unpaid work a viable political strategy of feminists. Women increasingly recognized the importance of acquiring the political and administrative tools to influence politics.

As the distributional conflicts in the welfare arena intensified in the 1980s and Helmut Kohl waged an election campaign based on introducing a *Wende* in German social policy after the elections in 1982, German feminists redirected their strategy toward the state. Their first focus was to have the state accept financial responsibility for the various local projects. Feminists were eager to have the project culture institutionalized within the state. Whereas in the 1970s the projects relied on self-financing and feminists were not paid at all, the 1980s saw a shift in the feminists' attitude toward more secure financing (Kontos 1992).

Building an "Alliance System"

A key step toward a more state-oriented politics came with the entrance of the Green Party into the Bundestag in 1983 and the first Red-Green coalition in the state of Hessen in 1985. Many Green feminists came either from the autonomous feminist movement or had experience with the feminist project culture (Schmid 1990). At the same time, the feminist activists in the movement realized that with the Greens in political power they now were able to build an "alliance system" that could help secure vitally important resources (Klandermans 1990). That this coalition between feminists in the Green Party and feminists in the autonomous movement was not always harmonious and was often regarded as little more than serving an "instrumental" purpose for acquiring state funding does not diminish the importance of this strategic change of feminists' strategy toward greater political visibility and increasing willingness to challenge the political power structure (Krieger 1990; Schmid 1990; Kulawik 1991–92).

These first steps into the arena of institutional politics were further facilitated by the increasing "feminization" of the Social Democratic

Party. This turn toward more a feminist politics within the SPD meant that the autonomous movement was able to broaden its alliance system and make coalitions, however tenuous, with feminists within the SPD. That the SPD made this turn to a more progressive women's politics had much to do with the intense pressure it felt from the Greens and their success in attracting young women voters by the mid-1980s (Markovits and Gorski 1993; Braunthal 1994; Weis 1995). This new competitive experience from the "new kid on the block" completely revolutionized the up to that moment rather nonfeminist Association of Social Democratic Women (ASF) within the SPD. The ASF, having rejected quotas until the late 1970s,[7] pursued a vigorous quota system that was finally adopted by the 1988 Party Convention to provide equal opportunities for women in the party selection of candidates (Braunthal 1994).[8]

Autonomous feminists found an additional, albeit controversial, "ally" in the Women's Affairs Offices within the administrative state apparatus. These "women's equality offices" (*Frauenbeauftragte*) further women's policies at the state and local levels. Although initiated in the 1970s, these offices mushroomed in the 1980s and had the task of "identifying women's particular concerns, to survey pending measures for their impact on women as a group, and to represent women's interests in the administration and implementation of policy" (Ferree 1991–92: 55; Ferree 1995). The offices contain mostly staff positions that report directly to the highest-ranking elected official, they have a small budget, and their responsibility is defined more in terms of influencing policy rather than making policy themselves. Ferree points out, however, that the real "power" of these offices is not in their formal position. Instead, their influence comes from the quality of the working relationship these *Frauenbeauftragte* can establish with the office of the elected official (Ferree 1995) and from whether they have an ally in the party or parties in power. In a CDU state the offices are often poorly equipped and staffed mainly by volunteers or part-time workers.

The relations between the autonomous feminist movement and the Women's Affairs Offices depend largely on whether the staff of the *Frauenbeauftragte* themselves come from movement-oriented backgrounds and are thus sensitized to feminist issues ranging from "improving services for

---

7. Braunthal points out that the feminists within the ASF rejected the quota because they argued "that quotas would endanger the emancipation movement; that to effectuate change women must become a political factor within the party in their own right; and that it would be insulting to women if they gained party positions on the basis of a quota system rather than on their qualifications" (Braunthal 1994: 177).

8. The resolution called for a 33 percent quota by 1988 and a 40 percent quota by 1994 in all SPD local, Länder, and national policy-making organs (Braunthal 1994: 179).

victims of domestic violence, to reviewing city planning initiatives for their impact on women (e.g., better lighting in parking garages to free taxi rides after dark)" (Ferree 1991–92; 1995: 107). Relations also hinge on whether the *Frauenbeauftragte* staff defines their responsibilities as representing women collectively. Those who come from a mainstream women's organization seem to be more geared toward increasing women's occupational status (Ferree 1995) and thus have less interest in the projects of the autonomous movement.

Autonomous feminists' relation to the *Politikfrauen* (institutionalized feminists) in the political establishment (political parties, administrative state apparatus, and labor unions) is one of "uneasy coexistence" (Roth and Ferree 1996). The loose coalition between the autonomous sector and *Politikfrauen* is largely an ad hoc arrangement and, depending on the political issues, is constantly being renegotiated. There have been costs for the autonomous movement in this state orientation. The "institutionalization of the autonomous feminist politics" (Lang 1993) has meant that the feminist movement has become more dependent on state resources for project funding. The state pays the wages of the activists, the office rents, and other project costs. In addition, Länder resources are often supplemented by federal subsidies that also pay for job creation and training programs. This financial support for the infrastructure of women's projects is largely financed through the federal Ministry of Women and Youth, which is then further distributed by the conservative federal Deutsche Frauenrat (German Women's Council) for final distribution to local recipients (Lang 1993; Young 1994).

It is indisputable that state financing of such projects has provided a substantial amount of money for new feminist projects. Yet being dependent on state resources has also meant the loss of some autonomy from the institutions that provide the grants. The selection criteria alone influence and shape the final outcome of state-financed projects and thereby limit the autonomy of the women's movement (Young 1994). State financing has also led to a depoliticization in the feminist movement. Lang (1993) has observed that the increasing competition for scarce resources between project groups has robbed the feminist movement of its collective voice and has increased internal segmentation and individual factions within the movement.

"Action Repertoires"

The increasing "institutionalization" has also shifted the movement's "action repertoires" to a combination of both conventional and unconventional means. The concept of action repertoire is helpful for our pur-

poses in explaining the different forms of action and the underlying strategies of the old and the new women's movements. The concept of action
repertoire was developed by Tilly (1986) to show that different action
repertoires are associated with different spatial and temporal locations.
For Tilly action repertoires are specific actions carried out by collective
actors over a specific period of time. Tarrow expands this concept and suggests that "actions are not only what people do when they are engaged in
conflict with others, it is what they know how to do and what others expect
them to do" (1994: 31). The strength of both Tilly's and Tarrow's
definition of action repertoire is their insight that actions of social actors
are not purely random. Instead, action repertoires are shaped by structural
variables and by the cultural context in which they originate.

If the nineteenth century is the "parliamentary age," it is not surprising that the first women's movement and the labor movement directed
their actions toward parliamentary representation (Tilly 1986). Only parliament had the political power to effect social change, and thus parliamentary elections became the focal point for movement mobilization
(Rucht 1990). Of course, the avenue of parliamentary agitation was formally closed for women until they received the right to vote in 1918. Nevertheless, even if women activists could not vote, their action repertoire
centered largely around election rallies, public meetings, and public
demonstrations (Frevert 1986). The proletarian movement had the additional weapon of participating in labor strikes, a repertoire that by
definition was not available to most bourgeois women.

If parliamentary actions symbolized hope for the movements of the
late nineteenth and early twentieth centuries, exactly the opposite seems to
be the case for today's social movements. Present social movements,
whether feminist or not, are much less confident that change will come
from either the "ballot" or the "bullet" (i.e., revolution). In this shift away
from parliamentary and revolutionary actions is a reorientation toward
local actions,[9] meaning that the action repertoire of the new social movements is much more diffuse. They rely on many forms of unconventional
action that include dramatic and highly visible events, mass demonstrations, rallies, marches, civil disobedience, highly visible court actions, disruptive tactics, blockades, sit-ins, sabotage, consciousness raising, provocations, and self-run communities/projects (Rucht 1990).

The autonomous feminist movement availed itself of virtually all
these actions. There are some actions, however, that have come to represent and be identified with certain time periods. The initial actions of the

---

9. It is interesting that Tilly (1986) sees the same shift occurring from the eighteenth to
the nineteenth century. The shift, however, is in the reverse direction. Action started to shift
from the local to the national sphere.

movement stand out in their intent to "shock." These included highly dramatic and visible events, beginning with the now-famous "tomato throwing" incident of 1968. Sigrid Rüger, a Socialist German Students' League (SDS) member, hurled three tomatoes against the smirking male delegates sitting at the podium at the Twenty-third Delegate Conference of the SDS in Frankfurt. This smug behavior was in response to the speech made by filmmaker Helke Sander of the then newly established Berliner Aktionsrat zur Befreiung der Frau (Berlin Action Committee for Women's Liberation), who talked about how women in everyday situations and in socialist organizations found recognition only if they adapted to male standards. Since the only reaction of males was a smirk—otherwise no comments— the tomatoes started to fly (Brand 1986; Anders 1988; Markovits and Gorski 1993). This tomato-throwing incident was not the invention of feminists. In fact, two years earlier feminists in the SDS were bombarded with tomatoes from their male comrades when they tried to push through a feminist resolution (Brand 1986).

This famous incident was followed by another highly visible action played out at the Twenty-fourth Delegate Congress of the SDS in Hannover. A group of SDS women organized in the Weiberrat (Broads' Council)[10] produced what has become a legendary flyer both for its irony and tastelessness. It pictures a nude woman (with definite witchy elements) reclining on a couch with an ax in her right hand. Above are six penises in various shapes mounted on the wall in place of the much-loved German deer antlers. The message needs no explanation. The eight feminist groups in the SDS defended the flyer and refused any kind of dialogue with the male comrades. This action increased the already existing aggression, if not anxiety, of males. By refusing to comment, the women used the standard action repertoire males had used to intimidate women in everyday situations and at political gatherings (Anders 1988).

While these actions were directed to their male comrades in the SDS, in 1971 feminists broadened their actions to shock the law-abiding conscience of German society. Three hundred and seventy-four German women confessed in the Hamburg journal *Der Stern* in June 1971 that they had had abortions. In this spectacular confession feminists signaled that illegal actions were an acceptable strategy if they furthered the interests of women. The period from 1971 to 1975 saw a continuation of these highly visible and dramatic actions, which included tribunals, street parties (*Strassenfeste*), demonstrations, openly announced journeys to foreign abortion clinics, and the publication of books about abortions. In

---

10. The highly derogatory name was selected by the group itself to draw attention to the inherent everyday "devaluation" of the term *Weiber* (broads).

addition, the first women's seminars were held in Berlin in 1974, and national and international congresses were initiated (Schwarzer 1981; Frevert 1986).

With the defeat of the liberalization of the abortion reforms that the SPD government had initiated in 1974, and which were declared unconstitutional by the Federal Constitutional Court in 1975, feminists started to move from this highly visible level of "big politics" to a "politics of autonomy."[11] In this phase women focused on building a countersociety both against the state and against males. This period saw the creation of a project culture independent of the state, with a strong emphasis on education and on consciousness-raising about feminist and, in particular, lesbian issues.

This move away from big politics should not be seen, however, as a "retreat inward" (Brand 1986). Exactly the opposite was the case. By creating the first women's shelters for battered women in 1976, feminists drew attention to a problem that had hitherto been completely neglected by the German authorities. This period of the politics of autonomy was foremost an attempt to create new public spaces and discursive resources on the issue of violence against women in the workplace, in public arenas, and, most important, in the family (Kulawik 1991–92). That feminists were organized in opposition to the state and males should not blind us to the fact that they availed themselves of "power-oriented" strategies (Rucht 1990) to politicize the "holiest cow" of Germany: the family.

Once again the 1980s saw a shift in the repertoire of the autonomous movement. In this era of the politics of diversity, feminists relied on both unconventional and conventional action repertoires, a move that was also visible in other social movements. The highly visible actions of the earliest period were less so in the 1980s. Nevertheless, civil disobedience and demonstrations, often in combination with antinuclear activists, peace groups, and environmental movements, continued to form an important repertoire for feminists. What was new was their greater involvement in institutional politics, which directed their action repertoires toward more conventional actions such as lobbying, petitions, political participation, pressure politics, bargaining, and political confrontation.

This shift does not mean that the autonomous movement is on its way to becoming another interest group but, rather, that the opportunity structure the Greens opened for feminists in the 1980s and to which the other

---

11. The law was to decriminalize abortions within the first twelve weeks of pregnancy, provided the pregnant woman agreed and the termination was carried out by a doctor. Yet, after the Constitutional Court's ruling, abortions were exempted from criminal prosecution only if one of these criteria were met: congenital defect, medical, rape, and social hardship (Maleck-Lewy 1995).

parties had to respond made it possible for feminists to engage in a double strategy. The majority of feminists continue to be engaged in projects at the local level. At the same time, a small group of feminists has started to focus more on the state and national levels to intervene in existing institutions to achieve political changes that are in the interest of feminists.

This combination of a more open political opportunity structure and the readiness of feminists to enter institutional politics is still a rather untested novelty. In fact, SPD leader Walter Momper's appointment of eight women—half of his cabinet— both from the SPD and the AL (coalition partner) in Berlin in January 1989 caused a media spectacle (Schaeffer-Hegel 1995).

That institutional feminists are not ready to abide by the conventional repertoire of parliamentary politics can be seen by some of the more headline-grabbing stories emerging from feminist politics within the Greens. A small circle of radical feminists in the Hamburg Green Party forced through a completely female slate for the election to the Hamburg parliament in 1986. This was all the more surprising since the Hamburg Green Party is 65.6 percent male. Feminists argued that "what was good for women was good for all humankind (including men)," and that an all-female slate was needed since men continued to hold the vast majority of power in society. In getting their slate approved they did not fear strong-arm tactics. In fact, they threatened to step down en masse, thereby making it impossible for the Greens to have enough women on the party list (Schmid 1990).

Of interest in this demand for an all-female slate is the combination of the use of both conventional and unconventional action repertoires. The fresh women of Hamburg, who initiated this slate, obviously were not averse to institutional politics. Yet they refused to accept the rules of parliamentary games. They even rejected the "zipper method" instituted by the Greens, which gives every other list place to women. Instead, they made up their own rules, while relying on conventional party pressure tactics to threaten "exit" if refused a "voice."

The Autonomous Feminist Movement in 1989

When the Wall collapsed in 1989, what was left of the autonomous feminist movement? Despite the blurring of the boundaries between autonomous politics and institutional politics, certain key aspects continue to define the movement. First, the informal, nonhierarchical movement structure characterized by networks of networks has become a permanent feature of the autonomous feminist movement. It continues to endorse an "anti-organizational ideology," shunning either an organizational center or the appointment of identifiable representatives. Its major communication networks remain the projects, feminist congresses, and the many feminist books, journals, calendars,[12] and newspapers that provide a ready exchange of ideas on German feminist theory and praxis.

The movement remains skeptical about the state, party politics, and men in general, although extreme anti-stateness and anti-maleness have subsided. Nevertheless, many feminists continue to believe that the present state structures are anti-women and that the integration of feminists within institutional politics will lead to co-optation rather than genuine social change. For many feminists active in the autonomous movement the transformation of social institutions remains a prerequisite for building an alternative to the present capitalist system. In equating the state and the economic system with values of "masculinity," the autonomous feminists have remained loyal to their radical feminist roots and the politics of difference.

Tracing the relationship between the opportunity structures of the West German political regime and the feminist movement has shown the why, how, and when of the autonomous movement's development. With the collapse of the Wall and with German unification, however, a different feminist group emerged in the former socialist state. The question that confronts us in the next section is the impact of the former GDR's political regime on East German feminist development. That feminism did not develop in the East under state socialism prior to the late 1980s was as important in shaping the East German feminist identity as was the development of such a movement in the West. How the political opportunity structures of East Germany shaped the organizational structures of the East German movement—its ideology, action repertoire, cultural frames of meaning, and the extent to which these groups gained access, or failed to gain access, to the political system—is the story of the next section.

The GDR: Women's Policies from Above

In constructing the "new women," the GDR looked backward toward the ideas of the proletarian women's movement. Clara Zetkin, the eminent

---

12. These calendars are geared to a feminist audience and list, in addition to the normal information found in calendars, addresses of public feminist centers and "autonomous networks" in virtually every city in Germany, including addresses for Austria and Switzerland. In addition, there are some references to feminist groups in other EU-countries and also overseas. Addresses are listed of women's archives and libraries, women's publishing houses and publications, as well as announcements of women's travel groups and vacation centers. Other calendars gear themselves to specific audiences such as lesbians and provide contact addresses in Germany, Europe, and overseas.

theorist of the proletarian women's movement at the turn of the century, as well as Friedrich Engels and August Bebel, provided a theory for the GDR leadership for the historical subordination of women (Kulke 1967; Schubert 1980). By following the path from proletarian roots, the East German leadership drew selectively on only one part of German history, disavowing not only the conservative bourgeois women's movement of the Kaiserreich and the Weimar Republic but also the National Socialist past. The GDR declared itself the true representative of the non–National Socialist part of Germany (Kulke 1967).

The GDR also looked westward and contrasted itself with the West Germans, who were at the same time looking East. The representation of women was always a competition between the newly emerging West and East German political systems (Moeller 1993). Fueled by the flames of the Cold War, it became a game between the "good" East Germans and the "bad" West Germans. One was constructed as continuing in the footsteps of all that was reactionary, including the women's question, in German history. The other identified with the proletarian past, its anti-conservative and anti-fascist image, and its emancipatory promise for women (Schubert 1980).

In emancipating women from their "historic" subordination, Marxists denied that the women's question could be solved within a capitalist system. Bebel (1990) points to the double oppression women suffer under capitalism: women are subordinated to and dependent on men, and they, like the proletarian worker, are economically exploited by capital. East German leaders built on Marxist insights that the abolition of private property is the answer to women's emancipation. These leaders suggested, with Engels (1972), that the legal inequality between men and women is not the cause but the effect of the economic discrimination against women. The socialist leaders started from the premise that the destruction of private property would lead to conditions that would free women from their subordination to bourgeois property relations. Women's emancipation, they argued, could only be realized in a socialist system in which the contradiction between capital and labor is abolished (Engels 1972; Bebel 1990). As long as property stayed in the hands of private capital, Zetkin (1960) had already argued fifty years earlier, the integration of women into the work force would only exchange "home slavery" for "wage slavery."

Women in the "Construction of Socialism"

This theoretical foundation for the emancipation of women left no independent action for women themselves in constructing their own identity. Emancipation was decreed "from above." The ideological commitment to solving the women's question from above was to some extent also born out of necessity. The Soviet Administration Zone (SMAD) immediately after 1945 was plagued with a shortage of labor.[13] Initially due to the number of war deaths and later due to the large number of able-bodied men leaving for the West, the labor of women became vital for the East German economy (Kulke 1967). Thus, the immediate appeal to women in the Soviet Administration Zone to enter the work force was a matter of practical necessity: the regime had to fill the factory floors, and women had to ensure their own physical survival.

To mobilize women the SMAD issued order no. 253 in August 1946 an equal pay regulation for blue- and white-collar workers irrespective of gender and age (Schubert 1980). The order was not immediately executed in the factories; nevertheless, it had great symbolic importance. The socialist leaders could assert that it had fulfilled one of the central bourgeois women's demands for achieving equality between men and women (Kulke 1967). In combination with the Law on the Protection of Mother and Child and the Rights of Women, which took effect on October 1, 1950, and first enabled women to combine work with motherhood, the GDR leadership proudly proclaimed that it was on its way to realizing the constitutional promise to make women equal to men (Demokratischer Frauenbund Deutschlands [DFD] 1989).

Not to be outdone by the West German Basic Law formally guaranteeing the equality of women and men, Article 7 of the Constitution of the GDR stated that "men and women are equal. All Laws and regulations, which are in non-conformity with the equality of women, are repealed" (qtd. in Schubert 1980: 37). Although both countries codified the formal rights of women in their respective constitutions, the SED leadership made the achievement of equality for women both a social and political task. As early as 1949, the GDR Constitution included in Article 18 the right to equal pay for equal work,[14] the protection of motherhood, and equal right to education and choice of professions (38). In its revised constitutions of 1968 and 1974 the GDR expanded on these rights and included in Article 20 that "men and women are equal and have the same rights in all spheres

---

13. The male "deficit" varied according to age groups but was most pronounced for those between eighteen and thirty. For example, in that age group there were 297 females to 100 males; the numbers were 241 to 100, respectively, for those between thirty and forty, 156 to 100 between forty and fifty; and 136 to 100 between fifty and sixty-five (Scholze and Arendt 1986: 19).

14. The American Office of Military Government also introduced the right of "equal pay for equal work" in its zone of occupation. This regulation found little support, however, and the Military Government did not enforce it. The male members of the Munich City Council insisted on differentiating between equal pay for equal performance and equal pay for equal work (Boehling 1995).

of social, political and personal life. The promotion of women particularly through professional training is a social and political task" (qtd. in Berghahn and Fritzsche 1991: 21).

This state-decreed reconfiguration of the East German woman into a worker-mother was not uniformly accepted by all East German women immediately after World War II. For many women the end of the war also reawakened their hope to reverse the trend of working in factories and offices for which they were mobilized in large numbers in the last months before Nazi capitulation (Tröger 1984; Bock 1992). To mobilize women into accepting this new role and facilitate their integration into the social-ist economy, the SED announced the creation of the Democratic Women's Union of Germany (DFD) on International Women's Day, March 8, 1947. The DFD became the official organ representing all women and women's issues until the very last moment of the GDR's existence.[15]

From its inception the DFD functioned as a "transmission belt" between the SED and women of the German Democratic Republic.[16] Its primary task was to persuade nonpolitical, nonworking women to become active in the labor process and agitate against the still existing bourgeois prejudice against working mothers. They fought against the widely accepted German stigma of the "raven mother" (*Rabenmutter*), a metaphorical term carrying the message that the young would be left "motherless" (Scholze and Arendt 1986; DFD 1989).

The GDR was successful in increasing women's participation rate from 40 percent (including women in educational training) in 1950 to 65 percent in 1957. In the same year women made up 44.4 percent of the entire work force. Nevertheless, enticing women to become socialist work-ers was not without problems. For example, of the 1,289,621 DFD mem-bers in 1957, 84 percent did not belong to any party, 41 percent did not work, and 75 percent were older than thirty (Scholze and Arendt 1986). The DFD's obvious function was to reach older, nonworking, and politi-cally uncommitted women. As more and more people fled to the West in the late 1950s, the DFD became an important instrument for organizing "housewife brigades" (*Hausfrauenbrigaden*), compensating for new labor shortages in agriculture, industry, the service industry, and health services. In the short term these women made up for the extreme labor shortages; in the long term it was hoped that the integration of women on a short-term

---

15. The Democratic Women's Union of Germany reconstituted itself in 1990 as the Democratic Women's League e.V. and continues to exist as five state associations with busi-ness offices in cities and counties (Rohnstock 1991).

16. The DFD was initially also active in West Germany. It was banned in 1957. At the time of its ban the West German DFD had twenty-eight thousand members (Scholze and Arendt 1986).

basis would lead to their eventual full integration in the labor force (DFD 1989).

There was never any illusion, however, that the DFD had any mandate to function outside of the SED. In fact, to forestall any possibility that women would acquire a power base outside the control of the SED, the party declared at the First Party Conference in 1949 that it would make women's issues (*Frauenarbeit*) the concern of the entire party. This decision meant that the SED did not entrust the organization of women to women themselves. In addition, the SED began to curb the political role of the DFD on the factory floors and eventually banned the DFD from factories altogether in 1949 (Schubert 1980; DFD 1989). With the DFD gone from the factories, working women lost the organization that gave them, at least initially, some power to intervene on their own behalf in the workplace (Schubert 1980). By 1963 the SED had decided to reorganize the DFD and to change its purpose from serving as a women's organization to carrying out social work in the newly established urban high-rise complexes and reaching out to rural women working on collectivized farms (Kulke 1967; Scholze and Arendt 1986).[17]

The Period of "Social Paternalism"

Immediately following the creation of the GDR, the leadership was mostly concerned with integrating women into the labor force. After it constructed the Wall in 1961, the GDR began its second phase of constructing socialism. The emphasis was no longer on simple integration; rather, the regime proposed a double strategy. First, it made the qualification and integration of women into technical professions the center of its new strategy (Diemer 1989). Second, it enacted measures to reduce the burden on working women and mothers (Kulke 1967). These new "women-friendly" policies included reducing the workweek and average working hours, introducing a paid "household day" for all full-time working women with families, permitting paid leave to take care of sick children, a year of unpaid mother's leave, and an extension of paid pregnancy leave from eleven to fourteen weeks (Kulke 1967; Scholze and Arendt 1986; DFD 1989).

Finally, a newly conceptualized "Family Statute Book of the GDR" went into effect in April 1966. For the first time the GDR spelled out the norms of socialist family life (Helwig 1982). The family in socialism was

---

17. The DFD did remain important at the international socialist level. The DFD, in conjunction with the International Democratic Women's Federation (IDFF), was key in organizing peace, antinuclear weapons, and anti-NATO conferences. These DFD representatives were seen as "peace ambassadors" for the GDR (DFD 1989).

defined as the "smallest cell in the society." Socialism could not do without the family, which remained the center of GDR society. The Statute Book differed from bourgeois Civil Codes in its emphasis on the economic independence of women and men, tied together in family relations. Thus, only in hardship cases of divorce did men have a responsibility to support women financially. The assumption was that the termination of personal relations between men and women also terminated economic relations (Schubert 1980).

This double strategy of stressing women's responsibilities for work and family shaped the identity of East German women (and men) in two important ways. First, the policies targeted to socialize the costs of child rearing and family relations did not include men. It never occurred to the SED to appeal to men as workers and fathers (Ferree 1993). Men could under special circumstances take advantage of the household day and also avail themselves of the baby year (Winkler 1990). The important point, however, is that women were targeted as the primary caretakers of children. Even in its impressive expansion in the 1970s of the social policies already on the books—the so-called Mommy Policies (*Muttipolitik*)[18]— the GDR continued to identify the responsibility for children as mothers' alone (Ferree 1993). Fathers did not have the stigma of being labeled "raven fathers" if they failed to protect the young.

Second, these policies were "given" to women by the state. Women themselves were never involved in the struggle to achieve their own emancipation. Even the very progressive abortion regulation in the early 1970s that legalized abortions on demand within the first trimester and provided free contraceptives had more to do with the state's goals to improve its demographics than with the right of women to choose freely. As more and more women joined the paid labor force (89 percent of all women and 75 percent of mothers in 1970), the birthrate started to decline. To reverse this trend the SED's strategy was to make childbirth more of a social responsibility while giving women a choice in their reproductive decisions (Scholze and Arendt 1986). In contrast to Western industrialized countries, in which the abortion issue figured as the fiercest struggle of feminists against the state and against the Catholic Church, the GDR "presented" East German women with a fait accompli.

---

18. These "Mommy Policies" included the further shortening of the workweek; maintaining the "household day"; increased vacation times; extension of pregnancy and childbirth leaves to six weeks prior to and twenty weeks after birth; a paid baby year, increasing to eighteen months after the third child; breaks for nursing mothers; extension of sick leave; expansion of daycare centers for all ages; free hot lunch and milk in schools and daycare centers; birth allowance of a thousand marks per child; child benefit per month; and marriage credit (Winkler 1990; Berghahn and Fritzsche 1991; Nickel 1993).

The costs of this state-decreed imposition of women's emancipation, however, have been extensive. The system of social paternalism that was fully in place by the 1970s meant that women were materially cared for but could not influence how their needs were met. Both "father state" and "mother party" were infallible and knew what was good for their children (Gerd 1989). Father state was indeed able to meet many of the individual concerns and demands of women, but the specific combination of social paternalism and its bureaucratic imposition from above produced a situation in which women were economically independent of males but still dependent on the state (Dölling 1994). Schäfer (1990) summed up this position in stating that GDR women were highly educated and self-confident in personal and professional matters but, in their continuing dependence on the state, could never achieve emancipation.

When the Wall collapsed in 1989, 78.1 percent of women were employed either as blue- or white-collar workers.[19] Despite its extensive efforts to promote women, the GDR failed to structure a nongendered labor process. The available figures[20] do show that, while some improvements were made to open previously male-dominated professions, gender-specific job segregation still existed in the GDR. Certain professions in the social services, retail, education, and postal and telephone service were largely feminized, yet women were significantly underrepresented in the heavy industries and in the mines. Gendered segregation also showed up in the wage structure: women consistently earned less than men. In 1988 the average wage of full-time working women was only DM 762 versus DM 1,009 for men (Nickel 1992: 45; see also Gensior, Maier, and Winter 1990).

Positive changes did occur, however, with regard to educating and training women. The younger generation was much more educated. The number of graduates from universities and technical schools increased from 8.1 percent in 1971 to 25.2 percent in 1989. The total number of women workers with diplomas certifying them for skilled work increased from 41 to 58.5 percent; the share of women with no professional training decreased from 44.4 percent in 1971 to 12.3 percent in 1989 (Winkler 1990). In other words, 87.7 percent of the youngest generation of GDR women had completed their education or occupational training.

The GDR prided itself on its highly educated female work force. At the same time, scholars noted a conservative return to traditional gender types after 1985 (Dölling 1990a; Merkel 1990a; Nickel 1993). In a perverse

---

19. If trainees and students are included, then the percentage of women engaged in the workforce is 91.2 percent (Winkler 1990).

20. The GDR did not publish any data on social or women's conditions. Only after the collapse of the regime did the GDR, under the pressure of the Women's Equality officer, Marina Beyer, in Lothar de Maizière's government, compile the *Frauenreport '90* (Winkler).

way the social policies targeting women increased their "double burden" in the home and the workplace and, more important, made this double burden publicly invisible. Already in 1969, Ilse Thiele, the chair of the DFD, proudly declared that the fundamental women's question had been solved (Scholze and Arendt 1986). Since the women's question had officially been declared nonexistent, the topic of women's emancipation was now passé, with the result that the SED daily, *Neues Deutschland,* declared in 1983 that "all who continue to write about this topic are men-haters and children-haters" (Schmitz-Köster 1991).

The increasing double burden of women in the 1980s started to appear also in some data on family relations (Helwig 1988). Not only were women more critical of their marriages than men; they also had higher expectations regarding their partners and family life (Bertram 1989). The best-educated women, raised on the promises of equality, were more dissatisfied with their partners and the division of labor in households than were women from working-class families (Gysi 1989).[21] Despite the more vocal dissatisfaction of women among the intelligentsia, women of all social groups felt more burdened than men, due to their juggling motherhood and work. Dissatisfaction was surely not unrelated to the economic contribution women made to family finances. Whereas women in the Federal Republic contribute only 18 percent to the family budget, women in the GDR contribute 40 percent (Maleck-Lewy 1990).

Given the general dissatisfaction of many women, coupled with their economic independence, it is not surprising that women most often initiated divorces. Most divorces occurred among couples under thirty-five years of age (Gysi 1989). A real shift seemed to have taken place in terms of women's attitudes toward family and children. There had been no decline in women's willingness to have children. Nearly 90 percent of women in the GDR had at least one child. And only 0.5 percent of women expressed the specific desire not to have children. A real jump occurred, however, in children born to single mothers. The percentage increased from 13.3 percent in 1970 to 34.4 percent in 1986. At the same time, the share of single-parent families had increased to 14.5 percent (13.7 percent mothers and 0.8 percent fathers) (Gysi 1989).

As the traditional family started to show signs of stress, the SED told women that their need for personal development was too demanding on males; women were urged to lower their expectations. Their high expectations and their general dissatisfaction were, according to the SED, the

---

21. Men did hardly more work in the family than their West German counterparts. Gysi (1989) shows that the majority of men were involved less than an hour with daily housework and that this work was divided according to gender-specific tasks. Men were mostly engaged in the care of the car and in small repairs around the house.

result of women's emotional "nature," based on the different socialization patterns of boys and girls. Having run out of ideas about how to solve the unresolved women's question in the 1980s, the GDR sided against women. More important, while the SED leadership had declared with Lenin that the women's question was a question of the entire party, it now proclaimed that women's dissatisfaction was a personal failure of individual women. The party no longer recognized the complaints as a social problem. Turning the women's question into an individual problem may have had the unintended consequence of making women political actors in the 1980s.

The Blossoming of East German Feminism in the 1980s

The state-decreed emancipation of East German women closed virtually all political opportunity structures for women to act collectively. Because the "public life in the GDR was not public" until 1989 (Bohley, interview), it was difficult for social movements to develop in such a hostile environment. A network of small, informal grassroots groups started to form, however, in the 1980s. These groups could not have emerged had they not had powerful "allies" in an otherwise highly antagonistic "conflict system" (Klandermans 1990). Under the protection of the Protestant Church and within the existing institutional structures of the universities, ecological, human rights, peace, lesbian, and feminist activists had created small, informal networks throughout the GDR. Yet these small networks had no institutional access to mass publics and the polity (Rucht 1994). Nor did resources exist to build either large organizations or public spaces to mobilize citizen support for the various agendas of these groups.[22] That the tremendous groundswell of frustration was able to manifest itself politically in the fall of 1989 was largely the result of this network of small informal groups, often unaware of one another's existence, throughout the GDR since the 1980s.

The feminist groups also fit this small-group pattern. That the feminist movement, barely one month after the collapse of the Wall, was able to create a national feminist organization, the Independent Women's League, is the result of these semipublic/semiprivate organizational activities. Women intellectuals were instrumental in creating a space for problematizing the issue of the continuing unsolved women's question

---

22. For an analysis of the emergence of the various groups and their activities in the 1980s, see Schwarz and Zenner 1990; Winkler 1990; Müller-Enbergs, Schulz, and Wielgohs 1991; Sillge 1991; Wuttke and Musiolek 1991; Forschungsjournal *Neue Soziale Bewegungen*, no. 1 (1992); Rüddenklau 1992; Haufe and Bruckmeier 1993; Meckel and Gutzeit 1994; and Joppke 1995.

throughout the 1980s. Women writers of the GDR played a key role in this politicization process of the younger generation (Lemke 1991). Authors such as Christa Wolf, Maxie Wander, Irmtraud Morgner, Sarah Kirsch, Brigitte Martin, and Helga Schubert[23] provided the language for feminists to free themselves from the official value system.[24] An internationally acclaimed "women's literature" emerged in the GDR with no equivalent in either the other Eastern European countries or in West Germany in the late 1970s.[25]

These writers reclaimed the "subjective authenticity" of women's experiences against the claim of a totalitarian male-oriented "objectivity" (Böck 1990). Whether these authors problematized the grand historical periods or problems of humanity (Christa Wolf in *Kassandra* and *No Place: Nowhere;* Irmtraud Morgner in *Trobadora* and *Amanda*), they did it from a woman's perspective. They used the "backward prophecy" deliberately to critique the present and to thematize history as dynamic, processual, and contradictory (Böck 1990). These women not only provided insights into cultural history; their intent was to mediate a consciousness for cultural history from the perspective of women. When Christa Wolf and Irmtraud Morgner spoke about war in classical antiquity, they used the social transformation process from the old matriarchy to a patriarchal system as the context to explain the increasing militarization of our time (Steiger 1990).

Irmtraud Morgner's wonderfully playful fantasies of the witches' world is symbolic of the despair over the present and at the same time a metaphor for survival. Witches are simultaneously excluded from this world and capable of intervening in the here and now; they change the world or escape into some imaginary place where they can forget the here and now, making them the embodiment of feminist resistance (Schmitz-Köster 1991; Steiger 1991). These metaphors of exclusion in a world they did not create and cannot shape gave feminists the conceptual tools to translate their dissatisfaction into political language. In addition, this

---

23. Other women writers are: Irina Liebmann, Roswitha Geppert, Monika Helmecke, Christa Müller, Helga Schütz, Maria Seidemann, Gerti Tetzner, Christine Wolter, Charlotte Worgitzky, Angela Krauß, Ursula Höntsch-Harendt, Christine Lambrecht, Sybille Muthesius, Doris Paschiller, Regine Röhner, Maja Wiens, Rosemaria Zeplin, Valerie Radtke, Beate Morgenstern, Renate Feyl, Brigitte Burmeister, Daniela Dahn (some of them cited in Böck 1990).

24. Women painters (Angela Hampel) and filmmakers increasingly centered their work on women as a point of departure from male artists (Schönfelt 1990).

25. Hanna Behrend, a retired English professor at the Humboldt University, Berlin, suggests that only African-American women have produced a similar genre of women's books (interview).

genre of literature personified women as individual subjects ready to intervene in historical processes.

Not surprisingly, female authors had a strong influence on female academics in the arts, linguistics, cultural studies, literature, and sociology (Dölling 1990b). In turn, they brought their students into contact with antisystemic politics. It is not accidental that many female activists in the fall of 1989 were teaching assistants, lecturers, permanent and short-term academic staff members, students, or professors at universities and research institutes. Nor is it accidental that at the Humboldt University, the Zentrum interdisziplinärer Frauenforschung (ZiF, Center for Interdisciplinary Women's Research); the *Humboldt Women;* and a weekly "women's breakfast" (*Weiberfrühstück*) were founded barely a month after the fall of the Wall (ZiF 1991).

The Humboldt University provided some, albeit very little, legitimacy for women to exchange ideas in small groups. One such feminist group started to form in the early 1980s. This group was established under very strict guidelines. It was properly registered at the university, and department chairs were informed of the participants' activities. This group consisted mainly of cultural theorists, but it provided a foundation of solidarity for other women who did not find supportive environments in their departments. These meetings offered a forum for discussing problems and frustrations and for engaging in theoretical discussions. It was the first time many participants realized that the problems they faced were shared by other women. Of equal importance were the theoretical insights they gained from one another (Dölling, interview).

Their action repertoire was quite limited, however. Feminists were able to meet and discuss issues in small circles, and this in itself was a new step. More important, they were able to reach students who in turn reached others. Thus, there was a multiplier effect in diffusing feminist ideas from this small group at the Humboldt University. They could not, however, reach a wider public to discuss the theoretical foundation of Marxist thought and problematize the relations between class and gender. Nor could they discuss publicly the problems of the GDR's forty-year state-decreed, and to many failed, emancipation.

Throughout the 1980s the SED remained opposed to all movement activities. Whereas the churches and some universities became part of the feminists' alliance system, the SED continued to form part of the conflict system (Klandermans 1990). In its opposition against feminist groups it relied on a double strategy. It marginalized them at the same time it co-opted them. Irene Dölling and Hildegardf Maria Nickel, active members of the feminist group at the Humboldt University since its inception, were asked to join the Scientific Committee of the research group Women in the

Socialist Society at the Academy of Science in Berlin in 1987 (Diskussion 1990). Invited as feminist scholars, they could not discuss feminist issues in this research group. They were permitted, however, to publish articles on gender issues in the *Weimarer Beiträge,* but this was a very select academic journal inaccessible to the general public (Hampele 1991). Hanna Behrend, professor of English, had to remove the names of Dölling and Nickel from her manuscript as late as 1989. Because Behrend's book was a school text intended for a wide audience, the publisher prohibited citation of Dölling's and Nickel's articles. Behrend summed up the situation, "I was able to cite American and British feminists, but not feminists from the GDR" (interview).

A very different and internationally well-known group, Women for Peace, and its successor, the Initiative for Peace and Human Rights, were also instrumental in shaping the general consciousness of women in the GDR in the 1980s. These two groups developed under the protection of the Protestant Church, though their goals were never fully condoned by the church hierarchy (Becker 1991; Richter and Zylla 1991; Meckel and Gutzeit 1994; Poppe 1995). These two groups differed, however, in both organizational structure and in action repertoire from the semipublic/ semiprivate feminist groups organized in the universities. Women for Peace was the first group to organize as a group at the national level and to appear publicly (Bohley, interview). No other organized group existed prior to 1983.[26] Second, Women for Peace also had contacts with human rights groups, ecological groups, and other peace groups. The successor organization, the Initiative for Peace and Human Rights, provided a more formal channel of communication by publishing the critical journal *Grenz-fall,* the first publication not published under the protection of the church. Third, its action repertoire included dramatic, visible actions that were geared to create national and international publicity.

Unlike their feminist sisters in the universities, these women activists did not shy away from confrontation with the state or from being arrested. The immediate external spark for the creation of Women for Peace was the 1979 NATO decision to station Pershing II and cruise missiles in Europe, and the Military Service Law of 1981 to conscript any women between the ages of eighteen and fifty for unarmed military service in case of war (Allen 1989; Kukutz 1995). It was in response to this law that women peace activists wrote a petition to Erich Honecker, which was signed by 150

---

26. I wonder if it is simply a matter of oversight that Bruckmeier (1993) and Semtner (1992) identify the group Initiative for Peace and Human Rights, created in 1986, as the oldest citizens' group in the GDR. According to Bärbel Bohley, it was Women for Peace that rightfully can claim the title of having been the first group to organize nationally as a citizens' group (interview).

cosigners stating that they reserve the "right to conscientious objection." In addition, women activists established contacts with other peace groups in the West protesting the stationing of tactical nuclear weapons in the West and East (Kukutz 1995).

Although external circumstances explain the creation of Women for Peace in 1982, many of the women activists had a long history of speaking out against the introduction of paramilitary training in schools and the introduction of war toys in daycare centers in the 1970s. That this was a very sensitive issue for the state can be seen by its quick reaction to close the independent daycare center operated by Ulrike Poppe, cofounder of the group, at the moment she was arrested in 1983. Poppe had created an alternative to the state-run centers, in which children were discouraged to play with war toys (Allen 1989).

Women for Peace also staged dramatic events in public places. They organized "political night prayers" to draw attention to the increasing danger of nuclear devastation. A symbolic mass die-in at the Alexanderplatz in Berlin in 1983 was meant to draw attention to the nuclear devastation of Hiroshima. In the same year black-clothed women organized a postcard action at the Alexanderplatz to protest the registration of medical personnel for war purposes (Winkler 1990; Hampele 1991).

Despite this visibility, Women for Peace never identified with feminist issues. Bärbel Bohley, one of the initiators of Women for Peace, suggested that being a woman was never the overriding criterion for creating this group; rather, the group was created for tactical reasons. "We thought as long as the state was a male society (*Männergesellschaft*), which they constructed and in which we only served as token women, we would challenge them and do something as women. Men occupied all the topics. Men were arrested and the entire struggle centered around men. Our interest was to discuss political topics, i.e., the militarization of the society and what can be done against it, among women." Leading women in Women for Peace such as Ulrike Poppe, Katja Havemann, and Bettina Rathenau were not only the wives of political dissidents; they also felt that they could make a unique contribution as Women for Peace (Bohley, interview).

Whether these women identified with feminist goals was less important than their organization as a women-only group. The SED's persecution of Women for Peace put them at the center of the struggle against the regime. This struggle gained national and international attention, which neither the academic nor lesbian groups had ever achieved. Thus, while these women did not address gender issues directly, their open struggle with the GDR regime furthered the potential for emancipation of GDR women as a whole in the 1980s. Understanding their role in developing a discourse and in providing an example of women's mobilization in the context of a monocratic and exclusionist socialist system is paramount for understanding why feminists could burst onto the scene in 1989 demanding not only social empowerment but a space in the political arena.

The development of women's academic groups, lesbian groups, and Women for Peace share several features. All originated in the 1980s and met in small groups; most of them were personally connected through friendships and their political work was intimately tied to their personal lives. Group meetings occurred in virtually all cities of the GDR, and the SED used strategies of intimidation and co-optation against them. These groups also demonstrate the recognition of diversity that started to appear in the GDR prior to 1989. No single issue existed that united all women as women. Rather, women organized as women depending on whether their interests dealt with a lesbian agenda, academic issues, or military matters. Their political actions were often symbolic, and yet these symbolic actions were readily understood by people as challenging the authority of the regime. This symbolic politics, which under the circumstances of a repressive regime stood for "real" politics, provided the groups with some notion of protection. The state was reluctant to suppress overtly these symbolic challenges to the existing authorities (Rucht 1994).

Only with the opening of the Wall did the various groups secure public space in which to organize and emerge into movements. Lesbians, female theologians, peace and human rights activists, and academic and church women came together on December 3, 1989, to create the Independent Women's League (UFV). This is not only the day when East German women expressed their desire to unite their "different voices" within a larger organization; it also signaled their intent to play an active role in the transformation of state and society (Schäfer, interview).

CHAPTER 2

The East German "Stateless State" Period and Feminist Mobilization

The Opening of the East German Political Opportunity Structure

The GDR's repressive political opportunity structure set the boundaries for collective action for informal social networks throughout the 1980s. The ever-present fear of state repression was too strong for the informal networks to challenge the regime (Neidhardt 1985). Hence, the majority of these informal social networks remained within the "safe" confines of the Protestant Church and universities. These groups, however, were able to constitute themselves as movements in the early summer months of 1989 as the East German political opportunity structure "broadened" and revealed the first signs of the state's vulnerability. This broadening was made possible by the increasing decline of the SED's political legitimacy. At least three circumstances show that the GDR system was no longer immune to the demands of the opposition.

First was the SED's overt manipulation of the local elections of May

---

The East German period of "statelessness" does not mean that there was no government. Hans Modrow formed a government on November 17 and, starting in January, entered into a "Government of National Responsibility" with the Central Round Table, which lasted until the parliamentary elections of March 1990. There was, however, no concept of a state. The only thing clear after November 9 was that the conditions for the authoritarian state had changed. The questions that were not resolved on November 9 were whether the new state was going to be a democratic socialist state, a radical democratic state, a party state, or a "movement" state; whether it would combine private ownership with public ownership; and, most important, whether it would remain independent of or enter into a federation with West Germany. Only the elections of March 18 clearly indicated that the "new" state in the GDR meant the institutionalization of Western-style democracy.

7, 1989. Officials reported that 99 percent of voters had approved the list of SED candidates. In its attempt to portray the local elections as a resounding victory for the regime, the leaders failed to admit that at least 10 to 15 percent either abstained from voting or voted against SED candidates (Jarausch 1994). For the SED to deny the existence of an opposition was all the more striking since members of the church grassroots groups, the Church from Below, and individuals who had applied for emigration, independently monitored polling stations in Berlin. In the evening they organized an election party at the Berlin Elisabeth Church and tabulated the results in front of nine West German media correspondents. The results were then printed on flyers and distributed among church members.

When Egon Krenz, the chairman of the Central Election Commission, announced the 98.89 percent approval rating for the regime on television at around midnight, those assembled at the church broke out in "ironic jubilation," which was duly reported the next day in the West German newspaper *Süddeutsche Zeitung.* In turn the official East German paper, the *Neue Deutschland,* blamed the Western media for creating the rumors of election manipulation (Wolle 1992).

The election fraud facilitated movement mobilization in two ways. First, it revealed the vulnerability of the SED. The party was unable to tolerate only an 80 or 90 percent approval rating of its candidates; rather than confront the existence of a growing opposition, it lied. This denial in itself was an expression of the state's increasing loss of legitimacy and its inability to deal with this new reality. Second, this event created a political space for other social actors to mobilize against the regime. In seizing opportunities for the opposition, the church group "created" opportunities for itself and for others (Tarrow 1994). Although publicizing the election fraud was a feat in itself, the legacy of this act was the public confrontation with the authorities. This sent a signal to others that some, however small, opportunity for opposition had been created.

Taking advantage of this newly won political space, the church groups called for additional protest rallies on the seventh of each month as a reminder of the election manipulation. Each month many young people in "nylon anoraks" assembled at the Berlin Alexanderplatz, and, each time, they were hauled away by the police who waited with water cannons in the side streets. Despite this police action, the numbers at the rallies increased every month. By the time of their fifth meeting, coinciding with the fortieth birthday of the German Democratic Republic, several thousand people had assembled (Wolle 1992).

The legitimacy of the SED was further weakened when the political leaders openly lent support to the Chinese government's suppression of the democratic students' uprising at Tiananmen Square in June 1989. As people watched on television the armed tanks rolling against the Chinese students, they were inadvertently reminded of the many uprisings in the East European countries and the brutal armed intervention by the Soviet forces (Wolle 1992). Disregarding its own history of violently crushing the 1953 uprising, the East German leadership reached out to Chinese party and state leaders and embarked on an exchange of visits in September and October. At his visit in Berlin, Quiao Shi, the leader of the Chinese delegation, thanked the GDR for its support and understanding in the PRC's suppression of the "counterrevolutionary uprising." Toasting the friendship between China and East Germany, Egon Krenz, the future successor to Erich Honecker, on October 1, 1989, proudly claimed that "we share the same ideals" (*Neues Forum Leipzig* 1989).

The experience with the election fraud and the SED's support for the Chinese suppression of the fledgling democratic uprising created an increasing "solidarity" among people against the regime. In an ironic twist of fate the East German opposition found its solidarity strengthened by the secretary-general of the Soviet Communist Party. Mikhail Gorbachev's speeches were now voluntarily read by people in the GDR, although Gorbachev and his "New Thinking" remained taboo subjects in the East German Politburo. Nothing less than a "Gorbachev cult" developed, with young East Germans importing T-shirts with "Gorbi" portraits from Hungary and then wearing them publicly in the GDR. This Gorbachev cult came into full bloom when East German and foreign dignitaries assembled to celebrate the fortieth anniversary of the founding of the GDR on October 7, 1989, and demonstrators not only shouted, "Gorbi, Gorbi!" They also shouted "Gorbi, help!" (Opp, Voss, and Gern 1995).

This anniversary celebration turned into a disaster and proved to be the final nail in the SED's coffin. Glaessner summed up the political elite's continued illusions about its forty years of achievements: "The celebrations became an embarrassing valedictory to a political and social system which had proved incapable of compromise or reform and of a political elite which mistook for reality its belief in its own proclamations of success" (1992: 42).

What was not visible to the dignitaries and the foreign guests was the brutal police actions against peaceful demonstrators assembled in the side streets; the brutality was targeted specifically against women. The intent was to provoke the male demonstrators into violent actions against the security forces. The day ended with 547 arrests, and the police violence continued well into the next day (Wolle 1992).

Gorbachev's prophetic inscription in the Berlin city guestbook, "life will punish those who arrive too late,"[1] fell on deaf ears in the GDR's leadership circle despite the visible decline of any remaining political authority of the Honecker regime. In the late summer months two interrelated aspects further weakened the leadership and finally burst open the political opportunity structure for movement activities. First, the by now well-known Monday demonstrations in Leipzig started on September 25. At this first rally around five thousand people demonstrated following a peace prayer at the Nicolas Church (Nikolaus Kirche) in the inner ring of the city; the number increased to seventy thousand on October 9 and reached over a half-million at its zenith on November 6.[2] In all, twenty-three Monday demonstrations took place between September 25 and March 12, 1990 (Voss 1995).[3]

These recurring Monday night demonstrations in Leipzig quickly spread throughout the GDR. No longer did demonstrators come only from dissident groups; an ever-wider circle of the previously apolitical population joined and voiced their growing dissatisfaction with the conditions of the GDR's "real socialism." These demonstrations in virtually every city provided a space for a hitherto bureaucratically suppressed society to constitute itself as active citizenry (Jarausch 1994).

Second, these large demonstrations and citizens' demands for political change were accentuated by the exit of hundreds of thousands of young GDR citizens, first via the Hungarian border then from the embassies in Warsaw and Prague to West Germany between August and October. Honecker's caustic remark "that one should not shed a tear for those who left" propelled some intellectuals to speak out, albeit rather late, in defense of the young people fleeing (Wolf 1990). The brutality of the GDR police in beating back those who tried to jump onto the trains coming from Prague and Warsaw and passing through Dresden between October 2 and 8 to hitch a ride to the West was beamed into the homes of East Germans, compliments of West German television.

Hirschman summarizes the preconditions for the revolutionary upris-

---

1. The German statement read, "Wer zu spät kommt, wird vom Leben bestraft."

2. The exact numbers of demonstrators will probably never be known. Since the demonstrations were illegal, there are no official statistics. In fact, Voss (1995) argues that the State Security (Stasi) probably stopped counting at some point.

3. That the demonstrations took place on Mondays has a history in the GDR. Since 1982 peace prayers had taken place in the Nicolas Church on Mondays. In 1989 people met for peace prayers at 5:00 P.M., followed by a gathering at the Karl-Marx-Place at around 6:00 P.M. and a march around the city on the Ring. This scenario was repeated for all twenty-three Leipzig demonstrations (Voss 1995).

ing in discussing the East Germans' "confederate strategy," "exit" and "voice":[4]

> The inability of the GDR, starting in the spring of 1989, to prevent a large-scale flight of its citizens to West Germany, via Hungary, Poland, or Czechoslovakia, signaled a novel, serious, and general decline in state authority. It was thus taken to imply a similar decline in the ability and readiness to repress voice—with the result that citizens started to demonstrate against the regime for the first time since June 1953. Precisely because the East German regime had made the repression of exit into the touchstone of its authority, its sudden incapacity to enforce its writ in this area meant a huge loss of face that emboldened people to other kinds of transgression. (1993: 187)

As the situation intensified in September and October of 1989, the citizenry split into two camps, those who elected to exit and those who chose voice. At the Leipzig Monday demonstrations these two options were reduced to the forces of "we want out" and the defiant "we're staying here" (Neues Forum Leipzig 1989). The conviction "we are here, we stay here, and we want to articulate what we still hope from this state" helped those who opted to stay overcome the despair engendered by "the exodus of the smiling youth who turned their backs on the GDR" (Wolf 1990: 77).

Focusing on exit and voice to explain why the regime crumbled in November 1989 tells us little about the role played by citizens' groups that remained in the country. Why and for what purpose did they demonstrate in virtually every city of the GDR? Why did their numbers increase from a few thousand demonstrators to a half-million by November 1989? And why did demonstrators in Leipzig take to the streets when there was every indication that the SED might use a "Chinese solution" on October 9, 1989 (Masur 1989; *TAZ,* October 24, 1989). This is not the place to explain the causes for the revolutionary uprising. Nevertheless, the citizens' groups that emerged in these last months of the GDR did influence the political contours of the revolutionary uprising. Granted their political

---

4. The controversy continues over whether or not to call the citizens' uprising a "revolution." In fact, many prominent members of the East German citizens' movement such as Gerd Poppe (Initiative of Peace and Human Rights) and Wolfgang Ullmann (Democracy Now) reject the notion that it was a revolution (Poppe interview, in Semtner 1992: 171; and Ullmann interview, in Stiftung Mitarbeit 1992: 12). Social scientists seem to struggle over what kind of revolution it was: a "catching-up revolution" (Habermas 1990); a "spontaneous revolution" (Opp 1991); a "protestant revolution" (Neubert 1991); an "unfinished revolution" (Schäuble 1991); and a "happy revolution" (Schäfer 1990). None of these terms provides a definition of the concept.

influence did not last much beyond the collapse of the Wall, yet the democratic awakening of the citizens' movements (*Bürgerbewegung*) had revolutionary consequences and ultimately broke the spell of the SED repression (Jarausch 1994).

Mobilization toward Collective Action

In this situation, in which "those that ruled" could no longer command and "those at the bottom" would no longer take commands, a loosely organized grassroots citizens' movement emerged. The creation of the Neues Forum (New Forum), with its appeal for an "Awakening '89" and a "democratic dialogue," gained the greatest public resonance in this period of general state demobilization. Well-known dissidents such as Bärbel Bohley, cofounder of Women for Peace and Initiative for Peace and Human Rights; Jens Reich, molecular biologist and cofounder of Initiative for Peace and Human Rights; the physicist Sebastian Pflugbein; and many others called for a dialogue on the "contradiction between the seriously unbalanced relations between state and society." The New Forum understood itself as providing an avenue to engage every single citizen in a debate irrespective of their social and political position. Appealing for a dialogue about "what the GDR had to do with socialism," the New Forum abstained from offering a ready-made reform package (Schulz 1991: 12). The process of a democratic dialogue became the political platform for the New Forum (Jarausch 1994).

On September 19 the New Forum demanded legal recognition as a movement in all administrative districts of the GDR. In requesting this political recognition, the New Forum was not only the first group to constitute itself as a social movement; this step also openly challenged the state to grant a political group, independent of the SED, political legitimacy. This recognition was denied until November 8. The GDR opposed the New Forum as an "enemy of the state," although the New Forum recognized the "two Germanies and rejected a capitalist social system" (Schulz 1991).

The New Forum did not remain without competition. Members of the citizen movement Democracy Now, a group that emerged from within the opposition in the Protestant Church, went public with an "appeal to become involved in our problems" on September 12. Its cofounders were a diverse group of intellectuals and included the historian Ulrike Poppe, pastor Wolfgang Ullmann, physicist Hans-Jürgen Fischbeck, and film director Konrad Weiss (Jarausch 1994). This group understood itself as neither a political party nor an association with a regular membership:

"We do not want a hierarchy. The group decides itself, who will speak for the group, and which priorities the group will follow. . . . We reject centralism." As a group, Democracy Now never rivaled the large membership of the New Forum. It never went much beyond four thousand members, in contrast to the two hundred thousand members of the New Forum in November (Wielgohs and Müller-Enbergs 1991: 119).

Unlike the New Forum, Democracy Now developed a programmatic thesis for a democratic transformation of the GDR. It called for a renewal of socialism. Rejecting state socialism, this group demanded in its three theses a shift from the authoritarian state to a republic, from nationalization to socialization of the means of production, and, finally, from exploitation and environmental degradation to compatible existence with nature (Wielgohs and Müller-Enbergs 1991).

Another more moderate church group formed two days later and called itself Demokratischer Aufbruch (Democratic Awakening). Formed mostly by the Protestant clergy, such as Friedrich Schorlemmer, Rainer Eppelmann, Bishop Gottfried Forck, and church lawyer Wolfgang Schnur, this group called for the end of SED dominance and proposed a "socialist society on a democratic basis." It differed from the previous group in that it continued to have ties to the church and thus projected a more conservative image than either the New Forum or Democracy Now (Jarausch 1994). Another group, the Vereinigte Linke (United Left), was also founded in the early movement-oriented days of September. The members came from diverse backgrounds on the Left and included labor union members independent of the official FDGB, members of the "Church from Below," women who subsequently formed the first women's autonomous group, Lila Offensive, others from the League of Independent Socialists, the Carnations, and also from the group Voices Against. In contrast to the other groups, the United Left openly identified itself as a Marxist, leftist, socialist group and remained reserved toward the Protestant Church, having shunned the protection of the church throughout the 1980s. In its reform goals it combined a socialist programmatic based on democratic, legal, and human rights, with the demand for an ecological transformation of capitalist societies. The United Left differed from the other social movements in that it was open to former reformed SED members (Wielgohs 1991).

Lila Offensive was the first independent women's group to emerge, on October 11, 1989; it constituted itself into a political union on December 2, 1989. Within barely a month members of this group developed a detailed theoretical paper with practical demands for the realization of a gender equal society. They caused an uproar at the, until then, largest non-

SED organized rally, on November 4, 1989, in Berlin. They made their premiere with a small "women's bloc," under the mottoes "Women in the Offensive," "Women belong in the House—in the Council House" (Die Frau gehört ins Haus—ins Rathaus!), "If you don't struggle, you remain in the kitchen" (Wer sich nicht wehrt, kommt an den Herd), "Women must enter politics," "Nothing can be done without women," and with a banner reading, "There are only two truths in the world: (1) Men are more intelligent than women. (2) The earth is a disk" (Kahlau 1990; Lila Offensive 1990; Hampele 1991).

In this "cat-and-mouse" game between a state whose authority was visibly withering away and a citizens' movement that had become ever bolder, the GDR leadership tried to forestall its own demise by making a halfhearted offer of reform. In a highly secret "palace coup" organized within the Politburo, Erich Honecker was ousted on October 17 as secretary-general of the SED. Also dismissed were Günter Mittag, the Politburo member responsible for the economy and secretary to the Central Committee; and Joachim Herrmann, Politburo member for agitation and propaganda. These dismissals were meant to liberate the party from the hard-liners around Honecker and install Egon Krenz as the secretary-general of the SED and later also as chairman of the State Council and National Defense Council. Yet to most GDR citizens Krenz was little more than "the loyal protegé of Erich Honecker and the man responsible for the ballot-rigging in the communal elections of the previous May" (Glaessner 1992; Bahrmann and Links 1994).

These cosmetic changes no longer satisfied the by now growing groundswell of popular dissatisfaction. The large November 4 demonstration in Berlin's Alexanderplatz with some five hundred thousand participants was the prelude to the final collapse of the GDR. Only three days after the Alexanderplatz demonstration, the cabinet of Willi Stoph resigned, followed the next day by the Central Committee's election of a new Politburo, which no longer included the SED hard-liners—Axen, Hager, Krolikowski, Mielke, Mückenberger, Neumann, Stoph, Sindermann, and Tisch (Glaessner 1992; Bahrmann and Links 1994). It was somewhat anticlimactic that the New Forum received legal recognition by the new government on November 8 (Schulz 1991).

The Wall finally collapsed the next day. Whether the GDR intended to open the Wall on that fateful night or whether it was an unplanned event is immaterial at this point (Schäuble 1991). It was the end of a forty-year experiment with state socialism in the GDR. The reform-oriented Dresden district secretary Hans Modrow was nominated to head the new government on November 12, and he introduced his new cabinet five days later. For the first time the government included, in addition to sixteen mostly moderate SED members, twelve ministers from the "bloc parties" (Jarausch 1994).[5]

The final end of the state party came on December 3. As a first step, the East German parliament (Volkskammer) deleted the SED's party monopoly status from the constitution (Thaysen 1990a). Two days later a revolt at the party grassroots forced the resignation of the entire Politburo of the SED—surely an unprecedented act in over seventy years of Communist Party history (Glaessner 1992). The fall of the Central Committee and the Politburo also forced Egon Krenz to give up political leadership as chairman of the State Council and the National Defense Council on December 6 (Bahrman and Links 1994). East Germans had joined, albeit belatedly, their sisters and brothers in other East European countries in throwing off the yoke of oppression.[6]

There are at least three aspects that distinguish the collapse of the GDR from those of other Eastern European countries. First, the large demonstrations and protests were not organized by any particular groups. The small number of opposition groups that had developed throughout the 1980s and the low membership numbers did not provide the organizational capacity to mobilize a large mass of citizens (Opp 1992). Second, the expectations of violence were great. Again and again, the leadership invoked a Chinese solution to cope with the "criminals," "rowdies," and "troublemakers" (*Störenfried*) (*Neues Forum Leipzig* 1989). Even after the opening of the Wall, the danger of violence did not subside. The Ministry of Security (MfS) continued to operate and its willingness to engage in violent action remained the "wild card" in this dangerous game (Ullmann, interview, in Maleck 1991). In addition, the swell of uncontrollable anger of ordinary citizens offered as much potential for violence as the threat of the Stasi. The peaceful outcome to this potentially violent situation was primarily because of the citizens' groups at the Central Round Table in Berlin (Thaysen 1990).[7]

Aside from the active involvement of the citizen groups to ensure a "peaceful revolution" and the nonorganized nature of the protests and

---

5. In addition to the SED, the GDR also had remnants of postwar parties: Christian (CDU); liberal (LDPD); nationalist (NDPD); and peasants' (DBD) parties. These parties were allied in the "democratic bloc" and controlled by the SED. There were also mass organizations such as the trade union (FDGB), party youth (FDJ), and women's league (DFD) that transmitted party directives (Jarausch 1994).

6. See Ash 1990; Offe 1994; and Joppke 1995 for a comparison of the different paths the communist collapse has taken in East Germany and other Eastern European countries.

7. The Central Round Table was created during the period of transformation from the SED regime to new forms of social and state institutions. At the Round Table the opposition groups and representatives of the old regime met jointly from December 7, 1989, until March 12, 1990 (Thaysen 1990a–c; 1992a).

demonstrations, a third factor sets the GDR apart from other Eastern European countries: the role of women. Women and men took to the streets to protest the political monopoly of the SED. They demanded "more democracy, and less bureaucracy," under the slogans "We are the people" and "The Stasi into production." Women also called out, however, "We need new men" (Schwarz 1990: 8) and "We need a testicle reform, away with the limp sacks"[8] (*Neues Forum Leipzig* 1989: 180).

As the opposition groups started to emerge and voice publicly their demand for more participation and democracy, women soon realized that political participation was reserved once again for men. There was silence around the question of women, and no "motherland was in sight" (Wolf 1990: 17, 104).

Feminists and the Lack of an Alliance System

Virtually none of the citizens' movements included women's issues in their platforms (Schulz 1991: 55). Of the newly organized citizens' movements (New Forum, Democracy Now, Democratic Awakening, Peace and Human Rights, and United Left) only United Left had a clearly stated position on women's issues from the very start of its draft program. The women's question did not even appear in the program and the statute of the New Forum. Only in its January version did the latter insert a demand for equal rights of men and women. The situation was no better in Peace and Human Rights and Democracy Now. In fact, among the eleven pages of small print of the Democracy Now program were a mere two and a half lines addressing women's issues (Kretschmar 1990).

Why did the citizens' movements have so little interest in addressing gender issues? The most plausible answer is one that we already encountered with members of Women for Peace. Women political activists did not see "males" as their enemies. Together with males they fought against the enemy: the state. Thus, East German women's identity, including feminists', was shaped by the belief that social transformation could only come with men and not against men (Merkel 1990b). Although women such as Bärbel Bohley (New Forum), Ulrike Poppe (Democracy Now), Ingrid Köppe (New Forum), and Vera Wollenberger (Greens-GDR) were some of the most powerful political activists during the citizen mobilization, they shared the belief that the emphasis on feminism was too restrictive and too exclusionary (Bohley, interview).

In addition, many academic feminists had ties to the SED and later to

---

8. The German translation is "Wir wollen Hodenreform. Weg mit den schlaffen Säcken!!"

the successor party, the PDS. Since the citizens' movement formed itself in strict demarcation from the existing regime, the closeness of many feminists to the SED made it difficult for women political activists organized in the citizens' movement to endorse feminism, which did not mean that they were indifferent to issues concerning women. Their overriding concern was to remain in opposition to the SED and its successor party, the PDS (Hampele 1996).

While the citizens' movements had no overt interest in issues concerning women, the new party leadership under Egon Krenz resurrected the traditional picture of women as saviors. In his first address as party leader Krenz appealed to women as "the indispensable support of our society and family." Finding themselves between the positions of either "being called upon again to rebuild the mess men left behind" or being left out altogether from the new project of state and social transformation, women chose the option of voice and demanded that the "awakening of the country has also to be the awakening of women" (Schwarz and Zenner 1990: 9).

Going It Alone

A public letter entitled "Does the Reform Bypass Women?" dated November 6, signaled the beginning of the independent women's movement in the GDR.[9] The letter, signed by journalists from the GDR women's journal *Für Dich,* and prominent feminist scholars,[10] demanded that the Central Committee discuss at the forthcoming Twelfth Party Congress of the SED a catalogue of demands. It asked for the transformation of the state apparatus, parties, and unions such that women's departments or commissions were created with real decision-making powers; the introduction of quotas in all areas of the economy, politics, state, and science; the right to form an independent women's association; and the creation of a Commission for "Women's Questions" at the parliamentary (Volkskammer) and executive levels. Finally, these feminists raised for the first time the demand that men be included in family and child-rearing policies (Schwarz and Zenner 1990).

The circulation of this letter mobilized women into action. They took the microphones at large citizens' demonstrations and read the letter. Crowds first received this message with amazement and then with much applause. With Walfriede Schmitt, a well-known GDR actress, the message hit like fire. She persuaded the women's group Lila Offensive to go

---

9. The feminists met on November 1, but the letter to the Central Committee of the SED was dated November 6.

10. The signatories of this letter were Irene Dölling, Gisela Ehrhardt, Jutta Gysi, Ute Kretzschmar, Hildegard Maria Nickel, Uta Röth, and Eva Schäfer.

public with its new program for a women-friendly GDR and sponsor a "women's spectacle" in the Volksbühne. Not only did members of Lila Offensive support this suggestion, they called for nothing less than the formation of an Independent Women's League at the planned gathering on December 3, 1989 (Schwarz and Zenner 1990: 13). The call sent a signal to the Democratic Women's League (DFD) that feminists would no longer accept the DFD's leadership on women's issues (Lila Offensive 1990).

This euphoria over the formation of an independent women's association was not limited to Berlin. Meetings and gatherings occurred in many parts of the GDR.[11] In fact, the regions of Thuringia and Saxony (Dresden) were known in the GDR as the "women-active areas of concentration" (*frauenbewegte Ballungsgebiet*) (Hampele 1996). Hampele makes the point that Berlin was not the center of women's activities prior to October 1989. She argues that only with the political upheavals targeted at the state and party apparatuses in Berlin did the center of women's activities move from the regions of Thuringia and Saxony to the national capital of Berlin. Nor were the activities limited to cities. Rural women of Mecklenburg, rejecting the position of the official women's association, organized the Movement of Independent Rural Women and later joined the UFV (Winkler 1990: 208).[12]

In Erfurt (Thuringia) many small women's groups, which did not know of one another's existence, formed into a citizen initiative called Women for Change. They developed a position paper that proposed the idea of creating networks with other groups and developed suggestions for legal reform; ecological programs; changes in the education system; reforms in the economy, health and social systems, arts and culture; and for demilitarization. On November 13, 1989, Women for Change sent out invitations to all women's groups for an informational and exchange meeting in Erfurt. This meeting took place one day prior to the Berlin women's spectacle, on December 2, 1989 (Schwarz and Zenner 1990; Hampele 1991). The women's spectacle in Berlin was looked upon with some misgiving in these women-active regions. They felt that their own endeavors to form networks had been hijacked by the Berlin groups and the decision to create a national Independent Women's League (Hampele 1996). It was the women's spectacle in Berlin on December 3, 1989, however, that gave rise to the first independent women's movement in the GDR.

---

11. For an account of the many different women's groups appearing in the fall of 1989, see Kahlau 1990; Winkler 1990: 203–13.

12. Unfortunately, no study exists that documents and analyzes these regional movements.

The opening salvo, "Without Women There Is No State,"[13] was, on the one hand, an expression of the fear that East German women would suffer the same plight of exclusion as did their sisters in other East European countries (Merkel 1990c). On the other, it served as an offensive strategy, signaling to other political parties and citizens' movements that there was no way around the women's issue. The euphoric gathering on December 3, 1989, was thus the outcome of both defensive and offensive calculations.

The Birth of the Independent Women's League: A Feminist Euphoria[14]

Around twelve hundred women, and a few men, gathered at the Volks-bühne in Berlin to create the Independent Women's League (UFV). Women who were present at this gathering nostalgically describe it as "the moment of euphoria" (interviews: Schäfer, Merkel, Böhm, Schwarz, Maleck-Lewy, Schindler, and Schenk). The meeting was intended to create nothing less than a "Happy Women's Revolution with Political Consequences" (Klotz 1992: 13). For this purpose around sixty different women's groups, initiatives, individuals, and party members met to demand to be involved in the transformation of the East German state and social relations. The collapse of the socialist regime seemed to these politically active women "a real opportunity to transform the society from a feminist perspective" (Schenk 1991: 124).

The conviction that women could offer an alternative political and social model is based on the specific experience women had in the GDR. They had witnessed the collapse of the patriarchal state and all the social institutions that had supported this state for over forty years. The state as apparatus of male control and domination collapsed, which symbolized to these feminists nothing less than the total delegitimation of male power

---

13. In selecting this slogan, East German feminists purposely expressed a double meaning. To use the words "Staat machen" is an inappropriate expression in German. By relying on this phraseology, feminists tried to send a signal to other political actors that "politics without women is not a good thing." The second meaning refers to the idea that "building a state" is a technical matter. In this notion of physically constructing a state, the idea is that such an action cannot be done without the involvement of women. The double meanings refer to, first, a normative appeal that states "should" not be built without women and, second, states "cannot" be built without women. I thank Birgit Sauer for pointing out the double meaning of this slogan.

14. I thank Anne Hampele for generously sharing her unpublished dissertation chapters on Free University, Berlin, Germany. This is the only comprehensive study of the UFV and its role during the unification process.

(Sauer 1994). Schäfer saw the "break-down of socialism as a declaration of the bankruptcy of patriarchal power structures" (1991a). The all-powerful state no longer was a state controlled by men. Because of the state's perceived power vacuum, coupled with the delegitimation of male power, women purposely united around the motto "Without Women There Is No State." Ina Merkel chose this motto for her statement to launch the Independent Women's League (Lila Offensive 1990).[15] This demand for the involvement of women at the very center of power politics not only set the new East German women's movement apart from other Eastern European countries; it also set the movement apart from the West German movement.

One reason for creating the Independent Women's League on December 3 had to do with the citizens' movement's call for "Round Table" discussions with the government. The proposal to create a Central Round Table came from the "contact groups," on November 11, and was, according to Thaysen, an expression of the fear of the "crisis-like situation in our country" (1990a: 188).[16] The initiators of the Round Table defined its institutional purpose as a control organ of the Modrow government. Wolfgang Ullmann (1992), a prominent participant, also saw these Round Tables as a forum to reconstitute new social and political structures outside the existing spheres of power. The first meeting of the Round Table was set for December 7.

Since feminists understood themselves as political actors demanding to be involved in the transformation of state and society and realized that the planned Round Table meetings would be the forum at which the transition from communism would be negotiated, they agreed that they had to create an organizational structure in order to participate in these negotiations. Eva Schäfer, one of the cofounders of the UFV, recounted the consensus among feminists: "If we did not participate at the discussions at the Round Table, we would be left without influence" (interview).

The feminist consensus was that gender relations are not synonymous with social relations (Merkel 1990b; Hampele 1991; Maleck-Lewy 1993). Reducing the gender question to its economic component, as the socialists had done for forty years, no longer provided an answer to the women's question for these activists (Kretschmar 1990). The women present at the theater articulated a vision of society in which the status and power hierarchies would no longer shape gender relations (Klotz 1992). In their

---

15. This statement then became known as the "Manifesto for the Independent Women's Movement."

16. The "contact group" consisted of the following citizen groups and political parties: Democratic Awakening, Democracy Now, Green Party, Initiative for Peace and Human Rights, SPD, and United Left.

endeavor to provide a different societal model these women consciously utilized the concept of feminism. Given this construct's negative connotation in the old GDR, this was a major step in breaking out of the official SED definition of the women's question (Schenk 1990). Feminism meant for these women not simply a critique of patriarchal power relations but also an alternative societal model: human, democratic, ecological, and socially fair (Helwerth 1994).

The founding meeting of the Independent Women's League also signaled its rejection of the official representative body, the Democratic Women's Federation of Germany (Sauer 1994). The UFV proclaimed it was "interested in working with the DFD on some issues, otherwise we understand ourselves as an alternative to the DFD" (Hampele 1996).

Despite the apparent loss of a large portion of its women's constituency, the DFD had material wealth at its disposal that the UFV did not have. The UFV approached the DFD and suggested negotiations to share financial resources and physical space at the Clara Zetkin House near the Humboldt University, a spacious building the DFD fully occupied. Yet Eva Rohmann, the newly installed secretary of the Executive Committee of the DFD, refused to part with any of its resources. Eva Schäfer, present at these negotiations, suggested that these meetings reflected a collision of two different women's cultures.[17] The DFD reflected the ethos of the SED party hierarchy and understood women's issues only as social issues; the UFV saw itself as an antihierarchical and antibureaucratic feminist organization (Schäfer, interview).[18]

The Organizational Structure of the UFV

The UFV understood itself as an organizational network for the diverse groups and initiatives that had sprung up during the 1980s and had been forced to remain isolated from one another (Klotz 1992). Its task was to organize women's politics among women's groups independent of political party structures (Hampele 1991; Maleck-Lewy 1993). Ina Merkel's "Manifesto for an Independent Women's Movement" was accepted by those present at the theater as the interim program between the initiation meeting of the UFV on December 3, 1989, and its formal constitution on February 17, 1990. This interim manifesto provided the basis for discus-

---

17. The two groups also differed in behavioral styles. Schäfer recounted that Rohmann was visibly upset when one of the UFV members started to breastfeed her child at the negotiations (Schäfer interview).

18. Noncooperation at the national level, however, did not "trickle down" to the regional and local levels, where members of the DFD and UFV continued to work together (Hampele 1996).

sions among the various groups to prepare drafts for a statute, structure, and program for the UFV.[19] The time until February was intended for collecting information and conducting discussions on the future of the UFV. No plans were made to impose organizational structures at this first meeting. Only a temporary Council for Coordination was created until the formal Congress convened in February to clarify further the organizational structure (Hampele 1991).

The statute of the UFV, accepted at the constitutive meeting on February 17, 1990, established the UFV on the basis of a government by soviets (*rätedemokratisch*). Translated for the UFV, this meant that the central organization was based on independent women's groups. A state congress was instituted as the highest decision-making body, and a Council of Coordination was the decision-making body between the yearly meetings of the state congress. Regional groups had the right to send two elected delegates to the Council of Coordination. A two-thirds majority was needed for decisions to pass. The council was to elect between five to ten spokeswomen authorized to speak for the UFV. Women in political positions were unpaid. Each woman was to pay a self-determined amount for membership dues. "Double membership" in other parties and/or organizations was permitted (Statute of the UFV, in Kahlau 1990: 62–66).

At their first constitutive meeting, however, the members of the UFV had to adjust to political reality. While they had agreed not to elect official spokeswomen of the organization, they found they had to do so (Schenk 1990). Because the Central Round Table was to meet in Berlin on December 7, 1989 (only four days after the UFV meeting), Ina Merkel suggested that provisional spokeswomen had to be elected so that the UFV could participate at the negotiations (Merkel 1990b). The first two elected were Ina Merkel and the actress Walfriede Schmitt, whose specific purpose was to represent the UFV at the Central Round Table. Political necessity thus imposed an organizational structure on the UFV at its first meeting.

The feminist conception of the new women's movement had considerable social support. No less than 3,030 dues-paying members were registered by August 1990 (Hampele 1991). The size of this core group indicates little about the large number of supporters and sympathizers the movement had. Social movement research has consistently shown that social movements typically generate a support base beyond the core membership. These nonmembers share some of the goals of the movement but are often not ready to become official members (Kaase 1990; Kuechler and Dalton 1990). Thus, it is difficult to give precise numbers of women sup-

---

19. The official statute and program were approved at the constitutional meeting of the UFV on February 17, 1990. See "Statute of the UFV" and "Program of the UFV," in Kahlau 1990.

porting the goals of the UFV. In fact, Kuechler and Dalton point out that there are four facets of movement support that should be kept analytically distinct: the core members; the larger segment of sympathizers; the movement-produced organizations; and the organizations and institutions external to the movement but which pursue similar goals (Kuechler and Dalton 1990: 278). Due to the absence of records, the number of these wider networks supporting the UFV will never be known.

Who Are the Members?

Hampele argues that the majority of women organized within the UFV were socialized in the 1970s and 1980s (Hampele 1996). Aside from some women in their early twenties and some over forty, the average age was between twenty-five and forty (Hampele 1996). Eva Schäfer, spokeswoman for the UFV, cites the generation between thirty and thirty-five as the most actively represented group in the UFV. This cohort also provided the subsequent spokeswomen of the organization (interview). In contrast to the age range of other citizens' groups, which Bohley has termed the "awakening of the forty-year-olds," the politically active members of the women's organizations were younger (Hampele 1996).[20] Despite their relative youth, these politically active women all had children (Merkel, interview).

The great diversity of women's groups gathering at the women's spectacle in the Volksbühne contrasted with a rather homogeneous socioeconomic profile of the members organized in these groups.[21] Hampele estimates that two-thirds of the women came from church-related backgrounds; one-third were intellectuals, including artists, journalists, and white-collar women. Least represented were blue-collar, rural women, and women from the natural sciences (interviews, cited in Hampele 1996). Among the white-collar workers women from typical female occupations such as nursing, medical staff, social services, and education seemed to be in the majority. This rather rudimentary profile of women attending the initial meeting shows that the majority were drawn from academia (mostly social sciences) and from the service sector.

In contrast to other citizens' movements, the UFV had fewer theologians and natural scientists. The question arises whether this particular membership profile explains why the UFV was more closely linked to the

---

20. For a sociological profile of the member of the New Forum, see Schulz 1991: 20–21.

21. Unfortunately, no breakdown exists of the occupational categories of women present at the original meeting on December 3, 1989. Only in 1990 did Daphne Hornig and Irina Meyer send out questionnaires to women present at the meeting to reconstruct some of the sociological data (Hampele 1996).

SED/PDS than were other citizens' groups (Hampele 1996). In contrast to other opposition groups such as the New Forum, Democracy Now, and Initiative for Peace and Human Rights, the UFV was haunted from its inception by the charge that it was too close to the SED and later to the PDS (Schäfer, interview).

The potential for conflict within the UFV was enormous. The UFV was split between women who had been politically active within the church, academics who had supported reform-oriented socialism, and women with a history of feminist organizing at the local level. Women coming from academia, the parties, and the churches were less ambivalent about power relations, and they did not hesitate to enter institutional politics. On the other hand, women organized in loose local networks had much more distant relations to institutional power. As a result, party, church, and academic women moved to occupy positions of power within the UFV (Schäfer, interview); women interested in grassroots democratic institution building found themselves on the margins of the UFV decision-making processes.

Additional potential conflict within the UFV arose from the women's varied backgrounds. While women with party, church, and academic backgrounds shared competence in public speaking and willingness to hold office, their initial alliance faltered along ideological lines. Women with ties to the churches who were embedded in a social-ethical tradition found themselves alienated from many female academics with close ties to the SED/PDS. Women organized in churches and those sharing a grassroots democratic understanding found common ground against the party and academically oriented women. These cross-cutting cleavages were there from the beginning of the UFV but were not openly addressed (Schäfer, interview).

The effect of the two lines of conflict—institutional power politics versus local movement politics and openness to women of the SED/PDS versus rejection—was that both church women and movement-oriented feminists either withdrew from the UFV or remained on the sidelines. The result was that the more movement-oriented wing from Saxony and Thuringia largely withdrew in the ensuing months, and the UFV membership was reduced to a Berlin concentration; it was academically oriented, with a focus on institutional politics, and had close ties to the PDS (Schäfer 1995; Hampele 1996).

The UFV's Identity

Four aspects of the UFV's self-definition merit particular attention. First, the UFV understood itself as an independent, political, and feminist organization representing East German interests. It did not understand itself "as a simple or incomplete repetition of the West German movement, nor a 'catching-up' movement, which copied the content and form of the West German movement" (Maleck-Lewy 1993: 1). Nor was it an all-German movement. In fact, West German feminists (without formal residence in East Germany) could not become members of the UFV (Hampele 1996).

Second, the UFV's usage of *independent* in its title meant independent from the SED and the DFD but not independent of state institutions (Sauer 1994). The UFV did not reject political participation in institutional politics. On the contrary, it constituted itself with the specific goal of participating in institutional politics. The slogan "Without Women There Is No State" was understood to indicate women's participation in the reconstitution of new socioeconomic and political institutions (Schäfer, interview). The UFV defined itself both as a representative for women's political interests and as oriented toward women's projects, including women's centers, cafés, feminist bookstores, lesbian clubs, and many other such endeavors (Schenk 1990). There was little support for the West German feminist's emphasis on the "politics of subjectivity" (Sauer 1994), whose "central substantive issues focused on male violence, control of women's sexuality and reproductive capacities, and unpaid housework" (Kulawik 1991–92: 68).

The UFV did not reject the locally based project movement. It did reject withdrawing into subcultural "niches," which was one of the identifying criteria for their Western sisters in the autonomous movement (Helwerth 1994; Schenk 1994). Instead, East German feminists wanted to change "the state" (Schenk, interview). They were never anti-state per se. They perceived the undemocratic socialist state as having been "misused" by the SED leadership. The SED's loss of legitimacy was thus seen as an opportunity for the citizens' movements to "use" the state for democratic ends (Sauer 1994). The founding mothers of the UFV claimed that the combination of institutionally active women (*Politikfrauen*) working in the political sphere and those engaged in projects (*Projektfrauen*) was necessary to transform the state and society (Schenk 1990).

Third, members of the UFV differed from their Western sisters in their approach to men. East German feminists always understood that a political and social transformation was possible only in conjunction with men (Merkel 1990b). A Lilo political pamphlet read: "We are fighting for a socialist society without patriarchal relations!—Together with men!" A conflict did arise over whether men could become members of the UFV; it was decided they could not but that various groups organized within the UFV were free to work with men (Schenk 1990). While the behavior of men was criticized and women insisted "We need new men!" East German feminists nevertheless emphasized that a new socialist society had to include men. This pro-male identity contrasts with the West German experience, in which feminism emerged in the conflict over abortion rights. Autonomy for the West German feminists always included autonomy from the male-dominated Left and from men generally (Gerhard 1992: 43).

Finally, the UFV stood for reformed socialism as an alternative to capitalism.[22] It stressed the transformation of the economy according to the criteria of efficiency and compatibility, along with ecological goals, a democratic restructuring of the political system, and cultural alternatives to the Western capitalist consumption model (Merkel 1990b; Schäfer 1991). Because it endorsed a reformed socialism, the UFV rejected German unification.[23] Ina Merkel called unification "three steps back for women." "It would mean that women had to fight again for the right to work, for daycare centers, and for meals at school." Instead of improving the social rights women had already achieved in the GDR, unification would mean losing the social advantages women had (Merkel 1990b).

The UFV started from the basic assumption that the social achievements of the GDR (right to work, reproductive freedom, economic independence, legal equality, socialization of child rearing, and rights to higher education) had to be preserved. Virtually all GDR women agreed that the right to work was the basic foundation upon which to build a new society and that reproductive freedom was a basic right of women. These two issues, which remained controversial in West Germany, had been resolved in the East (Schäfer 1991a). The members of the UFV, unlike their sisters in West Germany, no longer targeted their political struggle on liberalizing the abortion law and fighting for more daycare spaces. Instead, they focused their energies at the Central Round Table on building upon the social rights they possessed already (Schäfer 1991).

---

22. In this struggle for a reformed socialism the members of the Independent Women's League are not alone. In fact, Joppke (1995) argues that the dissidents of East Germany are an anomaly in comparison to other Eastern European dissidents. Whereas Eastern European dissidents gradually abandoned the hope of reformed communism, East German dissidents remained committed to a reformed socialism. For a critique of this argument, see Thaysen 1996.

23. It is interesting that more men than women left East Germany in the fall of 1989, unlike the period prior to the building of the Wall in 1961, when more women left than men. Alice Schwarzer reported at the official meeting of the UFV on February 17, 1990, that three-fourths of those who left East Germany were men (cited in Hampele 1996). There is evidence that women opted more often for the "we stay here" rather than the "we want out" strategy.

The Period of the Central Round Table

With the introduction of a Central Round Table a new era started in East German politics. The idea for Round Tables had originated in Poland and had also been tried in Hungary before it was instituted in Berlin (Ash 1994). These institutions have played an important role as "crisis instrument(s) for the establishment of democratic legitimacy" (Thaysen 1992a). Prototypical for such Round Tables is that legitimated decision-making majorities no longer exist. People come together at these Round Tables to address problems that, until that moment, could not have been decided without resorting to violence. Round Tables are thus "institutions of transformation of more or less closed political systems." They are the alternative to violence: "ballot, not bullet" (Thaysen 1992a: 8).

Thaysen argues that the period of the Round Table, starting on December 7 and ending with its sixteenth meeting on March 12, has to be seen as three distinct periods. The first period, starting in December until January 22, was a continuation of "the old power struggle." There were essentially two conflicts played out at the Round Table that divided the members into old and new forces. One was the struggle between members of the bloc parties represented in the Volkskammer and present at the Round Table and the opposition groups; the second was between the Modrow government and the opposition groups. The goal of the latter was to wrest power from the old forces and prevent their reemergence as a dominant political force. This meant forcing Modrow to disband the Office of National Security (AfNS)[24] and preventing him from institutionalizing a new secret police service. The defeat of the old forces was all the more important as a "Stasi coup" remained a real danger throughout January. In this first period Round Table members saw their role limited to controlling the Modrow government and refrained from any claim to lawmaking or executive functions (Thaysen 1990a).

The second period, starting January 8 and ending January 22, was characterized by a "political vacuum." Neither the opposition groups nor the government emerged as the sole power. As the GDR economy continued to deteriorate and more people left for the West—seventy-four thousand in January versus forty-three thousand in December (Jarausch 1994)—the government and the parliament continued to lose legitimacy. The Central Round Table, on the other hand, did not have legitimacy to make "laws." This period of the power vacuum only came to an end when in a "rhetorical masterwork" Ingrid Köppe (New Forum) forced the Mod-

---

24. The Office of National Security (AfNS) was the successor organization to the much hated Ministry of State Security (MfS).

row government to accept an ultimatum to appear at the Round Table and to disclose its reasons for not dissolving the Office of National Security (Thaysen and Kloth 1994). The ultimatum, which culminated in huge demonstrations outside the Volkskammer on January 11 and 12, and the storming of the Stasi headquarters in the Berlin-Lichtenberg Normannenstrasse on January 15, 1990, finally forced Modrow into abandoning his goal of instituting a new security apparatus (Thaysen 1992).

This showdown between the government and the Central Round Table ended with Modrow appearing twice at the Round Table, on January 15 and 22, at which he indicated his readiness to form a "Government of National Responsibility" with the opposition.[25] He offered the opposition "direct and responsible involvement in government by competent persons" and at his second visit asked the Round Table to "nominate persons who are willing to enter government as members of the Ministerial Council" (Glaessner 1992: 61). Modrow also invited members of the opposition to accompany him on his pending visit to Bonn.

The opposition entered the Modrow Government with eight ministers without portfolio on February 5. By cooperating with the Modrow government, the Central Round Table gave up its oppositional character and collaborated both as lawmakers and administrators. As a result, the Round Table was transformed from a "veto organ to an instance of government" (Thaysen 1990a). Participating in the Modrow Government did not mean being involved in equal power sharing. Thaysen portrays Modrow as a skillful tactician who understood to the very end how to instrumentalize members of the opposition. In this Government of National Responsibility, Modrow remained the captain of the boat. He understood how to steer the opposition closer to the government's position, reducing rather than increasing the flexibility of the opposition (Thaysen 1994; Thaysen and Kloth 1994).

The Central Round Table and the UFV's Struggle for Political Inclusion

The UFV was neither part of the original "contact group" that initiated the idea for a Round Table, nor was it invited to the first meeting on December 7.[26] It did, however, gain a seat at the Round Table at the very

---

25. See letter of Modrow's address to the members of the Central Round Table, in Herles and Rose 1990: 54–58.

26. At present none of the feminist participants have written about their experience at the Central Round Table. There are no documents or minutes about the discussions in the individual working groups of the Round Table. Thus, my insights are tentative and have to be updated and, if need be, corrected, as additional information becomes available.

first meeting. It is important for two reasons to focus on how the UFV came to sit at the Round Table: first, in order to demystify the story of the struggle to exclude the UFV from the Central Round Table. In fact, this struggle for inclusion was much more benign than what has since become "her-story." Second, the UFV's seating at the Central Round Table did not only shift power relations to the old forces at the Central Round Table, but, more important, the circumstances under which the UFV was initially admitted, and Ina Merkel's emphasis in her introduction that she still was a member of the SED, put the UFV, intentionally or not, closer to the SED/PDS than to the forces of opposition.

The contact group had arranged the seating at the Round Table so that each opposition group received two votes (except for the largest group, New Forum, which received three votes) and three votes went to each of the five groups of the old forces (Christian Democratic Union [CDU]; Democratic Farmers' Party [DBD]; Liberal Democratic Party [LDPD]; National Democratic Party [NDPD]; and the Socialist Unity Party [SED]). Thus, fifteen votes allocated to "new forces" of the opposition faced fifteen votes of the old forces of the National Front. Since the Round Table was conceptualized as a forum for communication between opposition groups and the politically dominant forces of the country, it made no claim to be representative of all existing opposition groups in the fall of 1989 (Ullmann, interview, Semtner 1992). Ullmann understood the Round Table as a "task group" of competent people with national reputations, "who knuckle down where, and because, there is a fire" (qtd. in Thaysen 1990a: 43).

The opposition's support for admitting the UFV at the first meeting on December 7, 1989, however, set in motion a chain reaction (Ullmann, interview, in Semtner 1992). It opened the Round Table to other mass organizations of the SED, such as the trade unions (FDGB) and the women's league (DFD)—groups that the opposition was eager to exclude (Thaysen 1992).

Members of the UFV had found out the night before that the Round Table was to have a preliminary meeting prior to the full meeting of the Round Table on December 7.[27] UFV members mobilized other women to appear the next morning in front of the Bonhoeffer House, East Berlin, in which the first meeting of the Central Round Table was to take place, in order to demand their right to representation. About ten women from the UFV and Lila Offensive arrived with a banner demanding to take part in

---

27. Eva Schäfer told me that the information about a preliminary meeting came from many sources. Since many of the members of the opposition groups knew one another personally, both members of the "Lila Offensive" and Ina Merkel had prior knowledge of the gathering.

the negotiations. Ibrahim Böhme from the SDP (later SPD), who person-ally knew Ina Merkel, told the feminist activists that if they were not admitted to the Round Table then "we shall refuse to take part."[28] Schäfer suggests that the personal contact between Ina Merkel (UFV) and Ibrahim Böhme (SDP) greatly facilitated that two members of the UFV (Ina Merkel and Eva Schäfer) were asked to participate in the preliminary negotiations.[29]

At these morning discussions only members of the opposition met. Their purpose was to reach some agreement for the negotiation phase at the full plenary meeting that afternoon. The presence of two UFV mem-bers at this preliminary meeting did not spark any controversy, according to Ina Merkel and Eva Schäfer. Thus, when the UFV arrived at the con-stitutive meeting of the Round Table in the afternoon, they in fact had already received the general approval of the opposition to take part in the negotiations of the Round Table. The misunderstanding and supposed "struggle" occurred when the church moderators, who had not been part of the preliminary meeting, questioned the presence of the UFV as well as the trade union and women's league, both of which were close to the SED. None of these groups and organizations had an official invitation.

Ibrahim Böhme and Wolfgang Ullmann strongly defended a change in the initial seating arrangements against the recalcitrant church modera-tors. A very long and tumultuous debate ensued about who had the right to admit new members to the Round Table—the church moderators as the hosts or the members of the Round Table—and whether new groups should be admitted at all and in what capacity. Would they gain full voting status or only observer status?

The as yet unpublished stenographic reports of the negotiations between the church leaders, the opposition, and the old forces over the seating arrangements at this first meeting are not without humor.[30] They also make clear the "iron" will of the mass organizations of the trade unions and the Democratic Women's Federation seeking to gain represen-tation at the Round Table. Both organizations claimed that with a mem-

---

28. This information comes from Eva Schäfer, who was present at the first meeting.

29. Thaysen suggested in his writings that the UFV had arrived only at the time of the full constitutive meeting of the Round Table in the afternoon. According to a personal dis-cussion with Uwe Thaysen, he did not have access to the information that UFV members had already participated at the preliminary meetings and had received the approval of the oppo-sition to take part in the negotiations at the Round Table.

30. At one point Ibrahim Böhme argued that he could not support seating five ecolog-ical groups and have the women's movement represented with only two "Jacks" (Hanseln), whereupon he corrected himself with much amusement of the audience and spoke of two "Jills" (Hanselinnen). Or, when Gregor Gysi, of the SED, justified admitting the mass farm-ers' organization with the comment that he hoped that everybody continues to be interested in eating (unpublished stenographic reports of the meetings of the Central Round Table).

bership of 9 million workers and 1.5 million women, they had a right to represent their constituencies at this new forum (Thaysen 1990a; Thaysen and Kloth 1994).

In fact, Eva Rohmann, the newly installed leader of the DFD, was visibly annoyed that, against a previous agreement of the "bloc parties" on November 28, 1989, the DFD was reduced to observer at the Round Table.[31] Rohmann not only voiced her strong displeasure but had telephoned a member of the Protestant Federation of Churches of the GDR prior to the meeting to inquire about why the initial agreement placing the DFD at the Round Table was to be disregarded. She then accused the Round Table of the same intolerance that the old forces were accused of practicing (unpublished stenographic report of the Central Round Table). This conflict over whether the DFD still had the right to represent the GDR's women and the insistence of the trade unions to represent the workers shows, as Thaysen forcefully states, that the commotion at the first meeting of the Round Table was staged by the mass organizations of the SED (Thaysen and Kloth 1994).

Once the opposition members had voiced their support for the UFV, the Round Table had little choice but to seat the trade unions; it did not want to seat the DFD, however. By admitting the UFV, it had outmaneuvered the DFD, admitting it as an observer without voting rights. Seating both the FDGB and the UFV, the opposition was only marginally able to neutralize the two additional votes of the trade unions (Thaysen 1990a). Starting with the second meeting, both the FDGB and the UFV were admitted with full voting rights.

A stipulation was attached, however, that voting members could not have a "double mandate" (*Schleppmandat*). They could not be members of the SED. This had the effect that Ina Merkel could not represent the UFV at the Round Table. In response to the church moderators that the new "guests" introduce themselves at the Central Round Table on December 7, Ina Merkel responded that she was the spokeswoman of the UFV and also an SED member (stenographic report of the Central Round Table). Once all the new groups and mass organizations of the SED had been admitted,[32] nineteen votes of the new forces faced nineteen votes of the old

---

31. Eva Schäfer provided this description in an interview with the author.

32. In addition to the FDGB and the UFV, the opposition group Green League (GL) and the SED mass organization VdgB (Farmers' Association) were added. Observer status was accorded in the first and subsequent meetings of the Round Table to: the DFD, consumption cooperatives (VdK); Free German Youth (FDJ), a mass organization of the SED; the Catholic laity movement; and the culture federation of the GDR (KBD, also a mass organization of the SED). This constellation of participants and groups with observer status remained to the very end, except for the admittance of the Domowina as "guests," representing the Sorb ethnic minority (Thaysen 1990a: 44).

forces. This new power constellation weakened the opposition (Thaysen and Kloth 1994).

Although Wolfgang Ullmann advocated the admission of the UFV, he suggests that the chain reaction set in motion at that point was, in hindsight, a mistake. The Round Table acquired a representational aura that was never the intent of its initiators (Ullmann, interview, in Semtner 1992).

A Time When "All Was Possible!"

The UFV's participation at all of the sixteen meetings of the Central Round Table and the subsequent appointment of UFV's Tatjana Böhm to Modrow's Government of National Responsibility was the UFV's moment of greatest political achievement.[33] Having a member of the UFV in a cabinet position gave feminist activists access to an arena of power—albeit a rapidly declining power—which they had never had before. From this vantage point gender issues became public issues. Feminist themes were introduced and considered at the Round Table because UFV members insisted on putting them on the agenda (Bläss, interview). Of the total 191 participants at the Central Round Table, 47 were women, 11 representing the UFV (Hampele 1996).

They demanded not only a space for feminist issues; they also refused to confine these issues to separate women's working groups at the Round Table (Merkel, interview). Feminist considerations were inherent in all issues; thus, feminist ideas had to be considered in all sixteen subcommittees of the Central Round Table (Schenk 1994).

The great achievement of these women was that they were "there," forcing the Central Round Table to consider the role of women in the drafts of the bills under consideration (Hampele 1991).[34] Members of the working group Gender Equality introduced a petition to draft the new

---

33. Tatjana Böhm, UFV, was one of eight ministers without portfolio appointed to join the Government of National Responsibility. These ministers were officially confirmed by the East German parliament on February 5.

34. Scholars have hardly taken note of the important role the UFV played at the Central Round Table. This neglect is exemplified by Semtner who summarizes the role of the UFV in two sentences. "The UFV focused on the equality of gender. They had prominent speakers, but the members fluctuated greatly at the meetings" (Semtner 1992: 45). Semtner derives this information from a CDU member. There is no mention of the *Social Charter,* nor is he familiar with the working group Gender Equality. He has a long footnote (51 n. 78) discussing that no such group existed, despite ample written and recorded evidence to the contrary. In an unbelievably ignorant interview he asked Uwe Thaysen if the Round Table had not been bogged down by too many unimportant details—that is, the resolution to formulate all drafts of legislative bills in gender neutral language. Fortunately, Thaysen answered that behind this supposedly "small point" was the entire question of women's emancipation. "For those who introduced this resolution it was of momentous significance" (132).

GDR election laws in pro-feminist language. They demanded inclusion of feminist forms of nouns, use of quotas in selecting political candidates, and an election commission with equal numbers of women and men. Of interest is that this petition was also endorsed by women representing the bloc parties and the mass organizations of the SED.[35] The UFV was also successful in persuading the Round Table to insert anti–sexual discrimination language into the drafts of the new constitution, the law on political party and citizen action groups, and the new election laws (Schenk 1991).

The Central Round Table in Berlin produced over one hundred legislative bills. These drafts were formulated and written in individual working groups set up by the Central Round Table to deal with particular issues. Altogether there were sixteen individual working groups.[36] According to a UFV document, feminists tried to have at least one member in each of the sixteen working groups (UFV document, n.d.). This meant

---

35. The petition was supported by the Democratic Farmers Party (DBD), the Liberal Democratic Party of Germany (LDPD), the Free German Federation of Unions (FDGB), the National Democratic Party of Germany, as well as the VdgB (Farmer's Association) (Round Table Document, Submission No. 13/30, 119–20, Federal Archive, Department Potsdam).

36. The sixteen working groups were: (1) issues concerning foreign citizens; (2) education, child rearing, youth; (3) equality issues (Women's Committee); (4) health and social issues; (5) media committee; (6) ecological conversion; (7) new constitution; (8) laws for political parties and citizen action groups (Parteien- und Vereinigungsgesetz); (9) committee for legal rights; (10) criminal law, code of criminal procedures, penal system, VP protection, and laws for rehabilitation; (11) social politics; (12) economy; (13) elections laws; (14) science; (15) security, and the (16) editorial group (Redaktionsgruppe) (UFV internal document, n.d.; Thaysen 1990a: 99; and listings of working groups at the Central Round Table from the Federal Archive in Potsdam). In many documents on the working groups at the Round Table the Control Committee Dissolution of the Office of National Security is listed as a subcommittee of the Central Round Table (see Hampele 1996; UFV documents). This is, however, inaccurate. The Control Committee was initiated by Ibrahim Böhme before the Central Round Table had met, and Böhme tried to connect it to the Round Table, a strategy that did not succeed (personal information from Uwe Thaysen). There is some discrepancy between Thaysen's sixteen working groups and my findings of sixteen. The discrepancy stems from the fact that Thaysen relies on information that lists the groups as they had been decided by the Round Table at the first, second, fourth, and eighth meetings. Yet some of the working groups never met, such as Frauenpolitik. Instead, the working group Gleichstellung der Geschlechter took the place of the working group Frauenpolitik. This subcommittee was also called Women's Committee. (Thaysen told me that he got this information from the Federal Archive in Potsdam, and my documents confirm that women's politics is listed as a separate working group.) The internal and more reliable UFV documents, however, do not show such a group. Second, Thaysen lists the working group on social and health issues twice (the second time as health and social issues). Subtracting from his original sixteen committees the two committees (health and social issues and women's politics), he actually is left with fourteen. If we add the science working group and the somewhat later established editorial group, which Thaysen does not list, then we have a combined number of sixteen working groups.

that women were rather thinly spread. Two members were selected to participate in the negotiations at the full assembly of the Central Round Table,[37] four women acted as advisors to the Round Table members, and at least one member (sometimes up to three) was present in the individual working groups. The UFV showed its strongest presence in the working groups on a New Constitution[38] and Gender Equality[39] (Hampele 1996). The latter group formed with the aim of developing a report on women's status in state and society; it was also supposed to design state policies to achieve gender equality.

Gender Equality drafted one of the most well-known documents associated with the Central Round Table. In a preliminary step the UFV had formulated the *Social Charter* at its constitutive meeting on February 17; it was then rewritten in the working group, introduced to the full assembly of the Central Round Table for further deliberations on March 5, and passed by the East German Parliament on March 7, 1990 (Hampele 1991). Thaysen has referred to the debates surrounding the *Social Charter* "as being more important than the actual debates on the new constitution which the Central Round Table also debated in one of the Working Groups" (interview). The *Social Charter* received much media publicity

---

37. Uta Röth and Walfriede Schmidt were the two members from the UFV selected to participate at the Round Table. Walfriede Schmidt attended only the first six meetings. Ute Röth attended every meeting except for the first, fourth, and fourteenth meetings. Other members, however, filled the vacancy. There were always at least two, sometimes even more, members of the UFV present at the negotiations at the Central Round Table (Central Round Table, Federal Archive, Department Potsdam).

38. The Round Table never completed the draft of the constitution. Despite the often repeated assertion that the Round Table approved a constitution "as the legacy of the German Democratic Republic, as the testament of the German Democratic Republic's people's identity," this is incorrect. The full assembly of the Round Table never voted on the substance of a GDR constitution. Because the date of the national elections was changed from May 6, 1990, to March 18, the working group was only able to present at the last meeting (March 12, 1990) "Points of View of the New Constitution." The plenary meeting of the Round Table gave a mandate to an editorial group to prepare a complete draft of the constitution once the Round Table ceased to exist. This draft was then submitted to the Volkskammer on April 4, 1990, and was never considered for parliamentary deliberations. (For a detailed account of the working group New Constitution and its development, see Thaysen 1993 [in English].)

39. The working group Gender Equality constituted itself on January 3, 1990. The UFV informed the full assembly of the Round Table at the sixth meeting (January 8, 1990) of the official status of the new group, its goals, next meeting, and the expected date of its forthcoming results. Apart from Christina Schenk, UFV, other groups present in the working group were: the peasant party (DBD); trade union (FDGB); Green League; Initiative for Peace and Human Rights (IFM); the Liberal Party (LDPD); Nationalist Party (NDPD); Social Democratic Party (SDP); the SED-PDS; United Left (VL); Democracy Now (DJ); Green Party; New Forum (NF); and the SED farmers mass association (VDgB). All representatives were women (Documents Round Table, 6. Meeting, Information No. 6, 46, Federal Archive, Department Potsdam).

because it was targeted to address the social question in the negotiations of the Monetary and Economic Union between the two Germanies.[40]

This political visibility provided the new women's movement with intense media coverage (Hampele 1996). East German television broadcast UFV meetings live, and UFV representatives appeared regularly on East German television. This media attention for the first time brought the issue of feminism into the homes of millions of people. In addition to television coverage the East German journal *Für Dich* and the daily newspaper *Berliner Zeitung* extensively reported the activities of the East German women's movement (Maleck-Lewy, interview). Reflecting on her experience at the Central Round Table and as cabinet minister, Tatjana Böhm said "it was a time when we believed everything was possible" (interview).

Political Strategies of the UFV

Having come to the Round Table with the express purpose of becoming involved in "state making," the UFV targeted the highest level of the state to ensure that women's issues would be at the center of restructuring the social and political arenas. On December 16, 1989, the UFV addressed a letter to Hans Modrow and demanded that equality officers (*Gleichstellungsbeauftragte*) be instituted at both the legislative and executive levels of government. At the legislative level they asked for an equality officer immediately subordinate to the parliamentary president, who was envisioned as exercising both control and appeal power (*Einspruchsrecht*) over pending legislation. At all lower levels the same model was to be instituted.

Second, the UFV demanded a state secretary for gender equality at the national executive level with authority equal to that of a minister.[41] No longer should women's questions be included under the Ministries for Health, Social Issues, and/or Family Politics. The state secretary's task was to propose laws to "achieve equality," function as coordinator for individual ministries and their equality officers, appeal laws contradicting the principle of equality, and create public awareness of gender issues.

---

40. The First State Treaty, as it became known, established a Monetary, Economic, and Social Union as "a first significant step towards the achievement of political unity according to Article 23." This treaty spelled out the terms of Eastern integration into the West German "social market economy." The preamble states its intention was "to introduce the social market economy in the German Democratic Republic as the basis for further economic and social development, with social compensation and social safeguards and responsibility towards the environment, and thereby constantly to improve the living and working conditions of its population." The treaty was signed on May 18 and went into effect on July 1, 1990 (Glaessner 1992: 176).

41. UFV members vacillated between the demand for a Ministry of Gender Equality and/or Women and a State Secretary for Gender Equality.

In order to ensure her independence the state secretary was to have her own budget. All territorial and local levels of government also were to institute such organizational structures. Finally, the UFV demanded inclusion as an equal partner in the creation and selection of a state secretary (letter to Modrow, dated December 16, 1989, UFV files).

Accompanied by three ministers (economy, finance, and work), Modrow did meet with a delegation of the UFV and the DFD on January 8. While UFV members did not achieve their goals, they believed that at least a dialogue had been started. The demand for an Office of the State Secretary was to be studied further, and information on equality officers was to be obtained from other West European regions (particularly those in Scandinavia). The UFV was successful in ensuring the participation of one officer of the Council of Ministers in the working group Gender Equality at the Round Table.

Modrow further agreed to make public statistical background material on GDR women, which had hitherto been a state secret. In addition, the officer of the Council of Ministers promised to initiate the publication of research findings on women accumulated over the years by the Academy of Science (Commitment Protocol, signed Dr. Korf, member of the Secretary of the Council of Ministers, dated January 16, 1990).[42]

The UFV pursued a double strategy at the Central Round Table. In a "Petition to the Round Table," dated December 21, 1989, the UFV continued its pressure to establish a Women's State Secretary for Gender Equality (Staatssekretariat zur Gleichstellung der Geschlechter). Making gender equality a constitutional right was considered the prerequisite for guaranteeing substantive rights for women. In addition, the working group Gender Equality met with the express understanding of developing a detailed program for achieving gender equality. This document was to be completed by the end of February. Another concern was the issue of economic reforms and the social implications of such reforms. Economic reform, feminists argued, could not be permitted to result in the loss of social status for women (UFV petition to the Round Table, dated December 21, 1989).

Utopian Visions

The *Social Charter* and the *Essential Features for the Equality of Women and Men* are the two most important documents providing insight into the

---

42. Marina Beyer, equality officer of the conservative government of Lothar de Maizière, who took office after the parliamentary elections in March, commissioned Gunnar Winkler to compile this information in *Women's Report '90* and the *Social Report '90* (Winkler 1990). These two reports were the first comprehensive data on the social and women's situation in the GDR.

new, more equitable social order envisioned by feminists at the Central Round Table. Neither document, however, had much political influence. First, the paper on the "Equality of Women and Men" was written on the assumption that an independent GDR would remain in existence. By the time the document was adopted by the Central Round Table, on March 5, the economy was close to collapse, the Modrow government had virtually lost all credibility, and the people had decided that they wanted to be "one Volk" with the more prosperous West Germans. They were "no longer interested in being historical guinea pigs." Instead, they were interested in "normalcy" and were eager to shake off an independent "GDR identity" (Thaysen 1990a).

Although the *Social Charter* was addressed to Bonn, urging the government there to consider the social question equally with economic questions in the negotiations over the Monetary and Economic Union between the two Germanies, it too was ignored (Hampele 1996). Unfortunately for the UFV, "reality" was going a different way. The decision to advance the first free East German parliamentary elections initially scheduled for May 6 to March 18, 1990, shifted the power struggle from the Central Round Table to a political party competition, an issue that will be addressed in the next chapter.[43] The UFV remained focused on the Round Table. In a critical retrospective Helwerth noted that, while the UFV concentrated on developing political grassroots concepts to change the GDR at the Central Round Table, the distribution of political power was negotiated somewhere else (*TAZ*, December 16, 1994). Believing that the center of power remained concentrated at the Central Round Table, they ignored, with the rest of the opposition movement, the change to West German party politics (Probst 1994). It is ironic that when the working group Gender Equality finally introduced two impressively detailed documents on social and gender equality at the full assembly of the *Round Table*, the important powerbrokers of the political parties and opposition movements had already left for the campaign trail (Round Table, Attendance List, Federal Archive, Department Potsdam).[44]

Although the *Social Charter* and the *Essential Features for the Equality of Women and Men* had little political significance, their novel and interesting ideas should not be "lost" just because history took a different turn.

---

43. One of the first demands of the opposition at the Central Round Table was to call for free parliamentary elections. At its first meeting the election date was set for May 6, 1990. Using the increasing instability in the country, Hans Modrow (PDS), with the support of Ibrahim Böhme (SPD), "forced" a recalcitrant opposition into advancing the election date to March 18 at a meeting called by Hans Modrow on January 28 (Thaysen 1990a).

44. They included Gregor Gysi, Wolfgang Berghofer, Lothar Bisky (PDS); Lothar de Maizière (CDU); Wolfgang Ullmann (Democracy Now); M. Gerlach (LDP); Ingrid Köppe (New Forum); and Ibrahim Böhme (SDP/SPD).

Essential Features for the Equality of Women and Men

This paper is one of the least mentioned documents in the literature on the Round Table. It was never debated by West German feminists (Maleck-Lewy 1992). At the center of this document is the feminist demand for *Gleichstellung* (making equal). This word, as Marx Ferree points out, "goes beyond making a claim for equal rights to actually charging the state with responsibility for producing gender equality" (1995: 95). The GDR had for forty years emphasized the "politics of equal rights" (*Gleichberecht-igungspolitik*). In contrast, the UFV set the accent on "creating equality" (*Gleichstellungspolitik*) (Kretschmar 1990; Maleck-Lewy 1991). This emphasis on creating equality goes beyond the formal demand for legal equality. Women demanded equal opportunities for participating in all social and political arenas and emphasized the autonomous personal development of women.[45] The existing male criteria for equality were rejected. Instead, women argued that "the different economic, structural, informal, psychological, cultural, political and social positions of women" had to form the basis for considering equality between the sexes (31). They pointed out that their grievances stem from women's specific place in male-dominated social relations.

That the linguistic differences between formal equality and creating equality are not simply academic became apparent in the platforms of conservative parties for the parliamentary elections in March. These parties supported formal equality for women but utilized the legal term for *equality,* instead of *Gleichstellung* (Kretschmar 1990; Winkler 1990: 214–23).

The document on creating gender equality was divided into three segments. The first part reiterated the importance of economic independence and of creating the conditions to combine work, partnership, and parenting for women and men. For the UFV the notion of creating equality always included changing men. It was not enough to become equal with men; men had to be included in this change. As a result, the paper on *Gleichstellung* emphasized not just the compatibility of work, partnership, and parenting for women alone; both women and men had to be included.

In order that men and women could combine work and other activities, the paper called for the provision of childcare and youth centers for all age groups. Since the GDR already had an extensive network of such facilities, feminists demanded a qualitative improvement of these centers. They built on their experience in the GDR that neither the need nor the cost for such centers was disputed. In addition, the paper made flexible working conditions a prerequisite for combining work with other activities.

---

45. "Gleichstellung of Women and Men," Round Table Vorlage 15/1, 31, Federal Archive, Department Potsdam.

The second part of the paper advocated structural changes within all political and economic institutions. Feminists had nothing less in mind than restructuring the state itself, known in Marxian terminology as the "superstructure." Maleck-Lewy (1992) refers to this part of the paper as having all the elements of a "concrete utopia." It reiterated some of the political demands made to Hans Modrow for a State Secretary of Gender Equality and for the creation of gender equality officers at all levels— national, local, regional, and municipal. The paper stipulated the creation of a parliamentary committee for *Gleichstellung* and the passing of a gender equality law.

In terms of economic restructuring the emphasis was on collective bargaining negotiations between the state and the unions to increase women's wages in accordance with a new definition of productivity based on comparable worth. At the same time, men were to have greater access to, and be encouraged to enter, the largely female-dominated service industry, while women were to be encouraged to enter the scientific and technical professions. In reshaping and restructuring both the political and economic arena to achieve a gender-equal society, the demand for quotas played an important role. The working group on Gender Equality concluded that without quotas the *Gleichstellung* between women and men was unattainable.

The final part of the paper deals with self-determination. Again, the economic independence of women and men was taken as the underlying condition ensuring *Gleichstellung* between women and men. Yet the members of the working group on Gender Equality pointed out that, despite their economic independence in the GDR, women (and men) continued to be represented by cultural stereotypes. They demanded a change in the use of these stereotypical gender roles in training programs and education. At the same time, they called for the inviolability of women's bodies, including changing the criminal codes to encompass violence against women and children and extending rape laws to marriage. The paper also expressed its opposition to the increasing commercialization of women's bodies and the expansion of pornography and prostitution.

The third segment on self-determination focused on a woman's right to decide freely on motherhood, including her right to end an unwanted pregnancy. Finally, the document on *Gleichstellung* targeted the media's role in perpetuating the "sexist" portrayal of women in word and deed. It recommended a public debate to discuss these issues. The State Secretary of Gender Equality and the various officers of gender equality were to play the central role in opposing sexist views in the media (paper on *Gleichstellung,* cited in Herles and Rose, 1990: 263–78).

The document on achieving equality was passed with one abstention at the plenary meeting of the Central Round Table and contained the addendum: "The members of the working group 'Gender Equality' expect that the essential features contained in the submitted paper will be considered by the present and future government of the GDR" (Maleck-Lewy 1992). The reference to "present" and "future" government of the GDR is particularly important. When feminists declared euphorically on December 3 that "Without Women There Is No State," they built on the assumption that an independent GDR would, at least for a time, continue to exist. This belief in a society based on democratic socialism is the starting point from which UFV members developed their concept for achieving the equality of women and men.

Of all recommendations offered in the *Gleichstellung* paper the system of gender equality officers had the most immediate impact. The reason for this is that gender equality officers have a tradition in West Germany going back to the 1970s. In response to the European Community directives mandating equal treatment for women in paid employment in 1975 and 1976, the federal parliament was forced "to bring the FRG into minimal compliance with European Community directives" (Ferree 1995: 98). The first West German women's affairs offices were set up in North Rhine–Westphalia in 1975, followed by the states of Hamburg and Hesse in 1979. Today there are over seven hundred women's affairs offices at all levels of government in the West. In the united Germany, there are approximately eleven hundred women's affair offices at all levels of government, including four hundred in the former GDR (Ferree 1991–92; 1995).

Since these gender equality officers had been accepted in the West and were considered noncontroversial, they were quickly installed in the former GDR. Quite often, these officers were elected by the local Round Tables, they participated in personnel decisions, cosigned important documents, and in some communities had certain veto rights. It was no coincidence that many equality officers were members of the UFV or were close to the women's movement (Maleck-Lewy 1992).

The Volkskammer subsequently passed a Municipal Constitution prior to the first communal elections in May 1990, mandating that every community and city with a population over ten thousand had to have a full-time gender equality officer. This Municipal Constitution is still in effect in most of the new states in the former German Democratic Republic today.

The Social Charter

In contrast to the little-known document on *Gleichstellung,* the *Social Charter* is one of the best-known documents emerging from the full assembly of the Round Table. This document no longer made any claim to advancing gender *Gleichstellung* between women and men. It was defensive in tone, seeking to save what possibly could be saved from the existing social policies in the GDR. This document was written from the vantage point that unification could no longer be avoided.

Once discussions over a possible union between the GDR/FRG began, the first step was to create the conditions for a Monetary and Economic Union,[46] the UFV submitted a petition to the full assembly of the Round Table on February 5 to support its requests that the government develop a Social Charter to regulate the "social standards" in both parts of Germany. Two days later the working group on Gender Equality of the Round Table formulated a resolution to call on women in both parts of Germany organized in political parties, unions, and political organizations to come to an understanding about the legal, economic, and social position of women (document in Hampele, 5/11, 1990).[47]

At its official meeting to constitute itself as a political organization and to introduce the program and statute on February 17, the UFV developed an outline for the *Social Charter* (document in Hampele, no. 5/12, 1990). This impetus for the *Social Charter* was directly related to the snub Hans Modrow and his ministers of the Government of National Responsibility had received in Bonn on February 13–14, 1990. Members of the Modrow government arrived in Bonn with negotiating positions prepared by the Round Table that declared that "the Round Table expects the Federal Republic of Germany as the economically and politically stronger partner in the process of union (*Einigungsprozess*) to undertake everything to stop a further destabilization of the situation in the GDR" (Thaysen 1990: 138).

The hope was for a financial "solidarity supplement" (*Solidarbeitrag*) between DM 10 and 15 billion, which had been vaguely promised by Kohl in Dresden in December (Thaysen 1990). Modrow and his eight ministers returned with empty hands; the snub in Bonn was perceived as a humiliation. Tatjana Böhm spoke of the "shock" of having had to face a different reality in Bonn. On his visits to the German Democratic Republic, Helmut Kohl never tired of paying homage to the citizens' role in bringing down the GDR and ushering in a peaceful revolution. In Bonn the citizens' "bravery" suddenly no longer played a role. More important, they were

---

46. The initial union was referred to as the Economic, Monetary, and Transportation Union. Only in the later stages of the negotiations was the term *transportation* exchanged for *social*. It has since become known as the Monetary, Economic, and Social Union.

47. This meeting did take place in February, issuing a catalogue of demands to be included in any future German/German negotiations. Despite plans to meet again, Hampele (1996) has found no record of such an additional meeting.

given to understand that they had no authority to make claims against the FRG (Böhm, interview). Antje Vollmer, the speaker of the West German Green parliamentary groups, also spoke of the "horror" effect this treatment had on the ministers, who had only recently been courted as members of the opposition (*TAZ,* February 15, 1990).

Thaysen suggested that this "humiliation" of East Germans in Bonn produced a "new GDR identity" at the Round Table. This new identity was defensive and is best expressed in the statement "We also have something to offer" (Thaysen 1990: 139).

Formulating the *Social Charter* was thus no longer seen as the confident and euphoric work of feminists who intended to restructure state and society. Instead, the *Social Charter* was an expression of retreat. The *Social Charter* was perceived as the last effort to influence the negotiations for the economic and monetary union of the two Germanies. Yet the UFV achieved one small symbolic victory. That *social* was added to the title of Monetary, Economic, and Transportation Union and that *transportation* was dropped was the result of the UFV's effort to draw attention to the importance of the social component in the transition to a market economy (Böhm, interview).

One aspect unites the *Gleichstellung* document and the *Social Charter.* Both documents are state-centered. Members of the UFV saw a pivotal role for the state for achieving *Gleichstellung* and for protecting them from the economic repercussions of an economic union with the Federal Republic of Germany. Feminists hoped by occupying key offices in the state they could thereby intervene in the process of gender relations. Even when they had given up any hope of success, they trusted the state to "protect" them from the forces of the market. In both situations, the state was the sun around which all hopes circled. The documents nonetheless differ both in content and in tone. The paper on *Gleichstellung* was written at a time when UFV members were convinced that they could still fill the void left by a delegitimized male power. They did not seek social protection; they intended to empower themselves. As such, it is a declaration of a feminist vision. While the social component in the paper on *Gleichstellung* is important, the gender issue is not reduced to the social issue. This is the key difference separating the two documents.

The *Social Charter* pleads for social protection in the name of all the socially weak groups in the GDR. The preamble demands a right to work; the democratization and "humanization" of working conditions; equality of gender and equality in child rearing; the right to free education and health service; the maintenance and expansion of social rights for older and handicapped people; and the right to social welfare.

The recommendations are somber with regard to charging the state to institute policies for gender equality. They do include the right of women to work and the adoption of affirmative action programs. There is no longer any mention, however, of quotas. Only once does the *Social Charter* demand quotas for the physically handicapped. In fact, affirmative action programs are only targeted to achieve "equal relations of women and men." Also absent is the rejection of the existing male criteria of equality. This document no longer expresses the hope of achieving gender equality.

Despite this weakness, the *Social Charter* remains an impressive document in the tradition of European social democracy. It bears the stamp of the many academics organized within the UFV. Both Tatjana Böhm (UFV) and Gerd Poppe (IFM), ministers in the Government of National Responsibility, introduced the document to the full assembly of the Central Round Table in Berlin. The East-CDU requested the addition of the protection of unborn life. In turn, it supported the right to state-funded abortions. The full assembly of the Round Table passed the *Social Charter* with suggestions for changes and additions on March 5. The Volkskammer adopted it on March 7, 1990.

The Limitations of "When All Is Possible!"

The UFV's achievements were simply phenomenal in this period of a stateless state. From December until February it created an umbrella organization to unite all feminists, gave itself a statute and program, gained a space at the Central Round Table and participated at many local Round Tables, participated in the Modrow government, wrote two important documents, and was involved in creating a local project culture throughout the GDR. These feminists not only had a vision for a women-friendly, radical, grassroots socialist democracy; they also had goals for restructuring every aspect of social relations to achieve a nongendered polity.

Yet the exceptional situation of the GDR also worked against the UFV. Increasing economic instability, lack of legitimacy of the parliament, power struggles between the old and the "reform" forces within the Modrow government, struggles between the Central Round Table and the Modrow regime, lack of legitimacy of the Round Table itself, disarray in the entire administrative and judiciary apparatus, and the power of West Germany to "manipulate" the "East German impatience" with the economic and political instability in the GDR introduced uncertainty and political disorientation (Thaysen 1990a; Jarausch 1994).

Two political trends emerged. The Modrow government and the opposition groups united around the common goal not to "sell out" the GDR to the Federal Republic. They wanted to stabilize the GDR first and then enter into discussions of unification as "equal partners" (Thaysen 1990a). The UFV shared this goal and called for the continuing independence of the GDR, citing the unfavorable situation of women in the FRG in comparison with their own situation (flyer, Call for Demonstration, December 17, 1989). At the same time, the masses had already decided that they preferred the consumerist model of the FRG and rejected any experiment with "radical democracy."

Given this duality of positions between the government and the opposition groups on the one side and the masses on the other, one could argue that the UFV, including the citizens' movements as a whole, utilized "collective action frames" that had lost "empirical credibility" (Snow and Benford 1988). The UFV was no longer able to find the appropriate symbols to appeal to women at a time when the majority of GDR citizens wanted to be united with the West. The UFV was increasingly unable to "frame" its grievances meaningfully to women about the causes of and responsibility for discrimination nor to propose solutions for it. The UFV continued to rely on cultural symbols that envisioned an independent, democratic, socialist state that was no longer desired in the East. These cultural symbols were all too familiar and no longer found cultural resonance with GDR women (Gamson and Modigliani 1989).

This lack of cultural resonance was no more evident than in the reception of both the documents on *Gleichstellung* and the *Social Charter*. The first document was geared to the transformation of an authoritarian GDR into an independent, radical, democratic women-friendly state. Thus, the UFV continued to utilize the master frame of a radical democracy when the majority of the population supported another frame that was "quick unification" (Rucht 1996).

The response to the *Social Charter* was no better. It did address itself to the new situation of possible unification. It was written, however, without the "host," who by then was the Federal Republic of Germany. Although the *Social Charter* was passed by the East German Volkskammer on March 7, the Volkskammer no longer had the political authority to lend any credence to its adoption of such a document. Nor did it have the financial means even to allocate the resources needed to finance the expansion of the social rights demanded in the *Social Charter*. The West German government, on the other hand, disregarded the document in toto.

The UFV was caught inside a tunnel at either end of which there was no light. The West German gender model of wife-mother for many GDR women was surely a step backward into an economic dependence they had not known in the GDR. On the other hand, creating a vision of a women-friendly, radical, socialist, grassroots democracy and having it accepted in the FRG was from the beginning a project that had to fail.

In summary, the GDR's institutional power vacuum did not provide the UFV with an opportunity structure for movement mobilization. Exactly the opposite happened. The general political and economic instability worked against the group. There was no reliable political alignment that could allow the UFV to orient its strategy, and there was no target to which to address demands.[48] Also missing were reliable allies that could have provided some protection for the UFV. In fact, one may even argue that the lack of political orientation pushed the UFV further into the orbit of the Modrow government and closer to the PDS. This in turn may have "frightened" many grassroots activists and led to a loss of membership in the long term. The period when all was possible ended with few political gains for the UFV.

---

48. This lack of orientation is a point Rucht (1996) makes about the entire GDR's citizens' movements.

CHAPTER 3

The Closing of the Political Opportunity Structure and Feminist Differentiation

The Changing Political Climate

Modrow's government of national responsibility failed to stem the increasing discontent of the people in the GDR. Three "dramatic changes" accelerated the general instability in February (Teltschik 1991). First, there was a real danger of economic collapse. On February 5 government reports disclosed that 1990 economic production was falling to the level of 1985, and 1989 per capita GNP was no more than a third of the West (DM 11,829 vs. 35,856). The economic picture looked equally dismal in terms of foreign trade. By 1989 the GDR had accumulated a foreign debt of $20.6 billion (Jarausch 1994). Lothar de Maizière, East-CDU Volkskammer deputy and member of the Central Round Table, and prime minister after the East German parliamentary elections of March 18, was surely not exaggerating when, in a February interview with the weekly West German journal *Der Spiegel,* he did not rule out economic collapse (Teltschik 1991).

The Modrow government, with Christa Luft (SED-PDS) as the new economic minister, introduced some market mechanisms, such as a joint venture law, introduction of private property, and more realistic pricing mechanisms. In March the government created the superorganization of the Treuhandanstalt to privatize state property including combines, farm collectives, trade organizations, and insurance companies. Given the outdated production system of the GDR and the state's complete bankruptcy, these halfhearted market measures were hardly enough to turn the economy around, nor did people believe that these measures would improve general living conditions anytime soon (Jarausch 1994).

In a last effort to stave off economic collapse the Modrow government, accompanied by the new ministers from the Round Table, went to Bonn on February 13–14 demanding a "solidarity contribution" from the West in order to stabilize the Eastern economy. Kohl, however, saw such a financial injection into the GDR economy as little more than an "economic futile election gift for Hans Modrow and the PDS" (Thaysen 1990: 138). The humiliation suffered in Bonn and Modrow's defiant speech that "I will not beg on my knees for such a solidarity contribution" did increase Modrow's political standing at the Central Round Table but did little to stem the further outflow of GDR citizens to the West.

The increasing exodus became a burden for both West and East. The East started to lose its most talented work force, and the West had difficulty coping with the large influx of people. The GDR lost 360,000 people between the Central Round Table's first meeting on December 7 and the election on March 18. In the first three weeks of January alone 40,000 GDR citizens had left for the West, and the daily numbers had increased from 2,000 in December to a high of 3,000 in February (Thaysen 1990a; Teltschik 1991).

Increasing economic deterioration and the mass exodus of people led to a third factor of instability. Modrow was faced with the increasing loss of governmental authority. His hesitancy in dissolving the state security, his intentions to rebuild a new security apparatus coupled with the government's inability to ease the economic decline, and the general inexperience of the opposition rendered any promise of democratic socialism unrealistic. People no longer trusted in the "Third Way" the Round Table and Modrow had promised. The new slogans appearing at pro-unification rallies expressed the increasing frustration of the general populace and their yearning for economic prosperity. The popular slogan "If the DM does not come to us, we will go to the DM" says it all.

A world lies between the heyday of November and December when the citizen movement could mobilize several hundred thousand people to demand a more humane social order and the mood in February, when the demonstrators turned their back on the movement. The voices in the street no longer wanted a GDR (Haug 1991).[1] Gone also were the days when Hans Modrow could confidently proclaim the continuing independence of the GDR. On November 17 he announced his plans for a "community of treaties" with West Germany putting German-German relations on a new level. Any cooperation with West Germany had to be based on the premise of the continuing existence of two independent states (Jarausch and

---

1. Stefan Heym, the famous East German writer, said that there were two kinds of people in the GDR: those who wanted a changed GDR and those who no longer wanted a GDR.

Gransow 1994). In advancing the concept of a treaty community, Modrow aimed at reconciliation with the West, thereby hoping to stabilize the East (Jarausch 1994).

Also gone was Kohl's hesitancy about the date of German unification. In his carefully crafted "Ten-Point-Plan" on November 28, he spoke about eventual unification without setting a concrete time. The plan started with "confederate structures," moving then to a German federal state (*deutscher Bundesstaat*), and finally to a united Germany (Teltschik 1991; Kohl 1992). In contrast to Modrow's plan, Kohl's Ten-Point-Plan started out with cooperation "as a stepping stone to unity," carefully avoiding specifying a particular timetable, only suggesting a "political direction" (Jarausch 1994: 68–70). But no sooner were these plans for a continuing independent GDR and German unification at some future time enunciated than more and more voices in the streets demanded "unification now." By December calls of "we are one people," instead of the citizen movement's slogan of "we are the people," became more frequent at large demonstrations in virtually every city of the GDR. Also new was the appearance of many West German black-red-gold flags at rallies at which the masses demanded, "Germany, united fatherland" (Deutschland einig Vaterland). These changes symbolized the turning point from an erstwhile minority calling for German unification into a majority by the end of January (*Neues Forum Leipzig* 1989).

The West was not an innocent bystander in this outburst of national feeling. Helmut Kohl understood only too well how to further the interests of the FRG by manipulating the impatience of the East Germans (Jarausch 1994). During his Dresden visit on December 19, while an exuberant crowd lined the streets, gathered on the rooftops, and mobbed the hotel entrance, Kohl told the East Germans: "Together we want to live in freedom. Germany, united fatherland" (Kohl 1992: 300).[2] Kohl's dislike for the SED-PDS government was no secret. Watching the storming of the Stasi headquarters on January 15 convinced Kohl that "concluding treaties with Modrow no longer makes any sense." Henceforth, his political instincts were guided by the desire "to push the SED-PDS out of the government as quickly as possible" (Jarausch 1994: 107).

The changing international environment also favored the voices in the street that no longer believed in the opposition's dream of a democratic socialism. Gorbachev's agreement to German unification after his initial misgivings about the developments in November 1989 and his assent to the "timing and manner" of German unification in Stravropol on Feb-

---

2. Seeing the exuberance of the crowd, Kohl turned to Rudolf Seiters and told him, "The matter is over" (Kohl 1992: 300). Unification for Kohl was from then on only a matter of time.

ruary 10 gave the green light to Bonn's negotiations over the terms of unifying the two countries (Teltschik 1991; Kirchner and Sperling 1992; Merkl 1993; Pond 1993; Jarausch 1994).

By the end of January the opposition and the government faced a paradoxical situation. The Central Round Table had set out in December to "represent" the interests of the people against SED rule, and it continued to function as the "people's representative" in Modrow's government of national responsibility. In the meantime "'the people' soon went their own ways" (Glaessner 1992: 63). Whether it was "DM-Nationalism" (Habermas [1991]) that won out in the short run no longer mattered. What mattered was that the "people" no longer accepted the authority of the people's representatives. In this dramatic context of economic collapse and increasing loss of political authority the campaign for the first free parliamentary elections in East Germany started to unfold in February.

The Parliamentary Election Campaign

Modrow imposed a heavy price on the opposition as a condition for participating in his government of national responsibility. As part of the bargain to create his second government, Modrow used the economic instability to persuade the Central Round Table to advance the election date from the previously set date of May 6 to March 18. This move showed once again Modrow's masterful strategy of governing through "divide and rule." This new date was negotiated with Ibrahim Böhme, East-SPD. Modrow admitted to Thaysen that the new date "was arranged between the SPD and PDS" (Thaysen 1990a: 91). This arrangement possibly violated the GDR constitution, and Wolfgang Ullmann from Democracy Now voiced concern over the presumed illegality of advancing the election date.

The old "bloc parties"—SED-PDS, CDU, DBD, LDPD, and NDPD—did not share these misgivings about the new election date. In fact, they saw a chance to defeat the fledgling citizen movements if the election were held earlier than planned. These well-established parties could rely on their organizational apparatuses and extensive financial resources to enter into the campaign. Except for the SED-PDS, the bloc parties could also hope for extensive help from the West. The situation was very different for the "new forces" of the citizen groups (Democracy Now, Green Party, Initiative for Peace and Human Rights, and the Independent Women's League). They did not have the organizational structures or financial resources to mobilize a campaign on such short notice, nor could they expect any help from the West.

Once again a political struggle emerged between the old and new forces, with one exception. The East-SPD counted as a new party, since it was only created in the fall of 1989. Unlike the other new kids on the bloc, the East-SPD could draw upon enormous financial infusions and organizational expertise from the West. For all practical purposes the East-SPD became virtually one party with the West-SPD on January 13 (Thaysen 1990a). In this horse-trading maneuver both the SPD and Modrow hoped to gain. Modrow was eager to see a parliamentary victory for the SPD. Such an outcome would have weakened Kohl's plans for quick unification on his terms. Except for Willy Brandt in the West-SPD, the social democratic leadership remained skeptical of German unification, and the SPD abstained from endorsing Kohl's Ten-Point Plan.[3] The SPD criticized the plan for not recognizing the Oder-Neiße border as a clear statement to Poland that Germany would not yield "one millimeter of discussion" on the border question. The SPD did offer an alternative plan in the Bundestag, including an additional point accepting the Oder-Neiße border and renouncing the modernization of short-range nuclear weapons. This alternative proposal was rejected by the majority in the West German parliament (*Kontrovers* 1991).

What did the SPD hope to gain from this horse trade with Modrow? Ibrahim Böhme figured that an early election could only work in favor of an SPD parliamentary victory (Thaysen 1990a). The SPD hoped that the general economic malaise and the West-SPD's candidate for chancellor Oskar Lafontaine's repeated warnings that the "social union" between the two countries was as important as "state unity" would attract voters for the East-SPD. The party also hoped that raising the social questions of unification would "reawaken" the historic legacy of East Germany as the social democratic stronghold during the Weimar Republic and turn this legacy into a present SPD victory. Finally, in the most opportunistic sense the East-SPD counted on the organizational infrastructure of the West to help overcome the "moral bonus" the citizen movements still enjoyed in the GDR and thus defeat them at the polls.

This new constellation of "power politics" created a new conflict line. No longer was the struggle limited to old versus new forces. Rather, it became a conflict between established parties—whether old or new—against the citizen movements (Thaysen 1990a; 1992; Thaysen and Kloth 1994). The Volkskammer election campaign thus signaled the start of a struggle between the "logic of party politics" and the "logic of citizen movements."

---

3. In fact, a generational break between Oskar Lafontaine and Willy Brandt erupted during the unification debate. Brandt asked Lafontaine at the Berlin Party Congress in December 1989 whether he was too "national" for him ("Ich war dir wohl zu national?"). Lafontaine answered yes (*Der Spiegel* 22 [1990]: 22–23).

The "Logic of Movements" versus the "Logic of Parties"

The election campaign abruptly changed the political opportunity structure for the UFV and all other citizen movements. No longer was the Central Round Table and Modrow's government of national responsibility the determining factor in East German politics. With the start of the election campaign, the West German political party system introduced a new set of rules that circumscribed movement activities. The introduction of Western-style political party competition in the Eastern elections introduced competing types of political organizations into the GDR. The loosely connected "networks of networks" now confronted well-organized and financed party organizations. That social movements are less equipped to survive in "routine politics" in which the name of the game is strong organizational structures, creating alliances and being able to reach compromises is not altogether a new insight (Rucht 1996).

The citizen movement's difficulty in maneuvering within this new political environment was not only the result of different organizational structures. The GDR also faced Western-style campaign rules that were part of the West German action repertoire of routine politics. The citizen movement had little experience with well-developed Western campaign tactics: advertising, campaign management, candidate nomination, ballot creation, speechwriting, media outreach, and writing party platforms. Such well-organized political campaigns developed for a Western political system soon dominated the entire East German political landscape.

The Central Round Table was still busily occupied with establishing the fundamental conditions for a democratic political system—writing a constitution, formulating new election and political party laws—when the campaign got under way (Thaysen 1990a, 1990b, 1990c). Thus, the East German political system lacked institutional structures to counter this invasion from the West.

Fearing West German interference in the election campaign, the Central Round Table voted twenty-two to nine that "as a matter of equal opportunities and fairness they would abstain from inviting guest speakers from the West until March 18" (Thaysen 1990a: 190; Jarausch 1994). The reality was altogether different. Guest speakers from West Germany massively intervened in the election campaign. Chancellor Helmut Kohl (CDU), Foreign Minister Hans-Dietrich Genscher (FDP), and former Chancellor Willy Brandt (SPD) drew crowds of several hundred thousand people in the cities of Leipzig, Cottbus, Dresden, Halle, Erfurt, and Karl-Marx-Stadt. By welcoming the Western help, the Eastern parties also gained access to the FRG media to broadcast their messages (Jarausch 1994).

Thaysen argues that, with the start of the election campaign, the polit-ical parties in the GDR were no longer in charge of their own affairs. Even if the timing and manner of German unification had not been decided, the mere fact that German unification was going to happen turned an East German election into a campaign that was no longer about electing East German deputies. The overriding game plan was to win at all costs (Thay-sen 1990a). In contrast to the period of the Central Round Table, in which the "actors" were more important than the existing "structures" (Rucht 1996), the start of the election campaign signaled the end of the "stateless state" period and a much less accessible political opportunity structure for movement activities.

The UFV and the West German Election Campaign:
A Moment of Closure

The UFV was confronted with three new challenges. First, the UFV had constituted itself as a "political association" (*politische Vereinigung*) and not as a political party.[4] The opening sentence of the statute reads, "The UFV understands itself as part of a world-wide women's movement to fight for the abolition of oppressive structures of domination and stands for a non-violent, democratic, ecologically sound, socially just, and a mul-ticultural world." Point 3 of its statement of principles states that the UFV "strives for *political offices* (*politisches Mandat*) for women in all decision-making bodies of society" (UFV Statute).

The UFV statute thus introduced a hybrid form of political organiza-tion that was neither a movement in the strict sense of abstaining from political office holding nor a party built around formal organizational structures. Constituting itself as neither a women's party nor a women's movement may have had advantages in the stateless state period of the GDR, but this hybrid organizational form proved much less advantageous and in many respects was a hindrance in the West German party system.

That these political associations could be at a disadvantage against the West German type of political parties was never understood by the cit-izen groups. They believed that by making the political associations equal to political parties they had won the battle. In fact, the Central Round Table was in the process of writing a new election law when a disagreement broke out between the Modrow government and the citizen movements.

---

4. "Political associations" were a distinct phenomenon of the East German transition period. This type of organization was not legal in West Germany. The Unification Treaty stipulated that political associations had to choose between the status of a political party or association (*Verein*) by October 1991. In response, the UFV decided to remain an association in September 1991 (Hampele 1994).

The government's position was to restrict the nomination of candidates only to political parties. In contrast, the opposition fought for less restrictive access to nominating political candidates. In the end the position of the citizen movements prevailed, and the electoral law of February 1990 recognized political associations and political parties as equal entities (Thaysen 1990a).

This success at the Central Round Table was a bittersweet victory for the citizen groups. It did facilitate the movement's participation in the elections, but it could not overcome the disadvantage of an organizational structure geared to the political system of democratic socialism. In the West German party system political parties are the mediators between the citizenry and the state, and there is no space for political associations. Being forced to compete on the basis of such asymmetrical starting conditions did not bode well for the UFV and the other citizen movements (Hampele 1992; Maleck-Lewy, interview).

The UFV and the Price of Freedom

The election campaign confronted the UFV with a second challenge for which it was not prepared: its claim as the sole representative of women. On February 24 women political activists from East and West met in Weißensee, East Berlin, to plan a challenge to the UFV. They called for the creation of a "Common Women's Federation." The signatories to this appeal included none other than Rita Süssmuth, West-CDU, and members of the East-CDU, Democratic Awakening, and the New Forum. The women's coalition emphasized in its organizational appeal that it intended to focus on the active promotion of women, job security for working women, support for low-income women pensioners, the situation of single mothers, and mechanisms to "create equality" for women (CDU appeal, dated February 17, 1990).

Two aspects of this increasing differentiation in the East German feminist movement merit attention. That a competing women's movement emerged and challenged the role of the UFV as the sole representative of women is not surprising. Such differentiations are the price of freedom and the hallmark of pluralist societies. What is new is that the women's appeal to create this organization, which appeared in the newspaper *Neue Zeit,* deliberately used the UFV's motto to launch the Independent Women's League on December 3. In heavy underlining the Common Women's Federation advertised its intended organizational meeting with the appeal "Without Women There Is No State."

The UFV reacted quickly to this misappropriation of its slogan and issued a press release that said, "Without Women There Is No State but:

please without the Ladies from the CDU-West." In the UFV's reply there is a clear reference to Ina Merkel's authorship of that phrase.[5] In addition, the UFV separated itself from this appeal of the Common Women's Federation by using the word *ladies* in its answer. It drew attention to its own identity as feminists and distinguished itself from the supposed "nonfeminist" challengers.

This challenge from non-UFV women went to the very heart of the UFV's self-definition. It understood itself as a coalition of feminists irrespective of differences in social status and religious and political views. With the appearance of this new competitor the UFV was suddenly confronted with acknowledging the variety of different feminisms within the movement itself. The assumption that all feminists had the same interests and identified with a political Left agenda of democratic socialism was no longer accepted (Hampele 1991).

Despite these differences between the UFV and the Common Women's Federation, an interesting aspect of mutual agreement existed. In the UFV's usage of the slogan "Without Women There Is No State" is an explicit understanding that the breakdown of socialism represented the total delegitimation of male power. Men were at the helm of the GDR state, and they were responsible for the shipwreck. Both women's groups agreed in declaring the complete bankruptcy of patriarchal power. In its appeal the Common Women's Federation stated, "For too long have women taken a back seat in shouldering political responsibility in our society—with the result that in the GDR a political system (*Gemeinwesen*) dominated by men collapsed" (appeal, February 17, 1990). This statement is not much different from the claim of the UFV that the GDR state was an apparatus of male control and domination.

Agreeing that males as political actors were delegitimized to run the state, feminists, although organized in ideologically different organizations, united around one goal: women had not only the right but also the responsibility to be involved in governing the state.

Internal Power Struggles: *Politikfrauen* versus *Projektfrauen*

The election campaign opened up a third conflict endemic to the UFV itself. The UFV linked two conceptions of feminist politics as necessary conditions for political effectiveness. It combined its grassroots involvement in local autonomous groups and projects with political engagement in institutions. Yet, by linking these two strategies, which the West Ger-

---

5. The press release read, "Ohne uns Frauen ist kein Staat zu machen (O-Ton Ina Merkel) aber: Bitte ohne die Damen von der CDU-West."

man movement by its self-definition of autonomy from the state rejected a priori, tensions between UFV members advocating the institutional road to power (*Politikfrauen*) versus the grassroots democratic advocates (*Projektfrauen*) started to emerge.

The UFV was thus confronted not only with the coexistence of movements and political parties at the macro level of GDR national politics; it had to face the same struggle within its own ranks. Whether the UFV was foremost a political organization seeking to intervene in institutional politics (realist) or whether it would remain an anti-institutional (fundamentalist) political association were questions far from settled when the UFV decided to enter the first free election campaign.

This realist versus fundamentalist controversy illustrates an important debate within democratic theory and dates back to the theoretical arguments between Bernstein, Luxemburg, Kautsky, and Lenin at the turn of the century (Offe 1990). This is not the place to argue the theoretical merits of either side. The reference to the debate is important only insofar as it shows that the struggle within the UFV was not unique. It is an old conflict within the Left that has not been resolved.

While the theoretical debate is still open, there seems to be a preference at the empirical level for the institutionalization of movement politics at least among many of the European environmental movements. The German Greens entered the political scene, as did the UFV, as an "anti-party party" that consisted of both extra-institutional and institutional practices (Kitschelt 1990; Offe 1990; Markovits and Gorski 1993). Yet the party was not able to satisfy either its realist or fundamentalist factions. The question of institutional accommodation versus anti-institutionalism not only haunted the Greens from its inception in the 1970s. In the "Fundi/Realo" struggle, as the conflict between the institutionalist versus the anti-institutionalist became known, the party nearly split in 1987 and remained stalemated for about three years. The institutional strategy won out only when the Fundis finally left the Greens in a grandstand exodus in early 1990 (Markovits and Gorski 1993).

Offe argues that there are rational calculations favoring the transformation from movement politics to institutional politics. He suggests that there cannot be any doubt that the institutional strategy has become the dominant one and that its attractions or, as its opponents would see it, its temptations have been sufficiently strong as to exert a continuous learning pressure in the direction of institutional accommodation (1990: 243). In Offe's argument the environmental movements benefited from political institutionalization, but the same cannot be said for feminist movements. The German autonomous feminist movement has remained autonomous from the state because it has not found "cultural resonance" for its feminist agenda among the established political parties. As I explained in the previous chapter, the West German autonomous groups continue to be linked to the local grassroots projects, except that these projects are now state funded. It is this controversy—whether the interests and needs of women are better served through institutional politics or by remaining grassroots oriented—that started to erupt just when the UFV decided to enter the parliamentary campaign.

This issue did not emerge during the UFV's political activities at the various Round Tables and in the cabinet of the Modrow government because of the stateless state nature of the East German transition period. The work of the institutional-oriented *Politikfrauen* was seen as complementary to the activities of the movement-oriented *Projektfrauen*. Women at the local level—engaged in establishing women's cafés, feminist libraries, counseling services, women's centers, and other such projects—worked together with the institutional women at the various Round Tables to gain local financial support, acquire physical space to house the projects, find the necessary personnel, and gain governmental permission for commercial enterprises. To establish a "project culture" at the local level, the expertise and the access of institutional feminists was needed. Women often occupied former offices of the local SED and claimed entire buildings of the state security to house the women's centers.[6] Such activities could only succeed if both movement-oriented *Projektfrauen* and *Politikfrauen* worked together. Given these conditions, separation between the movement-oriented factions within the UFV and the institutional feminists never developed.

The matter was altogether different when the campaign for the national elections started. The UFV's entire political energy became reoriented to the national level. The internal organizational structure of the UFV had to change to accommodate the national election campaign. Parliamentary groups formed within the UFV with their own agendas and interests. This extreme focus on the national level had the unintended consequence that the close communication and contacts between the locally engaged feminists and the institutional feminists declined. With the start of the election campaign the important contact persons for the UFV's campaign staff were no longer the local groups (Schäfer 1991).

Movement-oriented feminists complained that they were forced to accept political compromises negotiated at the national level, decisions in which they had no input and whose merit they did not understand (Schäfer, interview). Local feminists resented giving up the freedom not to

---

6. In Erfurt the first women's center of the GDR was established in the former "Stasi-Villa" ("Das erste DDR-Frauenzentrum—in der ehemaligen Stasi-Villa," *Frankfurter Rundschau,* February 27, 1990).

compromise on issues that were for many nonnegotiable. The price for engaging in routine politics was, as institutional feminists soon learned, to engage in compromises.

This pull between the logic of routine politics to compromise, and the grassroots feminists' willingness to take unpopular stances without arriving at bargained outcomes, is again not unique to the UFV. Democratic theory is built around the very notion of compromise. How to resolve these different logics has been one of the most divisive issues within movements that have striven for institutionalization while at the same time remaining wedded to a grassroots culture (Offe 1990; Rucht 1996).

Feminist institutional activists, on the other hand, voiced their frustration over local activists' lack of understanding for the burdens and constraints institutional women faced in this markedly changed political opportunity structure (Schenk 1991). Virtually all political activists expressed in interviews that they felt like "hunted animals." To create an entire infrastructure for the election campaigns, without any help from the West, proved a rather daunting experience. Christine Schenk, member of the first all-German parliament since 1990,[7] reflected on her frustration during the campaign: "We participated in four elections in 1990. There was no time to discuss the different perspectives between 'Politikfrauen' and 'Projektfrauen'" (interview).

The "Untimely" Election Campaign and the Search for Electoral Allies

The UFV had decided at its national meeting on January 2 to participate in the Volkskammer elections. At that time, however, the election date was still set for May 6. Advancing the election date meant nothing less than the complete fragmentation of the energies of the UFV. During February the UFV was confronted with writing its program and statute for the official constitutive meeting on February 17, participating at the plenary debates of the Central Round Table and in its various working groups, formulating the *Social Charter,* writing the paper on *Gleichstellung,* actively participating in drafting a new constitution, sitting in the Modrow cabinet, intervening in the abortion debate that started to surface in Bonn, and starting an election campaign. To intervene at all these points with a limited number of voluntary activists became an unmasterable task (Böhm, interview; Schäfer, interview).

As if these tasks were not daunting in themselves for a movement

---

7. Schenk first entered the German parliament as a UFV candidate (1990–94) and switched to the PDS in the parliamentary elections of 1994.

that could only draw upon the moral solidarity of its group members, the external environment also negatively influenced the political participation rate of feminist activists. More and more women feared losing their jobs. As a result, their individual concerns for economic survival took precedence over their collective concerns about the position of women in the newly emerging state. The spirit of the official constituting meeting of the UFV on February 17, 1990, had little in common with the "happy revolution with political consequences" in the fall of 1989. In February both atmospherically as well as historically something neared its end (Hampele 1991; Ina Merkel, interview; Schindler, interview, 1992). It is ironic that, at the moment when more feminists would have been needed to intervene at the national arena, feminist activists, and women generally, were overwhelmed by anxieties about the future and withdrew from political activities.

These fears about women's future role in a restructured East German economy convinced the UFV's institutional feminists to enter the election campaign. They saw as essential their presence in the first freely elected East German parliament. Once having decided to participate in the campaign, the UFV was then confronted with finding electoral allies. The other citizen groups such as the New Forum, Democracy Now, and the Initiative for Peace and Human Rights combined to form Coalition '90 (Bündnis 90) on February 6. Since political associations had the same status as political parties, none of the citizen groups transformed their organizations into parties. Coalition '90 encouraged other opposition groups to join the electoral alliance with the stipulation not to include political parties and groups with a Left political identity (Schulz 1991; Wielgohs, Schulz, and Müller-Enbergs 1992).

The UFV's perceived closeness to the PDS became a factor in excluding the UFV from the negotiations to form Coalition '90. There is even some evidence that a vote was taken among Coalition '90 members, who decided, nineteen to one, to exclude the UFV and the United Left from joining the election coalition.[8] In response to this exclusion from the electoral coalition, the UFV distanced itself from Coalition '90, charging that its election statement and priority goals were too unspecific (Schenk, interview, in *TAZ,* January 22, 1990).

Justifying in hindsight the exclusion of the UFV from Coalition '90, some members of Democracy Now have argued that it was only a matter of time before the Green Party–GDR and the UFV would have been asked to join the coalition. Others in Democracy Now feared that the

8. I thank Uwe Thaysen for this information. I found no written record, however, of this vote.

inclusion of the UFV might have alienated its Christian constituency, and some members of the New Forum objected to being aligned with feminism and a PDS-leaning Left (Hampele 1991; Schulz 1991).

In response to its exclusion the UFV entered an electoral alliance with the Green Party–GDR. This party was formed in the "more mature phase of upheaval" after the other citizen movements had already been established (Bruckmeier 1993). Realizing that environmental protection did not figure prominently enough in the goals of other citizen groups, environmental activists created the Green Party–GDR on November 5.[9] The focus of the Green Party was on ecological issues and on creating a parliamentary counterweight to other parties (Kühnel and Sallmon-Metzner 1991).

The Green Party–GDR was a suitable coalition partner for the UFV. Not only did it include a feminist statement in its call for creating the party, but its program made the emancipation of women a central element. The political activist Vera Wollenberger struggled for women's rights within the party and instituted a quota regulation for filling positions at the party executive level (Kühnel and Sallmon-Metzner 1991). As a coalition partner for the UFV, the Green Party–GDR, with its feminist stance, would be an advantage in the campaign. The only condition the Green Party set for its coalition with the UFV was its opposition to an electoral alliance with the far Left-leaning United Left (Vereinigte Linke).

Of the twenty-four citizen groups, parties, and coalitions entering the elections, the citizen movements and one party combined into three coalitions: (1) the United Left and the "Carnations"; (2) Coalition '90, which included the New Forum, Democracy Now, and the Initiative for Peace and Human Rights; and (3) the Green Party–GDR and the UFV. Thaysen (1990a) has referred to this dissolution process of the initial citizen movements as the "Weimarization" of the East German political process. The picture was altogether different in the traditional parties. While the opposition groups splintered going into the elections, the established parties moved in the opposite direction. The East-CDU, Democratic Awakening, and the DSU formed the winning coalition Alliance for Germany, and the liberal parties formed the Federation of Free Democrats.

Framing the Campaign Issues

The single most important election issue was the timing and mode of unification (Schulz 1991). That unification would happen was accepted—

9. The environmentalists split further with the creation of the Green League (Grüne Liga) on February 3, 1990. The league had a more "fundamentalist" movement orientation and did not want to limit its options to party politics. It was open to work with other environmental and nature groups and understood environmental issues foremost in terms of human survival (Kühnel and Sallmon-Metzner 1991: 195).

except by the United Left—by all East German parties and citizen movements. Even the UFV in its combined platform with the Green Party no longer rejected unity. The concern was to avoid a "quick uncontrolled unification" and to stress a slow and deliberate process of uniting the two countries.

The election platform of the Green-Lilac election coalition[10] combined both the Green Party's goals for creating an environmentally safe economic system and the UFV's emphasis on a socially just and women-friendly social system. The preamble also contains the demand for the gradual demilitarization of both Germanies and the integration of a united Germany within a European peace order. Altogether, the election platform singled out ten areas of concern to be addressed in transforming the GDR's political and social system: the economy, environmental protection, social policy, women, children and youth, underprivileged groups, cultural policies, education, science and research, and democracy.

The party platform endorsed a market economy but with strong social and environmental safeguards for achieving a society based on the values of solidarity rather than competition. It demanded the inclusion of a *Social Charter* for both Germanies that would take into account equal rights for women and men; the inclusion of previously excluded groups such as homosexuals, foreign citizens, the old and the sick; and the protection of the rights of children and youth. It also stressed its support for a constitutional state that included the rights of plebiscite and referenda. In its emphasis on a democratic social order the Green-Lilac coalition embodied the ideas of a grassroots democracy with citizen groups having control over public institutions and guaranteed access to all briefings and deliberations of the parliament, government, and economic institutions.

Many of the coalition's goals could also be found in the West German Green Party. The platform's indirect message, however, remained critical of German unification. In the preamble the platform refers to German unification as a process of "Anschluss." By using this terminology, the coalition indirectly linked the process of incorporating East Germany into the existing West German social system to Hitler's annexation of Austria in 1938.

Even if the coalition reluctantly accepted a slow process of unification, the UFV's position remained "clouded" by its strong anti-unification rhetoric prior to the election campaign. The UFV had organized a demonstration on December 17 "Against Unification" (Wider Vereinigung). In its flyer the UFV unfavorably compared the position of women in the FRG with their own situation and listed the disadvantages they would face if reunited with Germany. Unification would mean a

---

10. The alliance of the Green Party and the UFV was referred to as the "Green-Lilac" coalition in the election campaign.

return to the kitchen: only 54 percent of FRG women worked outside the home versus 91 percent GDR women. It would usher in mass unemployment: over 1 million FRG women were unemployed, and 400,000 were part of the labor reserve army. Reproductive rights would be jeopardized; there would be cuts in the social welfare state; and women's bodies would be subject to commercialization (*PornograVieh*).[11]

The UFV asked whether their only option was to end up once again where they had just come from ("to turn 360 degrees in a patriarchal circle?") instead of taking the end point of the GDR as a new starting point. Given their strong reservations about existing gender relations in the West and their desire to safeguard women's social rights achieved in the GDR, the UFV demanded the continuation of an independent GDR (Demonstration flyer, December 12, 1989).

Ina Merkel, a very talented public speaker, argued in January against unification because it would mean "three steps back for women" (1990b: 257). She warned her audience about the "fear that women again will be the new 'rubble women' to clear the debris of the collapsed socialism" (Merkel 1990d: 32). Her despair that women would fare well in the united Germany can be found in many of her campaign speeches. "We women have no fatherland to lose, because we never had one. And we don't have one to win either, because in this fatherland we would be forced to exchange our recently won individual freedom . . . against the bigoted dominance of a world ruled by money" (33–34).

The Greens/UFV advocated unification based on a "reciprocal reform process, which respects the sovereignty of both German states." In this demand the Green-Lilac coalition also found support among members of Coalition '90. Polling results showed that there was little difference between members of the Greens/UFV and Coalition '90 and their attitude toward unification. Both supported the overall goal of unification. Coalition '90's support was 88.3 percent versus 84.2 for the Greens/UFV. They both favored a slow process of unification, with 77.6 percent of Greens/UFV sympathizers agreeing with this position versus 75.1 percent of Coalition '90. These attitudes stood in marked contrast to those of the conservative Alliance for Germany. A high of 96.6 percent endorsed unification; only 39 percent endorsed a slow pace (Roth 1990: 383).

An unbridgeable gap between the opposition forces assembled at the

---

11. This very clever use of German language has no translation in English. The first part of the word refers to the syllable *pornogra-*, and *Vieh* (cattle) is substituted for *phy*.

Central Round Table and the demonstrators in the street became apparent as the election campaign unfolded. "The Round Table came to stand for a slow, conscious reflected merger on equal terms and with a constitutional assembly . . . while the demonstrators and those leaving the country represented the desire for a quick and unconditional take-over of the East by the Federal Republic" (Thaysen 1992: 81). The UFV and all the other citizen movements became the espousers of the old GDR identity, while the new identity was associated with the forces that won on March 18 (Thaysen and Kloth 1994).

Only 20.2 percent of the Alliance for Germany sympathizers identified themselves as GDR citizens; 78.2 percent as German citizens. Again, the picture was the opposite for the Greens/UFV: 69.5 percent identified as GDR citizens and only 30.5 percent as German citizens. Supporters of Coalition '90 divided rather evenly between a GDR and German identity (48.6 vs. 46.8 percent).

The results were again predictable when people were asked what they thought of socialism: 33.9 percent of the Greens/UFV and 35 percent of the Coalition '90 sympathizers thought highly of socialism, in contrast to only 12.1 percent of the members of the Alliance for Germany. When asked whether they were highly in favor of democracy as it existed in the Federal Republic, only 20.1 percent of UFV members answered yes. If the question were reworded, however, and *somewhat* was substituted for *highly,* then 74.1 percent of UFV members agreed that they were "somewhat" in favor of German democracy. Coalition '90 had a more favorable view with 40.7 percent approving the West German democratic system. The Alliance for Germany endorsed West German democracy by as much as 70 percent (Roth 1990: 386–87).

In subsequent polling results the Greens/UFV scored highest next to the PDS in their belief that unification would have a negative impact on the people in the GDR. The Greens/UFV affirmed this statement with 45 percent and the PDS with 55.6 percent. Supporters of the Alliance for Germany believed the opposite. Only 16.5 percent voiced concern that unification would have a negative impact. Coalition '90 supporters found themselves between the two extremes: 36.5 percent of its supporters believed that unification would be accompanied by negative effects (Roth 1990: 384).

Gender also affected attitudes toward unification. At the beginning of March around 88 percent of men supported unification versus 80 percent of women. The gap became even larger after the parliamentary elections. By the end of April men's support increased to 92 percent, whereas women's remained at 80 percent. Irrespective of political affiliation and citizen group involvement, the data show women as more cautious about unification than men (Förster and Roski 1990).

The Election Results and the Exclusion of the UFV

The rude awakening for all members of the opposition came with the election results on March 18. "There is no longer a GDR," the weekly journal *Der Spiegel* announced as it broke the news that the conservative Alliance for Germany had won with 48.1 percent of the vote.[12] The heavily favored SPD secured a disappointing second place, with 21.8 percent. The worst losses, however, came for the citizen coalitions. Coalition '90 received 2.9 and the Greens/UFV only 2.0 percent. In individual states the Greens/UFV received their strongest support in Berlin, with 2.7 percent, and in Brandenburg and Saxony-Anhalt with 2.1 percent; their poorest showing was in Saxony, with 1.7 percent. The Greens/UFV received the largest support from students (8.7 percent), intellectuals (3.2 percent), and white-collar workers (2.4 percent). The least support came from the self-employed (0.2 percent), managers (0.8 percent), and blue-collar workers (1.5 percent) (Roth 1990: 372–77). The highest support came from those under twenty-four years of age (4.9 percent) and those between twenty-nine and thirty-nine (2.8 percent). Support dropped in the forty-to-forty-nine-year-old group and declined even further among those over age fifty.[13]

Of all eligible women voters 46 percent voted for the Alliance for Germany, no different from the voting behavior of men (Schwarz 1993). Despite the fear of a collapsing economy, a large proportion of GDR women voters believed Kohl's promise of "flowering landscapes" rather than the warnings of the Social Democratic Party and the citizen movements that unification would also mean economic dislocation for many citizens.

These election results were a bitter defeat for the citizen movement as a whole. Yet the UFV faced an additional horror scenario. After having fought a rather brutal election campaign, not one of the eight seats won by the Green-Lilac coalition went to the UFV.[14] Due to the inexperience of the UFV, its members agreed at the preelection negotiations with the

---

12. *Der Spiegel* 12 (1990): 20–33.

13. For a detailed account of the election law and results, see Gibowski, *Zeitschrift für Parlamentsfragen* 1 (1990): 5–22.

14. Because the East German election laws did not contain a 5 percent "restrictive clause" for attaining a seat in the parliament, the Greens/UFV were able to get eight seats with only 2 percent of the vote.

Greens that all first places of the state party lists would be set aside for members of the Green Party (Hampele 1991). Due to the low percentage votes for the Greens/UFV, only the first places had any chance for gaining seats, thus being placed in second or third place prevented the UFV from gaining a single seat. The UFV was suddenly faced with the reality that it would not be represented in the first freely elected East German parliament (Schenk 1994).

The shock of having "given" away the election gains to the Green Party was evident in the interviews several years after the parliamentary elections. UFV members present at the preelection negotiations between the Greens and the UFV suggested that they could not fathom that by being placed second on the party list they would be at disadvantage. Invariably, women responded, "We simply did not understand the complexity of the West German election system" (Schäfer, interview). The UFV believed that it had an understanding with the Green Party that the Greens would fill two-thirds of the parliamentary seats and the UFV the remaining one-third. They were also under the impression that the distribution of list places would be negotiated in a "friendly manner" after the election (Hampele, interview).

Once the cold reality set in and the UFV realized that the Green Party occupied the first eight seats, the group demanded that at least three seats be vacated for the UFV. The Green Party refused to transfer any of the seats and declined all further negotiations. In response, the UFV canceled its election coalition with the Green Party. In its press declaration the UFV declared, "A Party—A Mafia," and not only accused the Green Party of violating democratic procedures but also of violating the pro-women stance it had supported in the platform. The Green Party responded with a statement of regret that the preelection negotiations had worked to the disadvantage of the UFV. Given that all eight Green Party candidates had agreed to accept the parliamentary seats, the party was unable to renegotiate the seat distribution (*Telegraph,* no. 6, March 30, 1990).

Frustration with the voters (they voted where the money was) and anger at the loss of access to political power was expressed overwhelmingly by members of the UFV after the elections (interviews: Christine Schenk, Tatjana Böhm, Ina Merkel, Eva Maleck-Lewy, Eva Schäfer, Christiane Schindler, Hanna Behrend). Having focused on institutional politics, the UFV faced the new reality of being excluded from the East German parliament. This exclusion went to the heart of the UFV, since it was founded on the premise of involvement in the process of "state making." The election outcome turned the erstwhile confident slogan "Without Women

There Is No State" into exactly the opposite. Ulrike Helwerth entitled a subsequent article: "Without Women There Is a State."[15]

Women's Political Representation in the New Government

The first secretly and freely elected East German parliament elected eighty women out of four hundred representatives, a total share of 20.5 percent. In the previous Volkskammer under the SED regime, women's share amounted to 32.2 percent. The lower number of women in the postcommunist parliament derived from the unwillingness of all the parties to adhere to agreed-upon election quotas ensuring one-third of the seats to women. The PDS entered the Volkskammer with the highest share of women deputies, with 42.4 percent, followed by the Green Party/UFV with 25 percent,[16] Democratic Awakening with 25 percent, and the SPD with 23.9 percent. The CDU had the lowest number of women deputies with 15.3 percent.

For the first time in the history of the East German parliament a woman, Sabine Bergmann-Pohl, of the CDU, was appointed to preside over the parliamentary procedures. The new government of Lothar de Maizière that took office after March 18 appointed four women to head the ministries of: Family and Women, Youth and Sport, Work and Social Issues, and Trade and Tourism (Winkler 1990).

On coming to power, de Maizière's government did fulfill one demand of the UFV. Although a state secretary for gender equality was never instituted, Marina Beyer was installed as equality officer in the Council of Ministers, subordinate to the newly established Ministry on Family and Women. Despite the presence of women at the highest level of government, the position of equality officer was never intended, as Marina Beyer has complained, to further the interests of women in the German unification process. She perceived the position of equality officer as a pacifier to the politically active women in the GDR (Beyer, interview). Most important, it was only an interim measure. On the day of German unification the Office of Equality Officer ceased to exist (Hampele 1991).

The conservative outcome of both the national elections on March 18 and the subsequent communal elections on May 6, 1990, had a drastic effect on the system of gender equality officers. Many UFV equality officers who had been in power during the time of the Central Round Table had to make room for the winning parties and their candidates. Along with administrative reforms the offices of the equality officers were

---

15. This article appeared in the weekly newspaper the *Freitag* on December 16, 1994.

16. The two women candidates, however, were members of the Green Party and not the UFV.

also reorganized and their powers curtailed. Except for the state of Brandenburg, where Regine Hildebrandt filled the Ministry for Social Issues and showed a political will to advance the system of gender officers,[17] the situation in the other *Länder* depended largely on the parties in power. Many feminists have argued that with the conservative election results these positions have been reduced to mere tokenism, with little power and few financial resources (Maleck-Lewy 1992).

East Faces West: The Increasing Importance of the West German Political Opportunity Structure

The victory of the conservative Alliance for Germany was a victory for Helmut Kohl and his goal for quick unification. There was no doubt after March 18 that the people had chosen national unity over socialist renewal. A new period in GDR history started. Lothar de Maizière's (CDU) coalition government,[18] confirmed by the Volkskammer on April 12, had the sole purpose of putting itself out of power on the day of unification. Having been given marching orders for dissolving itself, the East German state could no longer function as a "normal" state.

Given that access to decision-making arenas is central for determining movements' success in achieving stated objectives (Kitschelt 1985), the bizarre situation in the East German state precluded any such success. Even if the East German state had granted the UFV full access to the decision-making arenas after the March elections, no long-term impact would have resulted. The official political and economic state apparatuses of the German Democratic Republic ceased to exist on October 3. Using Kitschelt's (1985) distinction between access to participation and the "responsiveness of institutions to new inputs and their capacity to formulate and implement strategies of social control," once again we enter a twilight zone. Even if de Maizière's government had granted substantive feminist policy gains, these would have become null and void with unification.

We confront a situation that has no precedent in state theory. The East German state continued to be internationally recognized as a sovereign state but without any independent powers. Furthermore, a government was elected for the sole purpose of writing its own death sentence, and even in this endeavor the conditions for its death were set by its erstwhile enemy.

Conceptualizing the East German state after March as emasculated is

---

17. For more information on Hildebrandt, see her book-length interview in Schütt 1992.

18. Lothar de Maizière's government included the CDU, SPD, FDP, Democratic Awakening, and the DSU.

only one side of the calculation. In the fall of 1989 the UFV had argued that the East German state—symbolizing male power and domination—no longer had any legitimacy. The two periods resemble each other only superficially. Whereas feminists demanded to "occupy" state institutions in 1989 and to participate in reconstructing the state, there was no longer a vacuum to be filled by feminists in March. The new vacuum was already being occupied by the rules and regulations of the West German state system.

This new constellation did not arise against the wishes of the majority of the people. As Thaysen so wonderfully argued, the voice of the common people mattered for the first time in the history of the GDR. The "voices in the streets" had voted for German unity. The UFV, having constituted itself as an organization representing the interests of East German women, now faced a completely different opportunity structure. The rules and regulations no longer came from the Central Round Table or the East German government. Its new master was the state system of the FRG, a system that will be explained more fully in the next chapter.

At this point of reorientation from Eastern to Western institutions, the UFV confronted two new tasks that were absent in the stateless state period and in the period of the election campaigns. First, the UFV found itself once again in the opposition without access to the media (Schenk 1994). Moreover, it found itself in a totally schizophrenic situation. It continued to engage in political election campaigns at the local and state levels (May and October), limited to the territory of the GDR. At the same time, it had to reorient its focus and adjust its game plan to gain political access to the West German state system. In this situation the movement had to maneuver within two different institutional structures at one and the same time.

Second, the movement confronted no less a schizophrenic situation in its feminist identity. In the GDR election campaigns the UFV represented the identity and interests of GDR feminists. In entering the West German system, it confronted an autonomous West German feminist movement that had occupied the feminist space since the early 1970s. More important, the UFV came in contact with a feminist movement whose different historical experiences put it completely at odds with a GDR feminist identity. The negotiations for German unification were thus not a terrain limited only to East German feminists. Two movements confronted each other within one spatial territory.

The UFV in the Role of Opposition

The days were gone when the UFV had hoped it would actively pursue a "feminist strategy in parliament" (Schenk 1994). To make matters worse, the UFV found itself without recourse to the media. "The fourth level of power, the media, was no longer available to us" (Merkel 1990e). During the election campaign the UFV enjoyed celebrity status with the East German media, and also with the Western media in Berlin. Once the elections were over, "the doors to the media were shut" (Schäfer, interview). The UFV faced the unwelcome reality that political losers are of little interest. No newspaper except for the *Neue Deutschland* showed interest in the UFV (Maleck-Lewy, interview). With the loss of all political access points, Schenk reflected several years later "that with these setbacks we simply lost the possibility to intervene in national politics and structure a feminist discourse" (interview).

Women's issues did not disappear after the election, yet feminists could no longer define the public discourse. After the election the media and political parties became the public representative of women's interests. It is they who defined what was important. Thus, while women's issues continued to be present in the media and party discourse, they were filtered through a nonfeminist perspective. Instead of self-determination, feminists had to settle for representation by males (Maleck-Lewy, interview).

Second, the tensions between members of the UFV who had advocated the institutional road to power and the grassroots democratic advocates erupted openly after the election defeat. The strongly integrative and solidaristic impulses that pervaded the UFV prior to, and partly even during, the election campaign came to a screeching halt when the question once more surfaced whether the UFV should participate in the upcoming local elections of May 6.[19] During the parliamentary election campaign the larger interests of the UFV—to win—temporarily alleviated the tensions between the *Politikfrauen* and the *Projektfrauen*. After the Volkskammer election losses, the divergence between the two interests was no longer containable.

Institutional feminists came under attack for their style of decision making. Local autonomous groups, such as the Autonome Brennessel from Erfurt, had tried to address the authoritarian power structure within the UFV from its inception.[20] The UFV understood itself as nonbureaucratic and nonhierarchical, yet women belonging to the grassroots factions have increasingly critiqued the preponderant power position of institutional feminists in the central organization of the UFV in Berlin. Women

---

19. Two additional elections took place in 1990: the East German state parliamentary elections on October 14 and the federal elections to an all-German parliament on December 2.

20. This insight comes from some correspondence between the Autonome Brennessel and the UFV, in which these points were raised. Letters dated March 24, 1991, and January 19, 1992.

from the outer provinces complained that they were confronted with accomplished facts (Hampele 1996).

To alleviate some of these concerns from the grassroots movements, the UFV decided to create a Council of Spokespersons after the parliamentary elections. It was recognized that the State Coordination Council was an inappropriate mechanism for dealing with short-term decision making. Instituting a Council of Spokespersons meant de facto that the UFV had created an Executive Committee not foreseen in the statute of the UFV (Hampele 1996). With this additional organizational structure both the UFV's statute and program had become outdated. The call for a programmatic discussion on this topic fell on deaf ears. Nobody seemed to be interested in entering again into negotiations over defining the organizational structure of the UFV (Schäfer, interview; Maleck-Lewy, interview).

The Council of Spokespersons did provide a focal point for integrating and articulating the UFV's position. It was meant to counteract the increasing decentralizing tendencies within the movement (Hampele 1996). But the Executive Committee did little to provide more input for grassroots feminists. In fact, the opposite happened. The Executive Committee introduced hierarchical and bureaucratic structures of traditional political organizations. It is not surprising that the grassroots were hardly satisfied with changes that disempowered them even more. Increasingly, grassroots feminists perceived the central office of the UFV as little more than a support organization for the *Politikfrauen* (Schäfer 1991).

In this struggle over organizational structure the role of individual feminists also became an issue. The argument was repeatedly raised in interviews that institutional feminists understood themselves more as individuals and lone fighters organized in the UFV and less as solidaristic feminists representing the collective interests of the UFV. Implied in this argument is the accusation that individual feminists usurped the organizational structure of the UFV for their own ends. Whether the UFV was so different in this respect from other social movements remains an open question. It seems rather naive to assume that individuals running for political office enter such a marathon only to satisfy the interests of the collective. Yet to delve into this question about individuals' motives would require detailed information on psychological aspects of the UFV's group dynamic, which is simply not available.

Instead of debating the merits of the UFV's role as either pursuing institutional politics or functioning as a movement, the UFV decided to participate in the upcoming local elections in May, the state elections in October, and the federal elections in December. Despite the outdatedness of pursuing both institutional politics and autonomous projects at the local level (Schenk 1992), the *Politikfrauen* continued to argue that it was vital to be present in the inner sanctuaries of political power.

Reorientation to the Local Level

The decision to participate in the local elections was not just a question of entering another grueling campaign. More important, it meant that the UFV had to redirect the movement's resources from the national level to the local and state level. Realizing that the states (Saxony, Berlin, Brandenburg, Saxony-Anhalt, Mecklenburg-Vorpommern, and Thuringia) would be reconstituted as individual states (*Länder*) prior to unification, the UFV was forced to establish an infrastructure in these states to run election campaigns. New offices had to be created to run local and state campaigns, and new legal criteria had to be developed to hold these elections (Hampele, interview).

The energy that had previously been focused at the national level during the parliamentary campaign shifted now to the local level, which meant an even larger splintering of scarce movement resources, both human and financial. This shift to the local level did, however, empower the local activists to some extent. After the election defeat in March many feminists found the more practical hands-on approach of the project culture more attractive and withdrew from national politics. With the reorientation of the various election campaigns to the state and local levels, the grassroots political activists became important contact persons for helping in the campaign. In particular, the network of women equality officers and feminist members of the many local Round Tables provided a vital support infrastructure for institutional feminists in the election campaigns (Hampele 1991).

Yet these bridging actions between *Politikfrauen* and *Projektfrauen* did not last long. The disappointing results in the local elections furthered the disintegrative tendencies within the UFV. Despite a renewed effort to improve the election results for the UFV, the communal election outcomes of May 6 were not much better than the March elections.[21] In response to the disappointing showings, the GDR daily *Neues Deutschland* interviewed Christiane Schindler, UFV spokeswoman, asking the rhetorical

---

21. For the local election results, see Müller-Enbergs, Schulz, and Wielgohs 1990: 370–72. These election results are difficult to compare with the parliamentary elections. First, the UFV entered into many different coalitions with other citizens' movements depending on the local circumstances. Therefore, it is difficult to isolate the exact UFV percentage gains. Second, each voter had three votes to give to candidates of different parties or political associations. These peculiarities of the communal election rules make a precise comparison to either the parliamentary or state election outcomes difficult.

question: "Has the UFV disappeared?" (Hampele 1991: 253). Ina Merkel (1990e) could only suggest that "people voted again for the money."

Yet these results did not deter the *Politikfrauen* from once again entering the state election campaigns in October. The UFV entered into election coalitions with either the Greens, Coalition '90, or the New Forum. Only in Thuringia did the UFV run an independent campaign, achieving 0.68 percent of the second vote (1.06 percent of the first vote) (Feist and Hoffmann 1991). The UFV was able to gain some political representation, however, at these state elections. Having entered into coalition arrangements with other parties and movements, the UFV was able to gain one seat in each of three states (Schenk 1994).

Two points can be made concerning this struggle between the movement-oriented faction and the institutional feminists. First, institutional politics won out against the more movement-oriented faction. Even after the communal election losses, the grassroots faction was unable to persevere and force a withdrawal from further electoral races. The intent of grassroots feminists was to recoup the resources and reconsider the overall purpose of the UFV. That the political context had changed for the UFV since its creation on December 3 was evident. Schäfer argued that by May the initial UFV concept no longer fit the political reality. Many grassroots feminists were eager to open an internal debate about the future of the organizational structure of the UFV, its identity, goals, and political strategy. In this demand they failed (Schäfer, interview). Second, the gulf between *Politikfrauen* and *Projektfrauen* was also accentuated by their spatial separation. Institutional feminists were located mostly at the main office of the UFV in Berlin, and the *Projektfrauen* were much more widely distributed in the regional outskirts of Berlin and other cities. The advantage of Berlin was not only that there was a central office that provided a locus of communication. Given the centrality of Berlin, feminists were in constant contact with one another and with other like-minded groups and organizations. The grassroots feminists did not have these advantages. They were scattered throughout the GDR, and their trips to Berlin were infrequent. The only gathering points were the monthly UFV meetings and the congresses the UFV organized.

Although the internal UFV conflict can be framed as a struggle between different political understandings of institutional feminists and grassroots activists, at another level there is much evidence of a strong regional identity in the GDR that, in many of the interviews, was also expressed as anti-Berlin sentiment. That the feminist movement seemed to have been much stronger in the fall of 1989 in the "women-active centers" of Thuringia and Saxony than in Berlin and that the creation of a national Independent Women's League on December 3 was looked upon with some misgivings in these regions (Hampele 1996) suggests that the conflict was also regionally conditioned and may not just be limited to a conflict of institutional versus grassroots feminists.

The Changing Nature of the Project Culture

An altogether different question started to haunt the local project culture. Could these grassroots projects still be considered political activities that would lead to structural changes at the societal and cultural level (Sauer 1994)? Or did they increasingly turn into a psychological net for women who fell through the cracks in the change toward an "unsocial society" (Schäfer 1991)?

The UFV had always insisted that the local project culture was as important for achieving social change as was the institutional involvement in politics. This view was formulated at a time when economic collapse had not been foreseen. The creation of an "extraparliamentary women counterculture" envisioned that these local activities of women meeting collectively would: lead to the politicization of grievances rooted in women's particular location in social relations; draw attention to the increasing individualization of social problems; and encourage women to enter politics. Only such a counterculture, feminists argued, would create the necessary conditions for the development of a strong feminist movement that could exert political pressure (Schenk 1994).

This proactive vision of a project culture was no sooner enunciated as the economic situation started to deteriorate ever more drastically in the early summer of 1990. Women were not only afraid of company shutdowns and losing their jobs but also feared losing access to inexpensive childcare, the possibility of rising housing costs, and losing access to the completely free health service of the GDR. These fears touched on "social questions" concerning all women, and feminists were increasingly frustrated that the UFV became the unwilling custodian of the social question. Many feminists felt that, given this deteriorating economic context, all they could do was engage in "damage control to avoid the worst from happening" (Schenk 1991: 130).

This emphasis on the social question changed the nature of the project culture. Being no longer proactive, grassroots feminists increasingly reacted to the problems women faced in their communities. They offered "how-to" services for women who needed help in orienting themselves to situations they had never had to face before. The concept of unemployment and economic insecurity did not exist in the GDR. Citizens had a "right to work" with free access to all the social amenities, however deficient they were in comparison to Western standards, provided by "father state." Facing the loss of such amenities shifted the concern of many women to questions of survival. Whether the projects' reorientation to deal with social questions undermined the feminist demand to politicize grievances women faced everyday is a question that has to remain open for future research.[22]

East and West German Feminists Meet

If waging unfamiliar election campaigns and struggling over its own identity were not sufficiently vexing issues that increasingly undermined the ideological bond between the core members, the UFV confronted an altogether new and unexpected situation. Once the decision to unify the two countries was taken, the UFV had to orient itself toward the West German political system. This West orientation thrust the feminist movement onto foreign turf, already occupied by the West German autonomous feminist movement. Two feminist movements met who knew virtually nothing about each other, were socialized in two completely different ideological systems, and whose concepts about feminism had little in common (Schenk and Schindler 1993; Ferree 1994; Helwerth and Schwarz 1995).

Feminists from East and West did initially show great interest in meeting the "long lost," although never missed, sisters after the opening of the Wall. Prior to 1989 Western feminists, organized in the autonomous feminist movement, had shown little interest in their socialist sisters. For many the world stopped at the German-German border. The East Bloc was a seemingly dreary spot on the map to the right of "our" Europe (Graner and Jäger 1992). Nevertheless, the euphoria of the collapse of the Wall and the quick mobilization of East German feminists during the stateless state period was seen by many Western feminists as a possible infusion of energy to the rather stale movement the Western one had become by the end of the 1980s. In meeting the Eastern sisters, curiosity was mixed with incomprehension about a movement that immediately burst on the scene with a formal organizational structure and the demand to intervene politically. Given the West German autonomous feminist rejection of such organizational structures, the feeling toward these political activities of their Eastern sisters was quite ambivalent (Sauer, interview).

On the Eastern side there was also interest in getting to know the fem-

---

22. There is a complete lack of information on the local grassroots activities in the various regions of the former GDR. Many of these activities will remain forever "lost," since a reconstruction of such informal projects is at best a difficult undertaking eight years after unification. Unfortunately, feminist scholars have shown little interest in this topic.

inists from the West. Eastern feminists knew much more about their Western sisters. Many had read the feminist literature smuggled into the GDR and widely circulated during the 1980s and were thus eager to get to know feminists who had twenty years' experience in organizing and struggling against West German patriarchy. Thus, East German feminists met the sisters with great hopes to create a "united" feminist movement to counter the oncoming reality of "Germany, united fatherland" (Schenk and Schindler 1993: 136).

Many spontaneous meetings between Eastern and Western feminists took place immediately after the Wall collapsed. Some of these meetings occurred through friends in casual meetings on the streets or cafés; others were more formal meetings and seminars organized by Western and Eastern academics who often had personal contacts throughout the 1980s that had become more frequent and regularized prior to the fall of the Wall. Building on these contacts, feminist academics organized East-West meetings that took place either at the Free University (West Berlin), the Technical University (West Berlin), or the Humboldt University in East Berlin. The gatherings were still guided by the euphoric notion that the two feminist movements could formulate ideas on the future shape of a united Germany. Both sides agreed that women had to have guarantees for broad social and political rights to codetermination and safeguards for economic security in a united Germany (Faber and Meyer 1992; Kulke, Kopp-Degethoff, and Ramming 1992).

The initial euphoria soon gave way to an erstwhile feeling of incomprehension about each other's feminisms, which turned into outright hostility by the spring of 1990. The antagonism erupting at the first East-West feminist Congress at the Audimax of the Technical University in West Berlin openly signaled the rift that had been evident for some time between the two movements (Helwerth and Schwarz 1995). Nickel (1992) summed up this new feeling in the title of her article, "The Absence of a United Volk of Sisters." Similarly, Helwerth and Schwarz expressed this rift in their joint project on feminists in both parts of Germany, entitling it "Foreign Sisters." Terms such as *foreignness* and *strangeness* emerged with ever greater frequency to describe the movements' mutual feelings (Helwerth and Schwarz 1995).

After a short span of openness, a "new Wall"—as formidable as the former concrete Wall built by the SED in 1961—had been constructed between the two feminist movements. Even more perplexing is that this animosity has continued even after six years of German unity. In the meantime an extensive literature has emerged about the change from the initial euphoric embrace of the two sisters in the fall of 1989 and a final descent into the "ice age" by April 1990 (Böhm 1992; Hampele 1992; Nickel 1992; Schenk and Schindler 1993; Ferree 1994; Sauer 1994a; Helwerth and Schwarz 1995).

What were the commonalities upon which the two feminists could build, and what were the differences that separated them so relentlessly? Feminists from the West and East shared an ambivalence toward German unification, albeit for different reasons. East German feminists, as we saw in the rhetoric of the UFV, rejected unification because they feared the loss of their identity as workers and mothers. Despite the gendered nature of GDR social policies, they permitted women to combine work and motherhood. The introduction of the West German ideal of "wife-mother" meant that women would no longer have the right to work. East German women would also lose the right to reproductive freedom they had enjoyed since 1972. The right to work and the right to reproductive freedom were no longer part of a struggle in the former GDR; they had been accepted as settled. Becoming part of the West German political and social system meant once again that these issues had to be negotiated within a system that did not recognize these rights (Ferree 1994).

A second reason for East German feminists' ambivalence toward unification was their disappointment in not being able to realize their dream of building a "better" Germany. The UFV's demand to be involved in "state making" was not empty rhetoric. These feminists believed "that for the first time in the world's history we have a chance to develop a feminist polity" (Schenk 1991: 13). In hindsight these ideas may have been naive, as Tatjana Böhm readily admits today (interview). Nevertheless, East German feminists, as well as the entire East German civic movement, felt "robbed" of their chance to introduce a "Third Way" that would be neither capitalist nor socialist. This utopian vision for a democratic socialism was shared by the entire East German opposition movement (Joppke 1995). However critically one may view such visions, the fact remains that this hope was shattered with unification, and East German feminists had no choice but to enter a territory that was in every respect "foreign."

While the East was confronted with the transformation of its entire political and social system, the position of Western feminists did not change in any direct sense as a result of unification. Their anti-unification sentiments were based on altogether different considerations. They believed that unification would mean a rollback of the feminist accomplishments of the last twenty years (Sauer, interview). They often saw in their Eastern counterparts women who were conformist oriented, petit bourgeois "Muttis," fixated on men and not a bit radical. This stereotype of East German feminists was mirrored in the East, where West German feminists were seen as "women who were arrogant, knew everything better, were children and men haters, and on top of it dogmatic and intolerant" (Helwerth 1992: 9).[23] Several factors play key roles in this collision of different feminist identities. While the common language initially promised a sense of trust and agreement, it soon became apparent that, despite sharing a language, the feminists did not understand one another. The use of the same language, as Nickel (1992) has pointed out, hides different contexts, dissimilar meanings, and diversity of experiences and backgrounds embedded within a language structure. The different meaning systems carried in both the East and West German language reflected the different historical experiences of feminists in both countries. Although they shared a common German historical legacy, it is not of recent origin.

Even in terms of their common history, post–World War II leaders in both countries selected only those historical facts that suited them for reconstructing a national picture that always was in rivalry with the other. Thus, women in neither the East nor West had access to a "common history" not clouded by Cold War rhetoric.

The East, as was pointed out previously, abandoned all of what was seen as the conservative legacy of the bourgeois women's movement and instead celebrated the proletarian feminist roots of Clara Zetkin. Similarly, the West German post–World War II leaders rejected Marxian roots and instead renewed the cult of women as mothers and wives from the German Kaiserreich and Weimar Republic. Feminists tried to resurrect the common German historical legacy in 1989 only to find that "they did not know each other" (Nickel 1992). The feminist picture each side carried into the process of German unification was unrecognizable to the other.

Feminists from both sides did share a host of problems, both of a global and private nature, and the experience of patriarchy. But this patriarchy had taken different forms in the two countries (Nickel 1992: 41). Myra Marx Ferree has argued that the two feminisms that arose in postwar East and West Germany were primarily the result of different types of patriarchal state systems. East Germany reflected principles of public patriarchy, and West Germany those of private patriarchy. Public patriarchy refers to the dependence of women on the state, while private patriarchy encourages wives' dependence on their husbands. These different historical experiences shaped not only the identity of the different feminist movements but their aspirations as well (Ferree 1995).

---

23. That these stereotypes took on a life of their own can readily be seen in the title of the collaborative work between the West German Ulrike Helwerth and the East German Gislinde Schwarz, who entitled their new book *About Muttis and Women's Libbers* (Von Muttis und Emanzen). In this irony of wordplay they drew attention to the notion of unliberated Eastern mothers and liberated Western feminists.

Given these different historical experiences, the two movements differed in all major aspects of feminism. These included, as was pointed out before, the relationship to men, the organizational structure of the movement, relations to the state, belief in autonomy, and political strategies. Creating the Independent Women's League organized on the basis of a political association instilled in West German feminists hopes for reenergizing the feminist movement; at the same time, it met with disapproval. The autonomous feminist movement had from its inception rejected a formal organizational structure and shared with other new social movements the desire to remain organized in informal "networks of networks" without an identifiable center. The autonomous feminist movement has pursued its goals based on "high symbolic integration, little role specificity, and by means of variable forms of organization and action" (Kaase 1990: 85).

This self-identity of leaderless and centerless informal networks was interpreted by some institutional feminists in the East as "immaturity." Christine Schenk has found in the absence of such Western institutions the reasons that a common discussion over unification never got off the ground between the two movements. She in fact points to the desolate condition of the West German autonomous movement at the time of unification and criticizes its retreat into male-free niches and informal networks. "We had to recognize that for us the West German feminist movement did not exist in a form that enabled it to act as an influential political force" (Schenk and Schindler 1993: 138).

Schenk's attack on the organizational structure and identity of the autonomous feminist movement shows the frustration on both sides. The West German women's movement had no intention of ever playing the role envisioned by the UFV. It emphasized the formation of a separate political identity autonomous from political institutions (Kulawik 1991–92). Such differences in ideas about the structural forms of an organization and the political strategies of the movement are rooted in the different mental constructs and attitudes these feminists acquired over the last forty years.

The differences between the two feminist movements are not reducible to "misunderstandings" that can simply be corrected through a rational dialogue. These differences are the result of systemic differences inscribed in the attitudes feminists brought to the unification process. The feelings of animosity are thus not limited to stereotypes, although they are expressed as such. This is readily apparent in the stereotypical accusations over each other's relations to men. Autonomous feminists are stigmatized as "man-haters" and Eastern feminists are unliberated because of their supposed "fixation on men." These notions of how to relate to men, as either friend or foe, were the result of a specific historical constellation determining how the state shaped gender relations.

Solidarity between East German women and East German men did not develop because these men were necessarily more feminist but, rather, for two reasons. First, as Bohley has pointed out, the enemy in the GDR was never men as such but the state. Women and men, for better or worse, had to embark on this "marriage of convenience" in order to protect themselves from state repression. Bohley has made reference to the important function of "looking out for each other" in case members of the opposition got arrested (interview). These arrests affected women and men alike, as evidenced by the arrests of Bärbel Bohley and Ulrike Poppe (both mothers) in 1983.

Alison Lewis raised an additional factor that may have contributed to the feeling of solidarity among men and women. She focused on the socialist rhetoric with its emphasis on common working-class solidarity that included both men and women. She suggested that "to withdraw solidarity from men—even if it meant showing solidarity with similarly disadvantaged or oppressed social groups—was to side with the class enemy and thus turn against the working-class. Lack of solidarity was in extreme cases tantamount to class betrayal and high treason" (Lewis 1993: 269). Whether solidarity with men was the result of socialist ideology or because of women's experiences in the GDR is less important than the fact that these conditions were absent in the West. West German feminists never had the experience of solidarity with men organized in the Left or in political parties. Autonomous feminists' experience rests on their exclusion from the public sphere. In turn, they have constructed their identity around the notion of autonomy from both men and political institutions.

Only in this context can the conflict between Eastern and Western feminists over the use of the male and female form of nouns be understood. Western feminists have made the use of language one of the centers of their struggle, insisting that nouns had to be expressed in the feminine form in newspaper articles, job descriptions, and public announcements. By using only the male form of nouns, West German feminists argued that a "coded" message was transported that takes the male as the "norm." The masculine use of language, however, also constructed sexual differences that signified a hierarchical differentiation between men and women. Insisting on the use of feminine nouns was an attempt by Western feminists to point to relations of power inscribed in the meaning system of language (Scott 1988).

East German feminists were largely unsympathetic to this insistence on using female forms of nouns even in conversations with only women present. It was quite comical at times at meetings when Western feminists emphasized continually the "female form" and the other side continued in recognizing only the "male form." Maintaining such speech patterns signaled to each side either "backwardness" or "anti-male" attitudes. Eastern feminists' lack of sympathy for the Western insistence on changing speech habits may have had little to do with the feminist backwardness of East German feminists. Schenk (1993) has argued that East German feminists never experienced the sharp conflict that existed between men and women in the West. As a result, drawing attention to the specificity of "femaleness" in the terminology of language was hardly a high priority for East German feminists.

Differences between East and West German feminists showed up in many aspects of life: East German feminists had children; Western feminists were overwhelmingly childless. They differed in dress and hair styles; they differed in regional accent and in their use of language. By the spring of 1990 a feeling of "us" against "them" pervaded both movements. Facing a common "enemy" in the form of the West German state was not sufficient to unite the movement for the purpose of gaining access to the negotiations for German unity.

Except for sporadic meetings and some joint demonstrations particularly on the issue of abortion, an all-German feminist debate about issues such as the role of "women in the social welfare state," the maintenance of childcare centers, and the threat of extending the West German abortion regulations into the East German territory never took place during the negotiation period (Kulke, Kopp-Deggethoff, and Ramming 1992; Schenk 1993).

Attempts were made between feminists in the East and West to organize strategy meetings to intervene in the negotiations, as I will discuss in the next chapter, but there was little follow-up to such contacts.[24] The only issue that brought forth common action between East and West was on abortion rights in the months prior to unification (Schenk 1993). This issue lent itself to more cooperative activities, since the West German autonomous feminist movement had informal networks throughout Germany that had collaborated on reproductive rights since the 1970s.

In these meetings between East and West German feminists those from the East were at a disadvantage. Not only did they enter a territory that was foreign to them and occupied by the autonomous feminist movement; they were part of the "losers." The collapse of East German eco-

---

24. For example, an East-West Feminist Congress did take place in the Dynamo Sport Centrum on April 27–29, 1990, in East Berlin. This meeting was organized by the UFV, autonomous feminists from Munich calling themselves Women Cooperating with Women (Frauen Gehen zu Frauen), the Womeninfothek from Berlin, in collaboration with the West German Greens' Women's Foundation (Frauenanstiftung) (printed invitation, n.d.).

nomic and political institutions and their takeover by the prosperous West also affected the collective identity of feminists in that they were identified with a "losing regime" (Ferree 1994). Feminists complained that they had entered a "foreign country" (Schenk and Schindler 1993), they felt like "second-class citizens," or "third world citizens," and in their meetings with West German feminists the spear of "normal" patriarchal relations had reversed: West German feminists behaved like "men."

Irrespective of whether East German feminists were political actors participating in running the East German state at the time of the collapse—and the UFV signaled early on that "men" were the culprits in the socialist collapse—their collective identity was nevertheless that of East Germans. That full participation in the labor market belonged to the normal biography of an East German woman reflected at one and the same time the "heart of a socialist life style" (Nickel 1992). In portraying a worker-mother in positive terms, they could not find a language to transmit these pictures without the baggage of a devalued socialist system. For West German feminists these values found little cultural resonance, since they had never made participation in the labor market the sine qua non of feminism.

In the end national identity rather than feminist identity became the more important signifier. The UFV's emphasis on the continuation of an independent GDR and its rejection of the West German system had the unintended consequence that West and East Germans perceived each other first as "national" subjects and not as feminist subjects. In this context of two deeply divided feminist movements they now faced the daunting task of gaining access to the negotiation process for German unification.

CHAPTER 4

A Closed Opportunity Structure: German Unification and "Double Gender Marginalization"

The Rush to German Unity: **Article 23 versus Article 146**

With the consensus that all roads lead to unification, the question then became how to unify. Much has been written about the controversy whether to apply Article 23 or Article 146 of the German Basic Law (the Constitution) to unite the two Germanies (Lehmbruch 1990; Beyme 1991; Habermas 1991; Offe 1991; Merkl 1993; Huelshoff, Markovits, and Reich 1993; Jarausch 1994).[1] Article 23 made it possible for individual German states (like the Saarland in 1957) to join the federation. Going this route meant that the East German states would be incorporated into a united Germany without all German people having a chance to vote freely on the decision.[2] By contrast, Article 146 declared that the Basic Law would lose its validity on the day the German people chose to unify and ratify a new constitution (Brockmann 1991).[3] Article 23 thus permitted the incorporation of the GDR under the existing Basic Law, while Article 146 would lead to the replacement of the Basic Law. In short, applying Article 146

---

1. *The Rush to German Unity* (1994) is the title of Konrad H. Jarausch's pathbreaking book on German unity.

2. Article 23 states: "This Basic Law is valid for the time being in the area of the states of Baden, Bavaria, Bremen, Greater Berlin, Hamburg, Hesse, Lower Saxony, North Rhine-Westfalia, Rhineland Palatinate, Schleswig-Holstein, Württemberg-Baden, and Württemberg-Hohenzollern. In other parts of Germany it will take effect after their accession." This reference to "other parts" specifically was targeted to the Saarland, which acceded to the federation by plebiscite in 1957.

3. Article 146 states: "This Basic Law loses its validity on the day that a new constitution takes effect, concluded by the German people in free decision" (Brockmann 1991: 7–8 n. 8).

would have meant giving up the institutional structures of the "second Republic" (Lehmbruch 1990).

East and West German feminists strongly endorsed Article 146 to achieve German unity. They shared, with the entire East German opposition and the West German Left, the view that Article 146 would undo the "democratic deficit" of the Basic Law, which had never been ratified by the people in 1949. The hope was, as Habermas expressed, "When, if not now, will that day foreseen in Article 146 ever come?" (1991: 96). For West German feminists the concern was not so much that the Basic Law of 1949 had never been ratified. Instead, they hoped that this time around they would be equal participants in the drafting of a constitution that would place gender equality at the very center of the process. In 1949, after a lengthy battle and after mobilizing all of the German women's associations, Elisabeth Selbert, one of the four "founding mothers" in the West German Parliamentary Council, succeeded in including in the second reading the formal recognition of the equality between women and men in Article 3, Paragraph 2, of the Basic Law. As discussed in chapter 1, the article reads, "Men and women are equal." To have this moderate principle of equality included in the Basic Law stirred, to Selbert's surprise, great opposition among both the founding fathers and mothers in the Parliamentary Council. Thirty years later she recalled, "I took it for granted that after two world wars and the experiences that we women had in those decades, equal rights for women would make it through the political process without struggle and with no further ado" (qtd. in Moeller 1993: 40). The members of the Parliamentary Council feared nothing less than legal chaos if they sanctioned the inclusion of the equality principle in the Basic Law (Limbach and Eckert-Höfer 1993).

West German feminists have argued that the existing constitutional guarantee that men and women are equal has been insufficient to narrow the gap in political, social, and economic equality of West German men and women (Limbach and Eckert-Höfer 1993). They saw German unification via Article 146 as their chance to participate in formulating and implementing a Constitution that was based on a new "social contract" between women and men (Gerhard 1991). Feminists in the East and West shared the hope that the Constitutional Draft of the GDR, initiated by the Central Round Table in Berlin, would form the basis for an all-German constitution. Not only was there hope that a new constitution would overcome forty years of separate history and all the suffering inherent in this separation but also that women and men could freely decide on important rules structuring their lives together in a united Germany. The use of Article 23 dashed these hopes.

Wolfgang Schäuble, the leader of the CDU parliamentary group and the chief unity negotiator for the West German side, and from the beginning the staunchest advocate of Article 23, unabashedly set out his reasons for rejecting Article 146. Writing a new constitution was too time-consuming and would generate domestic uncertainties that could be carried into the European arena. "Only this way [Article 23] gave the chance for the necessary acceleration." This argument, however, was secondary to a more fundamental reason for rejecting Article 146. The majority of the FRG's political class believed that the Basic Law had proven itself and should not in any way be subject to alterations. For Schäuble it was a foregone conclusion that the majority in the Federal Republic and perhaps even a greater number of people in the GDR wanted the Basic Law "and did not want anything else" (1991: 55).

Schäuble asserted this position of "we want to keep what we have" and "we already have everything" most forcefully in an interview with the East German Markus Meckel (SPD). Meckel advocated the use of Article 146 to take into account the unique conditions people faced in the GDR and to permit these concerns to be reflected in a new constitution. He argued for the inclusion of the right to work, codetermination of workers, laws against factory lockouts, environmental protection, economic equality between women and men, and protection of privacy, among other things. Yet Schäuble saw no need to change the Basic Law. Unable to open the closed door, Meckel countered, "I only hear from you 'we already have everything'—as if there is no reason for improvement" (*Der Spiegel,* 12/1990: 57).

Schäuble's attitude reflected his fundamental distrust of participatory democracy. At the heart of the conflict raged a deep ideological division between those who advocated participatory democracy and the majority of the political class who continued to harbor a deep distrust of submitting fundamental constitutional decisions to popular control (Lehmbruch 1990). Germany's civil and political disintegration during the Weimar Republic and its tradition of *Obrigkeitsstaat*—the German tendency to submit to authority and regard duty and discipline as more important than liberty and individuality—has given rise to a state-centered version of democratic constitutionalism (Dyson 1977; Smith 1986). Built into the Basic Law is a strong distrust of the forces of civil society. In this etatist tradition the major tasks of the Basic Law were to tame, control, and contain "disruptive and potentially 'totalitarian' forces that might arise out of the conflicts of interest within civil society" (Offe 1990: 249). In contrast to the liberal notion of democracy, German democracy embraces the notion of a "combative democracy" (*wehrhafte Demokratie*), implying that the state would be able to combat any domestically disruptive forces through its monopoly of force (Hirsch 1986).

As Offe pointed out, the implications of these German philosophical, cultural, and legal traditions are expressed at one level in an "almost methodological elite distrust" in the citizenry. On another level the Basic Law is built on "institutional distancing from the citizenry" (Offe 1990: 249). Given this state-centered version of democracy, it is thus not surprising that the Basic Law contains strong provisions against any kind of referenda. In fact, Thaysen (1990d) has referred to the inherent "plebiscite phobia" contained in the Basic Law.

This plebiscite phobia is the basis for Schäuble's rejection of constitutional debate and ratification by all Germans. He argued that "the principles of representative democracy are now more than ever contained in the constitutional history of the West necessary to guarantee a stable order for freedom and democracy. Therefore I am against the plebiscitary experiment in our constitution." Pointedly, Schäuble stated that "with Article 146 everything is open, with Article 23 nothing" (*Der Spiegel,* 12/1990: 54). Article 23 did not risk the stability of the Bonn government.

Many Germans do not share this rejection of the right of referenda by the political class. According to a recent poll, almost 80 percent of West Germans favor the introduction of referenda into the Basic Law for important political questions. This is an increase of thirty percentage points over the 50 percent that had demanded a right to referenda in the 1980s (Schüttemeyer 1994). The collision between the people's will to be consulted on important questions such as rearmament and the placement of nuclear weapons on German territory and the rejection of such demands by the political class dates back to the 1950s (Koopmans 1995). Despite this public longing for more participatory democracy, the state has retained its suspicion of "das Volk" (Schüttemeyer 1994). Although the conservatives in the CDU and CSU continue to harbor a distrust of the citizenry, others believed that the Volk were ready for more democracy. Not only was the opposition party, the SPD, initially opposed to the use of Article 23, even the FDP—as a member of the coalition government—differed from Schäuble's position. Foreign Minister Hans-Dietrich Genscher openly contradicted Kohl's intentions to use Article 23, and the much-respected "great dame of the FDP," Hildegard Hamm-Brücher (MdB), suggested creating a Parliamentary Council with citizens from both the GDR and the FRG to draft a constitution, which would be ratified by the German people (*Frankfurter Rundschau,* March 3, 1990a).

Opposition to using Article 23 also came from East Germany. Little unanimity existed about how to structure German unity. As expected, the Central Round Table endorsed Article 146; the members had already voted against Article 23 on February 20, 1990, and coined the catchy phrase "Article 23—no connection under this number."[4] The East German Volkskammer put an end to these discussions on August 23, 1990, when it voted 80 percent in favor of Article 23.

The West German CDU/CSU-FDP, and ultimately the SPD, also voted in favor of incorporating the GDR under the fundamental principles of the Basic Law (Thaysen 1990d). Even the West German Left finally changed its position and advocated only minimal changes in the Basic Law. The fear of the political Right was at the center of this change. Many conservatives, particularly within the CSU, threatened using a constitutional debate to include more law and order clauses and to press for a more active German military role outside the present restrictions of Germany's military engagement to NATO territory. Given these fears of the Right and their conservative agenda, the West German Left finally came to accept that no change was better than a conservative change (Beyme 1993).

Many West German feminists believed that this decision to use Article 23 set the stage for the subsequent exclusion of women's demands during the unification process (Böttger 1991; Gerhard 1991; Maihofer 1991; Nimsch 1991). Antje Vollmer (MdB), of the Greens, concluded that the state still feared the "German in the Germans." Rejecting a constitutional convention and relying on Article 23 gave feminists two new challenges: the speed of unification and the secrecy around the negotiations for German unification.

The First Phase of Unification and Feminists' Exclusion: The State Treaty

Favoring Article 23 set in motion a two-stage process of unification. The first phase, the State Treaty, was finalized on May 18 to usher in the Monetary, Economic, and Social Union on July 1, 1990.[5] Altogether, seven principal legal instruments were negotiated to bring about a fusion of the two Germanies:

1. Currency Union Treaty (May 18—also known as First State Treaty)
2. Joint Declaration on Property Questions (June 15)

---

4. In German the phrase says: "Artikel 23—Kein Anschluß unter dieser Nummer," making reference to Hitler's *Anschluß* (annexation) of Austria in 1938 and the rejection of such a strategy by the Central Round Table.

5. The first talks on a Monetary, Economic, and Social Union had already been initiated during the Modrow government as early as February 20.

   3. All-German Treuhand Law (June 17)
   4. Länder Establishment Law (July 22)
   5. Electoral Treaty (August 3)
   6. Unification Treaty (August 31)
   7. Two-Plus-Four Treaty (September 12).
(Southern 1992: 42)

The First State Treaty regulated questions of economic rights and introduced the "social market economy" into the Eastern territory. The treaty was intended as a first step toward unity. In the preamble the parties to the treaty resolved "to achieve in freedom as soon as possible the unity of Germany within a European peace order" (State Treaty). The hallmark of the treaty was its provision to introduce the DM into the territory of the GDR, replacing the GDR currency, and authorizing the West German Bundesbank to oversee this currency transformation. Introducing the West German DM became the "trademark of the unification process" (Glaessner 1992: 96).

The First State Treaty was approved by the East German Volkskammer, 302 to 82 in the last week of May. Opposition came from members of the PDS, Coalition '90 and the Greens-GDR.[6] In a symbolic protest action against Western "expropriation" and "subjection" (Jarausch 1994: 147), the citizen movements organized a mock "funeral of the GDR" (BeeRDigung der DDR) in May 1990 at the Berlin Gethsemane Church to express disappointment at being excluded from the decision-making process of the treaty negotiations (Schulz 1991).

The West German parliament also approved the treaty 445 to 60. Opposition in the West came from the Greens and some SPD deputies. New Forum, in cooperation with Coalition '90 and the Greens, issued a "Common Explanation of the State Treaty," pointing to the grave social consequences that would result from the treaty. At the same time, the parliamentary groups of Coalition '90 / Greens in the East German parliament and the Greens in the Bundestag jointly made a public statement why they would vote against the State Treaty (Schulz 1991). In the Upper House of the West German Parliament (Bundesrat) only the SPD-led Länder of the Saarland, with Oskar Lafontaine as the minister president, and Lower Saxony, with the recently elected Gerhard Schröder, voted against the Monetary, Economic, and Social Union (Merkel 1993: 201).

The treaty addressed women's issues only in Article 19, which deals with issues of "unemployment insurance and employment promotion." It

---

   6. As discussed in chapter 3, the Greens-GDR had an election coalition with the UFV prior to the Volkskammer elections.

declares that "special importance shall be attached to an active labor market policy, such as vocational training and retraining. *Considerations shall be given to the interests of women and disabled persons*"[7] (State Treaty, in Glaessner 1992: 186). This scant attention to women's concerns jolted feminists in both the East and the West. They had called for an "East-West Women's Congress" to meet in East Berlin in April 1990 to develop common strategies for a future "East-West women's politics in a united Germany." With slogans such as "Everything's at stake" and "the all-German train threatens to run us over," feminists from the UFV and autonomous feminist groups from Munich and the West German Greens passed a resolution and submitted it to the governments and parliaments in both East and West Germany.

In this resolution they specifically criticized the social market economy because, they argued, it was based on unpaid labor of women in the home and the exploitation of women in child rearing and in caring for the old and the sick. They further stated that such a system denied women an independent material existence and put women at the mercy of personal relations and sexual exploitation. They also pointed out that German unification would mean a "historical step backward in the emancipatory process of women in the East and the West" and demanded specifically a constitutional council with equal representation of women and men to draft a new constitution embracing the basic values entailed in the draft of the East German Constitution of the Round Table (Resolution of East-West Women Congress, April 27–29, 1990).

It was all the more disappointing for feminists to wake up and realize that their demands had been completely ignored in the decision-making process of the first treaty. The members of the East-West Congress once again had proclaimed in their common statement that "politics [*Staatmachen*] is a public affair and not a confidential affair of governmental commissions." Thus, they reacted with "shock" when they realized that, despite constituting half of the population, they were addressed in the treaty as a marginal group needing special attention. Angrily, they responded, "We have Rights!"

In a highly collaborative effort between a wide spectrum of East German political women's groups and interest associations, women sent a statement to the deputies of the Volkskammer and the German Bundestag in which they protested their treatment as a marginal group and complained that neither the West German Ministry of Women nor the East German Ministry of Family and Women nor representatives of women's organizations and federations had been consulted in preparing the State

---

7. Emphasis in this sentence is added by the author.

Treaty. In their petition they specifically demanded that women be included in the decision-making process of German unification (statement dated May 19, 1990).[8]

This appeal to the legislatures in both parts of Germany spoke on behalf of feminists in the East and West. The opening sentence reads: "With outrage have women in the GDR and FRG taken note" (statement dated May 19, 1990). Yet it lists only the Deutsche Frauenrat as signatory, an umbrella association for West German women's groups.[9] The letter is not signed by any feminist groups from the West. A possible explanation for the absence of Western feminist signatures may have to do with time. The State Treaty was signed on May 18. The feminist statement to both legislatures followed the very next day. Wanting to respond immediately to the exclusion of women from the State Treaty, the East German feminists may have opted "to go it alone" for the sake of effectiveness. This is certainly a plausible explanation. It also seems to indicate, however, the continuing difficulty of feminists in both countries in devising a common strategy to intervene in the ongoing negotiations.

Although they tried to come together in April at the East-West Women's Congress to plan common strategies for an all-German feminist politics, the statement protesting the exclusion of women from the State Treaty showed that neither side had been able to build up networks that could be drawn upon when an immediate political reaction was of the utmost importance.

The Introduction of the DM and Its Immediate Effect on Women

The establishment of the social market economy meant that the Basic Law's premise of a "free democratic, federal, legal and social order" became the law of the land on July 1 and signaled the end of the economic sovereignty of the GDR, which therefore lost its material independence

---

8. This letter was signed by only one West German women's group, Deutsche Frauen-rat. The other signatories were from the East: the Democratic Women's League (DFD); the German League for Human Rights in the GDR; the Executive Committee of the Industrial Unions of Printing and Paper; the International Democratic Federation of Women (IDFF); the Women in the Liberal Party (BFD); the Independent Women's League (UFV); the East Berlin Center for Interdisciplinary Women's Research (Zif); the East German Farmers' Party (DBD); the East German Farmers' Association; the PDS; the Technical College of Trade Unions–Bernau; and the Club of Artists' Associations of the GDR.

9. In the Federal Republic several women's groups merged in 1951 to become the Deutsche Frauenrat (German Women's Council). The Women's Council, with about ten million members, is mainly a lobby group. It has never gained much political influence (Lemke 1994).

not on October 3, the day the Unification Treaty took effect, but on July 1, 1990 (Altvater 1991).

The introduction of the social market economy had several immediate, concrete effects on women. GDR women had a legally guaranteed right and duty to work. That this right also created a double burden for women—work and family —and failed to resolve the "women's question" in the GDR has been well documented (Nickel 1990a; 1990b; 1991–92; Maier 1991; Ferree 1993). Nevertheless, the labor laws provided women secure access to the labor market, economic independence, financial flexibility, and provisions for old age (Berghahn and Fritzsche 1991). If a company had to lay off workers, a transfer petition had to be filed that had to be agreed upon by both the company trade union representative and by the persons involved. Given these provisions, structural unemployment did not exist in the GDR.

Once the market economy was introduced and companies had to rationalize the industrial base, the old GDR norms no longer counted and citizens faced unemployment for the first time. The legacy of the GDR's gendered segregation of the labor market[10]—confining women to certain jobs and industrial sectors—translated immediately into a higher percentage of unemployed women than men. The collapse of the East German clothing industry, in which women were 81.4 percent of the workers, brought home the devaluation of women's skills in the new social market economy. Production shifted to high-quality articles, which meant that seamstresses had to adjust to new production conditions. Lower-quality production was immediately moved to low-wage countries. As a result, "Women experienced their dequalification virtually overnight" (Bast-Haider 1995: 59).[11]

Even before the West German regulations were introduced, companies started to lay off workers without the protections that were still in effect. In June 1990, 70 percent of all GDR citizens who were still employed were paid to work shorter hours or were paid to stay home (Kolinsky 1993). They entered what was called a *Warteschleife,* literally translated as "waiting loop," between employment and unemployment. The number of East German women employed decreased rapidly from the 86 percent in 1989 to 77 percent in April 1991. Women also fared rather poorly in terms of state support. Altogether, only 35.4 of the unemployed

---

10. There were about forty-eight jobs for which girls constituted a mere 1 to 5 percent of apprentices (e.g., plumber, fitter, control panel operator) (Nickel 1991–92: 36).

11. In 1989 the clothing industry employed 75,502 employees, of which 81.4 percent were women. The number of workers had fallen to 11,000 by the end of June 1993 (Bast-Haider 1995).

had a right to state support, and only 34 percent of them were women (Hampele 1990).

Given that 90 percent of GDR women were also mothers and about 30 percent were single parents, they were at a tremendous disadvantage in competing in a labor market with high regional imbalances demanding high flexibility and individual mobility (Nickel 1991–92). Moreover, according to the social policies of the GDR, mothers were given a year of job protection after giving birth to a child, in contrast to four months in the FRG. As a transition measure, a job guarantee was instituted for single mothers with children under the age of three (Berghahn and Fritzsche 1991).

The absence of seriously enforceable laws against sex and age discrimination in the West also negatively affected women's ability to gain access to the job creation programs (*Arbeitsbeschaffungsmaßnahmen*) and the retraining programs the FRG introduced as transition measures.[12] Increasingly, girls were closed out of apprenticeship positions, which in West Germany is necessary for entering the skilled professions. Girls were simply not considered by employers. Employers in the West can still express a preference for employees of a certain gender, which has a tremendous negative effect on women in the East. In 1991, 40 percent of the employment preferences listed were for men, 11 percent for women, and 41 percent as being open to either.[13] Government employment offices have quite openly advised women to seek retraining if they had nontraditional job qualifications (Ferree 1995).

East German women very quickly found that there was little room for women with children in the labor market of a social market economy. Employers often expressed their hostility to hiring women with young children, and women had to show that their children were enrolled in daycare in order to be considered "available to work." These rules are not applicable to West German fathers (Ferree 1995). It is thus not surprising that 45

---

12. Only in response to European Community antidiscrimination directives of 1975 and 1976 that advocated "equal pay for work of equal value and equal treatment of women and men regarding access, training, promotion, and working conditions" did West Germany pass, in 1980, an EEC-Adaptation Act. The European Court of Justice criticized this legislation, however, for its lack of enforcing mechanisms in 1984. "In 1985 the federal government provided guidelines, which were improved in 1990, for promoting women in recruitment, training, continued education, and employment, but again they were weak" (Lemke 1994: 272). Finally, in November 1993 the Constitutional Court once again strengthened the antidiscrimination law, in particular to make it easier for women to gain access to traditionally male jobs and sectors (Berghahn and Wilde 1996).

13. This ratio is even worse than in the West, where 25 percent of the jobs are listed for men, 12 percent are for women, and 65 percent are gender neutral (Ferree 1995).

percent of unemployed men in 1990 had found employment within a year, while only one in three women had found a job (Engelbrech 1994).

Feminists' Reaction to Their Exclusion

East German feminist activists did not give up. Although they were unable to influence the negotiations for the Monetary, Economic, and Social Union, they still hoped to influence the negotiations for the second treaty (Unification Treaty), which were in full swing during the summer of 1990. Of particular concern for feminists on both sides was the debate on how the differences between the abortion regulations in the East and West would be resolved. East German women had had the right to terminate a pregnancy within the first twelve weeks since the repeal of para. 218 of the 1871 Bourgeois Penal Code in 1972. Abortions involved inpatient treatment with full medical coverage, and women were permitted one abortion within a six-month period (Böhm 1991–92). In contrast, para. 218 remained in effect in West Germany.[14] The more liberal SPD/FDP legislation permitting women to have an abortion within the first three months had been declared unconstitutional by the Federal Constitutional Court in 1975. Since then women had to qualify under one of the four indicators (rape, fetal deformity, medical reasons, social hardship) to be exempted from criminal prosecution (Berghahn 1993a).

The East and West German negotiators of the German Unification Treaty faced the task of reconciling two fundamentally different approaches to the abortion issue. This was the only issue on which East and West German feminists consistently cooperated. Women in the West hoped that German unification would finally provide the chance to decriminalize abortions (Lemke 1993). At the same time, East German women feared that the restrictive West German abortion regulations would become applicable in their territory after unification. Women deputies of the West-SPD agreed with their Eastern sisters and rejected the transfer of the West German abortion law to the East. In a rare moment of cooperation both sides jointly organized demonstrations "Against 218." These demonstrations took place simultaneously in Bonn and Berlin on June 16, and smaller demonstrations took place throughout the summer months (Maleck-Lewy 1990a).

As the unification negotiations started to heat up during the summer, the UFV was suddenly confronted with a more difficult task. No longer was it the collective movement of feminist organizations it had been during

---

14. Para. 218 goes back to the 1871 *Reich Criminal Code Book,* in which "pregnant women who willfully aborted or killed a fetus in the womb were to be imprisoned for up to 5 years" (Maleck-Lewy 1995).

the fall of 1989 and spring of 1990 (Schindler 1992). Many of the church groups and *Projektfrauen* had withdrawn from the movement. In order to confront the new challenges of women's increasing unemployment rate and to intervene in the abortion debate, the UFV decided to institute a Frauenpolitischer Runder Tisch (FRT, Women's Political Round Table) in August 1990. This was an attempt to use the concept of the Central Round Table and to bring together a broad spectrum of political movements to increase women's influence over the Unification Treaty (Schindler, interview). Although the idea to establish these Round Tables came from the UFV, the participants at the Berlin Round Table included members from the Democratic Women's League, the New Forum, the Initiative for Peace and Human Rights, Democracy Now, United Left, the Farmers Association, the Green Party, the PDS, the SPD, and the CDU. A representative of the East German Ministry of Women and Family was also present during the discussions (Schindler 1992).

The Women's Political Round Table was not only conceptualized as a political mechanism but also, as with the UFV, as an alternative understanding of politics (Sauer 1994). The FRT was "an attempt to create networks of different extraparliamentary movements, interest representatives, and initiatives with the claim to intervene at the parliamentary level." The Women's Political Round Table defined itself as an "alternative political model in the extraparliamentary realm." Its conceptual statement "rejects the majority principle and a political understanding based on power politics and the principle of dominance." The FRT organized itself on the basis of consensus, and offered women a cooperative environment for discussing problems. The goals were to keep the gender debate in the public arena, to initiate and organize joint activities, and to gain influence at all political levels (FRT, Conceptual Statement, n.d).

The Round Table was financed through donations. It established two working groups: one concerned with the consequences of the Monetary, Economic, and Social Union that addressed questions of Women and the Labor Market and a second that dealt with the abortion regulation and called itself "Self-determined Reproduction."[15] The working groups held meetings to which they invited experts, and they published papers.[16] The

---

15. This idea of women's political Round Tables was imitated in many cities and localities in the former GDR and they continue to exist today. In Leipzig a "Round Table against Violence" was started. This idea of Round Tables was even taken up in the West. In West Berlin the "City Political Round Table for Women" was established in September 1990. In addition, a "Round Table from Below" was also created in West Berlin (Hampele 1991; Olbrich 1992; Schindler 1992; Schleusener, Balschuweit, and Schwind 1992).

16. For example, the pamphlets on "Work Promotion = Women's Promotion?" (Arbeitsförderung = Frauenförderung?), dated November 21, 1992; and "Women's Poverty in East Germany," dated February 29, 1992.

Women's Political Round Tables' main goal was to create public awareness of the unification negotiations. Whether through their organizational activities or by writing "open letters" to the representatives of the East German Volkskammer and the Bundestag, the Women's Political Round Table kept the focus on the Unification Treaty and the negative effect it would have on East German women (open letter, dated September 12, 1990).[17]

The Unification Treaty and Women

The treaty establishing political unity between the Federal Republic of Germany and the German Democratic Republic took effect on October 3, 1990; once again it was a somber day for feminists. The treaty made no reference to the many demands feminists had directed to the governments and parliaments in both countries. But, at the same time, German unification did bring tangible political improvements such as the introduction of parliamentary democracy and the extension of civil liberties to all East German citizens for the first time. Given their experience with an authoritarian state in which feminists could not even constitute themselves as a movement, the newly gained democratic rights were certainly a political gain.

The treaty between the Federal Republic of Germany and the German Democratic Republic consists of over a thousand pages of fine print with forty-five articles and three annexes (rules of procedures). The treaty deals with administrative law, criminal law, EU law, the accession date of the GDR into the FRG, constitutional changes, public property and debts, and social and cultural questions (Jarausch 1994: 174). The Unification Treaty even addressed the allotment rights of small gardens (*Kleingartenanlagen*)—a sign of German thoroughness—and declared that the existing regulations of 1983 would remain unaffected by the treaty (Thurich 1991a: 36).

On August 30 the West German "architect" Wolfgang Schäuble and the GDR state secretary Günter Krause signed the treaty.[18] The Volkskammer voted 299 for the treaty, 80 against, with 20 abstentions or absences on September 20. On the same day the West German Parliament also voted 440 for the treaty, 47 against, with 3 abstentions. The West German Upper House (Bundesrat) unanimously approved the treaty on September 21, 1990 (Thurich 1991a).

---

17. The Women's Political Round Table still exists today, and one of its main functions is to provide information and support to the only UFV representative in the Berlin Parliament, Sibyll Klotz (Sauer 1994).

18. The negotiations for the treaty started on July 6, 1990.

The treaty did include some, albeit minor, policy goals for women. The results were in no way commensurate, however, with the efforts women had expended on influencing the decision-making process. Feminist activists and institutional feminists in political parties and the parliament brought sufficient pressure to bear to insert in Article 31 of the Unification Treaty policy goals in regard to equal rights, reconciliation of work and family life, childcare, and the abortion regulations.

Article 31 introduced the nonbinding declaration that "it shall be the task of the all-German legislature to develop further the legislation on equal rights for men and women." Second, the article noted the different legal and institutional starting positions with regard to the employment of mothers and fathers and entrusted the all-German parliament to "shape the legal situation in such a way as to allow a reconciliation of family and occupational life." Third, it promised to contribute to the costs of maintaining the East German daycare centers for a transitional period up to June 30, 1991. Finally, Article 31 stipulated that an all-German legislature had to introduce an abortion regulation no later than December 31, 1992. Although the treaty left the different abortion regulations in East and West Germany intact until a new law was enacted, it did set up "counseling centers run by various agencies and offered blanket coverage" without delay in the Eastern territory. The article stipulated that "the counseling centers shall be provided with sufficient staff and funds to allow them to cope with the task of advising pregnant women and offering them necessary assistance, including beyond the time of confinement" (Verträge zur Einheit Deutschlands 1990: 60; Lemke 1993: 148–49).

The Unification Treaty also included an early retirement regulation for women over the age of fifty-five and men over the age of fifty-seven that was to be in effect until early 1993.[19] This regulation's effect was that the labor market became virtually closed for women over fifty. In reality the employment chances for women over the age of forty-five were already virtually nil. This early retirement measure was included in the Unification Treaty to cope with the unemployment rate that had started to skyrocket after the introduction of the Monetary, Economic, and Social Union in July, which set in motion the deindustrialization of the former GDR. For older women the regulation was devastating. It meant not only that they had been phased out of the labor market but also that they were forced into a life of premature retirement and domesticity in the new Germany (Kolinsky 1993).

In response to the meager results feminists had achieved in the

---

19. The age for men was reduced to fifty-five in 1991.

Unification Treaty, Uta Röth, the official UFV delegate to the Central Round Table in Berlin, noted that the East German feminist movement went from "awakening" (*Aufbruch*) to "upheaval" (*Umbruch*) to "collapse" (*Zusammenbruch*) (Schwarz 1993: 235). Measured against the UFV's mammoth political effort, the results were truly meager. Having created itself for the express purpose of intervening in politics, the UFV "failed" to have an impact on the negotiations for a united Germany. That the UFV failed, some may say, is evidence that "at the end of history" any utopias, feminist or otherwise, are destined to fail. This answer, while comfortable to political pragmatists, is also unsatisfactory, because it puts the existing political system of West Germany above scrutiny. Did the feminists' goals fail to materialize because of the UFV's internecine power struggles, their closeness to the PDS, their rivalries with the autonomous feminist movement in the West, or their political inexperience? Or did they fail because of the systematic exclusion of feminist concerns from German party and state politics?

Why did institutional feminists situated within the very heart of party and state power have so little influence? In shaping the outcome for women, these institutional feminists, as I will show shortly, fared no better than their sisters outside the political structures. Institutional feminists such as Rita Süssmuth (Christian Democratic Union), Renate Schmidt (Social Democratic Party), and Antje Vollmer (the Greens) all agreed that the unification politics of 1990 were associated with names of men. Süssmuth, president of the German Parliament and a member of the conservative CDU, stated in an interview that the men in Bonn determined the themes and timing of unification: "there is simply no evidence to speak of an equal representation of women during the unification process" (Süssmuth and Schubert 1992: 44). Like men, women would have pursued the overall goal of German unification; however, according to Süssmuth, they would have focused more on social and cultural issues in the negotiations. "It is not the same thing when men represent women's interests as when women are equally represented and assert their own right," she reflected, concluding in a rather frustrated tone, "men have virtually never thought of accepting women as their representative" (Süssmuth and Schubert 1992: 50). In a similar vein Schmidt conceded that, while there was no way back, "women did not want this kind of unification." She also acknowledged that women in the East were the losers: "East German women and women generally had something to lose during the unification process, and they did" (1994: 43). Despite their divergent political identities, Antje Vollmer joined her parliamentary colleagues and declared that the historical exclusion of women once the revolutionary dust had settled was nothing new: "The ladies disappear on the guillotines, into the canals (e.g., Rosa Luxemburg—B.Y.), into prisons, into the 'blues,' and into depressions" (1992: 29).

These voices have received support from an unlikely corner of German traditional political science. While Klaus von Beyme, a prolific West German political scientist, is rather critical of those pessimists who "claim German unification as a failure" (1995: 20), he nevertheless surprised readers in his updated classic *The Political System of the German Federal Republic after Unification.* On the next-to-last page of his voluminous work he offers without explanation: "It is women's politics which is most likely the 'real' loser of the peaceful revolution of 1989" (1993: 417). That's it. Nothing more, nothing less. Yet this declaration is important in its brevity for two reasons. First, it adds to the growing voices of women and some East German men (e.g., Wolfgang Ullmann) who have argued that the takeover of the West German legal system had clearly been a retrograde step for East German women (interview, in Maleck 1991: 93). Second, Beyme's statement provides a much-needed recognition in traditional political science, which up until now has failed to take note of the exclusion of women's and feminists' concerns during the unification process.

The question arises why politically active participants and their feminist agendas were swept aside during the unity negotiations. Why did the feminist agenda become a "nonevent"? How was unification negotiated? Who was included in the process? Who determined the themes to be included and/or excluded in the negotiations? Was the process of German unification so unique—what Dror (1968) would call "meta-policy-making"—that it was incommensurate with routine politics? Are we to assume that the feminist exclusion was little more than a sacrifice to the larger historic moment of uniting the two countries? That unification was a singular event—kept alive largely in the dreams of "sentimental old men" (Ziebura, Bonder, and Röttger 1992: 169)—is not disputed.

That the exclusion of feminist politics can be attributed to the extraordinary nature of unification is an altogether different matter. What the unification negotiations did demonstrate, with a force that is not "visible" during periods of routine politics, is the full extent of the exclusionary mechanisms of the West German state. The process itself reveals a systemic "gender bias" in the West German state system that blocked the access of East and West German feminists to the policy-making process of unification.

German Unification: "The Hour of the Executive"

Scholars have argued that the process of unification was "limited to few participants, highly expert-oriented and bureaucratized, confined to few administrative agencies, and taken out of popular control" (Lepsius 1994). Moreover, Lehmbruch noted that the two prevailing models of German decision making failed to explain the process of unification. Neither the model of the Federal Republic as a "semisovereign" state, in which the powers of the Länder and large interest associations constrain the central powers of the state, nor the "corporatist model" were able to explain the process of unification. Exactly the opposite of corporatist decision making seems to have taken place during the negotiating phase. The routine processes of interest intermediation through multilateral bargaining procedures were suspended at least, as Lehmbruch points out, until the later stages of the Unification Treaty (1991).

Two aspects of the decision-making process stand out. First, there was a "contraction of the structures of the state's decision-making strategies" (Lehmbruch 1991).[20] For example, the Unification Treaty was executed by bureaucrats in the chancellor's office. In fact, the "relevant ministers were not even asked for their opinions of all sections of the draft" (Müller-Rommel 1994: 165). Defense Minister Gerhard Stoltenberg was simply silenced in the Two-Plus-Four Treaty negotiations, which reestablished full German sovereignty in the international arena. The players in these treaty negotiations were Chancellor Helmut Kohl and Foreign Minister Hans-Dietrich Genscher. When Stoltenberg objected to Genscher's plan not to have military units of the Western alliance moved to the former territory of the GDR, he found himself the target of a sharp rebuke. Genscher explained this rebuke later as "a silencing of unhelpful public discussion at a delicate period" (Pond 1993: 182).[21]

The powerful German economic actors did not fare much better in the negotiations over the First State Treaty. The Bundesbank and interested ministers were informed of the negotiations, "but the details of the government policy had been worked out by the chancellor's staff in his office" (Müller-Rommel 1994). Bundesbank president Karl Otto Pöhl warned against a quick monetary union, but his advice was simply ignored (Busch 1991; Singer 1992). In fact, the decision to initiate the Monetary, Economic, and Social Union was executed despite the "massive reservations" expressed by the German Bundesbank (Priewe and Hickel 1991). Nor were many other highly respected economic institutions that regularly provide political advice to leaders consulted in the negotiations (Busch 1991).

---

20. Lehmbruch has characterized the first phase of German unification as the "Hour of the Executive," which extended from November 1989 and through the summer months of 1990.

21. It was Genscher who later reversed his position and came to endorse Stoltenberg's plan to move the military alliance onto the territory of the former East Germany.

"Kohl's Kitchen Cabinet of 1990" simply sidestepped the familiar multilateral modes of corporatist interest mediation (Ziebura, Bonder, and Röttger 1992) and embarked on a blitzkrieg strategy of unification (Haug 1991: 25). This was no more evident than in the drafting of the Ten-Point Plan at the end of November 1989, suggesting a possible unification at some future moment. This was done in total secrecy among Kohl's Kitchen Cabinet. Not even his foreign minister, Hans-Dietrich Genscher, knew of the preparation of this plan. At a nightly meeting at the chancellor's bungalow with his political trustees including Horst Teltschik, Rudolf Seiters, Hans Klein, Eduard Ackermann, Wolfgang Bergsdorf, Baldur Wagner, Norbert Prill, Michael Mertes, Stephan Eisel, Juliane Weber, and Wolfgang Gibowski, on November 23, the decision was taken to launch the initiative for German unification. It was Teltschik, with the support of Prill, Eisel, Mertes, and Gibowski, who persuaded Kohl to take the initiative. The actual drafting of the Ten-Point Plan was done by Horst Teltschik, Carl Duisburg, and Rüdiger Kaas from the working team Deutschlandpolitik, Peter Hartmann and Uwe Kaestner from the Office of the Federal Chancellory, as well as the speechwriters Norbert Prill and Michael Mertes (Teltschik 1991: 49–50).

The contraction of the structures of the state's decision-making strategies was seen once again during the negotiations for the Länder Establishment Law of July 1990. This treaty was to reestablish the five Länder in the Eastern territory that had been abolished by the GDR in 1952 and replaced by fourteen regions. The East German Länder were reconstituted on the basis of the five Länder that had existed in 1945 (Merkel 1993). The model of the semisovereign state stressed the importance of the Länder in the dispersion of executive power. According to Katzenstein, "the federal government has no choice but to negotiate and cooperate with centers of state power over which it has no control" (1987: 16). Heidrun Abromeit argues, however, that the treaty was single-handedly negotiated between the West German chief negotiator Wolfgang Schäuble and the East German State Secretary, Günter Krause. Little evidence exists for a "cooperative federalism" between the federal state and its Länder in this process (Abromeit 1992).

According to the Bundesrat president, Henning Voscherau, "German unification was a centralized process between Bonn and East Berlin at the expense of the Länder, who now have to cope with the results" (Abromeit 1992: 91). The states complained that they were forced to participate in the costs of unification but were not included in the decisions and preparations of these treaties, except in relation to the question of financial equalization between the old Länder and the new. In this instance Bonn and the West German states negotiated over the role of the new states and decided to exclude the new states from the revenue equalization measures that characterized the West German federal system until January 1995. Except for this instance, in which Bonn and the states formed a package deal against the new states (Abromeit 1992), the West German states were not even informed about the timing of many of the negotiations that led to the treaties. Johannes Rau, then minister president of the largest West German state, North Rhein–Westphalia, summarized Kohl's neglect of the states: "In comparison to what the Chancellor tells the States about the development of German unity, the contents of the 'Krefeld' telephone book is definitely exciting reading" (Sturm 1991: 161).

Aside from these centralizing tendencies of the state's decision-making structures, the strategy of "problem simplification" characterizes the first phase of the unification process (November 1989 until summer 1990). This entailed the exclusion of all important long-range issues from immediate consideration (Lehmbruch 1991). The idea of crisis conditions and an exceptional situation heightened the pressure for action. Under this scenario, problem simplification became the preferred mode of decision making. "Market ideology" became the instrument for achieving this problem simplification. Any political problem resulting from the economic transformation process was thus conveniently brushed aside, and market rationality was made responsible for the deindustrialization that began with the introduction of the Monetary, Economic, and Social Union. Conversely, the mismanagement of the socialist economy (*Mißwirtschaft*) was constantly invoked to absolve Bonn of political responsibility for the rising unemployment rates in the summer of 1990. Thus, the East Germans themselves were held responsible for the economic collapse.

Although the centralizing tendencies of the state's decision-making structures and problem simplification explain many aspects of the process of German unification, they fail to provide insight into feminist marginalization from the negotiations. Neither one sheds light on why proportionally more women than men lost their jobs in the transition to a social market economy and, more important, why women's unemployment rate is about a third higher than men's six years after unification. Second, the two aspects fail to explain why the substantive gender issue in the abortion debate in the West German parliament gave way to state legalistic reasoning instead of the more women-friendly discourse institutional feminists tried, but failed, to introduce.

The West German Political Opportunity Structure: A Double Gender Marginalization

I propose that the political marginalization of feminists during the unification negotiations was based on "double gender marginalization": feminists shared with other social forces the fate of general exclusion by the state and simultaneously faced selective exclusionary mechanisms in the German state and corporatist system that were gender specific. This double gender marginalization can best be demonstrated by a two-step process. Both the abortion debate surrounding the unification process and the focus on the institutional arrangement of the corporatist bargaining models demonstrate different institutional exclusionary mechanisms antithetical to women's political participation and concerns.

The abortion debate focuses on two important institutions of the German constitutional order: the German political party system organized around parliamentary groups (*Fraktionen*) in the Bundestag and the strong position of the Constitutional Court, with its power to review and challenge parliamentary legislation. The parliamentary groups acted both as "gatekeepers of legislation" (Schüttemeyer 1994) and as "gatekeepers of discursive practice" against the demands of institutional feminists in the political parties to frame the abortion issue in a more women-friendly way. The abortion issue also shows that the Federal Constitutional Court not only reflects a "substantive value commitment of the constitutional order" (Offe 1990: 249). German feminist legal scholars have argued that the court has become "a tool of conservative value commitments" defending the existing social order against the participatory demands of German women (Berghahn and Wilde 1996).

While the abortion issue focuses on the political party system and the role of the Constitutional Court, the emphasis on corporatist institutions highlights the exclusionary mechanisms of the growth-oriented class compromise of the bureaucratically organized corporatist welfare state (Kitschelt 1985). The answer to the question why East German women have fared so poorly in the transition to a social market economy and why it has been so difficult for West German women to gain equal access to the labor market can be found both in the bureaucratic nature of corporatist politics and the state's role in enforcing the class compromise between labor and capital. While corporatism is inclusionary toward economic actors concerned with the distribution of tangible goods and incomes, the bureaucratic nature of corporatist bargaining is, at the same time, exclusionary toward feminist concerns.

Separating the labor market issue associated with corporatist structures from the abortion issue debated in the state structures is only an analytical device to demonstrate the specific exclusionary mechanisms inherent in both the state structures and the corporatist institutions. As pointed out in the introduction, the corporate institutions only "appear" to be outside the state, but they are linked through the political parties and other channels to the state (Gramsci 1971). As a result, both the state structures (parliament, executive, judiciary, and the administrative apparatus) and the corporatist system form the "state in the inclusive system," blurring the boundaries between social forces and state structures. This state system in its inclusive sense explains the formal and informal institutional and cultural exclusionary mechanisms of the German state against feminist participation.

Exclusionary State Structures and the Abortion Debacle

By all accounts membership in NATO had the potential to derail the unification process. Instead, abortion became the most hotly contested issue during the unification negotiations (Maleck-Lewy and Ferree 1996). There were three competing positions on the abortion debate in the summer of 1990. First, the majority of East German women and men were eager to retain the liberal abortion regulations that had been in place in the GDR since 1972. The East German Minister for Women and Family, Christa Schmidt (East-CDU), worked closely with the UFV to defeat the West German attempt to change the East German abortion law. In cooperation with the UFV Schmidt organized a huge postcard initiative to demonstrate to the East German parliament the general support for the East German abortion regulations. Of the 26,500 postcards received in August 1990, only 508 women and men spoke in favor of the West German solution. On June 21, the day the State Treaty was given its first reading in the East German parliament, 17,260 signatures "against 218" were presented to the Volkskammer (Maleck-Lewy 1990a; Helwerth 1994).

The second position was that of the conservatives within the West German CDU and CSU, who wanted the West German law to take effect on the day of unification (Gerecht 1994). For these legislators the unification negotiations were a chance to narrow the provisions of the West German law even further and prohibit all abortions except for medical reasons. The CDU-East, however, did not share this position with its Western counterparts. With an overwhelmingly Protestant rather than Catholic membership (as in the CDU-West), the CDU-East was much more in tune with the GDR mainstream on the abortion issue. In its draft program the CDU-East stated "forbidding abortion and threatening punishment are not helping life" (Maleck-Lewy and Ferree 1996). Only the newly created DSU in the East agreed with its Bavarian sister party, the CSU, in favoring the rescission of the East German abortion regulations and declared "abortion is equal to murder."[22]

The third position was taken by Rita Süssmuth, West-CDU. She tried

---

22. "DDR-Regierung lehnt Übernahme des Paragraphen 218 ab," *Der Tagesspiegel,* July 13, 1990.

to formulate a compromise strategy between the East German trimester approach (*Fristenlösung*) and the West's restrictive regulations. This compromise entailed a trimester approach with mandatory counseling. A woman could have a legal abortion if, after mandatory counseling and a three-day "think period," she decided freely to go ahead with the procedure. Süssmuth also advocated providing a constitutional guarantee for the "protection of unborn lives" (*Schutz des ungeborenen Lebens*), and the extension of social policies to make it easier for families to have children.[23]

The East German government leader, Lothar de Maizière (East-CDU), supported Süssmuth's attempt to decriminalize abortion. Yet he favored a transition period until after the unification negotiations before negotiating a compromise (Gerecht 1994). In suggesting her compromise solution, Süssmuth hoped that a joint all-German abortion regulation could be agreed upon that would be included in the German Unification Treaty. This was not to happen. When Süssmuth tried to intervene in the negotiations and work toward a compromise that would have decriminalized abortion while offering counseling and help for pregnant women, Schäuble simply told her that, by addressing the abortion issue, she ran the risk of provoking the resistance of the CDU (1991: 233).

Schäuble had started to wonder aloud whether "German unity could fail because of the abortion issue!" (1991: 234). At that moment Helmut Kohl intervened personally and ordered the two chief negotiators of the Unification Treaty not to let the abortion issue derail the unification process. The orders from above instructed the negotiators to retain each state's law until the all-German Bundestag had passed a single law by the end of 1992 (Schäuble 1991).

The male negotiators then focused on the most abstract legal procedural question in discussing whether to punish West German women if they terminated a pregnancy in the East. The debate centered around whether international criminal law and the "place of residence" (*Wohnortprinzip*) or national law and its emphasis on the "site of crime" (*Tatortprinzip*) should apply. The question of women's rights never even figured in this bizarre legal wrangling. This debate was the ultimate triumph of male values of process over the more female-oriented values of content.

Although the site of crime was finally agreed upon by all parties, the CDU/CSU initially favored the place of residence, since East Germany was still an independent state and thus the site of crime was beyond the

---

23. "Kompromißvorschlag Frau Süssmuths im Streit um Abtreibungsregelung," *Der Tagesspiegel,* July 24, 1990.

reach of West German prosecutors. The fear of the conservatives was that the site of crime would encourage "abortion tourism" in the East (Riemer 1993).

The abortion debate highlights both the inability of institutional feminists to frame the discourse to their advantage and their inability to join forces across the political spectrum (Gerecht 1994; Sauer 1994). Süssmuth argued that, had women been permitted to participate fully in negotiating the Unification Treaty, there would not have been two competing legal norms regulating abortion in the two countries. Nor would there have been the bizarre legal wrangling about the site of crime. These discussions left most women legislators baffled. Süssmuth stated that neither women nor the public at large could understand why the abortion issue was reduced to such minor legal abstractions (Süssmuth and Schubert 1992). That this discussion had little to do with how women (even those who supported a pro-life position) tried to debate the issue can be ascertained from the parliamentary records. Yet women did not have the power to define the issue or to elevate it to the status of an important policy decision. The issues were framed by the party leaders in the "parliamentary groups" (*Fraktionen*), and institutional feminists simply lacked the support of their *Fraktionen* to frame the issue in a women-friendly manner. Thus, the actual framing of the issue was taken out of the hands of those who were most interested in reaching a compromise between the different regulations in the East and the West.

German institutional feminists tried to counter the male influence in the parliamentary "universe of political discourse" and define the abortion issue with an emphasis on less punishment and more women-friendly suggestions about how to resolve this complicated issue. The universe of political discourse remained inaccessible, however, to the discourse centered around feminist issues. This was even more evident in the second debate on abortion. As will be remembered, the Unification Treaty specified that the all-German legislatures had to introduce regulations no later than December 31, 1992, to achieve an all-German abortion regulation. The negotiations started once an all-German parliament had been elected.

In a study Birgit Sauer (1995) analyzed the discourse of the parliamentary debates of the all-German abortion law in 1992 and showed how quickly a hegemonic discourse around the concepts of "life," "protection of life," "the role of nature," "the polarization between men and women," "life and death," and "protection of life" versus "self-determination" marginalized the discourse of institutional feminists who spoke in favor of decriminalizing abortion. Even though more women deputies from all parties tended to support a more liberal position on abortion than did most men, they were unable to shift the discourse away from the protection of life. The idea that life starts at the moment of fertilization became the unquestioned consensus in the sixteen-hour parliamentary debates.[24] The question was no longer about the right of women; instead, two legal subjects—the fetus and the woman—were constructed who faced each other in struggle. In disassociating the pregnant woman from the fetus, the woman's role was reduced to that of merely providing the "environment" for the fetus.

Given this discursive construction about the independent nature of the fetus, it was not far to the next step of seeing the woman "endangering the fetus" through abortion, alcohol consumption, or drug abuse. The pregnant woman was thus imbued with power and aggression against the fetus from which the fetus had to be protected. The woman held the key to "life and death." Fantasies of the "bad mother" thus discursively entered into the abortion debate, and the notion of "destruction of human life and murder" entered the parliamentary rhetoric. From the destruction of human life the leap was made to compare abortions with the "destruction of Jews during the Holocaust." A CDU-West member warned his colleagues that the number of abortions in Germany are "holocaust numbers, which given German history weigh heavily upon the conscience of politicians, if we do not stop this avalanche of death" (Sauer 1995: 189).

Two situations resulted from this male-dominated discursive construction of the abortion debate. First, virtually all institutional feminists had to speak in favor of the protection of life in order not to fall into the discourse of murder. Supporters of the decriminalization of abortion, such as Renate Schmidt (SPD), Inge Wettig-Danielmeier (SPD), or Uta Würfel (FDP), all emphasized very poignantly the protection of life in addressing the plenary meetings of the Bundestag. Female deputies who still upheld the East German law, Petra Bläss (PDS) and Christine Schenk (UFV), found themselves marginalized. More important, the abortion debate also became an argument in absentia with communism. The East German right to abortion became the symbol of the "morally inferior" communist regime of the East. Thus the West German pro-life legislators subverted the "liberal" access to abortions of East Germans and the positive collective identity of East German women into a morally inferior system that lacked, as Schäuble had pointed out, "ethical socialization" (Maleck-Lewy and Ferree 1996).

This antifeminist construction of the abortion debate had a second effect. Once women were constructed as a "danger to the fetus," then the state had to become the protector of the fetus. In this we see the symbiosis

---

24. The debates started at 9:00 A.M. on June 25, 1992, and ended at 0:58 A.M. on June 26, 1992.

between the interests of men and the state. Males have an interest in sexual access to females, and the state to the reproductive capacity of women. Separating sexuality and procreation splits women's bodies into private and public arenas (Sauer 1995). This paradox between private and public women's bodies is resolved through the intervention of the state as protector of both the patriarchal rights of males and the rights of the state. The state becomes identified not with individual males but represents a system of masculinity that is inscribed in the norms and institutions of the state. In this conception the "state" not only becomes synonymous with "masculinity," but, more important, "state" and "man" appear as "culture," which has to moderate the female "nature" by disciplining and educating it (Sauer 1996).

The male German deputies thus were able to create a hegemonic discourse of either essentializing the woman as weak and in need of the protection of the male and the state or as the bad mother who endangers the fetus and thus forces the state to intervene to prevent the destruction of human life. In using this opposition between the rational culture of men and the state and the irrational nature of women, the relations between woman and fetus were no longer argued in terms of a rights discourse. A woman no longer had independent rights apart from the fetus. The relationship between the pregnant woman and the fetus was interpreted as a "relation of nature" that women had to accept as part of their biological destiny.

Once the discourse had been shaped by these symbolic constructs of the essentialist position of men and women, institutional feminists were unable to gain access to the universe of political discourse and frame the issues in a way that would have prevented two unreconcilable positions between murder and protection of human life being played out against each other.

The inability of women deputies to exert any leverage—even on issues where there was agreement across party lines—is all the more astounding if we consider the relatively high number of female deputies that sat in the German parliament. In 1990, the year the Unification Treaty was negotiated, women constituted 15 percent of the deputies. This share grew to 20.5 percent in the parliamentary elections of 1990 and to a phenomenal 26.3 percent in 1994. German female parliamentary representation now ranks between the Swedish zenith of over 40 percent and the American congressional representation of 10 percent. For Germany the large proportion of women deputies is quite an achievement given that their percentage in 1949 (6.8 percent) barely increased until 1983 (9.8 percent) and, in fact, decreased to 5.8 percent in the early seventies (Hoecker 1995).

The entrance of the Greens into the Bundestag and its mandate of quotas for women,[25] along with the SPD's introduction of quotas in 1988, "feminized" the parliament. The Greens entered the parliament with an unprecedented number of female deputies in 1983 (35.7 percent), increased its proportion of women to 56.8 percent in 1987, and expanded it to an all-time high of 59.2 percent after the 1994 elections. While not quite as spectacular, the SPD also doubled its proportion of women representatives from 16.1 percent in 1987 to 33.7 in 1994.[26] Only the CDU/CSU and FDP (with no quotas) trail far behind the other parties in female representation. The CDU/CSU increased the proportion of its women delegates from 7.7 percent in 1987 to 13.9 percent in 1990.[27] In the FDP the situation for women is rather bleak. Women increased their share from 12.5 percent in 1987 to 17 percent in 1994, but this is a decrease from their all-time high of 20.3 percent in 1990 (Hoecker 1995).

Despite the increasing feminization of the German Bundestag, at least numerically, institutional feminists were unable to join forces across party lines and formulate a compromise on abortion. Both the formal rules of party loyalty and the informal rules of the old boys' network that structure the parliamentary procedures of the *Fraktionsstaat* made it virtually impossible for party women to combine their energies and create a counterhegemony to the male-dominated party structures.

As pointed out previously, the German parliament is dominated by party groups inside the Bundestag. "Parliamentary groups are bodies made up of at least five percent of all Bundestag members who belong to the same party or to parties that, because of their common political goals, are not in competition with each other in any state" (Steffani 1990: 287). The major task of the *Fraktionen* is to represent the party in parliament. With the increasing importance of the parliamentary groups, party policy-making has shifted from the party leaders to the *Fraktion* leaders in the parliament. As a result, the *Fraktion*'s leaders have become more important in giving policy directives to the party; no longer does the party determine *Fraktion* policy (Steffani 1990; Schüttemeyer 1994; Braunthal 1996).

This shift from party policy-making to *Fraktion* policy–making was

---

25. The Greens' quota, "the zipper principle" as it became known, stipulates that the first place on the ballot and every subsequent uneven number have to go to a woman.

26. This increase is the result of the successful struggle of SPD women at the party conference in 1988 to secure a 40 percent quota in all SPD local, Länder, and national policy-making organs by 1994 (Braunthal 1994).

27. At the 1995 CDU Party convention the party executives introduced a 30 percent quota to increase the number of women in leadership positions and as deputies. Despite the predictions that this measure would succeed—even Helmut Kohl supported the quota—the attempt was defeated by the party delegates. The resolution failed by 6 votes to reach the 501 threshold required for passage. There were 495 votes for and 288 against it. "Kohl Rejected by Party on Women's Quota," *New York Times,* October 19, 1995.

made possible by the financial independence of the *Fraktionen* from party funding. *Fraktionen* are entitled to "payments from the federal budget according to their functions in parliament" (Schüttemeyer 1994: 39). Their operating budget thus comes from public funds. In 1990 the German taxpayers spent around DM 90 million on the *Fraktionen*, an increase of more than 45,000 percent since the 1950s. The sums of money allotted to the *Fraktionen* have increased, as the employment of research and legislative assistants has risen, and an oppositional "bonus" of 25 percent was introduced. This bonus is intended to compensate the minority *Fraktion* for not having access to the ministerial bureaucracies. There are over six hundred employees, not counting the individual deputies employed in the various *Fraktionen* (Schüttemeyer 1994).

These *Fraktionen* have become the primary force in organizing parliamentary operations in the Bundestag plenum and in the committees and are based on strong parliamentary party discipline of both the majority and minority parties. In virtually all *Fraktionen* policy initiatives flow from top to bottom. Given their central organizational role, the *Fraktionen* have become the gatekeepers of legislation (Schüttemeyer 1994). Within their structures interests are advanced. Any bill that reaches the parliamentary committees has already been scrutinized by the *Fraktionen*. No longer is the committee the clearinghouse for legislative proposals. Rather, a bill's life and death is decided in the parliamentary groups. Not surprisingly, the organizational structure of the *Fraktionen* is hierarchical and highly differentiated.

Individual members are bound by the decisions of the *Fraktionen*, but there is no absolute obligation to vote in line with party policy (*Fraktionszwang*). In fact, Article 38 of the Basic Law guarantees the individual deputy's freedom and autonomy from the *Fraktionen*. Nevertheless, a party has sufficient discriminatory measures, ranging from holding up certain assignments to excluding delegates from the parliamentary group, so that a member has every incentive to avoid diverging from the majority decision of the parliamentary group (*Fraktionsdisziplin*). Thus, the line between "party obligation" and "party discipline" is rather thin.

Given the power of the *Fraktionen*, it should not come as a surprise that not a single female deputy has been selected to lead a *Fraktion* in any of the parties. As in many other countries, the representation of German women declines as the power of the party office increases (Braunthal 1983; Feist 1986; Kolinsky 1993; Hoecker 1995). Herta Däubler-Gmelin, politically active in the SPD since her student days and one of the most renowned lawyers and legislators since 1972, suffered a bitter defeat in losing the *Fraktion* leadership election to her male rival, Hans-Ulrich Klose, in the fall of 1991. Had she won, Däubler-Gmelin would have been the first woman to occupy this position in the Bundestag. To argue, as many of her party colleagues did, that Däubler-Gmelin has a difficult "personality" and was thus "unsuitable" for the *Fraktion* leadership seems to be a character assassination applied more frequently to female deputies than to males. Inge Wettig Danielmeier, of the SPD, evaluated the defeat of her female colleague as the result of a decisive minority in the party who continue to reject a woman for the first place: "The fact remains that if the leading position is for a woman, then please no breakthrough into the real power domains!" (1992: 426).

Herta Däubler-Gmelin did score one big victory at the Party Conference in 1988. As the first woman ever in the history of the SPD, she was elected to the position of deputy party chair. Placing a woman in this important party position was only possible, however, because the SPD had instituted quotas for increasing the number of women party delegates and placing more women in party leadership positions (Braunthal 1994).

The dependence on male party members for gaining access to leadership positions is even worse in the CDU and FDP than in the SPD. The grand dame of the FDP, Hildegard Hamm-Brücher, bemoaned the fact that Irmgard Adam-Schwätzer failed by only eleven votes to become the first woman party chair of the FDP in 1988, after she had succeeded in becoming the first party secretary in the FDP's history in 1982 (Hamm-Brücher 1990). This defeat was even more remarkable since her competitor, Otto Count Lambsdorff, was found guilty and fined for a financial corruption scandal resulting from the combination of "money and politics" (Oltmanns 1990: 131). Yet not even Lambsdorff's shady party dealings could sway the party regulars to pass the leadership to a woman. Even Hamm-Brücher's nomination as the first woman presidential candidate in 1994 was nothing more than a symbolic act—symbolic because nominating the popular Hamm-Brücher gave a much needed boost to the FDP and created the impression that it was doing something for its women. At the same time, Hamm-Brücher was selected only because she had little chance of actually winning the office of the presidency.

Despite the visibility of Rita Süssmuth on women's issues in the CDU-West,[28] women's situation in the party remains one of subordination to the larger party goals. Professional women encounter reservations from both CDU male party members and from housewives, who still make up 50 percent of women party members. The rule in the CDU executive offices seems to be that women are included in the party executive meet-

---

28. Süssmuth's position on women's issues is very controversial within the CDU and does not have the backing of Chancellor Kohl. Instead, she represents the liberal wing of the CDU around Heiner Geißler.

ings, but the important positions and decisions remain in the hands of male party members. Males determine which women deputies articulate the interests of women in the party and how these interests are framed (Reichart-Dreyer 1995).

The party candidate selection procedures for political office are particularly disadvantageous for women. "In the West German electoral system, half the members of parliament win their seats outright as constituency candidates for their respective party while the other half is chosen from party lists" (Kolinsky 1993: 224). The safe seats are the direct seats and the first seats on the party lists. In virtually every party the safe seats go to male candidates, since the electoral districts are "strongly in the grip of men" (Maleck-Lewy and Penrose 1995; Reichart-Dreyer 1995). Even the Green's zipper principle of putting a woman in first place and in every subsequent uneven number has not guaranteed women safe seats. It did not stop the party regulars from putting a man in the first place in Bremen for the Bundestag election in 1990 (Krieger 1991).

Aside from the institutional exclusionary mechanism that starts with the candidate selection process for a parliamentary career and institutional feminists' inability to gain access to the inner domains of parliamentary political power, women also face a not-so-subtle cultural discrimination in all parties, which "mirrors the ethos of the general society" (Braunthal 1994: 188). German citizens scored the highest of the twelve European Community states (33.8 percent) in agreeing that "politics is foremost a matter for males" in 1987 (Hoecker 1995). In fact, the desire to see women participating in politics has even declined over the years. In various opinion polls the question was asked whether people support women's political engagement. In separating the answer according to sex, the percentage of women who agreed with this question increased from 32 percent in 1965 to 68 percent in 1971 and declined to 55 percent in 1990. Males started out at a lower level of support and also registered a marked decrease in 1990. The percentage of males agreeing with wanting to see women politically active increased from 27 percent to 56 percent in 1971 but declined to a horrendously low 34 percent in 1990 (31).[29]

That politics is a male domain is not new in Germany. At the turn of the century state theorists conceptualized "the state as the highest male bond," a justification and rationalization to keep the first women's move-

---

29. The increasing negative response rate of males toward female political participation indicates that generally men are more "threatened" by the increasing number of women entering politics. At the same time, these numbers have to be interpreted with caution. Hoecker pointed out that both women and men were less positive about men's participation in politics in the 1990s, in contrast to the 1960s and 1970s. This seems to indicate the general disillusion with politics starting in the 1980s.

ment at bay (Kreisky 1994). This cultural legacy of conceptualizing the state as the arena of male power continues to be embedded in the state structures as well as in the ethos of the general society. It is not surprising that female deputies across the party spectrum from the CDU to the Greens experience the West German political party culture as strongly male cliquish and exclusionary to women. They are made to feel as "foreigners" in politics. Women deputies complain that male elites have created the political rules to their own advantage (Hoecker 1995). "Women always feel they navigate in a strange land of politics," in which the informal rules provide males with all the power advantages (Krieger 1991).

Whether women confront the male "proletarian antifeminism" in the SPD with its prejudice against women participating in politics because "they are deemed to be unqualified or because their place should be at home" (Braunthal 1983: 177) or they are confronted with the culture of the bureaucratic and ritualistic ethos of the civil service (the essence of German statehood), these cultures have in common an orientation around "barroom politics" (*Stammtisch*). The male culture of meeting in smoke-filled rooms in the back of pubs has made it difficult for many women politicians to feel part of this "male clique culture" (Kolinsky 1993; Braunthal 1994). Women politicians are often repelled by this heavily male atmosphere. Behind the aura of a ritualistic cult and secrecy is the strong, not-so-hidden message that the "affairs of the state" are still a male domain.

Feminists have argued that this barroom politics is principally exclusionary to women (Krieger 1991). The times of party meetings alone, between 4:00 P.M. and 9:00 P.M., exclude many married women and women with children from attending (Reichart-Dreyer 1995). Many women party members not only reject the meetings in bars but are also not privy to the highly ritualistic male cult surrounding party politics. Belonging to either the proletarian culture or the highly respected German civil service is based on symbolic male-bonding rites that are built around alcohol and sexist jokes (Kreisky 1994). These rituals create a culture of insiders and outsiders. Only insiders gain access to power positions. Heide Simonis (SPD), the first female minister president of Schleswig-Holstein, recently declared that "the real decisions are made when the beer flows" (Hoecker 1995: 110).

By virtue of the hierarchical, closed, highly disciplined practices in the political parties and the parliamentary groups, women deputies have become outsiders within the power structure. Even if feminist concerns are shared across party lines, institutional feminists have virtually no repertoire to oppose decisions reached by the parliamentary group. A woman deputy always needs the support of the *Fraktionen* and male leaders to sanction her actions. "Without a parliamentary group she is a member without influence" (Steffani 1990: 288). From the perspective of feminist politics the *Fraktionen* have thus acted both as gatekeepers of legislation and as gatekeepers of discursive practices.

Given these formal and informal exclusionary mechanisms of German state institutions, it should come as no surprise that, despite the institutional feminists' efforts across party lines to formulate an abortion compromise, they failed. Herta Däublin-Gmelin invited women deputies from the East and West to meet in July 1990. Yet this cross-cooperation was not to last. At the moment when a draft of a "pregnancy support law" was to have been finalized, the FDP pulled out and declared it would submit its own draft proposal developed by party legal experts. Women from the SPD were particularly angry about this pull-out, because they had made extensive compromises in their positions on abortion to achieve this cross-party cooperation. The FDP's action had little to do with the substantive issue of abortion contained in the draft. The party leadership was eager to remain in the governmental coalition with the CDU/CSU and had decided at its Party Conference in September not to cooperate with the opposition if it went against the interests of the CDU/CSU. Once again specific party considerations took precedence over the interests of women across the political parties (Gerecht 1994).

The German Parliament created a Special Committee for the Protection of Unborn Life in October 1991 to draw up a legislative proposal.[30] Initially, six drafts were submitted to this Special Committee. These drafts supported positions anywhere from the complete deletion of para. 218 of the Criminal Law Code (supported by Coalition '90 / Greens and PDS / Left List), to the Group Werner (the minority position of the CDU/CSU), outlawing virtually all abortions except for medical emergencies (German Parliament, Legislative Proposals, Printed Paper 12,551; 12, 1178; 121179; 12/841; 12/696; 12/898). A seventh legislative proposal, the Group Resolution supported by members from several parliamentary groups (Gruppenantrag 12/2605), which was a cooperative endeavor led by Inge Wettig-Danielmeier (SPD) and Uta Würfel (FDP), was subsequently passed by the German Bundestag on June 26, 1992.[31]

---

30. This Special Committee had the following representatives: twenty deputies from the CDU/CSU Fraktion, ten from the SPD, five from the FDP, and one, respectively, from the PDS and Coalition '90 / the Greens.

31. The "Group Motion" was supported by 355 votes, with 284 votes against, and 16 abstentions. The SPD supported the motion by 232 out of 239 deputies; 73 out of 79 FDP deputies; 32 CDU/CSU (mostly East German CDU deputies) out of 268 deputies, 6 from Coalition '90 / Greens, 10 from the PDS/Left list, and 2 deputies without parliamentary group status (*fraktionslose*) (Sauer 1995; Gerecht 1994).

Given the very anti-women discursive parliamentary abortion debate, the party compromise bore the stamp of how *Fraktion* leaders had framed the discourse in the parliamentary debate. Abortions remained in principle a criminal act. The bill did not declare abortions within the first trimester illegal, however, if they were performed by a doctor after mandatory "anonymous" counseling (*Fristenlösung mit Beratungspflicht*).

With this formulation East German institutional feminists and women in the East lost the most. The UFV and PDS women deputies had demanded the removal of all restrictions from the penal code. They also fought against mandatory counseling and pushed for voluntary counseling (Maleck-Lewy 1995). They did not, however, have the support of the institutional feminists from the West-SPD or the FDP. Realizing that they would have to accept the continuation of the criminalization of abortion, if for no other reason than to forestall a Constitutional Court ruling against the parliamentary bill, as had happened in 1975,[32] the SPD feminists had to swallow the mandatory counseling geared to "the protection of life in the process of becoming" and had to accept the criminalization of abortion.

SPD members were able to mobilize some social family support measures, however, which they expressed in their guiding principles during the debate as "help instead of punishment." Aside from financial support for pregnancy prevention, family planning, and counseling, the law codified the legal right of every child to a space in a day care center—which was to start in 1996—but was delayed before the final vote until 1999 (Berghahn 1993b).[33]

Women deputies, irrespective of party, supported the more liberal proposals for abortion regulation, while proportionally more male deputies voted for the most restrictive draft of the Werner Group (Sauer 1994). The bill was passed by the Bundesrat on July 10, 1992, and signed by the Federal President on July 27, 1992. The first all-German abortion law was to take effect on August 5, 1992. Yet this never happened.

---

32. In response to the feminist movement and its demand for reform of the German abortion law, the SPD/FDP government passed a reform bill in 1974 that would have permitted abortions within the first twelve weeks, provided the abortion was carried out by a doctor. The Constitutional Court declared this law unconstitutional because it contradicted the obligation of the state to protect unborn life (Maleck-Lewy 1995).

33. Angela Merkel (CDU/CSU), at the time federal minister of women, estimated that the new law would mean providing 600,000 new places in daycare centers at a cost of DM 20 billion (20 Milliarden) (German Parliament, Stenographic Report, Minutes of the Plenary Protokol 12/99: 8246).

The Constitutional Court and Its Ruling

The Bavarian state Government and 248 CDU/CSU federal deputies (215 men and 33 women) appealed to the Federal Constitutional Court to rule on the constitutionality of the new law. The court issued an immediate injunction and declared that the law could not take effect as planned until it had issued a ruling (Berghahn 1993b). Yet the mandatory counseling provisions to encourage women to carry the fetus to full term took effect immediately (June 1993). Since the court found wanting the provision in the law that mandated "compulsory counseling with the final decision left to the woman," it set strict criteria for counseling centers and "described the criteria for counseling, including that it might take several sessions and involve close relatives and/or the father of the 'unborn,' among others" (Maleck-Lewy 1995: 70).

The shock was great when the Constitutional Court rejected with a clear 6 to 2 majority large parts of the Abortion Reform Act in May 1993. The court issued the macabre but very German ruling that abortions remain illegal yet exempt from punishment. While the final responsibility for deciding rests with women and abortions during the first twelve weeks after mandatory pro-life counseling that may require more than one session remain exempt from punishment, abortions remain unlawful (*rechtswidrig*) except in the special circumstances of medical indications, fetal deformities, or rape. The court struck down the possibility of allowing abortions in cases of social hardship, which had been permitted after the 1975 Constitutional ruling. Because abortions are illegal and only tolerated under very specific conditions, health insurance plans are now prohibited from paying for abortions unless there is a doctor's consent. In cases of financial need the social welfare agency will pay for the cost (Berghahn 1995; Maleck-Lewy 1995). This process, however, eliminates the anonymous nature of the mandatory counseling. The court also ruled that the counseling must be directed toward saving the unborn and that third parties (fathers, parents) can be punished if they interfere and/or deny support to a woman wishing to carry the fetus to term (Berghahn 1993b, 1993–94).

The ruling was a "slap in the face" particularly for women in the East. Women lost the right to freedom of choice after twenty-one years of self-determination.[34] Both Christina Schenk (Coalition '90 / Greens) and Petra

---

34. See Christel Hanewinckel, federal SPD deputy from Halle, cited in *Die Zeit,* "Die Frauen im Osten trifft die volle Härte des Karlsruher Urteils zum Paragraphen 218. Ausgegrenzt," June 11, 1993.

Bläss (PDS / Left List) stated that the compromise reached in the parliamentary Group Resolution was already a tremendous imposition on women in the East.[35] But they did not expect a further restriction by the Constitutional Court. In subsequent interviews Maleck-Lewy found a sense of confusion and dejection among East German women. "In every interview, women made the point that the new law can only be understood as a conservative and/or aggressive response to women's claim for autonomy, bringing them once again under the supervision and control of the state" (1995: 72).

In the West women had less to lose than their sisters in the East. The court's decision provoked approval, open criticism, or resignation. The two main architects of the parliamentary abortion compromise, Uta Würfel (FDP) and Inge Wettig-Danielmeister (SPD) declared the decision as "neither a victory nor a defeat" (Gerecht 1994). In a rather back-handed criticism of Uta Würfel the weekly news magazine *Der Spiegel* was quick to point out that she was the top candidate for the FDP in the European elections and thus "needed the support" of her male party colleagues.[36] The implication here is that she subordinated her pro-choice position, placing the "logic of the party" over the "logic of feminism."

The abortion debacle did initiate a blood feud between West German institutional and autonomous feminists and between East and West German feminists. Institutional feminists were attacked for not being radical enough during the parliamentary debates. Christina Schenk, of the UFV, argued that the women in the SPD "let themselves be outmaneuvered." Criticism also came from the Greens and the East German feminist movement. Waltraud Schoppe, of the Greens, "demanded to fight" instead of accepting the parliamentary pragmatism of the institutional feminists who tried to satisfy the criteria set by the constitutional restrictions of the 1975 ruling. In turn, East German feminists argued that the West German women negotiators failed to mobilize the grassroots women's movement. Maleck-Lewy reports an interview in which the East and West tensions are once again clearly visible:

> I think that the way the women leaders of the SPD and FDP handled this problem indicated fear that broad demonstrations could disturb their parliamentary negotiations, leading to the isolation of the demonstrators on the street. They don't like it that we are active here; they don't want to be disturbed by us. (1995: 72)

---

35. See Minutes of the Plenary Proceedings, German Parliament, Stenographic Report, 99th Meeting, 25 June 1992, 12/99.

36. "Flüchtige Kavaliere. Demütigung für die Frauen: Der nachgebesserte Paragraph 218 erschwert die Fristenlösung," *Der Spiegel* 21 (1994).

Inge Wettig-Danielmeier, of the SPD, responded in the daily Left German newspaper, the *TAZ,* and accused the autonomous feminists of "sitting on a moral high horse and looking down on the pragmatists."[37]

The only silver lining, at least to some West German women, was the court's ruling that the right to terminate or carry out a pregnancy was ultimately left up to the woman, despite the fact that this right could only be exercised after the woman had submitted to mandatory pro-life counseling. At the same time, the ruling brought forth a torrent of criticism from feminist and nonfeminist judicial scholars. Both the role of the Constitutional Court to review and challenge majority decisions of parliamentary legislation and its substantive value commitments to uphold a conservative constitutional order became a matter of dispute. First was the issue of "conflict of interest" among the judges themselves. Four of the eight judges on the court were practicing Catholics: Ernst-Wolfgang Böckenförde, Paul Kirchhof, Konrad Kruis, and Klaus Winter. For practicing Catholics abortion remains the "direct and intended killing of human life." Pope John Paul II has unilaterally proclaimed that abortions for Christians are synonymous with killing innocent life.[38] Not only was Judge Böckenförde (SPD) a devout Catholic, he belonged to the militant Judges' Association for Right to Life. Only in 1990 did he resign from this association. Judge Klaus Winter (CDU) has openly talked about the trimester approach as "luxury abortions." Another judge, Hans Hugo Klein (CDU), belonged to the group of parliamentary deputies who appealed to the Constitutional Court in 1974 to stop the reform abortion bill from taking effect. In addition, the Second Senate of the Court,[39] which was to hear the abortion case, had prepared an expert opinion in summer 1992 for the pro-life legal scholar, Rolf Stürner, in which the court's bias (*Befangenheit*) was quite evident.[40] Only one judge was known to be sympathetic to women's issues. Feminists could not expect any sup-

---

37. Inge Wettig-Danielmeier, "Da hat sich's ausgekämpft!" *TAZ,* June 3, 1992.

38. The Catholic Church has not always been dogmatically antiabortion. In fact, the change only occurred in 1869, when Pope Pius IX declared that the soul entered a fetus at the time of conception. Until then the church doctrine suggested that the soul entered the female fetus after eighty days and the male after forty days. Within this forty-to-eighty-day time span a pregnancy could be terminated. At the end of the eighteenth century the "killing" of a fetus was understood to take place only after the thirtieth week of pregnancy. Prior to that period the fetus was held as part of the "innards" (*Eingeweide*) of the woman (Sauer 1994b n. 21).

39. In Germany the Constitutional Court is made up of two Senates. The first Senate of the Federal Constitutional Court is mainly responsible for "basic rights and fundamental freedoms." The Second Senate, overwhelmingly more conservative, is primarily responsible for questions of constitutional law (Berghahn and Wilde 1996).

40. "Die Konterkapitäne von Karlsruhe," *Der Spiegel* 50 (1992).

port for their position even from the only woman judge (Karin Graßhof), who is a known conservative hard-liner who voted with the majority against the abortion reform act (Berghahn and Wilde 1996).

In response to the court's feared bias against any reforms of the abortion law, the Kiel minister, Gisela Böhrk, mobilized women from all political and social arenas to write an open letter to the Constitutional Court. Signatories to this letter ranged from Kohl cabinet member Irmgard Schwätzer (FDP), to women in political leadership from the SPD to the CDU in the old and the new states, to writers such as Monika Maron, film stars, as well as the former president of the Protestant Church Conference, Eleonore von Rotenhan. The signatories asked that Judge Bökkenförde and Judge Winter declare a conflict of interest and recuse themselves from the abortion ruling. As the petition from the women arrived in Karlsruhe, several professors with "power of attorney in legal proceedings" (*prozeßbevollmächtigte*) also asked for an informal investigation of the bias of the judges. The court ruled on its own bias in 1992 and declared that none of the judges had a conflict of interest (*Der Spiegel* 50/1992).

Not only was there a conflict of interest among the judges in the Second Senate, but there is virtually unanimous agreement that had the more liberal First Senate ruled on the case the result would have been different. Judge Jutta Limbach, who calls herself a "practicing feminist" and who is the present president of the First Senate, openly acknowledged that the First Senate would have ruled differently (*Der Spiegel* 50/1992).[41]

Although the bias of the court was heavily criticized, feminist scholars have also argued that the court violated its constitutional mandate to act as "the guardian of the Constitution," putting itself in the role of lawmaker. The court issued very detailed instructions about how the parliament could meet the constitutionality test of the law, thereby not restricting itself to consideration of general, abstract legal norms. In other words, the Constitutional Court decided legal policy (Berghahn 1993b). In suggesting that the Constitutional Court exceeded its competence, Christine Landfried drew attention to the "danger" such decisions pose to the parliamentary body's power to pass laws and how important it is to think about countermeasures to such abuse of power (Landfried 1995). Thus, the Constitutional Court has for some scholars become a threat to the democratic process of German politics.

Second, the court has imposed an absolute value standard in conformity with its own conservative interpretation and commitment to the German constitutional order. It gave preference to the "protection of unborn

---

41. Jutta Limbach was the keynote speaker at the German Studies Association Conference (Chicago, September 22, 1995) and affirmed her assertion that the First Senate's ruling would have been different.

life." In the Constitutional Court's earlier decision of 1975 it had elevated the fetus to an "independent legal entity" (*selbstständiges Rechtsgut*) and declared that a fetus deserves protection under Article 2, Paragraph 1, of the Basic Law, which states that "everyone shall have the right to the free development of the personality insofar as he does not violate the rights of others or offend against the constitutional order or against morality" (Basic Law 1991: 8).

While the 1975 court did not consider an unborn fetus as a person with legal rights guaranteed in the Basic Law, only that the fetus should enjoy the prevailing protection of the state, in the newest ruling the court explicitly states that the unborn should enjoy the same legal protection as the living. The fetus thus has the same legal status as a person "with the basic right of dignity and the right to life." Most important, the judges have invalidated the basic rights of pregnant women and subordinated these rights to the right to life of the fetus (Frommel 1992; Berghahn 1993b; 1994; 1995).

Where does the German abortion regulation stand after eight years of unification? The German president, Roman Herzog, signed a new version of the abortion bill into law on August 21, 1995, a measure passed by the Bundestag on June 29 and approved by the Bundesrat on July 14. The new law was written to reflect the Constitutional Court's emphasis on the protection of unborn life. Abortions remain illegal, but a woman will not be subject to criminal prosecution if the procedure takes place during the first twelve weeks and the woman attends compulsory counseling geared to the protection of unborn life. The national health service will pay the costs of abortions in cases that involve medical grounds and rape.[42]

Yet this is not the end of the saga. The state of Bavaria was not satisfied with the federal law and has imposed more severe restrictions on women who seek abortions. On June 12, 1996, not even a full year after the federal law had been in effect, the Bavarian state parliament followed the federal law in requiring a woman to attend a counseling session. In Bavaria, however, she will be required to state her reasons for seeking an abortion, something not required under the federal law; if she refuses, she will not receive the necessary certificate of attendance at the counseling session. Bavaria will also prohibit doctors from taking in more than 25 percent of their total revenues from abortions and will obligate them to a second counseling session with the pregnant woman.[43]

The Bavarian ruling has once again inflamed the abortion debate.

---

42. "After Much Conflict, Germany's New Abortion Law Goes into Effect," *Week in Germany,* September 8, 1995: 1.

43. "Bavaria Passes 'Counseling Law' for Women Seeking Abortion," *Week in Germany,* June 21, 1996.

The SPD, the Greens, and the FDP have threatened to appeal to the Constitutional Court to revoke the law. In a rare moment of agreement the daily moderate *Süddeutsche Zeitung* and the Left *TAZ* agreed that "a federal law is a federal law because it is applicable throughout the country. Bavaria, as we know, is part of the country" (*Süddeutsche Zeitung,* June 14, 1996). Similarly the *TAZ* responded that "Bavaria's violation of federal law is a scandal that no federal government can afford. Article 37 of the Basic Law gives the government the right to enforce compliance with federal statutes. Bonn has had no trouble doing this repeatedly with nuclear power issues" (June 11, 1996). As the *Süddeutsche Zeitung* points out, however, reality looks different from theory. Theoretically, Article 37 provides for situations in which states fail to comply with federal obligations: the federal coercion (*Bundeszwang*). But Bonn's realpolitik is altogether a different matter.

> Because the CSU governs in Bavaria, because the CSU is also part of the federal government and because the federal government doesn't want trouble. That's why the . . . CDU/CSU parliamentary group is trying to justify the Bavarian version of Section 218 . . . by saying that it only complements, but does not violate federal law.[44]

The outcry against the Bavarian "special treatment" (*Extrawurst*) has ranged from the senior editor of *Der Spiegel,* Rudolf Augstein, to Bavarian doctors and feminist and nonfeminist legal scholars. In the meantime, however, neither the SPD nor the FDP are sure whether they want to appeal to the Constitutional Court. The fear is that the court could accept the Bavarian interpretation of the law and force other states to comply with this more restrictive ruling. There is suspicion that the court's ruling on mandatory counseling is sufficiently contradictory that it could invite such an interpretation.[45] No further major challenge has been launched by any other parties involved in the abortion regulation signed into law in 1995 except for Bavaria.

Corporatism and Its Effect on Women

The exclusionary mechanisms against feminist participation, as I argued previously, are not limited to the formal structures of the parties and their parliamentary groups acting both as gatekeepers of legislation and gate-

---

44. *Süddeutsche Zeitung,* June 14, 1996, cited in ". . . Bavaria's Abortion Law," *Week in Germany,* June 21, 1996: 3.

45. "Kniefall vor dem Kardinal," *Der Spiegel* 25 (1996).

keepers of discursive practices against a feminist agenda. Nor can the entire explanation for feminists' marginalization be found in the strong position of the Constitutional Court and its conservative value commitments. These institutions are only one part, albeit an important one, of the difficulty German women confront in gaining access to the political decision-making structure. The "state in its inclusive sense" also includes the corporatist bargaining institutions that form the other part of the gendered opportunity structure women confront in the labor market. The combination of the formal and informal institutional exclusionary mechanisms and the marginalization of women from the corporatist class compromise form a "whole" explaining the gendered nature of the German state.

Since the introduction of the West German market economy, East German women have had a higher unemployment rate than men, and this has continued to be true. The total number of East German workers has dropped from about 9 million in 1989 to around 6.3 million in 1995,[46] and the number of employed women has decreased from 4.5 to 2.8 million (Ferree 1995). The total East German unemployment rate has increased from 14.2 percent in 1995 to 16.2 percent in May 1996 (Press and Information Office of the Federal Government, June 13, 1996). Yet this number is highly misleading. If the number of people engaged in federal and state work creation programs, training programs, and short-term jobs are included in the unemployment figures, the total East German unemployment rate would reach a high of 30 to 40 percent.[47]

The unemployment rate of 19.4 percent for East German women continues to be higher than the 13.3 percent for men in May 1996. Of the total number of unemployed, women account for 58 percent, a decline of 5 percent from the 63 percent registered in 1995 (Press and Information Office of the Federal Government, June 13, 1996).[48] This decline in the total number of unemployed again has to be read with caution. It does not

46. Kerstin Schwenn, "Dem Thema Arbeitslosigkeit kann sich niemand entziehen," *Frankfurter Allgemeine Zeitung,* July 21, 1995.

47. Kerstin Schwenn, *Frankfurter Allgemeine Zeitung,* July 21, 1995. The same estimate has also been given by *Der Spiegel* 28 (1996). In its July 8, 1996, publication *Der Spiegel* stated that the federal and state job creation programs are the largest "firms" providing jobs for East Germans, even in such boomtown cities as Leipzig ("Zaun hinter Chemnitz," *Der Spiegel* 28 [1996]).

48. Two social scientists, Walter Heering and Klaus Schröder, of the Free University of Berlin, came to the conclusion, however, that East German women had started with a 50 percent share of total unemployment in 1990 and that this number had increased to about 65 percent in December 1995. "Die DDR war kein Bollwerk der Emanzipation. Legenden und Wirklichkeit im ostdeutschen Transformationsprozeß: das Beispiel Frauenbeschäftigung," *Die Frankfurter Allgemeine Zeitung,* December 21, 1995.

mean that the position of women in the East German labor market has improved. Instead, the numerical improvement in the female numbers is the result of the sharply deteriorating employment situation for males in May 1996. Since the previous year the unemployment rate for blue-collar male workers has increased by 33 percent, for the young by 30 percent, and for those over fifty-five years by 64 percent (Press and Information Office of the Federal Government, June 13, 1996).

Overall, the situation of East German women remains worse than that of males. Females face a 6.1 percent higher unemployment rate, and they continue to be unemployed for longer periods of time. Whereas men on the average are unemployed for twenty-two weeks, females are unemployed for as long as thirty-six weeks (Press and Information Office of the Federal Government, June 13, 1996). According to the *Washington Post,* the long-term jobless rate for women was 69 percent in 1992, and this figure climbed to 77 percent in 1994.[49] The economic impact on young mothers has been equally devastating. They had an unemployment rate of 12 percent in 1991, compared with 48 percent in 1995.[50] Women also account for 98 percent of the total number of part-time unemployed, a figure that has not changed since the previous year (Press and Information Office of the Federal Government, June 13, 1996).[51]

Focusing on the changes in the percentage share of total employment instead of unemployment, the women's participation rate in the East German labor market accounted for 48 percent in 1990, declined to 44 percent in November 1993, and increased to 45 percent in November 1994. If we look at the total percentage of East German women employed, however, this number has dropped from around 90 percent in 1989 to 77 percent in April 1991 and decreased still further to 56 percent in 1993 (Schenk 1994).

Even worse for East German women is their much lower access to newly created jobs in the former GDR, of which women have been able to garner only 38 percent (Heering and Schröder, *Frankfurter Allgemeine Zeitung,* December 21, 1995). The inaccessibility of new jobs is all the more problematic for East German women, since 94 percent remain committed to their identity as workers.[52] East German women, who had an

49. Long-term unemployment is defined by the Federal Employment Office as being out of work for at least a year.

50. Rick Atkinson, "German Unification Lays Heavy Burden on Eastern Working Women," *Washington Post,* March 29, 1995.

51. This high number of unemployed female part-time workers is surely the result either of the declining full-time opportunities for women or the inability of mothers to work full-time given that the extensive social programs of the former GDR no longer exist in the united Germany.

52. Kerstin Schwenn, "Dem Thema Arbeitslosigkeit kann sich niemand entziehen," *Frankfurter Allgemeine Zeitung,* July 21, 1995.

employment rate of about 90 percent in the former GDR and who desire to remain in the job market, confront a West German political class with very different ideas about how to reduce the high unemployment rate in the East. The Institute for Economic Research in Halle (in the former East Germany) has concluded that unemployment will be reduced only if the supply of jobs is commensurate with demand ("participation in employment needs to be reduced"). Women are therefore told to withdraw from the labor market in order to reduce the number of job seekers. The percentage of job seekers in the East is 82 percent, while in the West it is only 70 percent. The difference in the rates is the result of the East German woman's identity as, and preference for, the worker-mother role (*Week in Germany,* July 7, 1995). East German women have shown little interest in staying home as housewives. In a 1991 opinion poll only 3 percent of former East German women could envision staying home and becoming full-time housewives (Notz 1992: 158).

Women's continuing demand to participate in the labor market and the government's response to deindustrialization and the highest unemployment rate since 1945 (Esping-Andersen 1995)—shrinking the labor force and inducing labor force exit—is a conflict whose full force both East and West German women are facing. Whether the only road for them is to return to the 1950s and tend to the family is an open, but not unlikely, outcome (Ostner 1994).

The picture for West German women in the labor market is not much better. The overall unemployment rate in West Germany was 9.8 percent in May 1996. The good news was that the rate for women was slightly lower than that of men: 9.5 percent versus 10 percent. Women were, as was also the case for East German women, unemployed longer than men: thirty-one weeks versus twenty-eight weeks for males. As in the East, women in the West make up the large majority—97 percent—of part-time job seekers.[53]

Nor does the labor market bode well for young women. Although they increased their employment by 6 percent from 1995, young men increased theirs by 17 percent. The Press and Information Office of the Federal Government acknowledges that young women's difficulty has to do with the "threshold problem" they experience in entering the traditionally male field of manufacturing (June 13, 1996).

---

53. In the West the high rate of part-time unemployment is of different origin from that in the East. The absence of full-time daycare facilities in the West and the closing of schools and kindergartens at midday has made it virtually impossible for mothers to work full-time. The number of female part-time job seekers has also increased among those who enter the labor market after bringing up their children and who are often no longer competitive for full-time jobs.

These different unemployment data between the East and West and between men and women tell only part of the story of the West German model of the social market economy. That model is built around suppressed female employment, with overall female labor participation still one of the lowest in Western Europe (Esping-Andersen 1995). The employment rate of German working-age women has risen from 51 percent in 1980 to 56 percent in the 1990s; women now account for 41 percent of the total labor force, with the sharpest growth in part-time jobs, taken by women who return to work after they have raised their children (Kolinsky 1993; Kurzer 1996).

In the West German corporatist model, with the "male breadwinner" on the one side and the wife-mother on the other, German social policy and industrial relations work in tandem. As Esping-Andersen pointed out, "The family's virtually complete dependence on the male earner's income and entitlements meant that unions came to battle for job security (seniority principles, the regulation of hiring and firing practice, and the 'family wage'" (Esping-Andersen 1995). Not surprisingly, the state's social policies are very male oriented.

The German social welfare state is generous in social benefits, including income maintenance targeted to the male breadwinner (accident, sickness, disability and old-age pensions, unemployment) and health care. The other side of the coin, however, is the underdevelopment of either private or state social care services that would benefit women and children.

While the Swedish daycare system covers around 50 percent of small children, no more than 1.4 percent are covered in Germany (Esping-Andersen 1995). The German idea of daycare has never been built around enabling families to cope with the dual task of employment and family. Instead, kindergartens for children between the ages of three and six were created as pedagogical institutions to provide a few hours of teaching each morning (Ostner 1994). As pointed out earlier, women are expected to be at home at lunchtime to provide meals and supervision for children who are in kindergarten or school only half-time (Kolinsky 1993). Since the "career housewife" is expected to attend to the old, the sick, and the young, public sector employment in health, education, and welfare services was only 7 percent in Germany at the end of the 1980s (Esping-Andersen 1995). In contrast to Sweden, which has expanded public employment opportunities for women and where women have benefited both as employees in the large public service sector and as clients of the extensive welfare state (Hernes 1987: 76), German women remain largely segregated in the private arena (Ostner 1994; Ferree 1995).

The ideological justification for this male-biased "standard worker family" model is continually reproduced and maintained within the bargaining structures of the corporatist model. Economic agreements are made in male-dominated hierarchical systems of elite bargaining among a limited number of class associations, recognized (if not created) by the state and granted a deliberative and representational monopoly in the policy formation and implementation process (Schmitter 1979).

These organizational structures have a very clear gender profile. Women are largely absent as leaders in labor unions and have virtually no presence in employers' associations, corporate boardrooms, state administrative structures (finance and economic ministries), or economic think tanks. Yet it is in these economic and professional organizations that key economic decisions about the public interest are made. They are made, however, for an economic production system oriented toward the male industrial worker: it was *his* job description and *his* wages that were at the center of the bargaining process between employers and unions and which provided the focus of state policies (Hagen and Jenson 1988).

Corporatist systems are at one and the same time inclusive and exclusive. This "selective corporatism" (Esser and Fach 1981), defined as an economic-social regulatory cartel consisting of the state administration, traditional political parties, and labor unions, defines the very essence of the achievement society. Those who are included in it gain material concessions and economic security. Excluded are the increasing numbers of unemployed, the unskilled, many foreign workers, those who do not adhere to the norms of an "achievement society," and the socially unfit (Hirsch 1986; 1990).

The situation for women in corporatism is more complex. They are not excluded from this compromise but are included only as dependents of their husbands and as career housewives. They have no independent economic existence in a system based on the male breadwinner and the family wage. Even if some women have benefited as employees of the welfare state, as consumers (childcare, health care, prenatal clinics) and as clients (recipients of social services) (Borchorst and Siim 1989), the jobs provided to women have been mostly at the bottom of the occupational hierarchy, low paid and low skilled, and they offer little upward mobility (Hagen and Jenson 1989). German women seem particularly overrepresented in the lower end of personal and "junk services" (Esping-Andersen 1990).

German labor and capital stand united in this exclusionary gender profile. Confronting each other as class antagonists at one level, capital and labor share a common Weltanschauung about the gendered division of labor at another level. Labor and capital hold onto a model of gender hierarchy in which men are the breadwinners and women play the secondary role in the home. The asymmetrical structure of gender relations in corporatist institutions is a reflection of the gender hierarchy in the economic division of labor. The concept of work continues to be associated with paid full-time employment, ignoring the unpaid work in the home. Work remains coupled to the norm of male work with a linear development from the completion of training to the time of retirement. There are no provisions in the normal career path for time off for reproduction. The corporatist model—based on the work profile tailored to the normal biography of males—not only devalues unpaid housework but also leads to a differentiated wage structure and gender-specific job segregation that is inscribed in the institutions of the German labor market (Kurz-Scherf 1996).

While labor unions in countries such as Sweden and Italy have been supportive of women's rights since the 1920s (Haas 1992; Beccalli 1994), German feminists have not been able to forge an alliance with the labor unions. The German Union Association (DGB) membership in the 1990s is more in tune with the German economic profile of the 1950s: male, middle-aged, and employed in manufacturing. Women are largely absent from the union rank and file; their overall union membership is only 18 percent (Kurzer 1996). The same proletarian antifeminism exists in the German labor unions as is found in the Social Democratic Party. The culture of the *Stammtisch* and male bonding is as prevalent and, in fact, has the same roots in the proletarian working-class movement of the late eighteenth century.

Given that the unions have continued to hold onto their patriarchal concept of work, Kurz-Scherf in a very critical article asked "whether the labor unions need a new concept of work? Or, whether women need a new labor union?" Criticizing the failed union politics in response to the crisis of the German work society, she not only accuses labor unions of "patriarchal blindness," she encourages women in labor unions to terminate their loyalty to the existing structures and create a new union that will represent the interests of women workers (Kurz-Scherf 1996).

Instead of coalition partners, German labor unions and the feminist movement confront each other as competitors and antagonists. This antagonism has led to the bizarre situation of the labor unions' failure to support the Women's Strike Day on March 8, 1994. Modeling their strike action on the example of the general strike of Icelandic women in 1975 and the strike of Swiss women in 1991, German feminists tried to stage a common action with feminists from the East (UFV) and West organizing a "warning strike" on March 8, 1994, to protest the "recreation of a larger Germany at the expense of refugees, the poor, the weak, and at the expense of women."[54]

---

54. Flyer of the announced warning strike, "Women Say No!" n.d.

Roth and Ferree (1996) have shown that the labor unions resisted the term *strike* for a protest event not tied to a specific workplace. Yet this strike was geared to draw attention to the "dismantling of civil rights, the reduction of social services and the increasing feminization of poverty, the backlash against women's rights, the increasing destruction of the environment and the expansion of German military participation" (flyer, "Women Say No!"). The Women's Strike Day was geared to bring together the autonomous feminist movement and institutional feminists in political parties, labor unions, and the government. Yet the union of public employees (ÖTV), the union of the communication workers (IG Medien), as well as the umbrella organization for all German unions (DGB) "invoked the letter of the law to legitimate their reluctance to use the word 'strike' for a women's protest event, even if many of the issues were economic. They were willing to endorse some sort of protest, but wanted to label the event a 'Women's Protest Day.'" Despite some collective action at work sites to support the women's action on March 8, "none of the union women were able to convince the male leadership to endorse the protest event and support a political strike of women" (Roth and Ferree 1996: 13–14).

The hostility toward the feminist movement is the result of the very nature of the welfare state compromise. The central organizing principle of the entire corporatist system is based on growth-oriented class compromise (Kitschelt 1985). Corporatist institutions bestow privileges on those who are included in the compromise at the expense of those who are seen as constraining economic growth. The feminist movement, with its emphasis on a model of production that includes reproduction and is based on solidarity instead of competition, its attacks on the male fetishization of technical progress and the antihumanism of "industrialism" (Kurz-Scherf 1996), is seen as endangering established relations between state and corporatist structures.

This antagonism between the German feminist movement and corporatist bodies is not easily resolvable. There are at least two colliding logics inherent in feminism and corporatism. One pits social gratification and qualitative "life chances" not produced by the market against stability and the equitable distribution of goods and services (Kitschelt 1985); the other is between the logic of movement politics and the logic of party politics. Feminists reject the bureaucratic, hierarchical organizational structure and stability-oriented economic goals of corporatist institutions, while corporatist actors disdain nonhierarchical networks of networks that reject institutional politics and pursue collective goods not subject to the logic of the market (Kitschelt 1985).

Corporatist bodies do not even have the resources to intervene in policy areas that deal with issues of identities, collectively shared meanings, the quest for community, the quality of life, autonomy, and individual social gratification. The three conventional modes of intervention of bureaucratic politics are, according to Offe: (1) legal regulation, bureaucratic surveillance, and the use of state-organized violence; (2) fiscal policy; and (3) the use of information and persuasion (1990: 247). These resources are ineffective, however, in addressing the concerns of feminists who do not subscribe to rational, utility-maximizing, economic criteria. These tools are geared to solve problems of economic distribution and "positive-sum game" situations—in which both labor and capital "give a little to get a lot" (Kitschelt 1985). No amount of legal and bureaucratic regulation and surveillance, fiscal incentives, or symbolic politics is likely to succeed in addressing the participatory demands and concerns of feminists.

Epilogue

The experience with double gender marginalization in the German state structures convinced some feminists from the East and West to create a "Feminist Party—The Women" in June 1995. The realization that feminists failed to "feminize politics" (Höcker 1987), and their shock at the ultimate abortion ruling of the Constitutional Court was in no small measure responsible for creating an "opposing force" to the existing exclusionary party and state structures. The idea of a German women's party has been discussed at least since 1919 (Feist 1986). Calling for a new party in Kassel, feminists referred to the "rigid," "inflexible," "stiff" structures of male-dominated parties and the loss of faith that women will achieve a 50 percent representation in these structures and gain "real" influence instead of the tokenism that seems to prevail at present. Luise Pusch summed up the feelings in addressing the women present to create the new party: "Working in male parties is wasted energy" (*TAZ*, June 12, 1995).

Feminists no longer wanted to make compromises with men. At the same time, they were also realistic and did not envision that millions of women would join the new party. Instead, they understood themselves as an opposing force (*Gegenmacht*) against the traditional parties. They intended to provide a support structure for those women in traditional parties who were forced to subordinate themselves to the larger goals of the party (*Neue Deutschland*, June 9, 1995).

That the creation of the feminist party is a reflection of the gendered opportunity structure of the German state should not come as a surprise. A different matter is whether this party will have much of a political impact. Any party seeking representation in the German federal and state parliaments has to overcome the 5 percent "restrictive clause" (*Sperr-*

klausel). Even if this hurdle can be overcome, it is difficult to see the access points this party could develop to enter the corporatist power structures. A feminist strategy focusing on a quantitative increase among women deputies in the parliament fails to take into account the substantial advantage in power and influence the corporatist institutions have in political decision making. How German feminists will "crack the nut" of this exclusionary state structure in its inclusive sense and gain access to the center of political decision making is a question that exceeds the scope of this study.

CHAPTER 5

The East and West German Women's Movements and the German State

Are Women the Losers of Unification?

"Women as the losers" of unification is certainly one part of reality. East German women gained political and civil liberties while at the same time forfeiting their reproductive rights, economic independence, and worker-mother identity. East German women had not envisioned this outcome in their joyous celebration after the fall of the Wall. In fact, feminists from both parts of the country had hoped that the collapse of real existing socialism would provide an opportunity to renegotiate gender relations in the new Germany. But the thesis of "East German women as the losers" is only half-true. Not only has there been a sharply rising economic disparity between men and women in the East eight years after unification but also an increasing differentiation among women themselves (Nickel 1994; Hüning and Nickel 1997). Female "winners" in the transformation to a liberal market economy are mostly from the younger generation, are highly educated, prefer a career over motherhood, are generally risk takers, and have often felt stifled in their career ambitions in the former GDR (Nickel 1994).

Nevertheless, the deep impact of economic insecurity on women can be seen in the unprecedented decline of the birthrate immediately after unification. The number of births in eastern Germany has dropped by two-thirds—from 220,000 in 1988 to roughly 70,000 in 1993. By 1994 the GDR had the lowest birthrate in the world. At 0.7 percent it has fallen below the already low birthrate of 1.4 percent in western Germany.[1] The fall was the largest ever in the industrialized world, comparable only to Berlin's between the war years of 1942 and 1946.[2] Participants in the forty-first meeting of the German Council on Psychosomatic Medicine described eastern Germany as the site of the "biggest birth strike in history" (Nickel, *Frankfurter Rundschau*). The birthrate has started to increase from the low of 70,000 in 1993 to 82,000 in 1995. This is, however, still below the 178,000 born in 1990.[3]

The extraordinary fall of the birthrate by itself speaks volumes about the economic insecurity East German women felt as a result of German unification.[4] Although the birthrate has stopped falling, a full three-quarters of East Germans interviewed in 1995 still feel that women remain disadvantaged in comparison with men. In fact, the level of dissatisfaction with women's situation has increased in the Eastern states by 14 percent between 1991 and 1993. Although dissatisfaction with the state of women's lives is not quite as low in the West, a hefty 62 percent there feel that equality between the sexes is far from being achieved in Germany today.[5]

Feminist scholars tread a fine line. It is very important to highlight the real imbalances of the gendered effects of unification, but it is equally important not to categorize all women as victims. By targeting women as the losers of unification, feminists themselves contribute to a static construction and understanding of gender relations: man as the historical subject and woman as the victim of structural and direct patriarchal domination. The victimization of women inherently reaffirms and reproduces how women are culturally constructed in our society: as beings of the second order for whom and over whom others decide (Dölling 1993).

Implicit in this image of women as the losers of unification is the assumption that the working and life world of East and West German women before unification was a "golden past" that unification has shattered. A wave of nostalgia for the many women-friendly social policies has swept the former GDR. These measures made it possible for women to

---

1. Hildegard Maria Nickel, "Die Ankunft der Ostdeutschen in einer verdampfenden Gesellschaft," *Frankfurter Rundschau,* November 30, 1994.

2. Judy Dempsey, "Scent of Self-Confidence," *Financial Times,* October 3, 1995.

3. The impact of this low birthrate on teachers will be felt very soon. In Saxony it is estimated that only 100,000 students will attend class in the year 2000 in comparison to the present 223,000. In the state of Brandenburg, 200 of the existing 650 elementary schools face the threat of closure ("Einfach Ruhe," *Der Spiegel* 25 [1996]).

4. As far as I know, there is no single study on the falling birthrate in East Germany.

5. This study was done on behalf of the Federal Ministry for the Family, Senior Citizens, Women and Youth ("Survey: Most Germans See Equality for Women as Far from Achieved," *Week in Germany,* May 10, 1996).

pursue both motherhood and work. At the same time, the gendered aspects of these state policies have hindered the emancipation of women (Dölling 1990; Schäfer 1990).

Nostalgia for the past is not confined to East German women. Nostalgia for the "feminist world" prior to unification has also developed among feminists in the Federal Republic. There is no doubt that economic distributional problems have increased with unity and that there has been a "backlash" against feminist gains made prior to 1990. The increasing participation of West German women in the post–World War II labor force has not been a success either. West German women before and after unification are still found at the bottom of the occupational hierarchy, in low-skilled and low-paid jobs. Looking back to 1989, the East German "happy revolution with political consequences" found a West German feminist movement that was more demoralized than energized by the politics of Bonn in the 1980s.

Despite the fact that feminists failed to influence the unification process, this defeat should not lead to political resignation. Instead, this historic moment offers feminists of East and West a chance to reflect on several theoretical aspects unification brought to the fore. The primary phenomenon accounting for the marginalization of women is the gendered opportunity structure of the state, with its exclusionary mechanisms adding up to double gender marginalization; the implications of this for postunification Germany will be discussed in a moment.

Secondary phenomena focused on possible shortcomings in the UFV itself also merit scrutiny. Was the UFV too state-centered in attempting to solve the "women's question"? What conception did East German feminists have of the state? Was it a conception looking backward to their own ideological socialist roots, grounded in teachings of how to conquer the bourgeois state, or was it a combination of looking backward for organizational guidance while at the same time being guided by Western feminism and its emphasis on autonomy? Stated differently, did East German feminists pursue strategies tied to the state system that clashed with their otherwise self-help-oriented and autonomous conceptions of gender politics? If so, did these contradictory strategies undermine the UFV's effectiveness? Moreover, what role did the conflict between movement politics and institutional politics play in the internal division of the UFV, and how can we account for the "communication problem" within the UFV?

The second issue concerns the tremendous animosity between the East and West German feminist movements that surfaced soon after the first euphoric meetings of November 1989. What role did this ideological conflict play in the "defeat" of a feminist agenda? Did the difficulties between East and West reduce the movements' effectiveness in launching a "common front" and speaking in a "common voice"? More important, what does this conflict tell us about feminist movement politics generally? Are these animosities specific to the East and West German movements? How do the different organizational structures of the East and West German movements, the action repertoire they used, the cultural frames they utilized to construct meaning, and the coalitions they made compare with feminist movements in other countries? Do both movements belong to what has been labeled by movement scholars as "new" movements, and what is specifically new about them?

In the remarks that follow three sets of issues will be addressed. First, I will provide an update and critical evaluation of the UFV and its feminist state vision and will discuss the nature of the internal conflicts of the feminist movement. Second, I will return to the question of the different Eastern and Western movements and derive some generalizations about their differences and about new social movements in general. Finally, I will address the issue of the double gender marginalization of the German state and derive some generalizations about the German state and feminist politics in the postunification era.

The UFV Today

Has the UFV degenerated into an empty "organizational shell," or does it continue to provide a "feminist political chance" (Hampele 1994)? If measured by organizational criteria such as membership numbers and institutional development, the evaluation tends to be rather negative. The UFV has lost a considerable number of its members. In Berlin alone the number of UFV members has decreased from a high point of over five hundred to below fifty.[6] As Zolberg (1972) has reminded us, however, a "period of total madness" also leaves lasting political accomplishments that are not immediately visible, including the "torrent of words" the feminist movement has spewed forth and dispersed throughout the GDR. These activities, in a country in which feminist discourse was prohibited, was surely a learning experience even for those GDR citizens who do not share a feminist perspective. Second, the many networks and informal acquaintances feminists have made during this period have left behind "alluvial deposits" that may generate new feminist growth in the future. By itself the involvement in feminist politics of a citizenry believed to be apolitical was an experience none of these feminists will ever forget.

---

6. The UFV does not provide an updated list of membership numbers. The information was given to me informally by UFV office staff in Berlin.

Third, the feminist visions and policy goals formulated in the *Social Charter* and the paper on "Creating Equality" were based on a political understanding of participatory democracy that existed neither in socialist systems nor in present-day liberal capitalist democracies. Feminists concluded that within the former socialist systems and the present liberal capitalist systems true gender equality is possible only at the margin. More substantive changes have eluded all feminist movements since the French Revolution. The intriguing aspect about the East German vision, despite its many flaws, was its conceptualization of an entirely new arrangement of state and civil society, however utopian, in which women and men are equal. Underlying this vision is a possibility for a world "in which gender should become less relevant and the abstractions of humanity more meaningful, through our actions as well as our words" (Phillips 1991: 7). In this sense the East German feminist vision may turn out a "successful miracle" necessary for the political transformation of German society (Zolberg 1972).

Despite the membership loss and the split of the East German women's movement, UFV presence continues to be felt at virtually all regional and local levels in a triple capacity. First, members of the UFV are represented politically in the federal parliament in Bonn,[7] many state parliaments, and city and county governments. Second, feminists continue to be active in the various local projects such as feminist bookstores, retraining opportunities, educational offerings, and many other such endeavors. Finally, UFV members continue to hold positions as gender equality officers at many public administrative levels, albeit with reduced political power. At the same time, the UFV has joined with other women's organizations in order to create umbrella organizations for various women's/feminist groups while retaining its status as an Independent Women's League.[8]

To provide a forum for communication the UFV has published an informative quarterly women's journal, *Weibblick,* since 1992, providing a regular exchange of information between women involved in projects and feminists in political offices, discussions on feminist theory and practice, as well as information on current national and regional activities and discus-

---

7. Christina Schenk (PDS) and Petra Bläss (PDS) are both UFV members. In fact, Schenk only changed to the PDS in the 1994 election. From 1990–94 she represented the UFV in the first all-German parliament.

8. For example, various women's groups in Saxony have united into the "Saxony Women's Forum," in which a representative of the UFV is the cashier, the chair is a member of the Round Table of Women, and the vice chair is from the League of Single Mothers and Fathers (Information from the Saxony Women's Forum, newsletter, no. 1 [1995]).

sions of future political actions. Feminists from both the East and West are represented in the pages of the *Weibblick* and share information.[9]

Anne Hampele (1994) insists that, despite its small membership, the UFV represents an innovation as a feminist association in the intermediate political arena; it links civil society and the state, "making politics" both as a protest movement and as an institutional actor. Hampele sees the political motor of local organizations in their initiating women's projects, mobilizing demonstrations, providing help in formulating state constitutions, writing laws on childcare centers, attending hearings and initiatives on labor market policies and states' women's equality laws, and organizing women's congresses.

The UFV has organized yearly congresses, which until 1993 remained largely restricted to the East. The 1993 UFV-Congress can be regarded as a watershed. It took place a week after the Constitutional Court's decree that the abortion compromise was unconstitutional. This congress was specifically organized as an East-West Women's Congress. The gathering was well attended by 350 participants from both sides of the former border; panels were composed of equal numbers of speakers from East and West Germany. The motto of the congress, "Against Individualization," expressed women's desire to draw attention to the increasing cutbacks in social programs, attacks on women's rights, as well as the need to resuscitate East-West feminist cooperation.

The UFV's intent was to turn the traditional East German Congress into an East-West affair (Maleck-Lewy 1993a). The congress also offered a chance for West German feminists to examine critically their own autonomous movement. The West German Ingrid Kurz-Scherf drew attention to the three weaknesses of the Western movement: "We have no program, no strategy, and no structure" (1993). Realizing the increasing political and economic marginalization of women in both parts of Germany, women passed a resolution to create a working forum to prepare a programmatic foundation for national feminist cooperation (*Frauenzusammenhang*) capable of political action. At the same time, it left open whether such feminist cooperation was to have the structure of a network, a stable, continuously working alliance, or even a political party (Maleck-Lewy 1993a; Hampele 1994a). The first meeting to establish all-German feminist cooperation was held in Kassel on June 23, 1993.

The immediate result of both the UFV-Congress and the meeting in Kassel was the preparation of a "women's strike" planned for International Women's Day, March 8, 1994. The idea of a women's strike was

9. Information printed in the *Weibblick* reveals a lively feminist political culture in the regions outside of Berlin from which one can infer that the East German feminist movement is more visible at the local than the national level.

simultaneously suggested by women in the West and East and was modeled after the successful strike of Swiss women in 1991 (Schindler 1993). The meeting in Kassel discussed the creation of a women's party at the Women's Day celebration in 1995. Both the women's strike in 1994 and the women's party in 1995 came to fruition. The strike urged women not to do housework, not to shop, not to go to work, not to smile, not to be nice, not to make coffee, and not to take care of children. With slogans such as "This is it," "We've had enough," and "We cancel the patriarchal consensus and start with a strike," women in the West and East organized a strike committee in Cologne/Bonn and at the UFV-Berlin headquarters (Strike Appeal, *Weibblick* 1993: 45–46).

The strike took place on March 8, 1994. It was not a centralized activity planned at the top from either Berlin or Cologne/Bonn. Instead, the strike activities were local affairs organized by community leaders, some labor unions, church women, and individually active women. The results of the strike were mixed. It demonstrated that women could still be mobilized. At the various decentralized strike activities several thousand women participated in the many public events, using transparencies and flyers to express their frustration over the increasing political and economic marginalization in the united Germany. Their energy was still visible at the first post-strike meeting evaluating the strike's effect (Hampele 1994).[10]

It was unclear, however, how much of this energy could be transferred into a stable mass of feminists willing to remain politically active. More important, the split between those who favored a feminist political party and those who preferred a national feminist action alliance (Feministisches Aktionsbündnis) once again showed the rift between those eager to pursue the institutionalization of movement politics and those who support grassroots networks. A follow-up meeting in Kassel in October 1994 decided to pursue a double strategy: create both a feminist political party and an informal alliance. For that purpose it established two working groups to draft rules and statutes for creating a party and a feminist action alliance. Despite these developments, the division of labor between the two organizations remains unclear.

Even more problematic is the continued split between Eastern and Western feminists. It cannot be overlooked that the last meeting in Kassel in October 1994 attracted mostly women from the West to plan the future activities of what was supposed to be an all-German endeavor. Hampele

---

10. The organizers of the strike, UFV-Berlin, Strike Committee Cologne/Bonn, and the women's foundation in the Greens: Frauenanstiftung e.V. Hamburg, published documentation of the strike, entitled *FrauenStreikTag 8. März '94* (Hamburg: Frauenanstiftung) in 1995.

suggested that, after the marathon political struggle of many East German feminists during the unification process, some seem to feel that "it is now time for those in the West to do the political work, we have done our share" (1994: 49; interview).

The UFV and Its Feminist State Vision

At a most fundamental level the UFV was a state-oriented political move-ment, not a cultural political movement. East German feminists put their trust in the state. The state was recognized as the major strategist for trans-forming relations in state and civil society. They saw the state as an instru-ment of male domination that could be conquered for feminist purposes. In their critique of the East German state feminists suggested that an elite group of males, tied together by their working-class background, their antifascist experience, and personal ties built either in the German con-centration camps or as "refugees" in the former Soviet Union, had con-quered the state in 1945 and maintained it until 1989. The state apparatus provided these males with important sources of political power and influence from which women were excluded. The obvious answer for the UFV was to wrest the power away from males and to conquer the state for itself. Once feminists had conquered the state, they could then create a gen-der-equal social system.

Feminists started with the proposition that they could rebuild on the ruins of the old state a totally new state structure that is neither socialist nor capitalist. In pursuing such a vision, they confronted a situation with-out historical parallels and without any theoretical guidance. The East German state simply "withered away." Marxist theories do not help in cre-ating a state on the ruins of a collapsed state. Karl Marx and his followers started from the assumption that there was a bourgeois state that had to be crushed. Even Marx was ambivalent about whether the state could be used as both "oppressor" of the working class and as an instrument for its lib-eration. In his writings on the class struggle in France, Marx does not take a clear position. In the *German Ideology,* on the other hand, Marx strongly denied that the (bourgeois) state could be used as an instrument for the lib-eration of the working class. Unfortunately, no Marxist has ever dealt with the theoretical question of how to wrest power from a socialist state.

Whether East German feminists were influenced by Marxist consider-ations of whether the state could be used simultaneously as oppressor and liberator is doubtful. The puzzling question remains why East German feminists were so state oriented. Is it the result of their socialist ideology, their experience in the GDR, or was it a tactical consideration to use the state as an instrument in this historic transformation process? I suggest that this state-centeredness is not unique to East German feminists and that it had to do with the feminists' personal experiences with the state under the GDR. Sam Barnes recently reported that the East Germans were the most state-centered of all the countries, based on a comparative study of East European countries. The situation is not that different in West Germany, where citizens are also inclined to defer to the state much more than Americans do (Thaysen, Davidson, and Livingston 1990). The reasons for the widespread East German state orientation may have as much to do with recent GDR history as it does with German history in general.

The second reason for the greater state-centeredness of East German feminists emerged from my interviews. Politically active women agreed that the only way to achieve "anything" in the former GDR was to go through the state. Many feminists had petitioned the state on behalf of the peace movement, lesbian causes, and environmental concerns and thus had contact with the state throughout the 1980s. The important aspect is not that political activists had contact with the state but that its response shaped their view of the state. The response may have come in the form of repression, denial of their petitions, delaying tactics, visits from state security personnel, granting petitions, and even changing existing laws, but what was important about state-individual relations was the responsiveness of the state. It created the "illusion" that the pressure of a small group of people could elicit a response from the state and even bring about political changes. This "cause-effect" relation between citizen groups and the state produced in the feminists a strong belief in the ability of the transformative power of the state (at least among the ones I interviewed). Thus, the feeling started to emerge that, "if only we could occupy these positions of power, we could transform the world!"

In their complaints about the West German state, East German feminists repeatedly mention the absence of a state response. From these non-responses a different East German feminist perception of the state emerges: "In the FRG everything is so far away. You are confronted with immense political and legal regulations without ever having the feeling of having any impact. In the GDR we at least got a response." Other interviews echo this feeling of distance from the West German state: "Everything illegal in the GDR is legal in the Federal Republic, but without any effect," and "citizens in the GDR were at least noticed even if it was only by the state security." Still others voiced frustration with the complexity of the German political system: "In the GDR it was not that complicated. New regulations were regularly published in the daily paper, *Neues Deutschland,* and with this information one could confront the authorities." Christine Schenk summarized her experience as a deputy within the all-German parliament and said: "The state in the FRG is like a rubber ball. You can stretch it, it will always return to its original position" (interview). These interviews show that it was not just GDR socialization or its socialist ideology that determined feminists' orientation toward the state. More important, it was their experience with the East German state and its responsiveness that shaped the feminists' inclination to view the state as an important "actor" in the transformation of social structures.

This state-centered feminist vision is nevertheless not without problems. East German feminists are not to be faulted for their failure to develop a feminist theory of the state. At the same time, their conception of the state is most wanting in its relations toward democracy. Althusser said the economy is "in the last instance" the determining factor in the political and ideological spheres. East German feminists have reversed the Althusserian notion and introduced a state-centered version of societal change that remains problematic, given German history with its "fetishization of the state" (Offe 1990).

Didn't East German feminists fall back upon the German legacy of conceptualizing a feminist vision that was state defined and state enforced and promulgated through constant "maternalistic" supervision, control, and education? How is this conception different from the present West German notion of democracy that Offe critiques as "often held to be a way of life, if not a state-defined and state-enforced *Weltanschauung* or 'constitutional culture' that must be promulgated through heavy doses of elite-supervised civic education" (1990: 249). The outcome of this West German state-centered conception of democracy is an inherent elitism and distrust of the citizenry. The East German feminists' notion of the state as a "motor" of societal change never addresses, however, the question of how to avoid domination. To speak with Agnes Heller

> if the state subsists, which type of state should it be, and which type of society should be related to this state? Where there is a state, there is power. If we are socialists, we have to consider the question: How is domination to be avoided? Where there is a state, there is no total freedom. Being socialists, we have to reconsider the question: How are human freedoms to be enlarged? Where there is a state, the public and private spheres can be unified only at the cost of tyranny. Whoever wants to avoid tyranny has to reconsider what kind of relations have to exist between state and society, the public and private sphere. If we cannot imagine a society expressing one homogeneous will, we have to assume the system of contracts which ensures that the will (and interests) of all has to be taken into consideration. Consequently, we have to presuppose democracy. (Heller 1988: 142)

That liberal democracy and the enfranchisement of women has not brought equality for women is hardly disputed today (Pateman 1988). Nevertheless, as Heller points out, socialists and feminists face a difficult task in formulating inclusive notions of democracy. Whether "gender" is an exclusionary category is a question beyond this analysis.

Although East German feminists never discussed how to achieve a feminist democratic socialist state, the conflict over this issue was not completely absent within the UFV. It was played out between those who adhered to an institutional and state-centered version of politics and those who adhered to a democratic, grassroots movement politics. The division between *Politikfrauen* and *Projektfrauen* was in the end a conflict about different notions of politics and different types of democracy.

The Internal Division within the UFV: *Politikfrauen* versus *Projektfrauen*

Officially, the UFV explains its rapidly diminishing membership by referring to factors external to the UFV. Because of the rapidly deteriorating economic situation, women are preoccupied with existential questions and have withdrawn into their private niches (interviews). With the increasing differentiation of demands, the few feminists remaining in the UFV are overstretched and overstressed. These two conditions reinforce each other. At one level this sounds quite plausible. Schäfer, however, rejects these externally induced assumptions—which she initially supported—and suggests that the problems are of an internal nature. Her thesis reflects the different conceptions of party versus movement politics. She argues that in the end the UFV pursued institutional politics that extracted compromises from the group at a cost that was too high for the UFV: "The UFV pursued goals at the expense of means. The separation between goals and means, form and content, political goals and individual path, led ultimately to the replacement of movement politics with the logic of party politics. In focusing on institutional politics the UFV substituted the male domination found in traditional parties with female domination in the ranks of the UFV" (Schäfer 1993: 19).

Feminist politics and the feminist self-conception of the UFV gave way, at least at the national level, to a fatal narrowing of the once open, pluralistic, and even erotic understanding of politics in the fall of 1989. The conflict within the UFV was not just reducible to a problem between institutional feminists and movement-oriented feminists. Rather, the erstwhile differentiation between these two factions led to devaluation and, consequently, to feelings of exclusion among feminists with a more grassroots, democratic, movement-oriented understanding of feminism. This conflict resulted finally in the "dissolution of the UFV as a political force" (interviews).

Projektfrauen felt that their interest in self-reflective processes to reach consensual decisions was sacrificed for the sake of political expediency; minority votes were no longer tolerated, and women used power as unreflectively as in any patriarchal society. These feelings of rejection of the grassroots, means-oriented movement led more feminists to desert the UFV. *Politikfrauen* responded that the speed of the political process was incompatible with the time frame for meeting the demands of the democratic grassroots feminists (Schenk 1993).

These different understandings of politics along with different political styles added further strain when the UFV raced from one election loss to the next. The UFV could not resolve the contradiction between the organizational demands for parliamentary representation at one level while remaining a grassroots movement without an institutional structure at another. The UFV hoped to do both, yet it succeeded at neither. Marginalizing one faction of the movement did not pay off in gains for the other. Electoral successes could not have stemmed the exodus of its grassroots support. Even if the UFV had won electorally, it could not have resolved the conflict without addressing the different conceptions of politics and their meaning for the UFV. That this debate within the UFV never took place has to do with interpersonal issues among the various members, which provides at least some answers about why intraorganizational rivalry reached such devastating heights.

The Communication Problem within the UFV

For an outsider to analyze the communication problems within the UFV is highly problematic. In the final analysis only those who "were there" and took part in the movement can provide the missing pieces. Because these issues are so personal, they are also the most difficult to bring to light. The following impressions remain tentative and are, of necessity, highly subjective.

Reference was made to three cross-cutting cleavages within the UFV. First, there were feminists who had been politically active within the Protestant Church. Second were academics who supported a reform-oriented socialism. Finally, there were feminists with a history of organizing at the local level and who came largely from regions outside of Berlin. Both academic and church women were articulate, good public speakers and willing to use institutional power. What separated academic from church feminists was their ideology. Many, though not all, academics were members of the SED and remained close to the PDS. This political biography contrasts with that of feminists organized in the church who were mostly involved in anti-SED actions and came from social-ethical traditions. The grassroots, movement-oriented feminists shared with the church members their distance from the SED/PDS, but they did not share the church feminists' easy relationship to institutional power. As a result of these cleavages, two major conflict lines divided the UFV. One was the previously discussed division between institutional power politics and grassroots politics, and the other was between those open to the PDS and those who rejected it. These conflict lines were there from the start of the UFV, but they worsened as feminists were unable and/or unwilling to discuss them.

In virtually every interview feminists referred to these conflicts within the UFV and their frustration about not being able to intervene and address them openly. Despite the increasing exodus first of feminist theologians and then of grassroots feminists (such as the Autonome Brennessel from Erfurt), this feminist bloodletting was accepted within the UFV without any discussion. Even when one of their most prominent founders and most articulate speakers, Ina Merkel, left in the spring of 1990, no internal soul-searching followed. Despite several interviews with Ina Merkel and other members of the UFV, it is unclear why she left the movement that so heavily bore her imprint. Why did Ina Merkel leave, and why did her departure not lead to an internal discussion and reflection about the future of the UFV?

There are several obvious explanations for the reluctance of the UFV to confront the internal divisions (the less obvious have to be provided by the members themselves). First is the much noted tendency among East Germans to avoid conflict.[11] The notion of a "debating culture" (*Streitkultur*), which has become such a prominent part of West German political culture, did not exist in the GDR. In a comparative profile of East and West Germans *Der Spiegel* reported that, even after five years of unification, East Germans continue to have more difficulty with open disagreements and confronting people they know.[12] This habit of conflict avoidance was sufficiently internalized by feminists that they were reluctant and unaccustomed to raising conflicts in open group situations (Penrose 1994).

Second, some interviewees were afraid of being branded "emotional" if they critiqued internal group dynamics. Like the political culture in the West, political discourse in the former GDR was based on a "rational logic," which elevated an objective rationality over subjective rhetoric

---

11. For a very interesting psychological profile of the East German psyche and how people have coped with unification, see Maaz 1990; 1991.

12. "Vor den Kopf geschlagen," *Der Spiegel* 29 (1995): 50–53.

(Kulke 1994). Feminists feared that, had they spoken up and criticized the "atmosphere surrounding how issues were discussed," they would have been reprimanded for raising "sensitivity issues" that had nothing to do with the larger political issue of how to win elections.

GDR socialization is once again an important guide to understanding this tendency not to speak up. The needs of the collectivity had priority over the subjective feelings of individuals: it was not the personal that counted but the political. In this regard feminists demonstrated the impact of GDR society in which collective goals ranked above individual subjectivity.

The most difficult division in the UFV stemmed from an inability to confront its own past. There were women who collaborated with the state security, whose husbands were high-ranking state security officers, others who ventured into the open and "confessed" their complicity (*Mittäterschaft*) with the SED regime, and still others who felt best served by a denial strategy. The silence around the question of the Stasi not only led to damaging distrust within the UFV, but many other issues were mediated through this suspicious climate of the Stasi. Suspecting—yet not knowing—produced an aggressive undercurrent that was often visible in personal interactions.

Attending some of the UFV meetings, I remember less about the programmatic points being raised; instead, I wrote in my notes about the "inability to communicate, long silences, little interaction, many isolated group fights, no response to the previous speaker, no eye contact, hostile body language expressed in moving the body away from the speaker, and the physical movement of chairs supposedly in response to the issues discussed." It was years later that I received some written documents about the UFV Congress in Leipzig in 1991 in which the Stasi discussion was finally aired in (what seemed to be) an unbelievably hostile environment. Reading today about the UFV's petition to exclude one member because of "serious and deliberate violations against the statute of the UFV" reminded me of what I had envisioned to be the language and political style of an SED functionary. The ironic thing was that it was the person who raised the accusations against a UFV member's supposed knowledge of her husband's complicity with the Stasi who was to be barred from the UFV and not the perpetrator against whom the accusations were launched.

This inability to deal with the future because of their past was also a problem that UFV members faced in interacting with politically active women from other East German opposition groups. Women activists who had been members of the New Forum, Democracy Now, Initiative for Peace and Human Rights, and Democratic Awakening and who had represented citizen groups at the Central Round Table had virtually no interaction with members of the UFV. Members of the opposition groups drew a rather sharp line between women who had been working in opposition to the SED in the 1980s and those who did not have this history. The UFV was not only perceived as "leftist-feminist"; it was also perceived as near to the PDS. This was not the case, however, in the beginning. As pointed out, the initial coming together on December 3, 1989, in the Volksbühne was a pluralistic and rather heterogeneous grouping of women from many walks of life, political orientations, lifestyles, and regions, encompassing even rural feminists. That the UFV became very Berlin-concentrated and heavily PDS-oriented resulted from its inability to deal with the internal cleavages, thereby sacrificing its development into a pluralistic and democratic political culture.

This critique of the UFV does not detract from its considerable achievements in creating an organizational structure and in its multiple attempts to gain access to both the political arena in East Germany and the policy-making process of unification negotiations. However remarkable its political engagement, the UFV made mistakes that should not be brushed aside only because it emerged as the "loser" of German unification. Equally important is why such animosity developed between the feminist movements in the East and the West and what these two feminist movements tell about new social movements in general, a topic that will be discussed next.

The Sisters Who Are Not a "Volk of Sisters"

The sisters who met for the first time in 1989 encountered one another as strangers. They shared a common German legacy, but even this legacy turned out to be different for the two movements. In the end being socialized into an East German socialist system and into a West German social market economy was more important for their identity than being feminists and being all-German. That one movement grew up in the shadows of an authoritarian state, in which the "public life was not public" (Bohley interview) and in which women together with men struggled against the state, and the other emerged repudiating the conservative notion of the West German ideal of women and the New Left's antifeminism shaped the very identity of the two feminist movements. They did not share the experience of having to conform either to the ideals of "worker-mother" or "wife-mother." The differences in their organizational structure (relying on formal mass organization versus informal "networks of networks"); framing of discourse (anti-male or pro-male); meanings of politics (institutionalization or anti-institutionalization); action repertoires to mobilize collective action; and alliance structures with other social forces result from the opportunity structures of the various state systems. That the West German feminists' identity was, and continues to be, anti-male and anti-state was the result of repressive and exclusionary state structures toward feminists' goals and the conservative political culture that has been part of the all-German historical legacy that reemerged after World War II. The formation of the "autonomous feminist movement" in the West is a response not only to an opportunity structure closed to issues that cut across class cleavages (Kitschelt 1985) but also to the gendered opportunity structure of the German "state in its inclusive sense." The inability to gain access to traditional party structures and the lack of coalition partners in the political parties, labor unions, and administrative structures has led to the creation of a "countersociety" independent of the established political structures. The feminist identity autonomous from males and the state constituted a new politics of organization that relies on networks of networks. These informal groups are linked through various levels of political and project networks providing a system of communication and information that challenges the organizational structures of traditional institutions.

West German feminists' insistence on an identity autonomous from the state is based on the belief that change cannot come through the institutions of the state. Only political activities outside the state, feminists argued, promised a challenge to the "family-, work-, and consumption-centered orientation" of the German post–World War II paradigm (Kulawik 1991–92).

The formation of an autonomous movement has to be understood as a political strategy of German feminists. This aspect is missed by new social movement scholars. Invariably, the German feminist movement is identified as a cultural movement with an expressive logic of action that corresponds to identity-oriented strategy. In dividing movements into power-oriented and identity-oriented movements, the political aspects of creating alternative lifestyles and different cultural codes are missed (Melucci 1989; Kaase 1990; Rucht 1990). Absent from such discussions are the gendered opportunity structures of the state. Although the German state is exclusionary to virtually all social movements, specific institutional mechanisms exist that are antithetical to feminists' concerns. Focusing simply on the general and specific strategies of movements and differentiating them according to "culture" and "power" misses the relational aspect between state structures and movement strategies. Feminists have created a countersociety outside the paradigm of old politics because the state structures were not accessible to feminists. Creating their own identity in separate spaces is thus not a cultural act but a highly political one.

Only by analyzing the opportunity structure of national regimes can we understand why the West German feminist movement is not a women's rights movement as is the case in the United States. American feminists were able to frame their grievances in a rights discourse that found cultural resonance in the larger American political environment. In their struggle for equal rights American feminists were able to draw upon an alliance system in the Democratic Party, the bureaucracies, and other social movements (Katzenstein 1987). West German feminists did not have political allies, until the Greens entered parliament in the early 1980s, nor was a rights discourse part of the toolchest of the German constitutional order. The more accessible political opportunity structure of the American state system shaped an American movement concerned with women's equality. In contrast, the German feminists' core value is "self-determination" and not equality.

In rejecting equality as a way to achieve social change, the autonomous feminist movement should be seen as a "cultural revolutionary women's emancipation movement" that goes beyond the single issue of women's rights (Brand 1986). The German feminist movement is emancipatory in a revolutionary sense in that the organization and the division of labor within capitalism is seen as a structure of domination. Women's social position is determined by its location as sexually oppressed, unpaid housewives in the capitalist division of labor. Only a transformation in the capitalist division of labor and the creation of an alternative economy based on solidarity is seen as an answer to the discrimination feminists face in the West German social market economy.

A women's rights discourse is not completely absent in West Germany. Women's rights activists are found within the traditional structures of the Social Democratic Party, the liberals, increasingly also in the CDU, and even in labor unions. These women's activists are not organized into women's lobby organizations to gain influence in state institutions, as is the case in the United States. The German women's rights activists, who increasingly also identify themselves as feminists, are individual activists who are situated within traditional institutions and—depending on the issues—are able to mobilize other women's rights activists and sometimes even the autonomous feminist movement for particular actions. Yet there are no permanent institutional structures that provide a "bridge" between the women's rights activists and the feminists. A first bridging action has emerged between the Green Party and the autonomous feminist movement due to their overlapping membership. Nevertheless, women's rights activists in the parties and the unions have become important, albeit only partial, allies for the autonomous feminist movement.

Given this complex differentiation between the autonomous feminist movement and the women's rights movement in West Germany, the picture becomes even more complicated in trying to identify the East German feminist movement. Is it a new social movement, and, if so, what is new about it? Social movement scholars have emphasized that in contrast to "old" politics, the novelty of new social movements is that the working class is no longer the actor, legal/political equality or economic demands are no longer central to their concerns, and their organizational forms are more informal and egalitarian than those in previous movements (Mayer 1991a). Feminist movements share with other new social movements (environmental, urban social, peace and disarmament, animal rights, squatter, and human rights and gay movements) a concept of politics broadened to include issues, spaces, and forms that previously belonged to the nonpolitical spheres of social life (Barnes et al. 1979; Kitschelt 1985; 1986; Dalton and Kuechler 1990; Roth 1991; 1994; Tarrow 1991). New social movements share an assumption that "the conflicts and contradictions of advanced industrial society can no longer be resolved in meaningful and promising ways through etatism, political regulation, and the proliferating inclusion of ever more claims and issues on the agenda of bureaucratic authorities" (Offe 1985: 819). As a result, the newness of these groups involves everything from an ideological rejection of "old politics" to an emphasis on the different political origins, structure, style, and goals of such movements (Dalton and Kuechler 1990). Moreover, the designation of "new" in these new social movements is justified "to the extent that they persist outside the universe of 'old' political parties and their electoral politics" and thus redefine the "boundaries of institutional politics" (Offe 1990: 232; 1987).

At the same time, Kontos has reminded us that the West German feminist movement is at one and the same time a new and old movement. The autonomous movement shares with new social movements many informal organizational aspects and different concept of politics. Yet they share the concerns of the old movement and struggle for distributional issues, economic equality, and reproductive rights—concerns that are part of the modern tradition of the nineteenth century. Issues of equality and the right to self-determination stretch from the first women's movement to the movement that emerged in the 1970s (Kontos 1986). As the criteria for new social movements do not completely fit the West German autonomous feminists, neither do they fit the East German movement. We find a hybrid form that, nevertheless, differs from that in the West. Aspects belonging to old politics include the East Germans' emphasis on state centeredness, large, formal, mass organizational structure with a program and statute, emphasis on economic and legal equality, belief in political regulation of social norms, and institutional strategy. At the same time, the East

German feminist movement shares with other new social movements its emphasis on a democratic, grassroots politics; an emphasis on emancipatory politics that goes beyond traditional party politics; unconventional strategies including demonstrations, rallies, marches, petitions, provocations, working projects; adhering to nontraditional gender roles; framing demands in an egalitarian rights discourse; and relying on interpersonal solidarity for movement mobilization. As a result, both institutionalized and uninstitutionalized ways characterize the strategies of the East German feminist movement to change the social order.[13]

Given this hybrid nature of the East German feminist movement, it may be best described as a "state revolutionary women's emancipation movement," in contrast to the West German "cultural revolutionary women's emancipation movement." Unlike the autonomous movement in the West, the Eastern feminists have been much less concerned with questions of subjectivity and body politics. The politics of subjectivity is expressed in "the personal is political," a slogan through which Western feminists called attention to the family as a gendered political space that is reproduced through state regulation. Given their economic independence from the family and the male, East German feminists have focused on revolutionary changes at the national political level in which the state was seen as the instrument of social transformation.

Frigga Haug (1990) referred to the disparities between the two movements as an "unevenness," or, as I categorized it, a "temporal asymmetry" (Young 1994). Not only did the histories of the two movements develop in spatially separated arenas; the movements also differed in their timing. The East German state-centered movement is embedded within the precepts of modernity. Its belief in the universal principles of equality and justice for both sexes, the reliance on large national organizations to achieve social and political changes, its collectivist orientation toward the national state as the guarantor of universal precepts of the enlightenment, and its visions of a "leftist-feminist" ideology have much in common with the movements of the early twentieth century. East German feminists set out to complete the "bisected modernity" that "withheld the universal principles of modernity—individual freedom and equality—from one gender at the time of birth and allocated it only to one sex" (Beck and Beck-Gernsheim 1990). In a very real sense the East German feminist project was to complete the process of modernity.

Here we find the most fundamental difference between the East and West German movements. The autonomous movement no longer believes

---

13. Kuechler and Dalton argue that "the term 'social movement' should be restricted to collective actors trying to change the given social order in uninstitutionalized ways" (Kuechler and Dalton 1990: 279).

that the bureaucratic state structures can solve the contradictions of advanced industrial capitalism through political regulation. Thus, West German feminism is foremost a "critique of modernization" (Brand et al., 1986; Mayer 1991c) embedded within the general social critique of the 1968 student movement. In contrast, the East German movement is best described as a type of "humanistic" feminism, with an emancipatory vision of a universal humanity for both women and men. This aspect of universal emancipation is completely absent in the autonomous feminist conception of social change.

It may well be that the "absence of 1968" in the East is the most crucial moment in differentiating the Eastern and Western feminist movements, since the West German feminist movement is an outgrowth of the student revolutionary period of 1968, with its rejection of an authoritarian state and male political culture and the emphasis on building a counterculture.

Comparing the temporal asymmetries shaped by the different opportunity structures of the two political regimes, it should not come as a surprise that, instead of creating a "common front" against the existing male political class, feminists met one another with distrust and misunderstanding during the unification negotiations. Feminists in the East reacted with skepticism to the initial curiosity and (even) sympathy West German feminists showed for the UFV, barring them from joining the East German organization and from speaking at some of the UFV congresses. While the reasons for the exclusion of the West German feminists may have been quite legitimate in that the UFV did not want to import the horrendous conflictual and separatist tendencies of the West German autonomous feminist movement and were eager to shield themselves from the Western habit of "knowing everything better" (*Besserwisserei*), the end result was that the UFV remained a closed East German phenomenon. Once the UFV did decide to become an all-German feminist organization it had lost its political importance, and the interest of West German feminists in the UFV declined accordingly (Hampele 1992).

Feminists in neither the East nor West have to this day been able to find common ground on questions such as their relations to the state and to men, organizational structure, political strategies, and how to formulate feminists goals for a united Germany.

The German State and Feminist Politics

Although the problems inherent within the UFV and the antagonism between East and West German movements are phenomena that may have contributed to the marginalization of feminists during the unification negotiations, nevertheless they are secondary. The primary reasons why not only the East and West German feminists but also the institutional feminists at the center of political power in West Germany were marginalized during the unification process are the specific exclusionary mechanisms found in the West German state structures and the corporatist institutions.

Utilizing a statist analysis of political opportunity structures has the advantage of discovering the effects of institutional constraints on the dynamics of feminist movement development. Access to the political sphere is dependent not only on the resources movements can extract from their environment and utilize for protest activities. Equally important is the movements' access to the public sphere and political decision making, which is governed by institutional rules encompassing specific patterns of interaction between interest groups, political parties, state agencies, and social movements (Kitschelt 1990).

Focusing on the extent to which national regimes impact on the resource development of movements, the extent to which social movements can gain access to the decision-making arenas, and, finally, the extent to which institutions can block such collective action suggests that there is a gender bias of the German state that makes its structures and corporatist institutions less amenable to feminist participation and political agendas. The double gender marginalization refers to formal and informal institutional and cultural exclusionary mechanisms that have acted both as "gatekeepers of legislation" and "gatekeepers of discursive practices" inherent in both the "parliamentary group state" and the system of corporatist interest intermediation.

Several conclusions follow from this finding. First, the exclusionary mechanisms that marginalized feminists during the unification process are not unique to the singular event of unification. Double gender marginalization is inherent in German state structures and has made feminist inroads a daunting experience in Germany. Unification has provided a snapshot of a "concentrated moment" that showed the full force of the bias of the German state toward feminist goals. The focus on the particular event of unification as a case study should not detract from the general insights it provides about the German state system and feminist politics.

Second, that the German state is biased against a feminist agenda does not mean that the state is altogether immune to the demands of feminists and women. For example, Article 3, Paragraph 2, of the German Basic Law was amended in 1993 in the Joint Constitutional Commission of the united Bundestag and Bundesrat, which had been charged in Article 5 of the Unification Treaty with deciding "whether and what constitutional amendments and alterations might be necessary after Germany's unification" (Thaysen 1993).[14] Article 3, Paragraph 2, reads now: "The state promotes the actual achievement of equality of women and men and works toward the removal of existing disadvantages." At the same time, the Joint Commission refused to alter Article 6 of the Basic Law, which continues to privilege marriage, particularly in the tax code, at the expense of the protection of families and children (Limbach 1991). Thus, while Article 3, Paragraph 2, extends the rights of women in the Basic Law, Article 6 continues to privilege the institution of marriage and works against the rights of women (Berghahn 1993b).

Women also achieved a major victory on marital rape legislation. After a twenty-five-year battle the German parliament in June 1997 officially made marital rape a crime. The new law removes much of the legal distinction between sexual violence within and outside marriage and imposes a minimum sentence of two years' imprisonment for both. Under this new law homosexual rapes are also covered.[15]

In addition, virtually all political parties have either enacted a quota system or are in the process of discussing one. Even Helmut Kohl has now become a convert and has supported a quota system in the CDU. In a vote of 609 to 297, delegates to the party's annual conference in Hannover in October 1996 agreed to reserve a minimum of one-third of party offices and parliamentary seats for women during the next five years.[16]

Even the Federal Constitutional Court, in particular the more liberal First Senate, has promulgated some progressive legislation extending the legal rights of women. In 1991 the court ruled against the "casting vote" (*Stichentscheid*) requiring a woman to take her husband's name upon marriage. Moreover, the First Senate declared in January 1992 the prohibition of night work for women incompatible with existing discrimination laws. Finally, in 1993 the First Senate strengthened the antidiscrimination laws in regard to women entering male professions (Berghahn and Wilde 1996).

These improvements for women do not detract from the general argument made that the center of German power is inaccessible and antithetical to feminist concerns. There is an inaccessible kernel around the very structure of German power, despite its "edges" becoming more open to the entrance of women into power positions. The German state can be

---

14. The commission consisted of sixty-four members of the Bundesrat and Bundestag (thirty-two of each house); twelve women were seated at the constitutive meeting on January 16, 1992, falling quite short of the 20.5 percent represented in the united German parliament (Limbach and Eckertz-Höfer 1993).

15. "Ehe: Vergewaltigung strafbar," *Das Parlament,* June 6, 1997; "Bundestag Approves Marital Rape Legislation," *Week in Germany,* May 17, 1996.

16. "CDU Adopts Quota System for Women within the Party, Back Tax Reform," *Week in Germany,* October 25, 1996.

compared metaphorically to an "apricot." Despite the soft and fleshy outside contours of the state structures that have opened the doors to large numbers of female deputies during the 1980s and have feminized the state, the power of the state has contracted inward into the parliamentary groups, the party *Stammtisch,* or the corporatist institutions, becoming, once again, exclusive of women's interests. This resistance to the institutionalization of feminists' demands continues to operate in the postunification German political system and confronts women with a largely closed gendered opportunity structure of the state.

CHAPTER 6

Democratization without Women: Comparisons to Other Eastern European Countries

Women and the Collapse of Socialism across Eastern Europe

The economic and political marginalization of East German women in the postcommunist transition has much in common with the position of women in other Eastern and Central European countries. Feminist scholars seem to agree that the introduction of liberal democracy and a free market economy in the former socialist countries (Poland, the Czech Republic, Slovakia, Bulgaria, Hungary, Rumania, Russia) did not usher in equal opportunities for women in the political arena or the economic sphere. Studies show that women face growing discrimination in the labor market, are the first to be fired and the last to be hired, experience more frequent and longer periods of unemployment, suffer from deteriorating social services and legal protection, experience the loss of identity as both workers and mothers, are virtually absent in the newly formed political institutions, face opposition to their reproductive rights, are subject to more physical and sexual violence, and witness an increasing commercialization and exploitation of the female body (Cviková 1993; Einhorn 1993; Posadskaya 1993; Sabadykina 1993; Wagnerová 1993; Rueschemeyer 1994; Siemienska 1994).

The marginalization of women in the former East European countries is all the more surprising given that the socialist systems did "release women in a tired, but not altogether in a bad shape" (Wagnerová 1993: 108). Under the socialist regime women did achieve high levels of educational standards and professional training, became economically independent, and attained a social status independent of men. By the late 1980s the educational level of younger women frequently surpassed that of males of their generation. This relatively high level of achieved equality across East-

ern Europe did little to help women gain representation in the newly
formed political institutions. In virtually no former Eastern European
country is the number of women deputies in the national parliaments
higher than 5 percent. The newly formed Czech Republic has, after its separation from Slovakia, the unique European distinction of not having a
single woman deputy in the national parliament. The political absence of
Czech women in the postsocialist era is all the more surprising given the
role they played in the opposition group "Charta 77." Eleven women
(nearly 29 percent) were speakers, out of a total of thirty-eight. The path
of the two sexes parted radically, however, after the "velvet revolution"
was over. Many males became ministers, and Václav Havel became president. In contrast, the former Czech women activists remain politically
absent in the postsocialist regime (Wagnerová 1993: 107).

Women across Eastern Europe share another common experience.
The "women's question" is no longer of interest to the postsocialist political class. Building a liberal democracy based on a "fraternal social contract" (Pateman 1989) and a free market economy has priority over the
women's question. If women figure in political debates, then they appear
as "spoilers." Leaders of many conservative and even social democratic
parties, and in particular the Catholic Church in Poland, have quite vocif-
erously suggested that women are, at least partially, to "blame" for the
scarcity of jobs and the present high unemployment rate. If women would
only return to the traditional role of staying home and tending the "nest,"
so the argument goes, the problems of high unemployment and the
demands for social services would decline. This would have a double
effect: it would take pressure off the labor market and ease the strain on
the Treasury.

Suggesting that women should return to the home is made in spite of
the overwhelming rejection by women of such a gendered "crisis solution."
Even in traditionally Catholic Polish society 35 percent of male and female
respondents rejected the model of women staying home in 1991 (Siemienska 1994). In East Germany the "emancipatory tendency" to stay in the
labor market has even increased between 1991 and 1997. According to the
latest report released by the Federal Statistical Office, the number of
women expressing any desire to "return to the kitchen" has decreased
from 33 percent in 1991 to 26 percent in 1997. This result shows that a
hefty 74 percent of East German women remain committed to their role as
"workers."[1] Despite the Federal Republic's hope that East German

---

1. The response between East Germany and Poland cannot be compared directly. The
Polish figures represent a nationwide sample of adults (over sixteen years), whereas the East
German figure refers to women only.

women would eventually accept the role of the West German "wife-mother" model, there is little indication that this is the case. Whereas only 26 percent of East German women want to return to the "hearth," the number of West German women endorsing the traditional separation between women and men remains at a high of 47 percent (*Die Tageszeitung,* May 23, 1997). Whether such comparisons between East and West support Alexandra Kolontay's vision of socialism's ability to create a "new woman" is a question that can only be answered in due time.

The East German Anomaly

At first glance there is sufficient evidence to suggest that many, albeit by far not all, women in both Eastern Europe and East Germany share a similar fate in being marginalized during the transition from planned economies to liberal democracies. This finding, however, is not altogether new nor theoretically all that interesting. Numerous studies already exist demonstrating the negative impact that the introduction of a free market economy had on many Eastern and Central European women. Moreover, there are plenty of historical instances when women activists took center stage at the revolutionary pinnacle only to be pushed back into oblivion when there was a return to "normal" politics.

The more interesting theoretical question is to isolate the specific formal and informal institutional and cultural mechanisms across the newly emerging liberal democracies that are antithetical to women's participation and concerns. If we take an institutional perspective as the starting point for understanding how specific gender regimes have operated in particular countries in shaping a gendered political opportunity structure, then we are able to go beyond the mere cataloguing of negative effects and come to understand the particular "gender biases" that characterize different political and social systems.

Focusing on an institutional perspective provides a theoretical compass to discover that, despite many commonalities women share across Eastern Europe, the East German case remains an anomaly in its transition to a liberal democratic system. No other Eastern European country had even the option of being integrated into an already existing highly efficient political and economic system. The entire state was simply absorbed by its wealthy cousin, its institutions were dismantled, and the West German system was placed in toto upon the rubble of the old East German centralized state. Other Eastern European countries were forced through trial and error to lay first the foundation for the legal and bureaucratic infrastructure on which the emerging liberal democratic social and economic systems were to be based. The East German experience is not only a singular event in modern history. It had a profound effect on how a preexisting West German gender order was reproduced in the East.

This transference of a preexisting gender order is simply neglected by traditional narratives of German unification. Mainstream political science focuses on a vast array of macropolitics and micropractices; they are constituted by men and in male-gendered terms. None of these accounts provide a formal and operational opening that makes women visible and permits their greater participation in the polity. They emphasize only political and bureaucratic dynamics and proceed to describe these processes as if they are inevitably gender neutral.

My starting point is to render visible what is now omitted from the narrative. I start with the assumption that gender operates as an "usherette" in reproducing particular gender orders that differ depending on the spatial and temporal location of analysis. Such an assumption postulates that all social systems are based on different "regimes of gender orders." Thus, "political regimes" are not just distinguished along a continuum of "open opportunity structures" and "closed opportunity structures," as the social movement literature suggests, but also along different regimes of gender. These gender orders or regimes operate in both structuring the social process and reproducing the symbolic order of every social system. A gendered operating framework rests on the assumption that regimes of gender orders are a functional requisite through which concrete individuals are reproduced and integrated into a given social order (Benhabib 1989). Important for our analysis is that processes of political and economic integration and transformation are always gender specific.

The different ways of transition to liberal democratic systems in Eastern Europe—either by transferring an entire set of existing institutions or creating new entities on the rubble of the old—provide the empirical arena for hypothesis testing. The question is not to look for winners and losers. Winners are surely also to be found among the many highly educated, mobile, single, younger women in both the former GDR and in Eastern Europe. Rather, the purpose of comparative work should focus on the relationship between movement development and the particular state structures. By delineating the gendered opportunity structures of the different states in the former Eastern European countries and their impacts on the formation and development of the women's movements, we can come closer to understanding the marginalization of women during the transition process.

The present study focusing on the particular integration of East German women into an already existing West German gendered political order is a first step in showing the specificity of the German regime of gender order and its operational codes that are an immanent part of the West German state structures and the system of corporatist interest intermediation. Only when we have comparative data from other Eastern European countries and their specific operational codes of gender regimes will we be able to understand more fully the process of marginalization of women after the collapse of socialism.

Appendix

Acquisition of Information

I gathered information for this book from several different sources. First, I conducted thirty-five open-ended, two- to three-hour interviews with a wide variety of feminists and women political activists mainly from East Germany but also with some West German activists (see Interviews below). I also interviewed two men from East Germany and one from West Germany who provided important additional information. Ten interviewees were interviewed at least twice, sometimes as many as four times, to check irregularities in information I received from other sources. The additional interviews also enabled me to compare statements across time. The interviews were done between 1990 and 1995.

I interviewed the founding mothers of the UFV; several spokeswomen for the UFV; a West Berlin feminist who belonged to the inner circles of the UFV[1] and who eventually wrote her dissertation on the UFV;[2] lesbian UFV members and political activists in the UFV; members of the Central Round Table in Berlin and members of the "Women, Political Round Table" in Berlin; a UFV cabinet member in the transition government of Hans Modrow; the equality officer in the Government of Lothar de Maizière; the founder of Women for Peace, cofounder of Initiative for Peace and Human Rights, and cofounder of the New Forum; a UFV deputy in the Bonn Bundestag; a feminist PDS deputy in the Bonn Bundestag; the West German science minister in the Senate of Berlin, who oversaw the restructuring process of the East German university system; the press secretary to the deputy mayor of Berlin and minister for work and women; West German feminist lawyers who wrote extensively about

---

1. The initial UFV statute barred West German feminists from joining the UFV except if their place of residence was in the East.

2. Anne Hampele's book-length manuscript on the UFV is the only in-depth study of the East German feminist movement that has been written up to now.

the abortion issues; and two feminist journalists from East and West Germany who collaborated on an East-West project interviewing thirty feminist activists between 1992 and March 1993.[3] In addition, I interviewed cofounders of feminists groups such as SOFI; Lila Offensive, and cofounders of the feminist group LISA within the PDS. I also interviewed a member of the public labor union Öffentliche Dienste, Transport und Verkehr (ÖTV) in Leipzig, who was involved in the closing of daycare centers and who provided some numbers on the administrative restructuring process in Leipzig and its effect on women public employees. I also interviewed the chair of the works council of the Leipzig Cotton Spinning Mills, a large regional employer of women that was in the process of being privatized. I interviewed some of the most prominent East German feminist academics who in the 1980s prepared the "groundswell" for the feminist activities of 1989 as well as affirmative action officers at East German and West German universities and members of university women's groups.

I also interviewed two East German men and one West German. One is now the chief editor and founder of the very respected East German social science journal *Berliner Debatte* and was one of the most important philosophical leaders of the project group Conception of a Modern Socialism in the 1980s. Another is an East German writer and historian. Finally, I interviewed a West German political scientist, Uwe Thaysen, who was the only West German present at all sixteen meetings of the Central Round Table in Berlin and who was permitted to make stenographic reports, which he is in the process of preparing for publication.

In addition, I conducted five interview sessions with groups of women from the East and West gathered for an evening or afternoon. After a question period a free-flowing discussion followed among the members of the group. These group discussions took place with the West Berlin Women's League; West Berlin Women for Peace; East German women faculty members at the Textile and Art College, Burg Giebichstein, Halle; a large group of East German women peace activists and church women at the Women's Center in Erfurt over an entire weekend; and political activists from the feminist group LISA within the PDS-Leipzig.

Before I discuss the interviewing method, it is important to realize that many women wore many of the same "hats." Thus, there were feminists who were UFV members as well as lesbians who worked at the Central Round Table in Berlin and at the Women's Political Round

---

3. This book, *Von Muttis und Emanzen, Feministinnen in Ost- und Westdeutschland,* was published in 1995 (Helwerth and Schwarz 1995).

Table and who then became party deputies in Bonn. Others started in the women's group Lila Offensive and then shifted to the UFV. Still others belonged to the SED, founded the feminist group LISA within the PDS, and then joined the UFV. Others entered the Bundestag as UFV deputies and then switched to the PDS. Some publicly admitted their collaboration with the state security Stasi and then became feminist grassroots activists. Some never officially admitted to being "informers" for the Stasi but were "relieved" of their positions. Others had family members involved in the state security apparatus. And, finally, some were leading UFV spokeswomen in the fall of 1989 and subsequently left the movement disenchanted.

Given the variety of experience of these feminists/women activists, I did not standardize the interviews. I did, however, ask all activists some variants of questions such as: What was their role in the opposition groups in the 1980s? Did they understand themselves as feminists, and what did that mean? How did East German feminism differ from that in the West? Were they active in the demonstrations during the period of "total madness"? Were they present at the founding of the UFV, and what role did they play in the organization? Did they endorse a feminist vision for the GDR, what did that entail, and how could it be implemented? In addition, I asked a host of questions about the electoral defeat of the citizen groups in March 1990: their attitudes toward German unification and toward a liberal market economy; their political participation in electoral politics; their insights into why feminists were marginalized during the unification process; the organizational and personality problems within the UFV; the reasons for the "cooling off" toward their respective sisters in the West. I structured some questions around their economic situation, whether they expected changes as a result of unification, about the impact unification had on women in the labor market, and why it was so difficult to organize East German women in spite of their deteriorating economic and social situation. And, finally, I asked them what future did they see for feminists in the East and the West, and what would the role be of the UFV in the postunification era?

Some interviews were targeted to attain specific information, in particular, from feminists who were members of the Bundestag and who were involved in the abortion debates or from women who served in the cabinet and governments in East Germany or who created the Women's Round Tables in Berlin or who were involved in local project groups or who ran for political office or who were involved in party candidate selection processes. An issue that always surfaced was the experience of well-known public feminists with the media.

I make no claim that the interviews are representative.[4] Selection of the interviewees was random and nonscientific, but one criterion was whether women, as feminists, were politically active and identified with the goals of the UFV. Interviewees were selected depending on their media "visibility," my ability to locate them, and their willingness to be interviewed. Often feminists were visible at one moment and were gone the next. One of the key activists at the Central Round Table whom I tried to locate got married, changed her name, moved to the West, and in the process supposedly destroyed the private documents she had collected as a participant at the Central Round Table.[5]

Despite the much-derided German habit of record keeping, feminists created their own experiences without much attention to records. For example, the exact number of East German (and some West German) feminist activists participating at their most exhilarating moment of creating the UFV, on December 3, will never be known. Only months later did the UFV try to reconstruct a rather incomplete sociological profile of the presumed attendees (Hampele 1996). Given the circumstances surrounding moments of political exhilaration, perhaps the "rigorous research procedures" advocated by political scientists are impossible to meet (Meier 1995). It is no wonder that "moments of madness have had a very bad press in the social sciences" (Zolberg 1972: 205).

The individual and group interviews provide fascinating material about different aspects of women's lives and experiences within three different state systems. In this study these interviews are used to guide an "interpretative and integrative" analysis of patterns of feminists' political engagement (Nelson 1994). The women's interviews provide insights into dimensions of their political activities in civil society, not only at the traditional level of formal politics. It is thus that the interviews furnish an important part of the present analysis. Only when it is appropriate to the analysis do I rely on direct quotations from the interviews.

As a second source of information, I used material collected in the UFV archives in Berlin, Leipzig, and Erfurt, and for information on the Central Round Table I visited the Federal Archive in Potsdam. The material available at the office of the Independent Women's League in Berlin is incomplete but contains appeals for demonstrations, flyers, the UFV statute and program, the electoral platforms of the UFV, and position papers written by UFV activists. They also contain newspaper clippings of

---

4. For a good overview of the various "verification/replication" standards in political science, see the articles in *PS: Political Science and Politics* 28, no. 3 (September 1995): 443–99.

5. This information was given to me by one of the key political activists within the UFV. I was not able to verify, however, whether she did, in fact, destroy her documents.

UFV events and some of the minutes of UFV meetings. I also visited the UFV offices in Berlin and Leipzig several times and spoke with staff members to get specific information.

The available material at the Federal Archive in Potsdam is restricted to the names and participants at the Central Round Table, the date of the formation of the various subgroups and their participants, and the official petitions to the Central Round Table and the groups who supported these petitions. Most of the documents concerning the subgroups of the Central Round Table in which feminists were active remain in the possession of individual participants.[6] I had access, however, to some sections of the unpublished stenographic reports of the minutes of the negotiations of the Central Round Table, which Uwe Thaysen kindly made available.

I also had access to some of the unpublished chapters of Anne Hampele's dissertation, whose work is a scholarly insider analysis of the UFV as a social experiment. Christine Kulke provided me with her unpublished dissertation, which was the first West German study dealing with East German women's policies in the immediate post–World War II period. This work provided excellent background material on the SED's handling of the women's question. In addition, some feminists furnished me with copies of reports from UFV meetings, which detail some of the bitter conflicts that raged within the UFV and concerned accusations having to do with family members working for the state security. These reports should have been part of the UFV archive but were not in the official files.

Of course, such a study cannot be written without relying on the many excellent daily and weekly German newspaper reports. Particularly, the article collections of the *TAZ* in the two *DDR Journal*s provided an easy overview of the important articles written on German unification between November 1989 and March 1990. I read many books and journal articles written in German and English on the process of German unification. I benefited greatly from many feminist writings and their analyses of various aspects of German unification and feminist politics. Except for some individual chapters in books,[7] however, not a single book-length analysis exists that deals with the situation of women in the former GDR and their "forced" cohabitation of political space with West German feminists and their joint experience during the process of unification.

---

6. At one interview in the home of a member of the Central Round Table, she confirmed that she had the material in her possession and would "write about her experience at the appropriate time."

7. One of the best and most extensive coverage dealing with women, politics, and society, before, during and after unification, can be found in Huelshoff, Markovits, and Reich 1993.

Finally, my personal impressions as a witness to the historic "hour" in Berlin in November 1989 and my continuous stay in Berlin until 1991 as an academic at the Free University of Berlin, and as a feminist and peace activist, provide a subjective context to this study.

Interviews by Author

Anders-Sailer. Member of Women's Group, University of Halle. Interview: January 1992.

Arnold, B., Gender equality officer, Leipzig University. Interview: July 1992.

Baer, Susanne. Lawyer and member of Women in Best Constitution, West Berlin. Interview: September 1992.

Behrend, Hanna. Professor of English, Humboldt University, UFV member. East Berlin. Interview: July 1992.

Berghahn, Sabine. Lawyer and member of Women in Best Constitution, West Berlin. Interviews: December 1989, June 1991, January 1992, January 1994.

Beyer, Marina. Equality officer in the government of Lothar de Maizière. Interview: April 1993.

Bläss, Petra. Member of German Parliament, PDS, and UFV member. Interview: April 1993.

Bohley, Bärbel. Founder of Women for Peace, cofounder of Initiative for Peace and Human Rights, and cofounder of the New Forum. Interview: April 1993.

Böhm, Tatjana. Cabinet member of the Modrow Government; member of SOFI and UFV; member of the Central Round Table; major activist on producing the *Social Charta;* member of the working group New Constitution, at the Central Round Table, East Berlin. Interview: January 1995.

Diedrich, Ulrike. Member of Alma, Women in the Sciences, Leipzig University. Interview: January 1992.

Dölling, Irene. Professor of cultural studies, Humboldt University; signatory of the public letter in the journal *Für Dich,* East Berlin; member of the Scientific Committee of the Research Group Women in Socialist Society at the Academy of Science in East Berlin; cofounder of the cultural feminist group at the Humboldt University that met during the 1980s. Interviews: December 1989, January 1992.

Färber, Christine. Gender equality officer, Free University of Berlin (West). Interview: January 1992.

Hampele, Anne. Member of the East-West Berlin Project Group Citizen Movement; West German participant in the UFV, West Berlin. Interviews: June 1982, January 1995.

Helwerth, Ulrike. Journalist, West Berlin. Interview: January 1994.

Hildebrandt, Karin. Former member of SOFI (Socialist Women's Initiative); economist at the former College of Economics (Hochschule für Ökonomie), East Berlin. Interview: January 1992.

Hüber, Christine. Architect, Leipzig. Interview: July 1992.

Kriszio, Marianne. Gender equality officer, Humboldt University, East Berlin. Interview: July 1994.

Land, Rainer. Philosopher; project group Conception of a Modern Socialism; founder and chief editor of *Berliner Debatte,* East Berlin. Interview: July 1994.

Lang, Sabine. Press secretary to Christine Bergman; deputy mayor of Berlin; and minister for Work and Women, Berlin. Interviews: January 1992, June 1992, June 1993, July 1994.

Ludwig, Johanna. Coeditor of *Einspruch. Leipziger Hefte,* Leipzig. Interviews: August 1992, January 1993.

Maleck-Lewy, Eva. Cofounder of LISA; later member of UFV, East Berlin. Interviews: January 1992, July 1992, June 1993, May 1994.

Merkel, Ina. Cofounder of UFV; author of UFV manifesto; participant at the first meeting at the Central Round Table; most important personality within the UFV, East Berlin. Interviews: February 1993, August 1994.

Nickel, Hildegard Maria. Professor of Sociology, Humboldt University; signatory of the public letter in the journal *Für Dich,* East Berlin; member of the Scientific Committee of the Research Group Women in Socialist Society at the Academy of Science in East-Berlin; member of the cultural feminist group at the Humboldt University that met during the 1980s. Interview: January 1992.

Petruschka, Gisela. Gender equality officer, Humboldt University, East Berlin. Interviews: January 1992, July 1992.

Petzold, Petra. ÖTV-Union (public labor union), Leipzig. Interview: July 1992.

Possekel, Ralf. Historian, writer, East Berlin. Interview: July 15, 1994.

Riedmüller, Barbara. Professor of political science, Free University of Berlin; minister for science in the West Berlin Senate. Interview: January 1992.

Sauer, Birgit. Member of the Committee for Basic Human Rights; West German feminist. Interviews: April 1990, January 1991, June 1993, July 1994.

Schäfer, Eva. Cofounder of Lila Offensive; cofounder of UFV; spokeswoman for the UFV; signatory of the public letter in the journal *Für Dich;* coauthor of the UFV statute; member of the Women Political Round Table; and present at the first meeting of the Central Round Table, East Berlin. Interviews: July 1994, January 1995.

Schenk, Christine. Member of Parliament (UFV 1990–94; PDS 1994); cofounder of Lila Offensive; cofounder of UFV; member of the working group Gender Equality at the Central Round Table, East Berlin. Interview: June 1992.

Schindler, Christiane. Spokeswoman for the UFV; cofounder of SOFI; co-initiator of the Women Political Round Table, East Berlin. Interview: June 1992.

Schindler, Karla. Chair of the Works Council, Leipzig Cotton Spinning Mills. Interview: July 1992.

Schwarz, Gislinde. Editor of the journal *Für Dich;* signatory of the public letter in the journal *Für Dich;* cofounder of UFV, East Berlin. Interview: January 1994.

Thaysen, Uwe. Political scientist; West German observer of the entire sixteen meetings at the Central Round Table in East Berlin; advisor to the Enquete Commission of the all-German Parliament on the "Reappraisal and the Effects of the SED-Dictatorship in Germany." Interview: May 1995.

Voth, Helga. Senate of Berlin, East Berlin. Interview: January 1992.

Group Interview Sessions

Berlin Women's League. West Berlin. Interview: July 1992.
Textile College. Burg Giebichstein. University of Halle, East Germany. Interview: January 1992.
LISA (PDS). Leipzig, East Germany. Interview: August 1992.
Women's Center. Erfurt, East Germany. Interview: February 1991.
Women for Peace. Martin Niemöller Haus, West Berlin. Interviews: August 1992.

Bibliography

Abromeit, Heidrun. 1992. *Der verkappte Einheitsstaat.* Opladen: Leske and Budrich.

Agnoli, Johannes. 1977. "Wahlkampf und Sozialer Konflikt." In *Auf dem Weg zum Einparteienstaat,* ed. Wolf-Dieter Narr. Opladen: Westdeutscher Verlag.

Allen, Bruce. 1989. *Germany East: Dissent and Opposition.* Montreal: Black Rose Books.

Allen, Judith. 1990. "Does Feminism Need a Theory of 'The State'?" In *Playing the State,* ed. Sophie Watson. London: Verso.

Altvater, Elmar. 1991. "'Soziale Marktwirtschaft' 1949 und 1989." *Leviathan, Sonderheft* 12:82–105.

———. 1992. "Die deutsche Währungsunion von 1990. Von den Schwierigkeiten der monetären Eingliederung in einen erfolgreichen Währungsraum." In *Entwickeln statt abwickeln,* ed. Werner Schulz and Ludger Volmer. Berlin: Ch. Links.

Anders, Ann. 1988. "Chronologie der gelaufenen Ereignisse." In *Autonome Frauen. Schlüsseltexte der Neuen Frauenbewegung seit 1968,* ed. Ann Anders. Frankfurt: Athenäums.

Anderson, Christopher, Karl Kaltenthaler, and Wolfgang Luthardt. 1993. *The Domestic Politics of German Unification.* Boulder: Lynne Rienner Publishers.

Anderson, Perry. 1976–77. "The Antinomies of Antonio Gramsci." *New Left Review,* no. 100: 65–77.

Andert, Reinhold, and Wolfgang Herzberg. 1991. *Der Sturz.* Berlin and Weimar: Aufbau-Verlag.

Arbeitsgruppe. 1990. "Neue Verfassung der DDR" des Runden Tisches, *Entwurf Verfassung der Deutschen Demokratischen Republik.* Berlin, April.

Arbeitskreis Verfassung des Frauenpolitischen Runden Tisches Berlin. 1992. *Macht—Verfassung—Demokratie.* Berlin.

Arendt, Hannah. 1968. *The Origins of Totalitarianism.* Cleveland and New York: World Publishing Company.

Argument extra, UFV. 1990. *Ohne Frauen ist kein Staat zu machen.* Hamburg: Argument-Verlag.

Arnold, Karl-Heinz. 1990. *Die ersten hundert Tage.* Dietz Verlag, Berlin.

Ash, Timothy Garton. 1990. *The Uses of Adversity.* Vintage: New York.
————. 1994. *In Europe's Name. Germany and the Divided Continent.* New York: Vintage Books.
Augstein, Rudolf. 1989. "Vereinigung der Sieger?" *Der Spiegel* 50:18.
————. 1990. "Bitte keinen Friedensvertrag!" *Der Spiegel* 10:22.
Baer, Susanne. 1992. "Grundrechte sind nicht genug." *Macht—Verfassung—Demokratie.* Berlin: Arbeitskreis Verfassung des Frauenpolitischen Runden Tisches Berlin.
Bagger, Ulrike. 1993. "Para. 218." *Weibblick* 13:38–40.
Bahrmann, Hannes, and Christoph Links. 1994. *Chronik der Wende. Die DDR zwischen 7. Oktober und 18. Dezember 1989.* Berlin: Ch. Links.
Barnes, Samuel, and Max Kaase. 1979. *Political Action: Mass Participation in Five Western Democracies.* Beverly Hills, Calif.: Sage Publications.
Basic Law for the Federal Republic of Germany. 1990. Bonn: Press and Information Office, revised document.
Bast-Haider, Kerstin. 1995. "The Economic Dimension of Social Change: Women in the East German Clothing Industry." *Social Politics* 2, no. 1 (spring): 51–61.
Bebel, August. 1990. *Die Frau und der Sozialismus.* Berlin: Dietz Verlag.
Beccalli, Bianca. 1994. "The Modern Women's Movement in Italy." *New Left Review* 204:86–112.
Beck, Ulrich, and Elisabeth Beck Gernsheim. 1990. *Das ganz normale Chaos der Liebe.* Frankfurt: Suhrkamp.
Becker, Manfred. 1991. "Auch die Kirchenleitung ist kein homogener Block gewesen." In *Mit Flugscharen gegen Schwerter,* ed. Manfred Richter and Elsbeth Zylla. Bremen: Ed. Temmen.
Beer, Ursula. 1984. *Theorien Geschlechtlicher Arbeitsteilung.* Frankfurt: Campus.
————, ed. 1987. *Klasse Geschlecht. Feministische Gesellschaftsanalyse und Wissenschaftskritik.* Bielefeld: AJZ-Verlag.
Beer, Ursula, and Jutta Chalupsky. 1993. "Vom Realsozialismus zum Privat- kapitalismus." In *Transformationen im Geschlechterverhältnis,* ed. Brigitte Aulenbacher and Monika Goldmann. Frankfurt: Campus Verlag.
Behrend, Hanna. 1990. "Die Hypertrophie des Vergangenen. Aufbruch und Elend der DDR-Frauen." *Das Argument,* no. 184 (November–December): 859–64.
Benhabib, Seyla. 1989. "Der verallgemeinerte und der konkrete Andere. Ansätze zu einer feministischen Moraltheorie." In *Denkverhältnisse, Feminismus und Kritik,* ed. Elisabeth List and Herlinde Studer. Frankfurt: Suhrkamp.
Bennholdt-Thomsen, Veronika. 1987. "Die Ökologiefrage ist eine Frauenfrage." In *Frauen und Ökologie. Gegen den Machbarkeitswahn,* ed. Die Grünen im Bundestag. Cologne: Cologne Volksblatt Verlag.
Berger, Suzanne, ed. 1981. *Organizing Interests in Western Europe.* Cambridge: Cambridge University Press.
Berghahn, Sabine. 1992. "Ehe, Familie, Lebensgemeinschaften." *Macht—Verfassung—Demokratie.* Berlin: Arbeitskreis Ver- fassung des Frauenpolitischen Runden Tisches Berlin.
————. 1993a. "Backlash made in Germany?—Frauenrechte drei Jahre nach der

Vereinigung." In *Frauen-Prisma.* Potsdam: Equality Council of the University Potsdam, November.

———. 1993a. "Frauen, Recht und langer Atem—Bilanz nach über 40 Jahren Gleichstellungsgebot in Deutschland." In Helwig and Nickel eds.

———. 1993b. "Demokratie und Geschlechterverhältnis nach dem zweiten Karlsruher Abtreibungsurteil." *Die Mitbestimmung* 7–8:34–37.

———. 1994. "Das zweite Abtreibungsurteil: weder Klarheit noch Konfliktlösung." Serie: Urteile des Bundesverfassungs- gerichts, November 1993–February 1994.

———. 1995. "Gender in the Legal Discourse in Post-unification Germany: Old and New Lines of Conflict." *Social Politics* 2, no. 1 (spring): 37–50.

Berghahn, Sabine, and Andrea Fritzsche. 1991. *Frauenrecht in Ost und West Deutschland.* Bilanz and Ausblick. Berlin: BasisDruck.

———. 1992. "Rechtspolitische Entwicklungsprozesse von Frauenrechten in Deutschland." *Nach der Vereinigung Deutschlands: Frauen fordern Ihr Recht.* Bonn: Friedrich Ebert Stiftung, Gesprächskreis Frauenpolitik.

Berghahn, Sabine, Helga Lukoschat, and Roscha Schmidt. 1993. "Spielräume nutzen. Kriterien für die gesetzgeberische Neuregelung nach dem Karlsruher Para. 218—Urteil und kritische Einschätzung des FDP-Entwurfs." Berlin: Frauenreferat von Bündnis 90 / Die Grünen Berlin, October.

Berghahn, Sabine, and Gabriele Wilde. 1996. "Die Karlsruher Macht über das Geschlechterverhältnis." In *Zwischen Machtkritik und Machtgewinn,* ed. Virginia Penrose and Clarissa Rudolph. Frankfurt and New York: Campus Verlag.

Berghofer, Wolfgang. 1989. Interview. "Das Vertrauen ist verloren." *Der Spiegel* 50:38–40.

Bertram, Barbara. 1989. *Typisch weiblich—Typisch männlich?* Berlin: Dietz Verlag.

Beyme, Klaus von. 1985. "Policy-Making in the Federal Republic of Germany: A Systematic Introduction." In *Policy and Politics in the Federal Republic of Germany,* ed. Klaus von Beyme and Manfred G. Schmidt. New York: St. Martin's Press.

———. 1990. "Die vergleichende Politikwissenschaft und der Paradigmenwechsel in der politischen Theorie." *Politische Vierteljahresschrift* 31, no. 3: 457–74.

———. 1990a. "Transition to Democracy—or Anschluss? The Two Germanies and Europe." *Government and Opposition* 25, no. 2 (spring): 170–90.

———. 1991. "The Legitimation of German Unification between National and Democratic Principles." *German Politics and Society* 22 (spring): 1–17.

———. 1991a. "Nationale Einheit und demokratische Legitimation. Plädoyer für ein zweistufiges Verfahren zur Legitimation der deutschen Einigung. In *Die Politik zur deutschen Einheit,* ed. Ulrike Liebert and Wolfgang Merkel. Opladen: Leske and Budrich.

———. 1992a. "Der Begriff der politischen Klasse–Eine neue Dimension der Elitenforschung?" *Politische Vierteljahresschrift,* no. 1: 4–32.

———. 1993 (1979). *Das politische System der Bundesrepublik Deutschland nach der Vereinigung,* Completely revised edition. Munich: Piper.

———. 1994. "The Failure of a Success Story: German Reunification in the Light of Policy Evaluation." MS. November.

Beyme, Klaus von, and Manfred G. Schmidt. 1985. *Policy and Politics in the Federal Republic of Germany.* New York: St. Martin's Press.

Biester, Elke, Barbara Holland-Cunz, and Birgit Sauer, eds. 1994. *Demokratie oder Androkratie? Theorie und Praxis demokratischer Herrschaft in der feministischen Diskussion.* Frankfurt and New York: Campus Verlag.

Bloh, Bernhard. 1990. "Testfall für Europa." *Die Zeit,* 8–16 February, 22.

Blüher, Hans. 1921. *Die Rolle der Erotik in der männlichen Gesellschaft. Eine Theorie der menschlichen Staatsbildung nach Wesen und Wert,* 2d ed. Jena: Diederichs.

Bobbio, Norberto. 1988. "Gramsci and the Concept of Civil Society." In *Civil Society and the State,* ed. John Keane. London: Verso.

Böck, Dorothea. 1990. "Ich schreibe, um herauszufinden, warum ich schreiben muß." *Feministische Studien,* no. 1 (May): 61–74.

Bock, Gisela. 1992. "Frauen und Geschlechterbeziehungen in der nationalsozialistischen Rassenpolitik." In *Nach Osten, Verdeckte Spuren nationalsozialistischer Verbrechen,* ed. Theresa Wobbe. Frankfurt a.M.: Neue Kritik.

Böckenförde, Ernst-Wolfgang, and Dieter Grimm. 1990. "Nachdenken über Deutschland." *Der Spiegel* 10:72–77.

Böckmann-Schewe, Lisa, Christine Kulke, and Anne Röhrig. 1994. "Wandel und Brüche in Lebensentwürfen von Frauen in den neuen Bundesländern." *Aus Politik und Zeitgeschichte.* B 6/94, February 11.

Boehling, Rebecca. 1995. "U.S. Democratization Plans, Gender Politics and the Revival of German Self-Government in Postwar Germany." Paper presented at the American Institute for Contemporary Studies, Johns Hopkins University, February.

Böhm, Tatjana. 1991. "Frauenfragen in der Verfassungsdiskussion." *Mehr Rechte für Frauen in einer neuen Verfassung.* Bonn: Friedrich Ebert Stiftung, December.

———. 1991–92. "The Abortion Question: A New Solution in Unified Germany." *German Politics and Society,* no. 24, 25 (winter): 135–41.

———. 1992. "Wo stehen wir Frauen nach 40 Jahren getrennter Geschichte in Deutschland West und Ost?" *Feministische Studien,* no. 2: 28–34.

———. 1992a. "DDR—Frauenrechte im Umbruch—Nur ein Rückblick?" *Macht—Verfassung—Demokratie.* Berlin: Arbeitskreis Verfassung des Frauenpolitischen Runden Tisches Berlin.

Böll, Heinrich. 1965. *Haus ohne Hüter.* Frankfurt a.M.: Ullstein.

Borchorst, Anette, and Birte Siim. 1987. "Women and the Advanced Welfare State—A New Kind of Patriarchal Power?" In *Women and the State,* ed. Anne Showstack Sassoon. London and New York: Routledge.

Böttger, Barbara. 1991. "Gleichberechtigung—ein uneingelöstes Versprechen." *Feministische Studien* (extra): 25–30.

Brand, Karl-Werner, Detlef Büsser, and Dieter Rucht. 1986. *Aufbruch in eine neue Gesellschaft: Neue soziale Bewegungen in der Bundesrepublik Deutschland.* Rev. ed. Frankfurt: Campus.

Braunthal, Gerard. 1994 (1983). *The German Social Democrats since 1969,* 2d ed. Boulder: Westview Press.

———. 1996. *Parties and Politics in Modern Germany.* Boulder: Westview Press.

Breuilly, John. 1992. *The State of Germany.* London: Longman.

Bridenthal, Renate, Atina Grossmann, and Marion Kaplan, eds. 1984. *When Biology Became Destiny: Women in Weimar and Nazi Germany.* New York: Monthly Review Press.

Brockmann, Stephen. 1991. "Introduction: The Reunification Debate." *New German Critique,* No. 52 (winter): 3–30.

Brown, Wendy. 1992. "Finding the Man in the State." *Feminist Studies* 18, no. 1 (spring): 7–34.

Bruckmeier, Karl. 1993. "Die Bürgerbewegungen der DDR im Herbst 1989." In *Die Bürgerbewegungen in der DDR und in den Ostdeutschen Ländern,* ed. Haufe and Bruckmeier. Opladen: Westdeutscher Verlag.

Bulmer, Simon. 1989. *The Changing Agenda of West German Public Policy.* Hants: Dartmouth.

Busch, Andreas. 1991. "Die deutsch-deutsche Währungsunion: Politisches Votum trotz ökonomischer Bedenken." In *Die Politik zur deutschen Einheit,* ed. Ulrike Liebert and Wolfgang Merkel. Opladen: Leske and Budrich.

Bütow, Birgit, and Heidi Stecker, eds. 1994. *EigenArtige Ostfrauen.* Bielefeld: Kleine Verlag.

Campbell, John L., J. Rogers Hollingsworth, and Leon N. Lindberg, eds. 1991. *Governance of the American Economy.* Cambridge: Cambridge University Press.

Carr, William. 1992. "The Unification of Germany." In *The State of Germany,* ed. John Breuilly. London: Longman.

Childs, David. 1983. *The GDR: Moscow's German Ally.* London: George Allen and Unwin.

Christ, Peter, and Klaus-Peter Schmid. 1990. "Hauptsache guter Wille." *Die Zeit,* February 8–16, p. 21.

Code, Lorraine. 1991. *What Can She Know? Feminist Theory and the Construction of Knowledge.* Ithaca and London: Cornell University Press.

Costain, Anne N., and W. Douglas Costain. 1987. "Strategy and Tactics of the Women's Movement in the United States and West Germany." In *The Women's Movements of the United States and Western Europe,* ed. Mary Katzenstein and Carol Mueller. Philadelphia: Temple University Press.

Cviková, Jana. 1993. "Ein Brief aus Bratislava: die slowakisch- tschechische Frauenzeitschrift 'ASPEKT.'" In *beiträge zur feministischen theorie und praxis* 34:113–16.

Dahlerup, Drude. 1980. "Approaches to the Study of Public Policy towards Women." Paper presented at the European Consortium for Political Research, Florence, Italy.

———. 1987. "Confusing Concepts—Confusing Reality: A Theoretical Discussion of the Patriarchal State." In *Women and the State,* ed. Anne Showstack Sassoon. London: Routledge.

Dalton, Russell J., and Manfred Kuechler, eds. 1990. *Challenging the Political Order: New Social and Political Movements in Western Democracies.* Oxford: Polity Press.

Dalton, Russell J., Manfred Kuechler, and Wilhelm Bürklin. 1990. "The Challenge of New Movements." In *Challenging the Political Order,* ed. Russell J. Dalton and Manfred Kuechler. Oxford: Polity Press.

Das Ende der Teilung. 1990. *Der Wandel in Deutschland und Osteuropa. Beiträge und Dokumente aus dem Europa-Archiv.* Bonn: Verlag für Internationale Politik, GmbH.

DDR. 1992. *Wer War Wer. Ein biographisches Lexikon.* Berlin: Links.

Demokratischer Frauenbund Deutschlands (DFD). 1989. *Geschichte des DFD.* Leipzig: Verlag für die Frau.

Deutsches Institut für Wirtschaftsforschung. 1995. Wochenbericht 23/95, "Aspekte der Arbeitsentwicklung in Ostdeutschland," June 8.

Die Verträge zur Einheit Deutschlands. 1990. *Staatsvertrag. Einigungsvertrag mit Anlangen. Wahlvertrag. Zwei-plus-Vier Vertrag. Partnerschaftsverträge.* 2d ed. Munich: C. H. Beck.

Diemer, Susanne. 1989. "Die 'neue Frau', aber der 'alte Mann' "? In *Politische Kultur in der DDR,* Hans-Georg Wehling. Stuttgart: W. Kohlhammer, GmbH.

Disch, Lisa. 1991. "Toward a Feminist Conception of Politics." *PS: Political Science and Politics* 24, no. 3 (September): 501–4.

Diskussion. 1990. "Atemschwelle—Versuche, Richtung zu gewinnen." Interview with Irene Dölling and Hildegard Maria Nickel, *Feministische Studien,* no. 1 (May): 90–106.

Diskussion. 1986. "Autonomie in den Institutionen?" *Feministische Studien,* no. 2: 134–46.

Dokumente zum Einigungsvertrag. 1990. Bonn: Press and Informations Office of the Federal Government.

Dölling, Irene. 1990. "Über den Patriarchalismus staatssozialistischer Gesellschaften und die Geschlechtsfrage im gesellschaftlichen Umbruch." In *Die Modernisierung moderner Gesellschaften,* ed. Wolfgang Zapf. Reports of the 25. German Sociology-Meeting. Frankfurt: Campus Verlag.

———. 1990a. "Frauen- und Männerbilder. Eine Analyse von Fotos in DDR-Zeitschriften." *Feministische Studien,* no. 1 (May): 35–49.

———. 1990b. "Frauenforschung." *Das Argument,* no. 180 (March–April): 267–71.

———. 1991. "Between Hope and Helplessness: Women in the GDR after the 'Turning Point.'" *Feminist Review* 39:3–15.

———. 1993. "Identitäten von Ost-Frauen im Transformations—prozeß—Probleme ostdeutscher Frauenforschung." MS for the Conference at the Goethe Haus, New York, "Women and German Unification." April.

———. 1994. "Zum Verhältnis von modernen und traditionalen Aspekten im Lebenszusammenhang von Frauen." *Berliner Debatte* 4: 29–35.

Dönhoff, Marion, Meinhard Miegel, Wilhelm Nölling, Helmut Schmidt, Richard Schröder, Wolfgang Thierse. 1992. *Ein Manifest. Weil das Land sich ändern muss.* Hamburg: Rowohlt.

Drakulic, Slavenka. 1993. *How We Survived Communism and Even Laughed.* New York: HarperPerennial.

Dror, Yehezkel. 1968. *Public Policy Making Reexamined.* Scranton: Chandler Publishing Company.

Duerst-Lahti, Georgia, and Rita Mae Kelly. 1995. *Gender Power, Leadership, and Governance.* Ann Arbor: University of Michigan Press.

Duverger, Maurice. 1995. *The Political Role of Women.* Paris: UNESCO.

Dyson, Kenneth. 1977. *Party, State, and Bureaucracy in Western Germany.* Beverly Hills, Calif.: Sage.

———. 1982. "West Germany: The Search for a Rationalist Consensus." In Jeremy Richardson, *Policy Styles in Western Europe.* London: George Allen and Unwin.

———. 1989. "Whither West German Broadcasting? The Transformation of a Policy Sector." In *The Changing Agenda of West German Public Policy,* ed. Simon Bulmer. Hants: Dartmouth.

Ebinger, Herma, Ursula Dauderstädt, and Bärbel Gerlind-Renner. 1992. "Weg mit 218." *Weibblick* 3–4:33–38.

Einhorn, Barbara. 1993. *Cinderella Goes to Market.* London: Verso.

Eisenstein, Hester. 1990. "Femocrats, Official Feminism and the Uses of Power." In *Playing the State,* ed. Sophie Watson. London: Verso.

Eisinger, Peter K. 1973. "The Conditions of Protest Behavior in American Cities." *American Political Science Review* 67:11–28.

Elshtain, Jean Bethke. 1981. *Public Man, Private Women: Women in Social and Political Thought.* Princeton: Princeton University Press.

Engelbrech, Gerhard. 1994. "Frauenerwerbslosigkeit in den neuen Bundes- ländern. Folgen und Auswege." *Aus Politik und Zeitgeschichte.* B 6/94, February 11.

Engels, Friedrich. 1972. *The Origin of the Family, Private Property and the State.* 1884. Reprint, New York: International Publishers.

Engler, Wolfgang. 1992. *Die zivilisatorische Lücke. Versuche über den Staatssozialismus.* Frankfurt: Suhrkamp.

Esping-Andersen, Gøsta. 1990. *The Three Worlds of Welfare Capitalism.* Princeton: Princeton University Press.

———. 1995. "Welfare States Without Work: The Impasse of Labor Shedding and Familialism in Continental European Social Policy." Working Paper 71.

Esser, Josef, and Wolfgang Fach. 1981. "Korporatistische Krisenregulierung im MODELL DEUTSCHLAND." In *Neokorporatismus,* ed. Ulrich von Alemann. Frankfurt and New York: Campus Verlag.

Evans, Peter B., Dietrich Rueschemeyer, and Theda Skocpol. 1985. *Bringing the State Back In.* Cambridge: Cambridge University Press.

Evans, Richard J. 1976. *The Feminist Movement in Germany, 1894–1933.* London and Beverly Hills: Sage.

Faber, Christel, and Traute Meyer, eds. 1992. *Unterm Neuen Kleid der Freiheit: Das Korsett der Einheit.* Berlin: Sigma.

Faludi, Susan. 1991. *Backlash: The Undeclared War against American Women.* New York: Crown.

Federal Institute for Employment, IAB Werkstattbericht. 1995. "Aktuelle Daten vom Arbeitsmarkt, Stand April 1995." No. 1.4/15. April.

Federal Institute for Employment. 1994. Informationen. "Frauen Ausbildung—Beschäftigung—Weiterbildung." 28/94.

Federal Institute for Employment. 1993. Informationen, "Frauen Ausbildung—Beschäftigung—Weiterbildung, Ihre Berufliche Zukunft." 50/93.

———. 1994. "Arbeitsmarktreport für Frauen." Nuremberg, January.

Federal Ministry for Women and Youth. 1991. Materialien zur Frauenpolitik, 12, "Integrationsprobleme von DDR- Übersiedlerinnen—Perspektiven, Erfahrungen, Strategien." June.

———. 1991. Materialien zur Frauenpolitik, 14, "Frauenfreundliche Arbeitszeitgestaltung—das verbandspolitische Forderungsumfeld." September.

———. 1991. Materialien zur Frauenpolitik, 15, "Betriebliche Maßnahmen zur Vereinbarkeit von Familie und Beruf sowie zur Förderung der Berufsrückkehr nach Zeiten ausschließlicher Familientätigkeit." November.

———. 1992. Materialien zur Frauenpolitik, 17, "Massnahmen des Bundesministeriums für Frauen und Jugend für Frauen in den Neuen Ländern." April.

———. 1992. Materialien zur Frauenpolitik, 19, "Erwerbschancen für Frauen aus landwirt- wirtschaftlichen Regionen der neuen Bundesländer." June.

———. 1994. Materialien zur Frauenpolitik, 44, "Modellversuch: 'Neue Wege der Arbeitsplatzbeschaffung: Gemeinweseno-rientierung erschließt Potentiale,'" October.

Feist, Ursula. 1986. "Die Amazonen sind noch fern. Das Wahlrecht der Frauen: Enttäuschungen und Chancen." *Feministische Studien,* No. 2: 91–106.

Feist, Ursula, and Hans-Jürgen Hoffmann. 1991. "Landtagswahlen in der ehemaligen DDR am 14. Oktober 1990: Förderalismus im wieder- vereinten Deutschland—Tradition und neue Konturen." *Zeitschrift für Parlamentsfragen,* no. 1: 5–34.

Feministische Studien, extra. 1991. *Frauen für eine neue Verfassung.*

Ferber, Marianne A., and Julie A. Nelson. 1993. "Introduction: The Social Construction of Economics and the Social Construction of Gender." In *Beyond Economic Man.* Chicago: University of Chicago Press.

Ferguson, Kathy. 1984. *The Feminist Case against Bureaucracy.* Philadelphia: Temple University Press

Ferree, Myra Marx. 1987. "Equality and Autonomy: Feminist Politics in the U.S. and West Germany." In *The Women's Movements of the United States and Western Europe,* ed. Mary Katzenstein and Carol Mueller. Philadelphia: Temple University Press.

———. 1991–92. "Institutionalizing Gender Equality: Feminist Politics and Equality Offices." *German Politics and Society Issue* 24–25 (winter 1991–92): 53–66.

————. 1993. "The Rise and Fall of 'Mommy Politics': Feminism and Unification in (East) Germany." *Feminist Studies* 19, no. 1 (spring 1993): 89–115.

————. 1994. "Institutionalisierung, Identität und politische Partizipation von Frauen in den Neuen Bundesländern." Paper delivered at the Congress of the German Association for Political Science, Potsdam, Germany, August 25–27.

————. 1994a. "The Time of Chaos Was the Best." Feminist Mobilization and Demobilization in East Germany. *Gender and Politics* 8, no. 4 (December): 597–623.

————. 1995. "Patriarchies and Feminisms: The Two Women's Movements of Post Unification Germany." *Social Politics* 2, no. 1 (spring 1995): 10–24.

Ferree, Myra Marx, and Brigitte Young. 1993. "Three Steps Back for Women: German Unification, Gender and University Reform." *PS: Political Science and Politics* 26:199–205.

Flax, Jane. 1990. "Postmodernism and Gender Relations in Feminist Theory." In *Feminism/Postmodernism,* ed. Linda J. Nicholson. New York and London: Routledge.

Forschungsjournal, Neue Soziale Bewegungen. 1992. Vol. 1.

Förster, Peter, and Günter Roski. 1990. *DDR zwischen Wende und Wahl.* Berlin: LinksDruck.

Fox Piven, Frances. 1984. "Women and the State: Ideology, Power, and the Welfare State." *Socialist Review* 74:11–19.

Fraenkel, Ernst. 1941. *The Dual State.* New York: Oxford University Press.

Frankfurter Rundschau. 1990. "Volk soll nicht über Einheit entscheiden." March 3, p. 1.

————. 1990a. "So wichtig wie die Mark sind Selbstachtung und Würde." March 3.

————. 1990a. "Genscher widerspricht Kohl." March 3, p. 1.

————. 1990. "Teltschik sorgt wieder für Wirbel." February 22, p. 1.

Fraser, Nancy, and Linda Gordon. 1994. "'Dependency' Demystified: Inscriptions of Power in a Keyword of the Welfare State." *Social Politics* 1, no. 1 (spring): 4–31.

Frauenpolitischer Runder Tisch. N.d. Selbstverständnis. UFV files.

————. 1990. Open Letter to the Representatives of the Volkskammer and the Bundestag, dated September 12.

————. N.d. W*as will er und was kann er?* Birgit Hartigs' Interview with Christiane Schindler. UFV files.

Frerichs, Petra, and Margareta Steinrücke, eds. 1993. *Soziale Ungleichheit und Geschlechterverhältnisse.* Opladen: Leske and Budrich.

Frevert, Ute. Frauen-Geschichte. 1986. *Zwischen Bürgerlicher Verbesserung und Neuer Weiblichkeit.* Frankfurt: Suhrkamp.

Frommel, Monika. 1991. "Frauen für eine neue Verfassung." *Mehr Rechte für Frauen in einer neuen Verfassung.* Bonn: Friedrich Ebert Stiftung, Gesprächskreis Frauenpolitik, no. 4 (December).

————. 1992. "Systematische Selbstentmachtung. Zum Para. 218 Kompromiß der Parteifrauen." *Links* (July–August): 6–7.

Funk, Nanette, and Magda Mueller. 1993. *Gender Politics and Post-Communism.* New York: Routledge.

Gamson, William. 1975. *The Strategy of Social Protest.* Homewood: Dorsey.

Gaus, Günter. 1983. *Wo Deutschland liegt.* Hamburg: Hoffmann und Campe Verlag.

———. 1990. *Zur Person Friedrich Schorlemmer, Lothar de Maizière, Gregor Gysi, Ingrid Köppe, Christoph Hein, Hans Modrow.* Berlin: Verlag Volk und Welt.

Geipel, Gary L., ed. 1993. *Germany in a New Era.* Indianapolis: Hudson Institute.

Gelb, Joyce. 1990. "Feminism and Political Action." In *Challenging the Political Order,* ed. Russell J. Dalton and Manfred Kuechler. Oxford: Polity Press.

Gensior, Sabine, Friederike Maier, and Gabriele Winter, eds. 1990. "Soziale Lage und Arbeit von Frauen in der DDR, Arbeitskreis Sozialwissenschaftliche Arbeitsmarktforschung." Working Paper 1990–6. Paderborn: University of Paderborn.

Gerecht, Cerstin. 1994. "Frauenpolitische Forderungen im Spannungsfeld von Interesse und Moral: Die Parteien und der Para. 218." In *Gleichstellungspolitik—Totem und Tabus,* ed. Elke Biester, Barbara Holland-Cunz, Eva Maleck-Lewy, Anja Ruf, Birgit Sauer. Frankfurt: Campus.

Gerhard, Ute. 1991. "Maßstäbe einer Verfassung auch für Frauen—eine andere Freiheit, Gleichheit, Würde." *Feministische Studien* (extra): 11–21.

———. 1991. *Unerhört.* Hamburg: Rowohlt.

———. 1991–92. "German Women and the Social Costs of Unification." *German Politics and Society,* nos. 24, 25 (winter): 16–33.

———. 1992. "Westdeutsche Frauenbewegung: Zwischen Autonomie und dem Recht auf Gleichheit." *Feministische Studien* 2 (November): 35–55.

———. 1994. "Die staatlich institutionalisierte 'Lösung' der Frauenfrage. Zur Geschichte der Geschlechterverhältnisse in der DDR." In *Sozialgeschichte der DDR,* ed. Hartmut Kaeble, Jürgen Kocka, Harmut Zwahr. Stuttgart: Klett Cotta.

Gerhard, Ute, Mechtild Jansen, Andrea Maihofer, Pia Schmid, and Irmgard Schultz, eds. 1990. *Differenz und Gleichheit.* Frankfurt: Ulrike Helmer Verlag.

German Parliament, 12th Legislative Period. 1992. Legislative Proposal of the "Fraktion" CDU/CSU, "Entwurf eines Gesetzes zum Schutz des ungeborenen Lebens." Printed Paper 12/1178 (new).

———. 1992. Legislative Proposal of the "Fraktion" SPD, "Entwurf eines Gesetzes zum Schutz des werdenden Lebens durch Förderung einer kinderfreundlichen Gesellschaft, durch rechtlich gewährleistete Hilfen für Familien und Schwangere sowie zur Sexualerziehung und zur Regelung des Schwangerschaftsabbruches." Printed Paper 12/841.

———. 1992. Legislative Proposal, "Entwurf eines Gesetzes zum Schutz der ungeborenen Kinder." Printed Paper 12/1179.

———. 1992. Legislative Proposal of the Deputies Christina Schenk, Dr. Klaus-Dieter Feige, Ingrid Köppe und the Group Bündnis 90 / Die Grünen, "Entwurf eines Gesetzes zur Sicherung der Entscheidungsfreiheit von Frauen beim Umgang mit ungewollten Schwangerschaften." Printed Paper 12/696.

———. 1992. Legislative Proposal of the Deputies Petra Bläss, Jutta Braband,

Ulla Jelpke, Andrea Lederer and the Group of the PDS / Linke Liste, "Entwurf eines Gesetzes zur Legalisierung des Schwangerschaftsabbruchs und zur Sicherung von Mindeststandards für Frauen zum Schwangerschaftsabbruch." Printed Paper 12/898.

————. 1992. Legislative Proposal, Printed Paper 12/2605, (new): 1–23.

————. 1992. Legislative Proposal of the "Fraktion" FDP, "Entwurf eines Gesetzes zum Schutz des werdenden Lebens, zur Förderung einer kinderfreundlicheren Gesellschaft, für Hilfen im Schwangerschaftskonflikt und zur Regelung des Schwangerschaftsabbruchs (Schwangeren- und Familienhilfegesetz)." Printed Paper 12/551.

German Parliament. 1992. Supplement to the Stenographic Record, 99th Session, *Supplement to the Minutes of Plenary Proceedings* 12/99, Bonn, June 25.

————. 1992. Stenographic Record. 99th Session, *Minutes of Plenary Proceedings* 12/99, Bonn, June 25th.

Gerstenberger, Heide. 1976. "Theory of the State." In *German Political Systems. Theory and Practice in the Two Germanies,* ed. Klaus von Beyme, Max Kaase, Ekkehart Krippendorff, Volker Rittberger, Kurt L. Shell. London: Sage Publications Ltd.

Gibowski, Wolfgang G. 1990. "Demokratischer (Neu-)Beginn in der DDR. Dokumentation und Analyse der Wahl vom 18. März 1990." *Zeitschrift für Parlamentsfragen,* 1/90: 5–22.

Giesen, Bernd, and Claus Leggewie, eds. 1991. *Experiment Vereinigung.* Berlin: Rotbuch Verlag.

Gildemeister, Regine, and Angelika Wetterer. 1992. "Wie Geschlechter Gemacht Werden." In *Traditionen Brüche,* ed. Gudrun-Axeli Knapp and Angelika Wetterer. Freiburg: Kore.

Gilligan, Carol. 1982. *In a Different Voice: Psychological Theory and Women's Development.* Cambridge: Harvard University Press.

Glaessner, Gert-Joachim. 1991. *Der Schwierige Weg zur Demokratie.* Opladen: Westdeutscher Verlag.

————.1992. *The Unification Process in Germany: From Dictatorship to Democracy.* New York: St. Martin's Press.

Goldthorpe, John H., ed. 1984. *Order and Conflict in Contemporary Capitalism.* Oxford: Clarendon Press.

Gordon, Linda, ed. 1990. *Women, the State, and Welfare.* Madison: University of Wisconsin Press.

Gramsci, Antonio. 1971. *Selections from the Prison Notebooks,* ed. and trans. Quintin Hoare and Geoffrey Nowell Smith. New York: International Publishers.

Graner, Claudia, and Susa M. Jäger. 1992. "Von der 'fröhlichen Revolution' zur Resignation? Einblicke und Ausblicke—die ostdeutsche Frauenbewegung aus westdeutscher Perspective." In Ludwig-Uhland-Institut für Empirische Kulturwissenschaft der Universität Tübingen / Institut für Europäische Ethnologie der Humboldt Universität zu Berlin: Blick-Wechsel Ost-West. Tübingen 1992.

Greven-Aschoff, Barbara. 1981. *Die bürgerliche Frauenbewegung in Deutschland 1894–1933.* Göttingen: Vandenhoeck and Ruprecht.

Gurr, Ted Robert. 1970. *Why Men Rebel.* Princeton, N.J.: Princeton University Press.

Graf von Krockow, Christian. 1994 (1998). *Die Stunde der Frauen.* Munich: Deutscher Taschenbuch Verlag GmbH.

Gransow, Volker, and Konrad H. Jarausch. 1991. *Die Deutsche Vereinigung. Dokumente zur Bürgerbewegung, Annäherung und Beitritt.* Köln: Verlag Wissenschaft und Politik.

Grass, Günter. 1990. *Two States—One Nation?* San Diego: Harcourt Brace Jovanovich.

Guggenberger, Bernd. 1991. "Wie 'zeitgemäß' ist die Verfassung? Ver- fassungsdenken im letzten Jahrzehnt vor dem 3. Jahrtausend." In *Eine Verfassung für Deutschland. Manifest Text Plädoyers,* ed. Bernd Guggenberger, Ulrich Preuß, and Wolfgang Ullmann. Munich: Carl Hanser Verlag.

Guggenberger, Bernd, Ulrich Preuß, and Wolfgang Ullmann, eds. 1991. *Eine Verfassung für Deutschland. Manifest Text Plädoyers.* Munich: Carl Hanser Verlag.

Gysi, Jutta. 1989. *Familienleben in der DDR.* Berlin: Akademie-Verlag.

Haas, Linda. 1992. *Equal Parenthood and Social Policy: A Study of Parental Leave in Sweden.* Albany: State University of New York Press.

Habermas. Jürgen. 1990. *Die Nachholende Revolution.* Frankfurt: Suhrkamp.

———. 1991. "Yet Again: German Identity." *New German Critique,* no. 51 (winter): 84–101.

Hagemann-White, Carol. 1987. "Können Frauen die Politik verändern?" *Aus Politik und Zeitgeschichte,* B 9–10:29–37.

Hagen, Elisabeth, and Jane Jenson. 1988. "Paradoxes and Promises, Work and Politics in the Postwar Years." In *Feminization of the Labor Force,* ed. Jane Jenson, Elisabeth Hagen, and Ceallaigh Reddy. New York: Oxford University Press.

Hamm-Brücher, Hildegard. 1990. "Seit 70 Jahren Abschied vom Männerwahlrecht. 1918 und die Folgen für Frauen in der Politik in Deutschland." In *Vater Staat und seine Frauen,* ed. Barbara Schaeffer-Hegel. Pfaffenweiler: Centaurus Verlagsgesellschaft.

Hall, Peter A. 1993. "Policy Paradigms, Social Learning, and the State." *Comparative Politics* 25, no. 3 (April): 275–96.

Hall, Peter. 1986. *Governing the Economy.* New York: Oxford University Press.

Hampele, Anne. 1990. "Auswirkungen der Rechtsangleichung für Frauen." *Links* (July–August): 22–24.

———. 1990a. *Ein Jahr Unabhängiger Frauenverband,* Teil I: *Ein dokumentarisches Lesebuch,* No. 47. Berlin: Berliner Arbeitshefte und Berichte zur Sozialwissenschaftlichen Forschung, November.

———. 1991. "Der Unabhängige Frauenverband." In *Von der Illegalität ins Parlament,* ed. Helmut Müller-Enbergs, Marianne Schulz, and Jan Wielgohs. Berlin: LinksDruck.

————. 1992. "Frauenbewegung in den Ländern der ehemaligen DDR." *Forschungsjournal Neue Soziale Bewegungen* 1:34–41.

————. 1992a. "Einige Überlegungen zur Situation des UFV." *Weibblick* 1:14–17.

————. 1994. "Überlegungen zum Unabhängigen Frauenverband." *Berliner Debatte* 4:71–82.

————. 1994a. "Bundesweiter Feministischer Zusammenschluß." *Weibblick,* no. 1 (December): 48–50.

————. 1996. "Der Unabhängige Frauenverband. Organisationslaufbahn eines Frauenpolitischen Experiments im deutsch-deutschen Vereinigungsprozeß." Dissertation, Free University Berlin.

Hampele, Anne, Helmut Müller-Enbergs, Marianne Schulz, and Jan Wielgohs. 1992. "Zwischen Anspruch, Realpolitik und Verklärung." *Forschungs- journal Neue Soziale Bewegungen,* no. 1: 24–33.

Harding, Sandra. 1984. "Is Gender a Variable in Conceptions of Rationality? A Survey of Issues." In Carol C. Gould, *Beyond Domination. New Perspectives on Women and Philosophy.* Rowman and Allanheld Publishers.

————. 1990. "Feminism, Science, and the Anti-Enlightenment Critiques." In *Feminism/Postmodern,* ed. Linda Nicholson. New York and London: Routledge.

————. 1991. *Whose Science? Whose Knowledge?* Ithaca: Cornell University Press.

Hartmann, Heidi. 1981. "The Unhappy Marriage of Marxism and Feminism: Towards a More Progressive Union." In *Women and Revolution,* ed. Lydia Sargent. Boston: South End Press.

Hartung, Sven, and Stefan Kadelbach. 1992. *Bürger, Recht, Staat.* Frankfurt: Fischer Taschenbuch.

Haufe, Gerda, and Karl Bruckmeier, eds. 1993. *Die Bürgerbewegungen in der DDR und in den Ostdeutschen Ländern.* Opladen: Westdeutscher Verlag.

Haug, Frigga. 1990. "Über die Frauenfrage als Systemfrage. Anmerkungen zum Frauen-Manifest von Ina Merkel." *Das Argument* 180:263–66.

Haug, Wolfgang Fritz. 1991. "The Surrender of the Fortress: Did the East German People Vote for the Restoration?" *Rethinking Marxism* (fall): 24–28.

Heidenheimer, Arnold J. 1986. "Politics, Policy and Policey as Concepts in English and Continental Languages: An Attempt to Explain Divergences." *Review of Politics* 48, no. 1 (winter 1986): 3–30.

Heller, Agnes. 1980. "On Formal Democracy." In *Civil Society and the State,* ed. John Keane. London, Verso.

Helwerth, Ulrike. 1994. "Ohne Frauen ist ein Staat zu machen." *Freitag,* December 16.

————. 1995. *FrauenStreikTag, 8. März, '94.* Berlin, Köln, Bonn, and Hamburg: UFV, Streikkomitee, FrauenAnstiftung.

Helwerth, Ulrike, and Gislinde Schwarz. 1995. *Von Muttis und Emanzen. Feministinnen in Ost- und Westdeutschland.* Frankfurt: Fischer.

Helwig, Gisela. 1982. *Frau und Familie in beiden deutschen Staaten.* Köln: Verlag Wissenschaft und Politik.

———. 1988. "Staat und Familie in der DDR." In *Die DDR in der Ära Honecker,* ed. Gert-Joachim Glaeßner. Opladen: Westdeutscher Verlag.

Helwig, Gisela, and Hildegard Maria Nickel, eds. 1993. *Frauen in Deutschland, 1945–1992.* Bonn: Bundeszentrale für politische Bildung.

Henzler, Herbert A., and Lothar Späth. 1993. *Sind die Deutschen noch zu retten?* Munich: C. Bertelsmann.

Hering, Heide. 1991. "'Frauen in bester Verfassung,' Das erste Jahr unserer Initiative in der Humanistischen Union." *Feministische Studien,* extra.

Herles, Helmut, and Ewald Rose. 1990. *Vom Runden Tisch zum Parlament.* Bonn: Bouvier Verlag.

Hernes, Helga Maria. 1987. "Women and the Welfare State: The Transition from Private to Public Dependence." In *Women and the State,* ed. Anne Showstack Sassoon. London: Routledge.

Hirsch, Joachim. 1986. *Der Sicherheitsstaat.* Frankfurt: Athenäum.

———. 1990. *Kapitalismus ohne Alternative?* Hamburg: VSA-Verlag.

Hirschman, Albert O. 1992. "Abwanderung, Widerspruch und das Schicksal der Deutschen Demokratischen Republik." *Leviathan* 3:330–58.

———. 1993. "Exit, Voice, and the Fate of the German Democratic Republic." *World Politics,* 45 (January): 173–202.

Höcker, Beate. 1987. "Politik, Noch Immer kein Beruf für Frauen?" *Aus Politik und Zeitgeschichte* B 9–10:3–14.

———. 1994. "Parlamentarierinnen im Deutschen Bundestag 1949 bis 1990. Ein Postskriptum zur Abgeordnetensoziologie." *Zeitschrift für Parlamentsfragen,* no. 4: 556–81.

Hofmann, Gunter. 1990. "Wer zahlt, hat auch das Sagen." *Die Zeit,* no. 8 (16 February): 2.

Holland-Cunz, Barbara. 1994. "Öffentlichkeit und Intimität—demokratietheoretische Überlegungen." In *Demokratie oder Androkratie? Theorie und Praxis demokratischer Herrschaft in der feministischen Diskussion,* ed. Elke Biester, Barbara Holland-Cunz, and Birgit Sauer. Frankfurt and New York: Campus Verlag.

Holzhauer, Johanna, and Agnes Steinbauer. 1994. *Frauen an der Macht. Profile prominenter Politikerinnen.* Frankfurt: Eichborn.

Huelshoff, Michael G., Andrei S. Markovits, and Simon Reich, eds. 1993. *From Bundesrepublik to Deutschland.* Ann Arbor: University of Michigan Press.

Hüning, Hasko, and Hildegard Maria Nickel (Hrsg.). 1997. *Grossbetrieblicher Dienstleistungssektor in den neuen Bundesländern.* Opladen: Leske and Budrich.

Inglehart, Ronald. 1977. *The Silent Revolution: Changing Values and Political Styles among Western Publics.* Princeton: Princeton University Press.

———. 1990. "Values, Ideology, and Cognitive Mobilization in New Social Movements." In *Challenging the Political Order,* ed. Russell J. Dalton and Manfred Kuechler. Oxford: Polity Press.

Institut für Demoskopie Allensbach, ed. 1995. *Frauen in Deutschland, Die Schering-Frauenstudie '93.* Köln: Bund Verlag. Institut für Wirtschaftsforschung,

Halle, Wirtschaft im Wandel, "Geschlechtsspezifische Differenzierung der Erwerbsbeteiligung." 4/1995.

Janssen-Jurreit, Marielouise. 1990. "Von Papa Staat zu Mama Staat." In *Vater Staat und seine Frauen,* ed. Barbara Schaeffer-Hegel. Pfaffenweiler: Centaurus-Verlagsgesellschaft.

Jarausch, Konrad H. 1994. *The Rush to German Unity.* New York and Oxford: Oxford University Press.

Jenson, Jane. 1985. "Struggling for Identity: The Women's Movement and the State in Western Europe." *West European Politics* 8, no. 4 (October): 5–18.

———. 1986. "Gender and reproduction: or babies and the state." *Studies in Political Economy,* 20 (summer 1986): 9–46.

———. 1989. "Paradigms and Political Discourse: Protective Legislation in France and the United States Before 1914." *Canadian Journal of Political Science* 22, no. 2 (June): 235–58.

———. 1991. "Ideas, Spaces and Times in Canadian Political Economy." *Studies in Political Economy* 36 (fall): 43–72.

Jenson, Jane, Elisabeth Hagen, and Ceallaigh Reddy, eds. 1988. *Feminization of the Labor Force.* New York: Oxford University Press.

Jesse, Eckhard. 1992. "Der innenpolitische Weg zur deutschen Einheit Zäsuren einer atemberaubenden Entwicklung." In *Die Gestaltung der Deutschen Einheit,* ed. Eckhard Jesse and Armin Mitter. Berlin: Bouvier.

Jesse, Eckhard, and Armin Mitter, eds. 1992. *Die Gestaltung der Deutschen Einheit.* Berlin: Bouvier.

Jessop, Bob. 1979. "Corporatism, Parliamentarism, and Social Democracy." In *Trends Toward Corporatist Intermediation,* ed. Philippe C. Schmitter and Gerhard Lehmbruch. Beverly Hills, Calif.: Sage.

———. 1990. *State Theory.* Cambridge: Polity Press.

———. 1994. "Recent Developments in State Theory: Approaches, Issues, and Agendas." MS.

Jonasdottir, Anna G. 1994. *Why Women Are Oppressed.* Philadelphia: Temple University Press.

Joas, Hans, and Martin Kohli. 1993. *Der Zusammenbruch der DDR.* Frankfurt: Suhrkamp.

Joppke, Christian. 1995. *East German Dissidents and the Revolution of 1989.* New York: New York University Press.

Kaase, Max. 1990. "Social Movements and Political Innovation." In *Challenging the Political Order,* ed. Russell J. Dalton and Manfred Kuechler. Oxford: Polity Press.

Kaelble, Hartmut, Jürgen Kocka, and Hartmut Zwahr. 1994. *Sozialgeschichte der DDR.* Stuttgart: Klett Cotta.

Kahlau, Cordula, ed. 1990. *Aufbruch! Frauenbewegung in der DDR.* Munich: Verlag Frauenoffensive.

Kaplan, Gisela. 1992. *Contemporary Western European Feminism.* New York: New York University Press.

Katzenstein, Mary Fainsod, and Carol McClurg Mueller. 1987. *The Women's*

Movements of the United States and Western Europe. Philadelphia: Temple University Press.

Katzenstein, Peter J. 1982. "West Germany as Number Two: Reflections on the German Model." In *The Political Economy of West Germany,* ed. Andrei S. Markovits. New York: Praeger.

———. 1987. *Policy and Politics in West Germany: The Growth of a Semisovereign State.* Philadelphia: Temple University Press.

———. 1988. "The Third West German Republic: Continuity in Change." *Journal of International Affairs* 41, no. 2 (summer): 325–44.

———. 1989. *Industry and Politics in West Germany.* Ithaca: Cornell University Press.

Keane, John, ed. 1988. *Civil Society and the State.* London: Verso.

Kelly, Rita Mae, and Georgia Duerst-Lahti. 1994. "Gender Paradigm for Studying Gender Power and Public Leadership: Changing the Way Stories Are Told and Heard." Paper presented at the American Political Science Association's Annual Meeting, New York, 1–4 September.

Kenawi, Samirah. N.d. "Ich weiss es wird einmal ein Wunder gescheh'n." UFV document.

Kirchheimer, Otto. 1966. "Germany: The Vanishing Opposition." In *Political Oppositions in Western Democracies,* ed. Robert A. Dahl. New Haven: Yale University Press.

Kitschelt, Herbert P. 1985. "New Social Movements in West Germany and the United States." *Political Power and Social Theory* 5:273–324.

———. 1986. "Political Opportunity Structures and Political Protest: Anti-Nuclear Movements in Four Democracies." *British Journal of Political Science* 16:57–85.

———. 1990. "New Social Movements and the Decline of Party Organizations." In *Challenging the Political Order,* ed. Russell J. Dalton and Manfred Kuechler. Oxford: Polity Press.

———. 1991. "Resource Mobilization: A Critique." In *Research on Social Movements. The State of the Art in Western Europe and the USA,* ed. Dieter Rucht. Boulder, Colo.: Westview.

Klandermans, Bert P. 1990. "Linking the 'Old' and 'New': Movement Networks in the Netherlands." In *Challenging the Political Order,* ed. Russell J. Dalton and Manfred Kuechler. Oxford: Polity Press.

Klandermans, Bert, Hanspeter Kriesi, and Sidney Tarrow, eds., 1988. *From Structure to Action: Comparing Social Movement Research across Cultures.* Greenwich, Conn.: JAI.

Klatt, Hartmut. 1986. "Reform und Perspektiven des Föderalismus in der Bundesrepublik Deutschland. Stärkung der Länder als Modernisierungskonzept." *Aus Politik und Zeitgeschichte,* no. 28: 3–21.

Klier, Freya. 1989. *Abreiß-Kalender. Ein deutsch-deutsches Tagebuch.* Munich: Knaur.

Klinger, Cornelia. 1986. "Déjà-Vu oder die Frage nach den Emanzipationsstrategien im Vergleich zwischen der ersten und zweiten Frauenbewegung." *Kommune* 12/1986: 57–72.

Klotz, Sibyll. 1992. "Die Verschiedenheit als Chance." *Weibblick* 1:13–14.

———. 1992a. "Frauenprojekte Ost—Anpassung oder Widerspruch?" In *20 Jahre und (k)ein bißchen weiser? Bilanz und Perspektiven der Frauenprojektbewegung,* ed. Arbeitskreis Autonomer Frauenprojekte. Brennpunkt-Dokumentation No. 18, Bonn: Stiftung Mitarbeit: 67–73.

Knapp, Gudrun-Axeli. 1992. "Macht und Geschlecht." In *Traditionen Brüche,* ed. Gudrun-Axeli Knapp and Angelika Wetterer. Freiburg: Kore.

Köcher, Renate. 1991. "Reste der Teilung." *Die politische Meinung,* no. 255 (2): 47–52.

Kohl, Helmut. 1992. *Die Deutsche Einheit.* Bergisch Gladbach: Gustav Lübbe Verlag.

Kohler-Koch, Beate, ed. 1992. *Staat und Demokratie in Europa.* Opladen: Leske and Budrich.

Kolinsky, Eva. 1989. *Women in Contemporary Germany. Life, Work and Politics.* Oxford: Berg Publishers.

Kolontay, Alexandra. 1920. *Communism and the Family.* San Francisco: Richmond Record.

Kontos, Sylvia. 1986. "Modernisierung der Subsumtionspolitik. Die Frauenbewegung in den Theorien neuer sozialer Bewegungen." *Feministische Studien* 2:34–49.

———. 1990. "Zum Verhältnis von Autonomie und Partizipation in der Politik der neuen Frauenbewegung." In *Vater Staat und Seine Frauen,* ed. Barbara Schaeffer-Hegel. Pfaffenweiler: Centaurus-Verlagsgesellschaft.

———. 1994. "Jenseits patriarchaler Alternativen: Grenzen der Gleichstellungspolitik." In *Gleichstellungspolitik—Totem und Tabus,* ed. Elke Biester, Barbara Holland-Cunz, Eva Maleck-Lewy, Anja Ruf, and Birgit Sauer. Frankfurt and New York: Campus Verlag.

Kontrovers. 1991. *Die Wende in der DDR.* Bonn: Bundeszentrale für politische Bildung.

Koonz, Claudia. 1987. *Mothers in the Fatherland.* New York: St. Martin's Press.

Koopmans, Ruud. 1995. *Democracy from Below. New Social Movements and the Political System in West Germany.* Boulder: Westview Press.

Kreisky. Eva. 1991. "Der Staat als 'Männerbund,' Der Versuch einer Staatssicht." In *Staat aus feministischer Sicht,* ed. Elke Biester, Brigitte Geißel, Sabine Lang, Birgit Sauer, Petra Schäfter, and Brigitte Young. Berlin: Free University.

———. 1993. "Der Staat ohne Geschlecht? Ansätze feministischer Staatskritik und feministischer Staats- erklärung." In *Österreichische Zeitschrift für Politikwissenschaft,* no. 1: 23–35.

———. 1994. "Das ewig Männerbündische? Zur Standardform von Staat und Politik." In *Wozu Politikwissenschaft? über das Neue in der Politik,* ed. Claus Leggewie. Darmstadt: Wissenschaftlilche Buchgesellschaft.

Kretschmar, Ute. 1990. "Gleichstellung statt Gleichberechtigung." In *Wir wollen mehr als ein "Vaterland,"* ed. Gislind Schwarz and Christine Zenner. Hamburg: Rohwolt.

Krieger, Verena. 1991. *Was bleibt von den Grünen?* Hamburg: Konkret Literatur Verlag.

Kuczynski, Jürgen 1963. *Frauenarbeit Geschichte der Lage der Arbeiter,* bk. 18. Berlin: Akademie-Verlag.

Kuechler, Manfred, and Russell J. Dalton. 1990. "New Social Movements and the Political Order: Inducing Change for Long-term Stability?" In *Challenging the Political Order,* ed. Russell J. Dalton and Manfred Kuechler. Oxford: Polity Press.

Kühnel, Wolfgang, and Carola Sallmon-Metzner. 1991. "Grüne Partei und Grüne Liga." In *Von der Illegalität ins Parlament,* ed. Helmut Müller-Enbergs, Marianne Schulz, and Jan Wielgohs. Berlin: LinksDruck.

Kukutz, Irena. 1995. "'Nicht Rädchen, sondern Sand im Getriebe, den Kreis der Gewalt zu durchbrechen.' Frauenwiderstand in der DDR in den achtziger Jahren." In *Zwischen Selbstbehauptung und Anpassung,* ed. Ulrike Poppe, Rainer Eckert, and Ilko-Sascha Kowalczuk. Berlin: Ch. Links 1995.

Kulawik, Teresa. 1991–92. "Autonomous Mothers? West German Feminism Reconsidered." *German Politics and Society,* nos. 24–25 (winter): 67–86.

Kulke, Christine. 1967. *Die Berufstätigkeit der Frauen in der industriellen Produktion der DDR—zur Theorie und Praxis der Frauenarbeitspolitik der SED.* Ph.D. diss., Free University, Berlin.

———. 1994. "Politische Rationalität, Demokratisierung und Geschlechterpolitik." In *Demokratie oder Androkratie?,* ed. Elke Biester, Barbara Holland-Cunz, and Birgit Sauer. Frankfurt: Campus Verlag.

Kulke, Christine, Heidi Kopp-Degethoff, and Ulrike Ramming, eds. 1992. *Wider das Schlichte Vergessen.* Berlin: Orlanda Frauenverlag.

Kurz-Scherf, Ingrid. 1993. "Frauenbewegung West: In den Wechseljahren?!" Presentation at the UFV-Congress, June 4–6.

———. 1996. "Krise der Arbeit—Krise der Gewerkschaften." *Weibblick,* no. 25 (February–March): 20–29.

Kurzer, Paulette. 1996. "At Odds: Women and Unions in the Labor Markets of Germany and Japan." MS. Dept. of Political Science, University of Arizona, Tucson.

Lafontaine, Oskar. 1990. Interview. "Eine eminente Fehlentscheidung." *Der Spiegel* 22:26–29.

Land, Rainer, and Ralf Possekel. 1992. "Intellektuelle aus der DDR- Kulturelle Identität und Umbruch." *Berliner Debatte,* 1/1992: 86–95.

———. 1994. *Namenlose Stimmen waren uns voraus.* Bochum: Dr. Dieter Winkler Verlag.

Landfried, Christine. 1995. "Architektur der Unterkomplexität: Politische Willensbildung und Entscheidungsstrukturen im Prozeß der deutschen Einigung." In *Einigung und Zerfall, Deutschland und Europa nach dem Ende des Ost-West-Konflikts,* ed. Gerhard Lehmbruch. 19th Scientific Congress of the German Association of Political Science. Opladen: Leske and Budrich.

Lang, Sabine. 1994. "Politische Öffentlichkeit und Demokratie, Überlegungen zur Verschränkung von Androzentrismus und öffentlicher Teilhabe." In

Demokratie oder Androkratie? Theorie und Praxis demokratischer Herrschaft in der feministischen Diskussion, ed. Elke Biester, Barbara Holland- Cunz, and Birgit Sauer. Frankfurt: Campus Verlag.

Laufer, Heinz, and Ursula Münch. 1992. "Die Neugestaltung der bundes- staatlichen Ordnung." In *Die Gestaltung der Deutschen Einheit,* ed. Eckhard Jesse and Armin Mitter. Berlin: Bouvier.

Laver, Michael, and Kenneth A. Shepsle, eds. 1994. *Cabinet Ministers and Parlia- mentary Government.* Cambridge: Cambridge University Press.

Lehmbruch, Gerhard. 1979. "Liberal Corporatism and Party Government." In *Trends Toward Corporatist Intermediation,* ed. Philippe C. Schmitter and Ger- hard Lehmbruch. Beverly Hills, Calif.: Sage.

———. 1984. "Concertation and the Structure of Corporatist Networks." In *Order and Conflict in Contemporary Capitalism,* ed. John H. Goldthorpe. Oxford: Clarendon Press.

———. 1990. Die improvisierte Vereinigung: Die Dritte deutsche Republik." *Leviathan* 4 (December 1990): 462–86.

———. 1991. "Die Deutsche Vereinigung: Strukturen und Strategien." *Politische Vierteljahresschrift* 31, no. 4: 585–604.

———. 1992. "Die deutsche Vereinigung. Strukturen der Politikentwicklung und strategische Anpassungsprozesse." In *Staat und Demokratie in Europa, 18,* ed. Beate Kohler-Koch. Scientific Congress of the German Association for Polit- ical Science. Opladen: Leske and Budrich.

Lehmbruch, Gerhard, and Philippe C. Schmitter, eds. 1982. *Patterns of Corpo- ratist Policy-Making.* London: Sage Modern Politics Series, vol. 7.

Leif, Thomas, Hans-Josef Legrand, and Ansgar Klein. 1992. *Die politische Klasse in Deutschland.* Bonn: Bourvier Verlag.

Lemke, Christiane. 1989. "Eine politische Doppelkultur." In *Politische Kultur in der DDR,* ed. Hans-Georg Wehling. Stuttgart: W. Kohlhammer, GmbH.

———. 1991. *Die Ursachen des Umbruchs 1989.* Opladen: Westdeutscher Verlag.

———. 1993. "Old Troubles and New Uncertainties: Women and Politics in United Germany." In *From Bundesrepublik to Deutschland,* ed. Michael G. Huelshoff, Andrei S. Markovits, and Simon Reich. Ann Arbor: University of Michigan Press.

———. 1994. "Women and Politics: The New Federal Republic of Germany." In *Women and Politics Worldwide,* ed. Barbara Nelson and Najma Chowdhury. New Haven: Yale University Press.

Lerner, Gerda. 1986. *The Creation of Patriarchy.* New York: Oxford University Press.

Liebert, Ulrike, and Wolfgang Merkel, eds. 1991. *Die Politik zur deutschen Einheit.* Opladen: Leske and Budrich.

Lila Offensive. 1990. *Frauen in die Offensive.* Berlin: Dietz Verlag.

Limbach, Jutta, and Marion Eckertz-Höfer, eds. 1993. *Frauenrechte im Grundge- setz des geeinten Deutschland.* Baden-Baden: Nomos.

Limbach, Jutta. 1991. "Zur Rechtsstellung von Eltern und Kindern." *Feminist- ische Studien,* extra.

Lovenduski, Joni. 1986. *Women and European Politics.* Amherst: University of Massachusetts Press.

Maaz, Hans-Joachim. 1990. *Der Gefühlsstau. Ein Psychogramm der DDR.* Berlin: Argon Verlag.

———. 1991. *Das Gestürzte Volk. Die Verunglückte Einheit.* Berlin: Argon Verlag.

MacKinnon, Catherine A. 1982–83. "Feminism, Marxism, Method, and the State: Toward Feminist Jurisprudence." *Signs* 8:635–58.

———. 1989. *Toward a Feminist Theory of the State.* Cambridge: Harvard University Press.

Maier, Charles S. 1982. "Bonn ist doch Weimar: Informal Reflections on the Historical Legacy of the Federal Republic." In *The Political Economy of West Germany,* ed. Andrei S. Markovits. New York: Praeger.

Maier, Friederike. 1991. "Geschlechterverhältnisse der DDR im Umbruch—Zur Bedeutung von Arbeitsmarkt und Sozialpolitik." *Zeitschrift für Sozialreform,* nos. 11–12 (November–December): 648–62.

Maihofer, Andrea. 1991. "Eine notwendige Ergänzung des Gleichberechtigungsartikels, *Feministische Studien* (extra): 38–45.

Maleck, Bernhard. 1991. *Wolfgang Ullmann: "Ich werde nicht schweigen."* Berlin: Dietz.

Maleck-Lewy, Eva. 1990. "Gleichstellung kontra Patriarchat." In *Gleichstellungspolitik in der DDR und BRD.* Berlin: Humboldt University, Zentrum interdisziplinärer Frauenforschung.

———. 1990a. "Frauen in der DDR gegen Par. 218." *Links,* August 7.

———. 1993. "'Ohne Frauen ist kein Staat zu machen.' Die Ostdeutsche Frauenbewegung auf der Suche nach ihrer Geschichte und Zukunft." MS.

———. 1993a. "Wi(e)der die Vereinzelung!" Bericht über den 5. Kongreß des Unabhängigen Frauenverbandes (UFV) vom 4. bis 6. Juni 1993 in Berlin." In *Rundbrief, Netzwerk politikwissenschaftlich und politisch arbeitender Frauen und Arbeitskreis "Politik und Geschlecht" in der Deutschen Vereinigung für Politische Wissenschaft,* no. 4 (October).

———. 1995. "Between Self-determination and State Supervision: Women and the Abortion Law in Post-unification Germany." *Social Politics* 2, no. 1 (spring): 62–75.

Maleck-Lewy, Eva, and Myra Marx Ferree. 1996. "Talking about Women and Wombs: Discourse about Abortion and Reproductive Rights in the GDR during and after the "Wende." Paper prepared for the Conference on Gender and Eastern Europe, American Council of Learned Societies, Il Ciocco, Italy, June.

Maleck-Lewy, Eva, and Virginia Penrose, eds. 1995. *Gefährtinnen der Macht. Politische Partizipation von Frauen im vereinigten Deutschland—eine Zwischenbilanz.* Berlin: Edition Sigma 1995.

Markovits, Andrei S. 1982. "Introduction: Model Germany—A Cursory Overview of a Complex Construct." In *The Political Economy of West Germany.* New York: Praeger.

———, ed. 1982. *The Political Economy of West Germany.* New York: Praeger.

Markovits, Andrei S., and Philip S. Gorski. 1993. *The German Left: Red Green and Beyond.* New York: Oxford University Press.

Markovits, Andrei S., and Simon Reich. 1991. "Should Europe Fear the Germans." *German Politics and Society,* no. 23 (summer): 1–20.

Masur, Kurt. 1989. Interview, *Neues Forum Leipzig.* Leipzig: Forum Verlag: 273–77.

Mayer, Margit. 1991a. "Social Movement Research in the United States: A European Perspective." *International Journal of Politics, Culture and Society* 4, no. 4: 459–80.

———. 1991b. "Social Movement Research and Social Movement Practice: The U.S. Pattern." In *Research on Social Movements: The State of the Art in Western Europe and the USA,* ed. Dieter Rucht. Frankfurt and Boulder: Campus Verlag and Westview Press.

———. 1991c. "Politics in the Post-Fordist City." *Socialist Review* 21, no. 1: 105–24.

———. 1993. "The Career of Urban Social Movements in West Germany." In *Mobilizing Politics in the Era of the Global City,* ed. Robert Fisher and Joseph Kline, London and Beverly Hills: Sage.

Mayntz, Renate. 1980. "Executive Leadership in Germany: Dispersion of Power or 'Kanzlerdemokratie'?" In *Presidents and Prime Ministers,* ed. Richard Rose and Ezra N. Suleiman. Washington, D.C.: American Enterprise Institute.

Mayntz, Renate, and Fritz Scharpf. 1975. *Policy-Making in the German Federal Bureaucracy.* New York: Elsevier.

McAdam, Doug, John D. McCarthy, and Mayer N. Zald, eds. 1996. *Comparative Perspectives on Social Movements: Political Opportunities, Mobilizing Structures, and Cultural Framings.* Cambridge, U.K., and New York: Cambridge University Press.

McAdams, James A. 1993. *Germany Divided: From the Wall to Reunification.* Princeton: Princeton University Press.

McCarthy, John, and Mayer N. Zald. 1977. "Resource Mobilization and Social Movements: A Partial Theory." *American Journal of Sociology* 82, no. 6: 1212–41.

Meckel, Markus, and Martin Gutzeit. 1994. *Opposition in der DDR.* Köln: Bund Verlag.

Meier, Kenneth J. 1995. "Replication: A View from the Streets." *PS: Political Science and Politics* 28, no. 3 (September): 456–59.

Meinhof, Ulrike M. 1988. "Die Frauen im SDS oder In eigener Sache." In *Autonome Frauen. Schlüsseltext der Neuen Frauenbewegung seit 1968,* ed. Ann Anders. Frankfurt: Athenäums.

Melucci, Alberto. 1984. "An End to Social Movements?" *Social Science Information,* 23:819–35.

———. 1988. "Getting Involved: Identity and Mobilization in Social Movements." In *From Structure to Action: Comparing Social Movement Research across Cultures,* ed. Bert Klandermans, Hanspeter Kriesi, and Sidney Tarrow. Greenwich, Conn.: JAI.

———. 1989. *Nomads of the Present: Social Movements and Individual Needs in Contemporary Society.* Philadelphia: Temple University Press.

Merkel, Ina. 1990. *. . . und Du: Frau an der Werkbank.* Berlin: Elefanten Press.

———. 1990a. "Frauenpolitische Strategien in der DDR." In "Soziale Lage und Arbeit von Frauen in der DDR, Arbeitskreis Sozialwissenschaftliche Arbeitsmarktforschung," ed. Sabine Gensior, Frederike Maier, and Gabriele Winter. Working Paper 1990–6. Paderborn: University of Paderborn.

———. 1990b. "Ohne Frauen ist kein Staat zu machen." *Das Argument* 180 (March–April): 255–62.

———. 1990c. "Wie Alles Anfing." *Argument extra, Ohne Frauen ist kein Staat zu machen.* Argument Verlag.

———. 1990d. "Frauen haben kein Vaterland." *Argument extra, Ohne Frauen ist kein Staat zu machen.* Argument Verlag.

———. 1990e. "Trick des Westens heißt: Teile und herrsche." Interview. *Die Tageszeitung,* May 12.

———. 1991–92. "Another Kind of Woman." *German Politics and Society* 24–25 (winter): 1–9.

———. 1994. "Leitbilder und Lebensweisen von Frauen in der DDR." In *Sozialgeschichte der DDR,* ed. Hartmut Kaelble, Jürgen Kocka, and Hartmut Zwahr. Stuttgart: Klett Cotta.

Merkl, Peter H. 1963. *The Origin of the West German Republic.* New York: Oxford University Press.

———. 1993. *German Unification in the European Context.* Pennsylvania: Pennsylvania State University Press.

Meuschel, Sigrid. 1992. *Legitimation und Parteiherrschaft in der DDR.* Frankfurt: Suhrkamp.

———. 1993. "Revolution in der DDR. Versuch einer sozialwissenschaftlichen Interpreation." In *Der Zusammenbruch der DDR,* ed. Hans Joas and Martin Kohli. Frankfurt: Suhrkamp.

Meyer, Birgit. 1992. "Die 'unpolitische' Frau. Politische Partizipation von Frauen oder: Haben Frauen ein anderes Verständnis von Politik?" *Aus Politik und Zeitgeschichte,* B 25–26/92, June 12: 3–18.

Meyer, Gerd. 1989. "Der Versorgte Mensch." In *Politische Kultur in der DDR,* ed. Hans-Georg Wehling. Stuttgart: W. Kohlhammer, GmbH.

Mies, Maria. 1987. "Konturen einer Ökofeministischen Gesellschaft." In *Frauen und Ökologie. Gegen den Machbarkeitswahn,* ed. Die Grünen im Bundestag. Cologne: Cologne Volksblatt Verlag.

Miliband, Ralph. 1969. *The State in Capitalist Society.* New York: Basic Book.

Misselwitz, Ruth. 1994. "Ruth Misselwitz im Gespräch." *Weibblick,* no. 16:55–57.

Modrow, Hans, et al. 1992. *Zwei Staaten. Zwei Paktsysteme und ihre Grenze.* Berlin: Oktoberdruck.

Moeller, Robert G. 1993. *Protecting Motherhood.* Berkeley: University of California Press.

Mörbitz, Eghard. 1990. "Kein Blankoscheck aus Moskau." Frankfurter Rundschau, February 22, 3.

Morgner, Irmtraud. 1991. "Die großen Veränderungen beginnen leise." In *Irmtraud Morgners Hexische Weltfahrt,* ed. Kristine von Soden. Berlin: Elefanten Press.

Morris, Aldon D., and Carol McClurg Mueller, eds. 1992. *Frontiers in Social Movement Theory.* New Haven: Yale University Press.

Müller-Enbergs, Helmut, Marianne Schulz, and Jan Wielgohs, eds. 1991. *Von der Illegalität ins Parlament.* Berlin: LinksDruck.

Müller-Rommel, Ferdinand. 1994. "The Role of German Ministers in Cabinet Decision Making." In *Cabinet Ministers and Parliamentary Government,* ed. Michael Laver and Kenneth A. Shepsle. Cambridge: Cambridge University Press.

Münch, Ingo von. 1991. *Dokumente der Wiedervereinigung Deutschlands.* Stuttgart: Alfred Kröner Verlag.

Narr, Wolf-Dieter, ed. 1977. *Auf dem Wege zum Einparteienstaat.* Opladen: Westdeutscher Verlag.

———. 1977. "Parteienstaat in der BRD—ein Koloß auf tönernden Füßen, aber mit stählernen Zähnen." In *Auf dem Weg zum Einparteienstaat,* ed. Wolf-Dieter Narr. Opladen: Westdeutscher Verlag.

Nave-Herz, Rosemarie. 1988. *Die Geschichte der Frauenbewegung in Deutschland.* Bonn: Bundeszentrale fur politische Bildung.

Neidhardt, Friedhelm. 1985. "Einige Ideen zu einer allgemeinen Theorie sozialer Bewegungen." In *Sozialstrukturen im Umbruch: Karl Martin Bolte zum 60. Geburtstag,* ed. Stefan Hradil. Opladen: Westdeutscher Verlag.

Neidhardt, Friedhelm, and Dieter Rucht. 1993. "Auf dem Weg in die 'Bewegungsgesellschaft'?" *Soziale Welt '93,* no. 3: 305–26.

Nelson, Barbara J. 1990. The Origins of the Two-Channel Welfare State: Workmen's Compensation and Mother's Aid." In *Women, the State, and Welfare,* ed. Linda Gordon. Madison: University of Wisconsin Press.

———. 1992. "The Role of Sex and Gender in Comparative Political Analysis: Individuals, Institutions, and Regimes." *American Political Science Review* 86, no. 2 (June): 491–95.

Nelson, Barbara J., and Najma Chowdhury. 1994. *Women and Politics Worldwide.* New Haven: Yale University Press.

Neubert, E. 1991. "Protestantische Kultur und DDR-Revolution." *Politik und Zeitgeschichte.* B 19/91 (May 3): 21–29.

Neues Forum Leipzig. 1989. *Jetzt oder nie—Demokratie! Leipziger Herbst '89.* Leipzig: Forum Verlag Leipzig.

Neugebauer, Gero. 1990. "Socialcharta contra Sozialreport. Entwürfe zu Wunsch und Wirklichkeit der DDR-Sozialpolitik." *Zeitschrift für Parlamentsfragen,* no. 1: 146–49.

Nicholson, Linda, ed. 1990. *Feminism/Postmodernism.* New York and London: Routledge.

Nickel, Hildegard Maria. 1989. "Sex-Role Socialization in Relationships as a

Function of the Division of Labor." In *The Quality of Life in the German Democratic Republic,* ed. Marilyn Rueschmeyer and Christiane Lemke. New York: M. E. Sharpe.

———. 1990. "Frauen in der DDR." *Aus Politik und Zeitgeschichte.* B 16–17 (April 13): 39–45.

———. 1990a. "Geschlechtertrennung durch Arbeitsteilung. Berufs- und Familienarbeit in der DDR." *Feministische Studien* no. 1: 10–19.

———. 1990b. "Zur sozialen Lage von Frauen in der DDR." In "Soziale Lage und Arbeit von Frauen in der DDR, Arbeitkreis, Sozialwissenschaftliche, Arbeitmarktforschung," ed. Sabine Gensior, Frederike Maier, and Gabriele Winter. Working Paper 1990–6. Paderborn: University of Paderborn.

———. 1991–92. "Women in the German Democratic Republic and in the New Federal States: Looking Backwards and Forwards." *German Politics and Society* 24–25 (winter): 34–52.

———. 1992. "Modernisierungsbrüche im Einigungsprozeß—(k)ein einig Volk von Schwestern." In *Wider das Schlichte Vergessen,* ed. Christine Kulke, Heidi Kopp-Degethoff, and Ulrike Ramming. Berlin: Orlanda Frauenverlag.

———. 1993. "Women in the German Democratic Republic and in the New Federal States: Looking Backward and Forward (Five Theses)." In *Gender Politics and Post-Communism,* ed. Nanette Funk and Magda Mueller. New York: Routledge.

———. 1993. "'Mitgestalterinnen des Sozialismus'—Frauenarbeit in der DDR." In *Frauen in Deutschland 1945–1992,* ed. Gisela Helwig and Hildegard Maria Nickel. Bonn: Bundeszentrale für Politische Bildung.

———. 1994. "Mit dem DDR-Gleichstellungsvorsprung in die bundesdeutsche Modernisierungsfalle? Deutschlands Frauen nach der Wende." *Berliner Debatte* 4:3–14.

Nimsch, Margarethe. 1991. "Eine neue Verfassung für Frauen. Ohne Frauenrechte keine Verfassungsreform." *Feministische Studien* (extra): 7–10.

Notz, Gisela. 1992. "Frauen in den neuen Ländern, (Haus-)Wirtschaft ist keine Alternative." In *Entwickeln statt abwickeln,* ed. Werner Schulz and Ludger Volmer. Berlin: Ch. Links, Verlag.

Offe, Claus. 1974. "Structural Problems of the Capitalist State." In *German Political Studies,* vol. 1, ed. Klaus v. Beyme. London: Sage Publications.

———. 1981. "The Attribution of Public Status in Interest Groups: Observations on the West German case." In *Organizing Interests in Western Europe,* ed. Suzanne Berger. Cambridge: Cambridge University Press.

———. 1985. "New Social Movements: Challenging the Boundaries of Institutional Politics." *Social Research* 52, no. 4 (winter): 817–68.

———. 1990. "Reflections on the Institutional Self- transformation of Movement Politics: A Tentative Stage Model." In *Challenging the Political Order,* ed. Russell J. Dalton and Manfred Kuechler. Oxford: Polity Press.

———. 1991. "Prosperity, Nation, Republic: Aspects of the Unique German Journey from Socialism to Capitalism." *German Politics and Society* 22 (spring): 18–32.

———. 1994. *Der Tunnel am Ende des Lichts.* Frankfurt and New York: Campus.

Olbrich, Anne Katrin. 1992. "Der Runde Tisch der Frauen in Dresden." In *Der Runde Tisch—ein neues Demokratiemodell?* Documentation of a Conference in the Dresden City Council, November 29–December 1, 1992, ed. Stiftung Mitarbeit. Bonn: Stiftung Mitarbeit.

Oltmanns, Reimar. 1990. *Frauen an der Macht. Marie Schlei. Renate Schmidt. Irmgard Adam-Schwaetzer. Rita Süssmuth. Antje Vollmer.* Frankfurt: Anton Hain.

Opp, Karl-Dieter. 1991. "Zu den Ursachen einer spontanen Revolution." In Kölner *Zeitschrift für Soziologie und Sozialpsychologie,* 43:302–21.

———. 1992. "Wie erklärt man die Revolution in der DDR." *Forschungsjournal, Neue Soziale Bewegungen* 1:16–23.

Opp, Karl-Dieter, Peter Voss, and Christiane Gern. 1995. *Origins of a Spontaneous Revolution: East Germany, 1989.* Ann Arbor: University of Michigan Press.

Ostner, Ilona. 1994. "Back to the Fifties: Gender and Welfare in Unified Germany." *Social Politics* 1, no. 1 (spring): 32–59.

———. 1991–92. "Ideas, Institutions, Traditions—West German Women's Experience, 1945–1990." *German Politics and Society* 24–25 (winter): 87–99.

Outshoorn, Joyce. 1994. "State Feminism and 'Femocrats' in the Netherlands." Paper presented at the Annual Meeting of the American Political Science Association, September 1–4.

Panitch, Leo. 1979. "The Development of Coporatism in Liberal Democracies." In *Trends toward Corporatist Intermediation,* ed. Philippe C. Schmitter and Gerhard Lehmbruch. Beverly Hills, Calif.: Sage.

Pateman, Carole. 1988. *The Sexual Contract.* Cambridge: Polity Press.

———. 1988a. "The Patriarchal Welfare State." In *Democracy and the Welfare State,* ed. Amy Gutman. Princeton: Princeton University Press.

———. 1988b. "The Fraternal Social Contract." In *Civil Society and the State,* ed. John Keane. London: Verso.

———. 1989. *The Disorder of Women.* Stanford: Stanford University Press.

Paterson, William E., and David Southern. 1991. *Governing Germany.* New York: W. W. Norton.

Penrose, Virginia. 1993. *Orientierungsmuster des Karriereverhaltens deutscher Politikerinnen, Ein Ost-West Vergleich.* Bielefeld: Kleine Verlag GmbH.

———. 1993. "The Political Participation of GDR Women during the Wende." In *Studies in GDR Culture and Society,* ed. Gerber G. Woods. 11–12: 37–52.

———. 1994. "Differenzen im Demokratieverständnis ost- und westdeutscher Politikerinnen:" In *Demokratie oder Androkratie?,* ed. Elke Biester, Barbara Holland-Cunz, and Birgit Sauer. Frankfurt: Campus.

Pfarr, Heide. 1991. "Quotierung ein Reizwort auch in der Verfassung." *Feministische Studien* (extra): 30–32.

Phillips, Anne. 1987. *Feminism and Equality.* New York: New York University Press.

———. 1991. *Engendering Democracy.* Cambridge: Polity Press.

Pond, Elizabeth. 1993. *Beyond the Wall.* Washington, D.C.: Brookings Institution.

Poppe, Ulrike. 1995. "Der Weg ist das Ziel." Zum Selbstverständnis und der politischen Rolle oppositioneller Gruppen der achtziger Jahre." In *Zwischen Selb-*

stbehauptung und Anpassung, ed. Ulrike Poppe, Rainer Eckert, Ilko-Sascha Kowalczuk. Berlin: Ch. Links.

Poppe, Ulrike, Rainer Eckert, and Ilko-Sascha Kowalczuk, eds. 1995. *Zwischen Selbstbehauptung und Anpassung.* Berlin: Ch. Links.

Posadskaya, Anastasia. 1993. "Übergangszeit in Rußland. Demokratisierung ohne Frauen." In *beiträge zur feministischen theorie und praxis:* 34:93–97.

Preuß, Ulrich K. 1990. "Grundgesetz-Chauvinismus oder . . . neue gesamtdeutsche Verfassung?" *Die Tageszeitung,* March 3, 2–3.

———. 1991. "Brauchen wir eine neue Verfassung?" In *Eine Verfassung für Deutschland. Manifest Text Plädoyers,* ed. Bernd Guggenberger, Ulrich Preuß, and Wolfgang Ulmann. Munich: Carl Hanser Verlag.

Priewe, Jan, and Rudolf Hickel. 1991. *Der Preis der Einheit.* Frankfurt: Fischer.

Probst, Lothar. 1994. "Das Modell Runder Tisch." In *Die real- existierende post-sozialistische Gesellschaft.* Berlin: Wissenschaftliche Konferenz der Branden-burgischen Landeszentrale für politische Bilding.

Reichart-Dreyer, Ingrid. 1995. "Partizipation von Frauen in der CDU." In *Gefährtinnen der Macht. Politische Partizipation von Frauen im vereinigten Deutschland—eine Zwischenbilanz,* ed. Eva Maleck-Lewy and Virginia Pen-rose. Berlin: Ed. Sigma.

Richardson, Jeremy. 1982. *Policy Styles in Western Europe.* London: George Allen and Unwin, 1982.

Richter, Manfred, and Elsbeth Zylla, eds. 1991. *Mit Pfugscharen gegen Schwerter. Erfahrungen in der Evangelischen Kirche in der DDR, 1949–1990.* Bremen: Edition Temmen.

Riedmüller, Barbara. 1988. "Das Neue an der Frauenbewegung. Versuch einer Wirkungsanalyse der neuen Frauenbewegung." In *Frauensituation. Verän-derungen in den letzten zwanzig Jahren,* ed. Uta Gerhardt and Yvonne Schütze. Frankfurt a.M.: Suhrkamp.

Riemer, Jeremiah M. 1993. "Reproduction and Reunification: The Politics of Abortion in United Germany." In *From Bundesrepublik to Deutschland,* ed. Michael G. Huelshoff, Andrei S. Markovits, and Simon Reich. Ann Arbor: University of Michigan Press.

Rohnstock, Katrin. Handbuch. 1991. *Wegweiser für Frauen in den fünf neuen Bun-desländern.* Berlin: BasisDruck.

Rossanda, Rossana. 1990. "Differenz und Gleichheit" In *Differenz und Gleichheit,* ed. Ute Gerhard, Mechtild Jansen, Andrea Maihofer, Pia Schmid, and Irm-gard Schultz. Frankfurt: Ulrike Helmer Verlag.

Roth, Dieter. 1990. "Die Wahlen zur Volkskammer in der DDR. Der Versuch einer Erklärung." *Politische Vierteljahreschrift* no. 3: 369–93.

Roth, Roland. 1991. "Local Green Politics in West German Cities." *International Journal of Urban and Regional Research* 15, no. 1: 75–89.

———. 1994. *Demokratie von unten. Neue soziale Bewegungen auf dem Wege zur politischen Institution.* Köln: Bund-Verlag.

Roth, Silke, and Myra Marx Ferree. 1996. "Sisterhood and Solidarity? Mobilizing for the WomensStrikeDay in Germany, March 8, 1994." Paper presented at the Eastern Sociological Society, Boston, Mass.

Rowbotham, Sheila. 1979. "The Trouble with 'Patriarchy.'" *New Statesman,* December.

Rucht, Dieter. 1988. "Themes, Logics, and Arenas of Social Movements: A Structural Approach." In *From Structure to Action: Comparing Social Movement Research across Cultures,* ed. B. Klandermans, H. Kriesi, and S. Tarrow. Greenwich, Conn.: JAI.

———. 1990. "The Strategies and Action Repertoires of New Movements." In *Challenging the Political Order,* ed. Russell J. Dalton and Manfred Kuechler. Oxford: Polity Press.

Rucht, Dieter. 1994. "German Unification, Democratization and the Role of Social Movements: A Missed Opportunity?" Paper presented at the International Political Science Association in Berlin, August 21–25.

———. 1996. "German Unification, Democratization, and the Role of Social Movements: A Missed Opportunity?" *Mobilization* 1, no. 1: 36–62.

———, ed. 1991. *Research on Social Movements: The State of the Art in Western Europe and the USA.* Frankfurt and Boulder: Campus Verlag and Westview Press.

Rueschemeyer, Marilyn. 1988. "New Family Forms in a State Socialist Society." *Journal of Family Issues* 9, no. 3 (September): 354–71.

———, ed. 1994. *Women in the Politics of Postcommunist Eastern Europe.* New York: M. E. Sharpe.

Rueschemeyer, Marilyn, and Christiane Lemke. 1989. *The Quality of Life in the German Democratic Republic.* New York: M. E. Sharpe.

Rüddenklau, Wolfgang. 1992. *Störenfried.* Berlin: BasisDruck 1992.

Sabadykina, Jelena. 1993. "Frauen im heutigen Rußland am Beispiel von Sankt-Petersburg." *Beiträge zur feministischen Theorie und Praxis* 34:99–106.

Sander, Helke. 1988. "Rede des 'Aktionsrates zur Befreiung der Frauen,'" In *Autonome Frauen. Schlüsseltexte der Neuen Frauenbeweung seit 1968,* ed. Ann Anders. Frankfurt: Athenäums.

Sapiro, Virginia. 1981. "Research Frontier Essay: When Are Interests Interesting? The Problem of Political Representation of Women." *APSR* 75:701–16.

Sarkar, Saral. 1993. *Green-Alternative Politics in West Germany.* Vol. 1: *The New Social Movements.* Tokyo and New York: United Nations University Press.

Sauer, Birgit. 1995. "Der 'Runde Tisch' und die Raumaufteilung der Demokratie. Eine politische Institution des Übergangs?" In *Politische Soziologie. Sonderheft der Kölner Zeitschrift für Soziologie und Sozialpsychologie,* ed. Brigitta Nedelmann.

———. 1994. "Macht- oder Kulturorientierung? Politische Motivationen und Zielsetzungen im Unabhängigen Frauenverband (UFV)." MS.

———. 1994a. "Was heißt und zu welchem Zwecke partizipieren wir? Kritische Anmerkungen zur Partizipationsforschung." In *Demokratie oder Androkratie?* ed. Elke Biester, Barbara Holland-Cunz, and Birgit Sauer. Frankfurt: Campus.

———. 1994a. "Totem und Tabus. Zur Neubestimmung von Gleichstellungspolitik. Eine Einführung." In *Gleichstellungspolitik—Totem und Tabus,* ed. Elke

Biester, Barbara Holland-Cunz, Eva Maleck-Lewy, Anja Ruf, and Birgit Sauer. Frankfurt: Campus.

———. 1995. "'Doing Gender.' Das Parlament als Ort der Ge-schlechterkonstruktion. Eine Analyse der Bundestagsdebatte um die Neuregelung des Schwangerschaftsabbruches." In *Sprache des Parlaments und Semiotik der Demokratie. Studien zur politischen Kommunikation in der Moderne,* ed. Andreas Dörner and Ludgern Voigt. Berlin: Walter de Gruyter.

Schabowski, Günter. 1991. *Das Politbüro.* Hamburg: Rowohlt.

Schaeffer-Hegel, Barbara. 1995. *Frauen mit Macht. Zum Wandel der politischen Kultur durch die Präsenz von Frauen in Führungs- Positionen.* Pfaffenweiler: Centaurus Verlag.

———, ed. 1990. *Vater Staat und seine Frauen. Beiträge zur politischen Theorie.* Pfaffenweiler: Centaurus-Verlagsgesellschaft.

———, ed. 1988. *Frauen und Macht. Der alltägliche Beitrag der Frauen zur Politik des Patriarchats.* Pfaffenweiler: Centaurus-Verlagsgesellschaft.

Schäfer, Eva. 1993. "Wie ich Feministische Politik verstehe." *Weibblick,* no. 11: 18–22.

———. 1991. "Drei Schritte zurück in der Frauenfrage—zum Wandel von Frauenleben in der ehemaligen DDR." Paper presented at the UFV Congress, March 8–10.

———. 1991a. "Frauen und Politik—zum Politikverständnis innerhalb der Unabhängigen Frauenbewegung der ehemaligen DDR." MS. April 7.

———. 1990. "Die fröhliche Revolution der Frauen." In *Wir wollen mehr als ein "Vaterland,"* ed. Gislinde Schwarz and Christine Zenner. Hamburg: Rowohlt.

———. 1990. "'Wer sich nicht wehrt, kommt an den Herd!'"*Das Argument* 180 (March–April): 273–80.

Scharpf, Fritz W. 1984. "Economic and Institutional Constraints of Full-Employment Strategies: Sweden, Austria, and West Germany, 1973–1982." In *Order and Conflict in Contemporary Capitalism,* ed. John H. Goldthorpe. Oxford: Clarendon Press.

———. 1987. *Crisis and Choice in European Social Democracy.* Ithaca: Cornell University Press.

———. 1990. "Holzweg, nicht Königsweg." *Die Zeit,* March 12–16, p. 55.

———. 1991. "Entwicklungslinien des bundesdeutschen Föderalismus." *Leviathan,* Sonderheft 12:146–59.

Schäuble, Wolfgang. 1991. *Der Vertrag. Wie ich über die deutsche Einheit verhandelte.* Stuttgart: Deutsche Verlags-Anstalt.

Schäuble, Wolfgang, and Markus Meckel. 1990. Interview. *Der Spiegel* 12:48–57.

Schenk, Christina. 1994. "Feministische Politik im Bundestag—Erfahrungen und Perspektiven" In *Demokratie oder Androkratie?,* ed. Elke Biester, Barbara Holland-Cunz, and Birgit Sauer. Frankfurt and New York: St. Martin's Press.

———. 1994. "Der Politikbegriff von ostdeutschen Frauen am Beispiel des Unabhängigen Frauenverbandes (UFV)." In *EigenArtige Ostfrauen,* ed. Birgit Bütow and Heidi Stecker. Bielefeld: Kleine Verlag.

———. 1993. "Ein paar Gedanken . . . zum UFV und eine Entgegnung auf den

Beitrag von Eva Schäfer, "Wie ich feministische Politik verstehe." *Weibblick,* no. 12: 34–40.

———. 1993. "Lesbians and Their Emancipation in the Former German Democratic Republic: Past and Future." In *Gender Politics and Post-Communism,* ed. Nanette Funk and Magda Mueller. New York: Routledge.

———. 1992. "Eine Möglichkeit Politik zu machen." *Weibblick* 5:6–9.

———. 1991. "Experiment UFV." In *Irmtraud Morgners Hexische Weltfahrt,* ed. Kristine von Soden. Berlin: Elefanten Press.

———. 1990. "Experiment Unabhängiger Frauenverband." *Das Argument* 184 (November–December): 847–57.

———. 1990a. "Die haben unsere Kompromißbereitschaft ausgereizt bis zum Ende." *Die Tageszeitung,* October 10.

Schenk, Sabine. 1994. "Eastern Women in the Unified Germany. Modernisation or De-Modernisation in Gender Stratification?" Sabine Schenk, Commission for the Research on Social and Political Changes in the New Federal States of Germany, Halle, Germany, MS.

Schiller, Karl. 1990. Interview mit Professor Karl Schiller über Wirtschaftsreformen. *Der Spiegel* 3:51–56.

———. 1994. *Der Schwierige Weg in die offene Gesellschaft.* Berlin: Siedler Verlag.

Schindler, Christiane. 1992. "Frauen Runde Tische—Ein Sinnvolles Politikmodell?!" *Weibblick* 5:13–16.

———. 1993. "Frauenstreik zum Frauentag." *Weibblick,* no. 12: 33–34.

Schleusener, Anita, Heide Balschuweit, and Sieglinde Schwind. 1992. "Der Runde Tisch der Frauen in Aue/Sachsen." In *Von der Illegalität ins Parlament,* ed. Helmut Müller-Enbergs, Marianne Schulz, and Jan Wielgohs. Berlin: Links-Druck.

Schulz, Marianne. 1991. "Neues Forum. Von der illegalen Opposition zur legalen Marginalität." In *Der Runde Tisch—ein neues Demokratiemodell?* Documentation of a Conference in the Dresden City Council, November 29–December 1, 1992, ed. Stiftung Mitarbeit. Bonn: Stiftung Mitarbeit.

Schmid, Carol. 1990. "Women in the West German Green Party: The Uneasy Alliance of Ecology and Feminism." In *Women and Social Protest,* ed. Guida West and Rhoda Lois Blumberg. New York: Oxford University Press.

Schmid, Thomas. 1990. *Staatsbegräbnis.* Berlin: Rotbuch Verlag.

Schmidt, Helmut. 1993. *Handeln für Deutschland.* Berlin: Rohwohlt.

Schmidt, Manfred G., ed. 1988. *Staatstätigkeit. Politische Vierteljahresschrift* Special Issue 19.

Schmidt, Renate. 1991. "Neue Rechte für Frauen in Gesamtdeutschland." *Nach der Vereinigung Deutschlands: Frauen fordern Ihr Recht.* Bonn: Friedrich Ebert Stiftung, Gesprächskreis Frauenpolitik, January.

———. 1994. "Jenseits des Patriarchats." In *Perspektiven für Deutschland,* ed. Warnfried Dettling. Munich: Knaur.

Schmitter, Philippe C., and Gerhard Lehmbruch. 1979. *Trends toward Corporatist Intermediation.* Beverly Hills, Calif.: Sage.

Schmitz-Köster, Dorothee. 1991. "Hexen, Weltfahrer und die Schöne Melusine."

In *Irmtraud Morgners Hexische Weltfahrt,* ed. Kristine von Soden. Berlin: Elefanten Press.

Schöler-Macher, Bärbel. 1992. "Elite ohne Frauen. Erfahrungen von Poltikerinnen mit einer männlichen geprägten Alltagswirklichkeit in Parteien und Parlamenten." In *Die politische Klasse in Deutschland,* ed. Thomas Leif, Hans-Josef Legrand, and Ansgar Klein. Bonn: Bouvier Verlag.

Scholze, Siegfried, and Hans-Jürgen Arendt. 1986. *Zur Rolle der Frau in der Geschichte der DDR.* Leipzig: Verlag für die Frau.

Schönfeldt, Beate. 1990. "'Die Frauenfrage ist eine Frage von Übermorgen.' Regisseurinnen in der DDR und ihre Filme, *Feministische Studien,* no. 1 (May): 50–60.

Schröder, Monika. 1991. "Deutschland in Europa." In *Der Schwierige Weg zur Demokratie,* ed. Gert-Joachim Glaessner. Opladen: Westdeutscher Verlag.

Schubert, Friedel. 1980. *Die Frau in der DDR.* Opladen: Leske Verlag und Budrich GmbH.

Schulz, Werner, and Ludger Volmer, eds. 1992. *Entwickeln statt abwickeln.* Berlin: Ch. Links.

Schulze, Karla. 1992. "Weg mit 218—Bildung von Meinung und Wissen." *Weibblick* 3–4:38–40.

Schütt, Hans-Dieter. 1992. *Regine Hildebrandt: "Bloß nicht aufgeben!"* Berlin: Dietz.

Schüttemeyer, Suzanne S. 1994. "Hierarchy and Efficiency in the Bundestag: The German Answer for Institutionalizing Parliament." In *Parliaments in the Modern World,* ed. Gary W. Copeland and Samuel C. Patterson. Ann Arbor: University of Michigan Press.

Schwarz, Gislinde. 1990a. "Aufbruch der Hexen." In *Aufbruch! Frauenbewegung in der DDR,* ed. Cordula Kahlau. Munich: Frauenoffensive.

Schwarz, Gislinde, and Christine Zenner, eds. 1990. *Wir wollen mehr als ein "Vaterland."* Hamburg: Rohwolt.

Schwarzer, Alice. 1977. *Der "kleine Unterschied" und seine großen Folgen.* Frankfurt: Fischer.

———. 1981. *10 Jahre Frauenbewegung. So fing es an!* Cologne: Emma-Frauenverlag.

———. 1993. "218-Reform 5 Nach 12." *Emma,* no. 1 (January–February): 68–69.

Scott, Joan Wallach. 1988. *Gender and the Politics of History.* New York: Columbia University Press.

Seibel, Wolfgang. 1993. "Verwaltungsintegration im vereinigten Deutschland." In *Verwaltungsreform und Verwaltungspolitik im Prozeß der deutschen Einigung,* ed. Wolfgang Seibel, Arthur Benz, and Heinrich Mäding. Baden-Baden: Nomos Verlagsgesellschaft.

Seibel, Wolfgang, Arthur Benz, and Heinrich Mäding, eds. 1993. *Verwaltungsreform und Verwaltungspolitik im Prozeß der deutschen Einigung.* Baden-Baden: Nomos Verlagsgesellschaft.

Seifert, Jürgen. 1990. "Die Bundesrepublik behält alles in der Hand." *Frankfurter Rundschau,* March 20.

Semtner, Klemens. 1992. *Der Runde Tisch in der DDR.* Munich: Tuduv-Verlag.

Shonfield, Andrew. 1979. "Organisierte freie Marktwirtschaft: Bundes-republik Deutschland." In *Die Bundesrepublik Deutschland. Entstehung Entwicklung Struktur,* ed. Wolf-Dieter Narr and Dietrich Thränhardt. Königstein: Anton Hain Meisenheim GmbH.

———. 1980 (1965). *Modern Capitalism.* London: Oxford University Press.

Showstack Sassoon, Anne. 1987. "Women's New Social Role: Contradictions of the Welfare State." In *Women and the State.* London: Routledge.

———, ed. 1987. *Women and the State.* London: Routledge.

Singer, Otto. 1992. "The Politics and Economics of German Unification: From Currency Union to Economic Dichotomy." *German Politics* 1 (April): 78–94.

Skocpol, Theda. 1992. *Protecting Soldiers and Mothers.* Cambridge: Harvard University Press.

Smith, Gordon. 1982. *Democracy in Western Germany. Parties and Politics in the Federal Republic,* 2d ed. New York: Holmes and Meier.

Smith, Gordon, William E. Paterson, and Peter H. Merkl, eds. 1989. *Developments in West German Politics.* Durham: Duke University Press.

Snow, David A., and Robert D. Benford. 1992. "Master Frames and Cycles of Protest." In *Frontiers in Social Movement,* ed. Aldon D. Morris and Carol McClurg Mueller. New Haven: Yale University Press.

Snow, David A., and Robert D. Benford. 1988. "Ideology, Frame Resonance, and Participant Mobilization." In *From Structure to Action: Comparing Social Movement Research across Cultures,* ed. B. Klandermans, H. Kriesi, and S. Tarrow. Greenwich, Conn.: JAI.

Soden, Kristine von. 1991. *Irmtraud Morgners Hexische Weltfahrt.* Berlin: Elefanten Press.

Sombart, Nicolaus. 1988. "Männerbund und politische Kultur in Deutschland." In *Typisch deutsch: Die deutsche Jugendbewegung,* ed. J. H. Knoll and J. H. Schoeps. Opladen: Leske and Budrich.

Sommerkorn, Ingrid, with R. Nave-Herz and Christine Kulke. 1970. *Women's Careers: Experience from East and West Germany.* London: P E P, October.

Sontheimer, Kurt. 1993. *Grundzüge des politischen Systems der neuen Bundesrepublik Deutschland.* Munich: Piper.

Southern, David. 1992. "The Constitutional Framework of the New Germany." *German Politics* 1 (April): 31–49.

Sozialistische Fraueninitiative (SOFI). 1990. "Positionspapier zur Vereinigung der beiden deutschen Staaten." *Feministische Studien* 1 (May 1990): 143–47.

Spiegel, Der. 1989. "Die Siegermächte warnen Bonn." 50:16–19.

———. 1989a. "Vieles ist möglich." 50:19–21.

———. 1989b. "Die Macht liegt auf der Straße." 50:22–26.

———. 1989c. "Jedes Pissoir beherrscht." 50:27–29.

———. 1990. "Auf den Kohl eindreschen." 22:21–25.

———. 1990. "Deutschlandpolitik: Bonn befürchtet eine neue Übersiedler-Welle." 3:16–18.

———. 1990. "Erst Mitleid, dann zuschlagen." 3:19–28.

Steffani, Winfried. 1990. "Parties (Parliamentary Groups) and Committees in the Bundestag." In *The U.S. Congress and the German Bundestag,* ed. Uwe Thaysen, Roger H. Davidson, and Robert Gerald Livingston. Boulder: Westview Press.

Steiger, Christine. 1991. "Alle Macht den Hexen." In *Irmtraud Morgners Hexische Welfahrt,* ed. Kristine von Soden. Berlin: Elefanten Press.

Steinmo, Sven, Kathleen Thelen, and Frank Longstreth. 1992. *Structuring Politics. Historical Institutionalism in Comparative Analysis.* Cambridge: Cambridge University Press.

Stephan, Cora. 1993. *Der Betroffenheitskult, Eine politische Sittengeschichte.* Berlin: Rowohlt.

Stern, Fritz. 1993. "Freedom and Its Discontents." *Foreign Affairs,* September–October: 108–25.

Stern, Susan, ed. 1991. *Meet United Germany.* Frankfurt: Frankfurter Allgemeine Zeitung GmbH, Information Services and Atlantik- Brücke e.V.

Stetson, Dorothy McBride, and Amy G. Mazur, eds. 1995. *Comparative State Feminism.* Thousand Oaks, Calif.: Sage Publications.

Stiftung Mitarbeit. 1992. *Der Runde Tisch—ein neues Demokratiemodell?* Documentation of a Conference in the Dresden City Council, November 29–December 1. Bonn: Stiftung Mitarbeit.

Streeck, Wolfgang. 1984. "Neo-Corporatist Industrial Relations and the Economic Crisis in West Germany." In *Order and Conflict in Contemporary Capitalism,* ed. John H. Goldthorpe. Oxford: Clarendon Press.

Streeck, Wolfgang, and Philippe C. Schmitter. 1985. *Private Interest Government.* London: Sage Publication.

Sturm, Roland. 1991. "Die Zukunft des deutschen Föderalismus." In *Die Politik zur deutschen Einheit,* ed. Ulrike Liebert and Wolfgang Merkel. Opladen: Leske and Budrich.

Süssmuth, Rita, and Helga Schubert. 1992. *Bezahlen die Frauen die Wiedervereingiung?* Munich: Piper.

Szabo, Stephen F. 1992. *The Diplomacy of German Unification.* New York: St. Martin's Press.

Tageszeitung, Die. 1989. *DDR Journal, Zur Novemberrevolution.* August–December.

———. 1989. "Feuert's Magazin leer bis zur letzten Mumpel!" October 24.

———. 1990. *DDR Journal* No. 2, *Die Wende der Wende,* January–March, Von der Öffnung des Brandenburger Tores zur Öffnung der Wahlurnen.

———. 1990. "Frauen-Nachhilfe für Regierung Modrow." February 9.

———. 1991. "Eine neue Verfassung für das vereinte Deutschland." June 15.

Tarrow, Sidney. 1989. "Struggle, Politics and Reform: Collective Action, Social Movements and Cycles of Protest." Cornell University, Western Societies Paper, no. 21.

———. 1994. *Power in Movement. Social Movements, Collective Action and Politics.* Cambridge: Cambridge University Press.

Tatur, Melanie. 1992. "Why Is There No Women's Movement in Eastern

Europe?" In *Democracy and Civil Society in Eastern Europe,* ed. P. G. Lewis. London: Macmillan.

Teltschik, Horst. 1991. *329 Tage.* Berlin: Siedler Verlag.

Thaysen, Uwe. Forthcoming. Stenographic Report. Round Table. Minutes of the Negotiations of the Central Round Table of the GDR in East Berlin, December 7, 1989–March 16.

———. 1996. "Revisionisten statt Dissidenten?" Book Review. *Politik* 2 (spring): 10–12.

———. 1994. "Rückzug, Verschleierung—und Rückkehr?" *Recht und Politik* 30:143–49.

———. 1993. "A New Constitution for a New Germany?" *German Studies Review,* 2 (May): 299–310.

———. 1992. "The GDR on Its Way into Democracy." In *German Unification: The Challenge,* ed. Dieter Grosser. Oxford: Oxford University Press.

———. 1992a. "Runde Tische—Kriseninstrument zur Herstellung demokratischer Legitimität." In *Der Runde Tisch—ein neues Demokratiemodell?* Documentation of a Conference in the Dresden City Council, November 29–December 1, 1992, ed. Stiftung Mitarbeit. Bonn: Stiftung Mitarbeit.

———. 1992b. Interview. In *Der Runde Tisch in der DDR,* ed. Klemens Semtner. Munich: Tudov-Verlag.

———. 1990a. *Der Runde Tisch. Oder: Wo blieb das Volk?* Opladen: Westdeutscher Verlag.

———. 1990b. *Der Runde Tisch. Oder: Wer war das Volk? Zeitschrift für Parlamentsfragen,* Part 1, no. 1: 71–101.

———. 1990c. *Der Runde Tisch: Oder: Wer war das Volk. Zeitschrift für Parlamentsfragen,* Part 2, no. 2: 257–308.

———. 1990d. "Representation in the Federal Republic of Germany." In *The U.S. Congress and the German Bundestag,* ed. Uwe Thaysen, Roger H. Davidson, and Robert Gerald Livingston. Boulder: Westview Press.

———. 1990d. "Entwicklung und Perspektiven seit dem 9. November 1989," *Information zur politischen Bildung,* 3. Quarter, 30–35.

———. 1986. "Fraktionsstaat—Oder was sonst? Zum Verhältnis von Partei und Demokratie in der Bundesrepublik Deutschland." In *Parteiendemokratie,* ed. Peter Haungs and Eckhard Jesse. Special issue of the weekly *Das Parlament.* 13/20 September 1986.

Thaysen, Uwe, Roger H. Davidson, and Robert Gerald Livingston, eds. 1990. *The U.S. Congress and the German Bundestag.* Boulder: Westview Press.

Thaysen, Uwe, together with Hans Michale Kloth. 1994. *Der Runde Tisch und die Entmachtung der SED.* Expert's Report for the Enquete Commission for the German Parliament, "Reappraisal and the Effects of the SED-Dictatorship in Germany." Lüneburg: University of Lüneburg.

Thielecke, F. 1993. "Der Habitus im Veränderungsprozeß eines Versicherungsunternehmens." Dissertation Humboldt University, Berlin, Department of Social Sciences.

Thierse, Wolfgang. 1994. "Fremde im eigenen Land. Nach der Einheit die Entfremdung?" In *Perspektiven für Deutschland,* ed. Warnfried Dettling. Munich: Knaur.

Third Sommer University for Women 1978 e.V., ed. 1979. *Frauen und Mütter.* Berlin: Basis Verlag.

Thurich, Eckart. 1991. "Politik der Wiedervereinigung oder Anerkennung des Status quo." *Informationen zur politischen Bildung,* 4. Quarter, 23–39.

Tiemann, Heinrich, and Josef Schmid. 1991. "Von der Revolution zur Einheit: Die staatlichen Ebene als Handlungsrahmen für Parteien und Verbände." In *Wiedervereinigung als Organisationsproblem: Gesamtdeutsche Zusammenschlüsse von Parteien und Verbänden,* ed. Frank Löbler, Josef Schmid, and Heinrich Tiemann. Bochum: Universitätsverlag Dr. N. Brockmeyer.

Tilly, Charles. 1978. *From Mobilization to Revolution.* Reading, Mass.: Addison-Wesley.

———. 1986. *The Contentious French.* Cambridge: Harvard University Press.

Tröger, Annemarie. 1984. "The Creation of a Female Assembly-Line Proletariat." In *When Biology Became Destiny,* ed. Renate Bridenthal, Atina Grossmann, and Marion Kaplan. New York: Monthly Review Press.

Twain, Mark. 1880. "The Awful German Language."

UFV Papers, UFV Archive Berlin.

Ullmann, Wolfgang. 1990. Interview. "Gesamtdeutsche Verfassungsdebatte statt Wahlkampf." *Die Tageszeitung,* March 3, p. 3.

———. 1991. "Das Volk muß die Möglichkeit haben, ja zu sagen." In *Eine Verfassung für Deutschland. Manifest Text Plädoyers,* ed. Bernd Guggenberger, Ulrich Preuß, and Wolfgang Ullmann. Munich: Carl Hanser Verlag.

———. 1992. "Umfassende Beratungen jenseits der Machtstrukturen." In *Der Runde Tische—ein neues Demokratiemodell?* Documentation of a Conference in the Dresden City Council, November 29–December 1, 1992, ed. Stiftung Mitarbeit. Bonn: Stiftung Mitarbeit.

———. 1993. "Freiheit für die deutschen Länder. Vom Grundgesetz zur gesamtdeutschen Verfassung." In *Umverteilen,* ed. Rudolf Hickel and Ernst-Ulrich Huster and Heribert Kohl. Köln: Bund Verlag.

Unabhängiger Frauenverband Berlin, Streikkomitee Köln/Bonn, FrauenAnstifung e.V. Hamburg. 1995. *FrauenStreikTag 8. März '94,* ed. Ulrike Helwerth. Hamburg: FrauenAnstiftung.

Verfassungsentwurf für die DDR. 1990. *Arbeitsgruppe "Neue Verfassung der DDR" des Runden Tisches.* Berlin: BasisDruck.

Verträge (Die) zur Einheit Deutschlands. 1990. *Staatsvertrag, Einigungsvertrag mit Anlagen, Wahlvertrag, Zwei-plus-Vier Vertrag, Partnerschaftsverträge,* 2d ed. Munich: Beck-Texte im Deutschen Taschenbuch Verlag.

Vollmer. Antje. 1986. "Die schöne Macht und ein Hauch von Identität." *Feministische Studien,* no. 2: 107–9.

———. 1991. *Die schöne Macht der Vernunft.* Berlin: Verlag der Nation.

Voss, Peter. 1995. "Citizens against the State: Political Protest in the GDR." In *Origins of a Spontaneous Revolution: East Germany, 1989.* ed. Karl-Dieter Opp, Peter Voss, and Christiane Gern. Ann Arbor: University of Michigan Press.

Wagnerová, Alena. 1993. "Der Sozialismus entläßt die tschechischen Frauen." In *beiträge zur feministischen theorie und praxis:* 34:107–12.

Watson, Sophie, ed. 1990. *Playing the State.* London: Verso.

Wehling, Hans-Georg. 1989. *Politische Kultur in der DDR.* Stuttgart: W. Kohlhammer, GmbH.

Weber, Max. 1978. *Economy and Society,* ed. Guenther Roth and Claus Wittich. Berkeley: University of California Press.

Weis, Petra. 1995. "Hürdenlauf an die Macht? Politische Partizipation von Frauen in der SPD und die Quote." In *Gefährtinnen der Macht,* ed. Eva Maleck-Lewy and Virginia Penrose. Berlin: Edition Sigma.

Weller, Konrad. 1991. *Das Sexuelle in der deutsch-deutschen Vereinigung.* Leipzig: Forum Verlag.

Werlhof, Claudia von. 1990. "Mit Frauen ist kein Staat zu machen, Thesen zur politologischen Frauenforschung, Eine kritische Bilanz." In Widerspruch, *Beiträge zur sozialistischen Politik* 19:105–15.

Wettig-Danielmeier, Inge. 1992. "Die Quote. Eine 'Erfolgsstory' auf dem Prüfstand." In *Die politische Klasse in Deutschland,* ed. Thomas Leif, Hans-Josef Legrand, and Ansgar Klein, Bonn: Bouvier Verlag.

Wieczorek-Zeul, Heidemarie (SPD). 1994. In *Frauen an der Macht,* ed. Johanna Holzhauer and Agnes Steinbauer. Frankfurt: Eichborn.

Wielgohs, Jan. 1991. "Die Vereinigte Linke. Zwischen Tradition und Experiment." In *Von der Illegalität ins Parlament,* ed. Helmut Müller-Enbergs, Marianne Schulz, and Jan Wielgohs. Berlin: LinksDruck.

Wielgohs, Jan, and Helmut Müller-Enbergs. 1991. "Die Bürgerbewegung Demokratie Jetzt." In *Von der Illegalität ins Parlament,* ed. Helmut Müller-Enbergs, Marianne Schulz, and Jan Wielgohs. Berlin: LinksDruck.

Wielgohs, Jan, Marianne Schulz, and Helmut Müller-Enbergs. 1992. *Bündnis 90, Entstehung, Entwicklung, Perspektiven.* Berlin: Gesellschaft für sozialwissenschaftliche Forschung und Publizistik.

Wielgohs, Jan, Marianne Schulz, and Anne Hampele. 1990. "Auszug aus der amtlichen Statistik zur Kommunalwahl." In *Ein Jahr Unabhängiger Frauenverband,* Teil I: *Ein dokumentarisches Lesebuch,* No. 47, ed. Anne Hampele. Berlin: Berliner Arbeitshefte und Berichte sur Sozialwissenschaftlichen Forschung, November.

Will, Rosemarie. 1995. "Die Revolution ist vorbei." *Die Wochenpost,* February 23.

Wilson, Frank L. 1990. "Neo-corporatism and the Rise of New Social Movements." In *Challenging the Political Order,* ed. Russell J. Dalton and Manfred Kuechler. Oxford: Polity Press.

Winkler, Gunnar, ed. 1990. *Frauenreport '90.* Berlin: Die Wirtschaft.

Wobbe, Theresa. 1989. *Gleichheit und Differenz. Politische Strategien von Frauenrechtlerinnen um die Jahrhundertwende.* Frankfurt a.M.: Campus.

Wolf, Christa. 1990. *Reden im Herbst.* Berlin: Aufbau-Verlag.

Wolffsohn, Michael. 1992. "Der außenpolitische Weg zur deutschen Einheit." In *Die Gestaltung der Deutschen Einheit,* ed. Eckhard Jesse and Armin Mitter. Berlin: Bouvier.

Wolle, Stefan. 1992. "Der Weg in den Zusammenbruch: Die DDR vom Januar bis zum Oktober 1989." In *Die Gestaltung der Deutschen Einheit,* ed. Eckhard Jesse and Armin Mitter. Berlin: Bouvier.

Wollmann, Helmut. 1984. "Policy Analysis: Some Observations on the West German Scene." *Policy Sciences* 17:27–47.

Wuttke, Carola, and Berndt Musiolek. 1991. *Parteien und politische Bewegungen im letzten Jahr der DDR.* Berlin: BasisDruck.

Young, Brigitte. 1996. "The German State and Feminist Politics: A Double Gender Marginalization." *Social Politics* (summer/fall) Vol. 3, nos. 2–3: 159–84.

———. 1996a. "An Illiberal Liberal German State: The 'Fraktionsstaat,'" Paper presented at the 10th International Conference of Europeanists, Chicago, March.

———. "Asynchronitäten der deutsch-deutschen Frauenbewegung." *Prokla* 94 (March): 49–63.

Young, Iris Marion. 1990. *Justice and the Politics of Difference.* Princeton: Princeton University Press.

———. 1994. "Gender as Seriality: Thinking about Women as a Social Collective." *Signs* 19, no. 3 (spring): 713–38.

Zapf, Wolfgang. 1995. "Two Different Speeds in East and West Germany." MS.

Zeit, Die. 1990. "Inflation ist die größte Gefahr." February 8–16, p. 23.

———. 1990a. "Anwalt der Bürgerbewegung. Wolfgang Ullmann von Demokratie Jetzt möchte einen Bund deutscher Länder errichten." February 8–16.

Zetkin, Clara. 1960. *Ausgewählte Reden und Schriften* (Berlin), 2, no. 2.

———. 1979. *Zur Geschichte der proletarischen Frauenbewegung Deutschlands.* Frankfurt a.M.: Marxistische Blätter Verlag.

Ziebura, Gilbert, Michael Bonder, and Bernd Röttger. 1992. *Deutschland in einer neuen Weltära.* Opladen: Leske and Budrich.

ZiF. 1991. *Bulletin* no. 2. Berlin: Zentrum interdisziplinärer Frauenforschung, Humboldt University.

Zolberg, Aristide R. 1972. "Moment of Madness." *Politics and Society* (winter): 183–207.

Zysman, John. 1983. *Governments, Markets and Growth: Financial Systems and the Politics of Industrial Change.* Ithaca, N.Y.: Cornell University Press.

Index